Uncle Sam's
Policemen

Uncle Sam's Policemen

The Pursuit of Fugitives across Borders

Katherine Unterman

Harvard University Press

Cambridge, Massachusetts
London, England
2015

Library of Congress Cataloging-in-Publication Data
Unterman, Katherine, 1976–
    Uncle Sam's policemen : the pursuit of fugitives across borders /
Katherine Unterman.
        pages cm
    Includes bibliographical references and index.
    ISBN 978-0-674-73692-4 (hardcover : alk. paper)
    1. Fugitives from justice—United States—History.   2. Extradition—
United States—History.   3. International crimes—History.   I. Title.
    HV6791.U57   2015
    364.3—dc23   2015002112

For my father,

Robert Unterman

Contents

Introduction: Crimes of Mobility   1

1   The Embezzlement Epidemic   14

2   Detectives without Borders   47

3   An Empire of Justice   75

4   Extradition Havens   101

5   Asylum No More   127

6   Camouflaged Extradition   160

7   From the Pinkertons to the FBI   183

Epilogue: How Rendition Became Extraordinary   210

Notes   221

Acknowledgments   263

Index   267

INTRODUCTION
Crimes of Mobility

*I*N AN EARLY SCENE of Jules Verne's 1873 best seller *Around the World in Eighty Days*, members of a London social club discuss a robbery that occurred at the Bank of England three days earlier. Andrew Stuart, an engineer, maintains that the odds of a successful escape are in the thief's favor, but Gauthier Ralph, one of the bank's directors, disagrees. A description of the robber had been sent all over the world, Ralph explains, so "where can he fly to? No country is safe for him." Continuing his paean to modern policing, Ralph asserts: "The world has grown smaller, since a man can now go round it ten times more quickly than a hundred years ago. And that is why the search for this thief will be more likely to succeed." But, as Stuart quickly responds, improved transportation works both ways; it is "also why the thief can get away more easily." And so the wager that began Phileas Fogg's eighty-day journey around the world started with a simple debate: Did the new technologies of the nineteenth century—railroads, steamships, telegraphs—provide more of a benefit to the fugitive or the policeman? Did they lead to a more orderly or a more criminal society?[1]

Around the World in Eighty Days was written by a French author and featured a British protagonist, but Americans shared its fascination with the speed of modern travel. Eager to claim the mantle of modernity, American adventurers enthusiastically sought to outdo the fictional Phileas Fogg. In 1889, a young female journalist known as Nellie Bly, funded by Joseph Pulitzer's *New York World*, beat Verne's imaginary record by more than a week. Bly's newspaper reports, later published as the collection *Around the World in Seventy-Two Days*,

1

demonstrated that it was possible for even a solitary female traveler to circle the globe. Could criminal fugitives also reach the other side of the world with such ease?[2]

By the last third of the nineteenth century, recent technologies made the crossing of international borders more feasible than ever before. Steamboat lines navigated the oceans, railroad tracks traversed countries, and the electric telegraph enabled rapid communication between continents. And each year these international networks grew tighter. Prior to the 1880s, a train trip from New York to Montreal had taken more than twenty-four hours; now it took twelve, and the journey from Kansas City to the Mexican border could be made in only six and a half hours. Commercial transoceanic steamships offered to take passengers from the United States to locales as exotic as Europe, South America, and Asia in only a few days' or weeks' travel time. A steamship from San Francisco, heading west, could reach Yokohama, Japan, in seventeen days; Sydney, Australia, in four weeks; and even Calcutta, India, in forty-seven days. Heading south, it would arrive in Panama after fifteen days and in Peru after another week. From New York, a steamer might head south to Central America (nine days) or east to Liverpool (ten to twelve days). Americans often described these new, faster technologies through the trope of a shrinking world: the globe seemed to be getting smaller. In a phenomenon that geographer David Harvey calls "time-space compression," a decrease in travel time was commonly perceived and articulated as a decrease in space.[3]

Technological innovations could make the policeman's job easier. Thomas Edison promoted his early experiments with wireless communications as a benefit to international policing. With such technology, Edison claimed, "escaping criminals would have small chance of evading detection by skipping off to countries [that] might give them safe harbor." The electric telegraph enabled detectives to send descriptions of a suspect around the world in seconds, and photographs and fingerprint cards allowed for easier identification. An 1890 article outlined for readers just why it was that "this world is getting too small to hold certain kinds of bad people": America's advanced technology, particularly the telegraph; international

cooperation between police agencies; the intelligence and persever-
ance of American detectives; and the expansion of extradition law.[4]

Like Verne's Andrew Stuart, however, not everyone was certain
that modern technology favored law enforcement. The facility of
modern travel was thrilling, but it also could feel threatening. "The
same line of railroad now often runs through many different countries," observed William Gammell, a professor of history and political economy at Brown University. "Steam navigation has bridged
the broadest rivers, and has closely connected the opposite shores
even of the Atlantic." For Gammell, writing in 1880, these transportation networks were a source of peril, not promise. They meant
that fugitives had an easier time getting away and getting farther
from the grip of American law. "The perpetrator of a crime may now
reach a distant land almost before his guilt is discovered," he lamented. The whole world had become a potential safe haven.[5]

John Bassett Moore, then assistant secretary of state, noted the
shrinking world with alarm in an 1890 report, writing that "improved means of travel which modern invention has afforded and
the consequent case of flight have made the extradition of criminals
a subject of constantly growing importance. A person commits an
atrocious offense and in a few hours at most may be beyond the
confines of the country." Here, then, was the administrative challenge: trying to apply *national* laws to increasingly *transnational*
people. Laws stopped at the border, but people did not. The problem,
in short, was one of jurisdiction. Federal, state, and local laws helped
to structure a particular social and moral order by endorsing some
acts as acceptable and condemning others as criminal. Yet these laws
were inherently limited by jurisdictional boundaries, with the international border as the ultimate legal barrier. Fugitives demonstrated
just how easy it was to subvert American law, and the social order it
supported, merely by crossing the international border. In fact,
people could cross more easily than ever before, while legislation remained stymied at the international line.[6]

Compared to European nations, the United States was slow to address the problem of international fugitives. In the early nineteenth
century, envisioning itself as a nation of asylum, the United States
refused to enter into extradition treaties. Meanwhile, France and

Great Britain took the lead in negotiating such compacts with their European neighbors. But with the acceleration of international trade and transport, Americans began to chafe at the ease with which fugitives could escape state-sanctioned justice. Not only did railroads and steamships allow offenders to travel abroad with unprecedented speed and convenience, but newly urbanized cities also meant that criminals could disappear into anonymity. By the 1880s, the crisis of international fugitives—both entering and leaving the country—had become acute. While the United States had signed a few extradition treaties in the 1840s and 1850s, it now began pursuing fugitives in earnest.

If improvements in transportation made it easier to escape the grip of the law, it was a certain type of fugitive who evoked particular anxiety: those who stood as scapegoats for the social instabilities of the day. Thus, it was not so much the conventional murderer or sneak thief who raised alarms about cross-border escape. Rather, it was those who committed new crimes, whom old laws were often ill-equipped to reach. Embezzlers, for instance, represented the turbulent rise of corporate capitalism, the corruption of the Gilded Age, and the uncertainty of one's social station in a changing economy. "Family deserters"—men who abandoned their wives and children—evoked anxieties about being uprooted from the kinship networks that had held families together in rural communities or immigrant homelands. Anarchists and other foreign radicals conjured fears of a shady, mysterious underworld that seemed to export violence across borders. The science of criminology during this era encouraged these transnational anxieties. Instead of viewing crime simply as the breaking of a law, influential criminologists like Cesare Lombroso rooted it in the body, as an inherited trait—the "born criminal," who carried his criminality from country to country. The whole world began to seem, as Michel Foucault put it, like "a borderless society of dangerous criminals." And if the lawbreaker knew no borders, then law enforcers should know no borders either.[7]

By letting criminals pass but stopping the laws meant to control them, the border seemed to cause instability. The "facility of escape" across international borders "has been a standing encouragement to crime," complained the *Independent* in 1888. "This condition of things *makes* criminals." Late nineteenth-century Americans pro-jected their fears about social instability onto border crossings, fix-ating not only on immigrants entering the United States but also on fugitives trying to escape the country. It is no coincidence that the passport regime arose at the same time as the extradition regime, as both were ways of addressing and trying to restrain international mobility. Extradition treaties and the subsequent pursuit of Amer-ican fugitives abroad aimed not only to secure the nation's physical borders but also to stabilize the cultural boundaries of citizenship and national identity during an era of increasing mobility, demo-graphic flux, and social upheaval.[8]

In these cases, reaching out and apprehending fugitives abroad was seen as critical to maintaining tranquility at home. At the turn of the twentieth century, a time when Americans fiercely debated whether their nation should take colonies, most forms of foreign interven-tion were highly visible and contested. Yet the goal of law enforce-ment seemed so commonsensical that Americans neglected to think of it as a form of foreign intervention in its own right. Obscuring the international ramifications of their missions, law enforcers gen-erally defined and legitimized cross-border policing as a matter of national criminal justice. Reaching out beyond the borders of the United States, they explained, was a project with domestic aims, not international or imperialist ones. Thus, Americans often treated in-ternational policing as a unilateral project, without fully acknowl-edging the ways their actions affected other nations. Policy makers justified it as an extension of domestic criminal justice, jurists legiti-mized it in the authoritative language of law, and journalists praised it as stabilizing society. In the name of law and order within the boundaries of the nation, it was necessary to reach America's policing power out beyond them.

✳

Legally and politically, rendition means the transfer of a criminal suspect from one jurisdiction to another. Extradition, a set of legal procedures governed by treaty and statute, is the most regulated form of rendition between countries. Extradition treaties embodied the tenets of late nineteenth-century international law, which placed an emphasis on the territorial sovereignty and sovereign equality of all "civilized nations." In keeping with this ideology, extradition treaties were bilateral agreements that respected the territorial integrity of each nation. They also smoothed over the process of surrendering fugitives by specifying a set of fixed procedures. These extradition compacts were part of a larger nineteenth-century proliferation of international treaties, what might be called a vogue for treaty making, reflecting a faith in treaties to solve international tangles from postal service to trademark law. In 1840, the United States was not party to a single extradition treaty; by 1900, it had fifty-eight agreements with thirty-six nations.[9]

In practice, however, turn-of-the-century law enforcers often searched for ways to circumvent the terms of extradition treaties. They turned to more informal types of rendition, apprehending cross-border fugitives through abduction, for instance, or unofficial surrender outside the terms of a treaty. A criminal suspect might be deported into the hands of waiting law enforcers, a practice known as "disguised extradition." Or, during the time when the United States practiced extraterritorial jurisdiction in supposedly "uncivilized" countries, a U.S. consul might unilaterally take custody of a fugitive. Indeed, looking at the entire spectrum of rendition techniques reveals a range of power relations, from bilateral cooperation to legal coercion to explicit force. Rather than an age of inviolable borders, this was a time when American detectives frequently breached the boundaries of other nations. In a system ostensibly grounded in bilateral equality and cooperation, the United States pressured other countries to sign treaties or hand over fugitives—though it was not always able to dictate the terms.[10]

Rendition may have become widespread in the last decades of the nineteenth century, but Americans' concern with catching international fugitives did not originate during the Gilded Age. Americans had long had an interest in capturing cross-border fugitives, particularly fugitive slaves who escaped into Canada, Mexico, and Spanish Florida. In their attempts to retrieve fugitive slaves from across international borders, slave owners employed some of the same tactics that would be used to target fugitive criminals in the postbellum years, including extradition and abduction. However, these ad hoc attempts to retrieve fugitive slaves from across international borders met with limited success. Most of the time, extradition requests were denied. Mexico had a clear policy that refused to extradite fugitive slaves for any reason, and Canada had strict legal requirements for extradition that made it difficult for slave owners to make a successful case. Hired slave catchers occasionally kidnapped fugitive slaves who had escaped across international borders, though Canada and Mexico vigorously objected to the violation of their territorial sovereignty. It was not until after the Civil War that the international rendition of fugitives became more organized, streamlined, and commonplace.[11]

Rendition was not only a set of practices; it also entailed a new type of geographical and legal consciousness among late nineteenth-century Americans. As transportation networks linked distant places, Americans exhibited a novel style of geographical thinking, as cities hundreds of miles from an international boundary developed the same law enforcement concerns as border towns. The pursuit of an international fugitive blurred the distinction between international relations and local law enforcement. Ordinary policing became internationalized: questions of who could cross the border, how they could cross the border, and which laws could be enforced across the border emerged as pressing and local issues throughout the nation. If "the frontier region is the only place where international law enforcement is often synonymous with local law enforcement," as Peter Andreas and Ethan Nadelmann assert, then cities like New York, Chicago, and St. Louis became, in effect, border towns.[12]

Widely covered in the news and popular fiction, international searches gave rise to a new way of thinking about the role of the United States in the world. While extradition treaties provided the legal means to pursue fugitives across international borders, the public discourse surrounding such pursuits encouraged Americans to view the entire world as legitimately subject to U.S. laws and norms. As maps and atlases became more readily accessible, Americans began to visualize the world not just in terms of markets or formal territorial possessions but also in a jurisdictional sense. There was a popular obsession with the spaces where U.S. extradition law did not reach, such as Canada in the 1880s and Honduras in the 1890s and early 1900s. However, late nineteenth-century

Americans expressed a confidence that U.S. law covered, or would soon cover, the entire globe. For Uncle Sam's policemen, the world was borderless.[13]

Empire was implicitly part of this new consciousness. Underneath claims of inward-looking, domestic goals a subtext revealed America's vision of itself as a rising power on the world stage. Newspapers regularly bragged about the abilities of U.S. law enforcement, emphasizing that the United States' capabilities were surpassing those of Britain, once the undisputed world power. No other country had a detective service like the Pinkertons, who claimed their work superior to Scotland Yard's, or an investigator like William J. Burns, the private eye who called himself "the American Sherlock Holmes." The popular press helped Americans envision the law's limitless reach. Territories outside the United States were conceptualized as spaces where the American policeman could act as he pleased. International manhunts enabled the United States to project global power without the formal trappings of territorial imperialism. It was a dominion not of territory but of justice, wherein the reach of American law extended far beyond the nation's geographical borders.[14]

Of course, the United States was not the only country with a fugitive problem. Great Britain and France had signed nearly as many extradition treaties, occasionally used alternate rendition tactics like abduction and deportation, and celebrated sensational captures. Yet, at least rhetorically, American manhunts were distinctive. For many Americans, extradition was more than an obscure judicial matter; it was a sign of national greatness. The United States could not boast that the sun never set on its empire the way that Britain could. But it could make the claim, as H. C. Potter did in 1899, that "no criminal can outrun the law or the hand of Justice, wherever he goes." Mainstream newspapers, politicians, and novelists repeated the myth that there was nowhere in the world where a fugitive could hide from U.S. law. By taking pride in the expansion of extradition, Americans could imagine themselves in a triumphant, far-reaching international role without the controversy of formal empire. Other great powers had territorial empires; the United States had an empire of justice.[15]

Although the State Department often sanctioned these cross-border ventures, they were largely carried out by private, nonstate actors, at least until the 1920s. Banks and corporations frequently hired private detectives like those from the famed Pinkerton National Detective Agency to track down thieves and defrauders who fled the country. Today, the Pinkertons are most often remembered for their work breaking strikes and infiltrating unions, but they also generated substantial business conducting manhunts, both domestic and international. In contrast, municipal police forces lacked the manpower and organization to engage in distant investigations. Apart from the Treasury Department's Secret Service, created to suppress counterfeiting, there was no federal investigative force prior to the creation of the Bureau of Investigation (later renamed the FBI) in 1908 to deal with these departures.[16]

As strikebreakers, union busters, and man hunters, the Pinkertons were employed in the service of policing capitalism. This private army for hire was not accountable to the American people; it answered only to the banks and corporations wealthy enough to pay the hefty price tag. Most often, these clients commissioned them to track down financial felons, like thieves and embezzlers. The Pinkertons had few qualms about crossing borders, transgressing lines of sovereignty, and using tactics like fraud and abduction to catch a fugitive for a client. As Allan Pinkerton often stated: "We will pursue you to the ends of the earth," by any means necessary. This left open the question of which legal rules, if any, restrained these mercenaries of capital. Politicians may have debated whether the Constitution followed the flag, but when it came to the practice of international manhunts, the real question was: Does the Constitution follow the coin?[17]

Over time, it became increasingly apparent that the legal constraints that restrained police at home would not hold back American agents operating abroad. As the stopping point of national jurisdiction, international borders initially seemed to restrict the process of law enforcement. Circa 1880, American jurists and law enforcers were paralyzed because they viewed the international border as a rigid jurisdictional boundary; U.S. law was absolute on one side and nonexistent on the other, and their authority seemed to stop at the

international line. But by the early twentieth century, this type of
strictly territorial thinking evolved into a more expansive notion of
jurisdiction. American agents came to realize that the pursuit of
fugitives did not need to stop at the border; rather, they could re-
write what the borders meant so their policing could extend as far as
they needed it to go. They discovered that the crossing of international borders actually served to augment power, as they would not
be held to the same legal and constitutional standards as they were
at home. For instance, a kidnapping that would have been illegal
within U.S. borders was acceptable outside of them.

As a result, rendition increased in the last decades of the nineteenth
century, whether by extradition, abduction, or other means. In the
1870s, it had been difficult to retrieve fugitives from across borders.
Law enforcers in the borderlands brought back a handful each year
from Mexico and Canada, but more distant searches were unfeasible.
But by the early 1900s, American detectives were delivering dozens
of outlaws annually from places as far away as Japan, Morocco, and
Brazil. Although this was never truly a worldwide reach, as so many
Americans imagined, it was certainly a much-expanded one.

※

This trajectory coincides with the growth of American power on a
global stage. During the last quarter of the nineteenth century,
American markets spread across the world, and in 1898, the United
States demonstrated its stature as a global power by acquiring colonies. But a commercial and formal empire was not the only way to
project American power outward. American policemen also reached
across international borders, extending their power and influence
into other countries. In time, American law enforcers came to treat
the Western Hemisphere—the space where the United States so
often rehearsed imperial strategies—as part of their criminal jurisdiction. Eventually, they expanded this legal reach to encompass the
entire globe.

While histories of U.S. empire generally concentrate on military,
economic, or cultural dominance, law also was a crucial instrument
that helped to further American power. The Insular Cases, a series
of Supreme Court decisions in the early twentieth century, most

clearly exemplified the link between law and empire, as they directly addressed the constitutional status of colonial possessions. But law is not only a matter of statutes and court cases; it also includes the way that law enforcement functioned on the ground. American actors set legal norms and used the law to legitimize their actions abroad, redefining global spaces as part of the orbit of American policing. By considering the pursuit of fugitives in conjunction with other permutations of American empire—economic, cultural, military— we gain a fuller understanding of how the United States has wielded power around the world during the last century. To this day, Uncle Sam continues to breach the borders of other countries in order to catch his man.[18]

Yet U.S. power was never absolute or unidirectional; other governments variously collaborated with or struggled against it according to their own national interests. The vision of a world with nowhere to hide was an idealized aspiration that did not account for contention or resistance. Uncle Sam did not simply reach; he pushed, and sometimes other countries pushed back. Certain spots gained infamy as popular destinations for fugitives, including, at different times, Argentina and Brazil, Costa Rica and Honduras, Morocco and Egypt—wherever there was no extradition with the United States. These countries resisted State Department pressure in the name of sovereignty, and also because they benefited from sheltering American fugitives, thanks to the capital these émigrés invested in their new homelands. Fugitive funds helped build the railroads of Canada, Peru, Chile, and Costa Rica, among other places. The resistance to American power also sent a political message. At a time when the United States dominated economic policy in the Western Hemisphere, refusing to extradite was a way of standing up to U.S. hegemony in the region.

Rendition worked in both directions, and other countries demanded the return of those who were seeking sanctuary in the United States as well. Once an asylum for fugitives from other nations, the United States now began to hand over people who previously had been protected within its borders. In some ways, this was a concession, a growing pain that accompanied the spread of extradition, which, after all, was a bilateral process. But this was also a demonstration of strength. Americans were frustrated with the number of foreign criminals seeking refuge on their shores. As Ivan Shearer put it, "a State which did not take effective measures against the incursion of foreign criminals would quickly find itself a seething haven for the undesirables of other lands." Just as passports, immigration laws, and border patrols enabled the state to regulate who entered the nation, so too did deportation and extradition allow it to control who was permitted to stay. Immigration, deportation, and extradition laws often were used interchangeably to achieve the same end: policing inclusion into the nation. Loosening its own self-regulations over who was extraditable, the state gained greater flexibility to decide who would be entitled to its protection.[19]

✻

The legacies of Uncle Sam's late nineteenth- and early twentieth-century policemen are still with us. Consider the story of Joseph W. Folk, who ran for St. Louis district attorney in 1901 on a pledge to clean up public corruption. After he took office, many were surprised to discover that he actually meant it. While awaiting trial for bribery the next year, two of St. Louis's most notorious aldermen escaped across the international border to Mexico. Folk took his predicament to President Theodore Roosevelt, himself an avowed enemy of corruption. Roosevelt reacted like a sheriff stopped at the county line, shaking his fist in frustration because he could not follow the absconding outlaws across. In his 1903 message to Congress, he declared: "It should be the policy of the United States to leave *no place on earth* where a corrupt man fleeing from this country can rest in peace."[20]

Twenty-first-century Americans heard the same sort of rhetoric when their commander in chief spoke about the war on terror. After 9/11, President George W. Bush vowed that there would be nowhere in the world where America's enemies could hide from U.S. justice. "We're engaged in a global struggle," Bush proclaimed in a 2006 speech. "We had to find the terrorists hiding in America and across the world before they were able to strike our country again." Like Roosevelt, Bush pictured the long arm of U.S. law extending around the world, the entire globe a part of the American policeman's beat.

Speaking more than a century apart, the two presidents faced vastly different geopolitical situations. But both believed it was crucial that the United States be able to exercise its police power beyond its geographical borders.[21]

In many ways, international manhunts changed from Roosevelt's day to Bush's. Organizations like Interpol (International Criminal Police Organization), for example, now enable the exchange of criminal information among 190 member nations. New technologies like television and the Internet allow law enforcers to solicit assistance from the public. However obvious the transformations, though, it is even more striking to note the continuities with the late nineteenth century, when the United States first began to pursue international fugitives with vigor. The legacies fall into three categories: tactical, or the mechanics of manhunts; cultural, or the idea that there was nowhere to hide from American law; and legal, or the court decisions that enabled law enforcers to reach across borders with impunity. In one of the most remarkable links between the past and the present, a Supreme Court case from 1886, dealing with international abduction, has been used in the twenty-first century to defend U.S. rendition practices in the war on terror. Thus, it is important to examine international manhunts in the late nineteenth and early twentieth centuries, not only to understand how they evolved in the context of the Gilded Age and Progressive Era but also to comprehend the origins of our practices, assumptions, and justifications today.[22]

1

The Embezzlement Epidemic

RICHARD S. SCOTT, a paying teller at New York's Manhattan Bank, left work on the evening of June 1, 1885, his pockets stuffed with cash. Instead of going home, he headed straight to Grand Central Station and boarded the overnight train to Montreal. The next morning, when he failed to show up to work, Scott's employers grew alarmed. In an emergency meeting, the president of the bank ordered the clerks to check the books. Sure enough, along with the trusted teller, $160,000 was missing. But by then it was too late. Scott was already over the Canadian border and out of reach.[1]

Scott made off with more money than most, but his story was all too common. Nearly every week, newspapers reported another clerk, cashier, or bank teller who embezzled from his employer's coffers, then escaped the country. More than two thousand of these white-collar criminals fled the United States during the 1880s alone. In cities like New York, St. Louis, and Chicago, business leaders diagnosed the crime spree as an "epidemic." The press gave various monikers to these financial fugitives, but most often they were simply called "boodlers." Derived from the Dutch word *boedel*, meaning property or goods, "boodle" was a common nineteenth-century American colloquialism for ill-gotten gains. But the label "boodler" indicated more than just corruption; it also signified international flight. Staying one step ahead of extradition treaties, boodlers took advantage of jurisdictional divides to get away with their crimes.[2]

Boodlers left the United States for destinations around the globe, but during the 1880s, they most frequently headed north to Canada. According to the treaty between the United States and Great Britain, which controlled Canada's foreign affairs, embezzlement was not an extraditable offense. Canada would hand over murderers, arsonists, or common thieves, but not embezzlers. As a result, boodlers in Canada often lived openly and conspicuously, making no secret of their identities, bringing their families to live with them, and even granting interviews to American reporters. Though both the U.S. and British governments sought to amend the extradition treaty, the wheels of diplomacy moved slowly, and it took nearly a decade to make the change. In the meantime, American banks and businesses lost tens of millions of dollars to the boodlers, who either speculated away or outright swiped funds from their places of employment.[3]

The boodler phenomenon was symptomatic of a late nineteenth-century crisis of mobility. Increased mobility and global interconnectedness were nothing new—indeed, they had been growing throughout the nineteenth century—but in the 1880s, they produced a wave of international fugitives unlike anything America had seen before. Direct international rail lines built in the 1870s and 1880s made travel faster and easier, allowing fugitives from major U.S. cities to cross the Canadian border in just a few hours. American society also experienced new forms of mobility in the fluidity of capital, the increasing flexibility of one's social station, and the rapid dissemination of information. This revolution in mobility was key to the growth of American corporate and finance capitalism during the Gilded Age. Yet, ironically, the very mobility that allowed this economic system to thrive also threatened it by creating new opportunities for crime and escape. The boodler crisis emerged when laws failed to keep up with rapidly changing social and economic conditions.[4]

The clerk was a pivotal figure in the emergence of modern American capitalism in the nineteenth century, but studies have overlooked his corrupt variant. During the 1880s, however, the banking and business communities were all too aware of the boodler's presence. They experimented with new ways to extend policing across international lines, seeking to discipline a labor force that was endangering the nation's financial stability. For moral reformers, lawmakers, and the interests of capital, the Canadian border represented a threat to order by offering freedom to thieves, temptation to ordinary clerks, and a refuge to scoundrels. However, redefining physical boundaries was only one facet of their challenge. The other was to confirm the morality of remaining within one's proper social boundaries: play by the rules, be content with your lot, and do not steal from the rich. The firming of physical borders helped reaffirm the moral borders of the Gilded Age social order.[5]

❋

In 1842, the United States and Great Britain inserted an extradition agreement into the Webster-Ashburton Treaty. The primary purpose of the treaty was to resolve persisting border disputes and to diffuse tensions along the U.S.-Canadian line, and the extradition clause furthered the goal of order and tranquility along the shared boundary. Article 10 named seven extraditable offenses: murder, assault with intent to commit murder, piracy, arson, robbery, forgery, and the passing of forged paper. This list was carefully constructed so as not to allow for the surrender of fugitive slaves, at Britain's insistence, or political prisoners. Despite the list's brevity, both signatories felt optimistic that it was inclusive enough to suppress the most serious and common crimes along the border, especially cross-border raids. Edward Everett, Daniel Webster's successor as secretary of state, marveled that "no more was heard of border forays . . . or violences offered or retaliated across the line." The extradition provision was a success, at least initially.[6]

By the 1870s, however, the seven enumerated offenses that once served the border so well started to seem inadequate. New felonies—some of which had not even been criminalized in 1842—had become prevalent. When three members of William M. "Boss" Tweed's Tammany Ring fled to Canada in 1871, accused of taking more than $100 million of city funds, the New York district attorney discovered that he could not demand their extradition on either embezzlement or bribery charges, as neither crime was named in the treaty. In 1876, legal scholar David Dudley Field suggested the inclusion of more than a dozen additional offenses to the U.S.-British extradition agreement, among them bigamy, kidnapping, counterfeiting, and various acts of fraud.[7]

The offenses that Field singled out shared a common trait—they all depended on modern means of mobility. Each of these acts required the capacity to change one's identity, to relocate, to falsify one's past. The second half of the nineteenth century saw a great deal of geographical movement: from Europe to the United States, from the East Coast to the West, from rural to urban areas. Because so many migrants and immigrants were uprooted from their native communities and distant from their families, swindlers could show up in new locations without arousing suspicion. Everyone was on the move; everyone was a stranger.

Embezzlement was most often cited as an offense that needed to be added to the extradition treaty. Although its statutory roots originated in eighteenth-century England, embezzlement was the quintessential Gilded Age crime, fostered by the rapid growth of cities, the rise of corporate and finance capitalism, the expansion of the national banking system, and particularly the birth of the urban managerial class. Differentiating it from robbery or larceny, the 1864 New York criminal code defined embezzlement as "the fraudulent appropriation of property *by a person to whom it has been entrusted.*" Embezzlers had lawful custody over the property of others, generally through their employment; the crime of robbery, in contrast, involved unlawfully taking possession of another's property. Embezzlement was the crime of the paper pushers: the clerks, managers, cashiers, and bureaucrats hired to balance company books and handle other people's money. With the growth of corporations, banks, and government agencies in the decades after the Civil War, the demand for these office workers swelled. Between 1870 and 1900, the number of clerical workers in the United States increased by roughly 300 percent.[8]

Embezzlement and urbanization grew alongside each other. As more wealth concentrated in cities, clerical workers had access to ever greater sums of money. Like Herman Melville's Bartleby, these clerks often exercised tremendous power over everyday matters in the office, with almost complete responsibility over the books and finances. A cautionary article in *Century* magazine listed the different ways that bank cashiers could steal funds. They might dip into the safe, steal checks and bonds, falsify the ledgers, or bury their withdrawals deep within complex columns of double-entry bookkeeping. An indication of its prevalence, the crime of embezzlement possessed a variety of popular monikers—hypothecation, peculation, defalcation, default.[9]

Embezzlement rates shot up in the early 1880s. U.S. banks reported twenty-nine embezzlements in 1880, amounting to $1,481,472. By 1885, there were sixty-six reported cases, adding up to $3,477,536. The official numbers only represented a fraction of the actual totals, though. Most banks tried to keep embezzlements quiet, afraid of losing the public's confidence and triggering a run of withdrawals. Businesses and financial firms tested new ways of monitoring funds: external audits, rotating duties, fidelity bonds insuring the honesty of employees. In 1883, James Ritty patented the first cash register, designed to prevent cashier fraud. Despite these safeguards, however, the sums of money stolen by employees more than doubled during the first half of the 1880s, while the amounts retrieved declined. Embezzlers were taking their loot across the international border and out of the grasp of U.S. law enforcers.[10]

In part, American fugitives of the early 1880s chose Canada as a destination because it had recently become much faster and easier to get there. Advances in transportation reduced the travel time between major American and Canadian cities, enabling more commercial dealings but also increasing opportunities for criminals to escape. The Grand Trunk Railway's "Great International Route" between New York and Montreal, completed in 1882, halved the travel time between the two cities. The trip previously had taken more than a day and required a transfer and often a long delay in St. Albans, Vermont, or Portland, Maine. Now, passengers and goods could make the direct journey overnight, in less than thirteen hours. Newly constructed railway lines also decreased the travel time between Chicago and Toronto, and Boston and Quebec.[11]

These new international rail lines had an unintended effect on law enforcement: they essentially turned the major commercial centers of the U.S. Northeast and Midwest into border towns. Communities in close geographic proximity to the international border faced the challenge of transnational crime on a daily basis; the fugitive who crossed international lines to evade the law was a familiar figure in northern Vermont and along the Rio Grande. Now, cities like New York and Chicago faced similar problems. In an era before passports were common or border patrols existed, American law enforcers already were grappling with the challenge of applying national laws to transnational populations.[12]

Not all boodlers fled to Canada. Many attempted to vanish into the West, others escaped to Europe, and some headed south to Mexico or beyond. International railway lines also connected American cities to Mexico; however, it never approached Canada's popularity as a destination for financial fugitives. Canada was closer to the major northeastern cities and presented less of a linguistic and cultural shock. More important, Mexico extradited. The U.S.-Mexican extradition treaty, written more than twenty years after the Webster-Ashburton Treaty, included more "modern" crimes such as embezzlement. Even in questionable cases, Mexican president Porfirio Díaz usually cooperated with U.S. extradition requests, eager to demonstrate the strength of Mexican law and order to foreign investors. The most significant boodler traffic to Mexico was on the ferry from New Orleans to Veracruz. In central Mexico, where U.S. and Mexican law enforcers communicated less than in the borderlands, a boodler might evade capture. In general, however, even Texas boodlers headed to Canada.[13]

The stabilization of the U.S. greenback also helped trigger the boodler phenomenon. Like the improved transportation networks, this too was a double-edged sword. Greater capital mobility enabled the expansion of American investment abroad, but it also created the potential for illicit capital flows. On purely practical grounds, the lightness of paper currency permitted individuals to carry large sums of money. In gold, the $160,000 taken by Richard S. Scott, the Manhattan Bank teller, would have weighed 483 pounds. Prior to the 1880s, however, it was hard to spend U.S. dollars abroad because the notes were not backed by specie. American traveler Gilbert Haven had difficulty finding a single Canadian merchant who would accept his banknotes in 1878. The U.S. Treasury returned to a gold standard in 1879, guaranteeing that greenbacks were redeemable for payments in gold. By 1891, the *Canadian Guide-Book* assured tourists that "the traveler who is well supplied with American bank-notes will find no difficulty with the currency. American bills are good all over Canada."[14]

Beyond the opportunity and means, there was also a rise in knowledge about the asylum Canada inadvertently offered. Prior to the 1880s, many Americans simply did not realize the limitations of the law. However, a series of high-profile cases in the mid-1880s informed the public of how much U.S.-British extradition law lagged behind social change. The most notorious case was that of John Chester Eno, the thirty-three-year-old president of the Second National Bank of New York. Between 1881 and 1884, Eno lost more than $4 million of bank deposits in speculative ventures, mainly in the stock market and railroads. Each time he made a withdrawal, Eno falsely recorded it in the bank's books as a legitimate loan. The more money he lost, the riskier the next investment he chose, in the hopes of recouping his losses. In May 1884, when Eno realized that the Second National's safe was almost empty, he wrote a bank check to himself for the remaining $95,000, cashed it, and got on a train to Quebec.[15]

Eno's defection made headlines across the United States, thanks to the rapid spread of information through telegraph lines and a much-expanded press. This media attention was due in part to his family's wealth; his father, Amos, was a successful real estate investor who built Manhattan's Fifth Avenue Hotel. Mostly, though, Eno's actions received media scrutiny because of their widespread severe repercussions. The week before his embezzlement, two shocks had destabilized New York banking: the collapse of the Marine National Bank, which held deposits of $4.5 million, and the failure of the Grant and Ward brokerage firm, cofounded by former U.S. president Ulysses S. Grant. The news of Eno's embezzlement was the final straw, triggering a heavy run on New York banks. "The wildest kind of panic raged," reported the *Commercial and Financial Chronicle*, "and securities were thrown overboard regardless of price." Stock prices tumbled, and the Metropolitan Bank and six brokerage houses closed their doors. Events in New York had financial consequences around the nation. The panic of May 14, 1884, was the nation's largest financial disaster since the Panic of 1873, and it confirmed just how destructive a boodler could be. The stability of

American banking and finance was at stake, yet Eno was safe in Canada.[16]

Wanting to set an example, New York district attorney Peter B. Olney convinced the State Department to request Eno's extradition, not for embezzlement but instead on the charge of forgery. The strategy was clearly a gamble, but Olney believed it was the only way to discourage future boodlers. Canada could not act on the basis of comity, voluntarily handing Eno over, since both U.S. and British authorities held that a judge's power to extradite was strictly limited to the terms of the treaty. After a prolonged hearing, however, the Superior Court of Quebec ruled that the false records Eno had entered into the Second National's books did not amount to the common-law crime of forgery. Rejecting the State Department's request, Judge Louis-Bonaventure Caron ordered Eno's release. As long as he remained on Canadian soil, Eno was a free man.[17]

Judge Caron did not deny the State Department's request out of sympathy for Eno. Many Canadians were eager to rid their country of American fugitives, and also hoped for access to the handful of Canadian boodlers living in the United States. The boodler phenomenon went in both directions. Canadian embezzlers sought asylum in the United States as well, yet their numbers were much smaller and Canada never made a serious effort to retrieve them. But even frustrated American jurists admitted that Judge Caron had made the correct legal ruling. Neither the United States nor Canada wanted the boodlers to find a refuge, but everyone's hands were tied. Banks and corporations that wanted to pursue fugitives like Eno relied on judicial procedures.[18]

Ironically, Eno's hearing provided potential boodlers with a thorough education in the limits of extradition law. Newspapers clarified the reasons why Eno was secure in Canada and cataloged which crimes were and were not listed in the treaty. In the months after Eno's trial, there was a sharp spike in the number of embezzlers fleeing to Canada. By 1885, scores of American fugitives lived openly and visibly in the Dominion. Many took their families along with them, kept their names, and made no effort to conceal their whereabouts. Melville Stone fancied himself a "detective journalist" when he set out to find Chicago embezzler Avery Moore, but his hunt required little detective work. Stone easily discovered Moore in the border town of Sarnia, Ontario, registered at a hotel under his own name.[19]

The Eno case revealed just how much the law lagged behind social realities, especially when a crime involved crossing international borders. Domestically, the U.S. Constitution mandated that states had a duty to deliver fugitives to each other. Article 4, section 2 stated: "A Person charged in any State with Treason, Felony, or other Crime, who shall flee from Justice, and be found in another State, shall on demand of the executive Authority of the State from which he fled, be delivered up, to be removed to the State having Jurisdiction of the Crime." But it was harder to thwart international escape, and revising extradition treaties was a sluggish, difficult process. Extradition was intended to affirm a state's sovereignty and strengthen its international law enforcement abilities. Instead of empowering the United States and Canada, however, the extradition laws were paralyzing them.[20]

Boodlers were often criticized for "laughing at the law" and disregarding legality. In fact, it was just the opposite: They acted with a careful consideration of the law and a deep confidence in it. For the boodlers to show themselves so openly—when the United States desperately wanted them and Canada wanted to be rid of them—they had to truly believe that both states had no choice but to acquiesce to the dictates of the extradition treaty. Beyond demonstrating a profound faith in the rule of law, the boodlers also highlighted the dialectical relationship between law and lawlessness. While extradition law was meant to bring order to the international border, it inadvertently inspired and encouraged new crimes. The boodlers did not represent the breakdown of law at the U.S.-Canadian border; rather, they exposed the drawbacks of rigid adherence to legal codes that could not keep pace with social transformations. The boodler problem did not exist independent from extradition law; it was actually created by the law, in the gray area at the meeting point of two sovereign powers.[21]

✻

At the 1885 convention of the American Bankers Association, one of the leading items on the agenda was the upsetting rise in embezzlements during the previous three years. In one of six papers on the matter, Wharton business professor Albert S. Bolles argued that the problem was not careless oversight but the lure of temptation. As a preventative measure, he suggested dismissing employees who were partial to gambling, horse races, or fancy clothes. But the most seductive temptation, and the hardest to combat, was the looming presence of the Canadian border. "The chances for escape . . . by running away," Bolles complained, "are so great that persons with an evil intent do not fear of feeling the power of the States." He cursed the example set by the embezzler in Canada, who lived "almost within sight of the scene of his crime, where he can look at his victims and mock them, and yet live in security." Canadian asylum not only precluded punishment, but actually encouraged crime.[22]

Bolles's widely reprinted speech echoed a common refrain: that international mobility brought about domestic instability. The border was a convenient scapegoat for fears and anxieties about an unsteady social order because it seemed to undermine the law. For those with the power to decide which acts should be criminalized, the international border posed a threat for a simple reason. People could cross more easily than ever before, while legislation remained stymied at the international line.

The border's allure alarmed those who most acutely felt the effects of boodlers' transgressions: banks and corporations, as well as the insurance companies that covered these institutions' losses. Larger banks could survive, though at a great cost, but smaller banks often had to close their doors permanently after a serious embezzlement. An annual report issued by the comptroller of the currency listed banks across the country—from Massachusetts to North Carolina to Minnesota—that failed after a clerk, cashier, bookkeeper, or even president absconded to Canada. "The business community is, and has been, suffering for a number of years from an epidemic of a particular class of crimes," explained Edward S. Washburn, a representative from the Chicago Board of Trade, at a national meeting in 1887. These crimes "bring financial ruin to the victims, and always exert a most pernicious and demoralizing influence upon the community at large. Almost every day we read in the papers that some one who has been filling an office of trust has gone to join the

American colony in Canada." For the sake of the health of the U.S. economy, this "epidemic" needed to be contained and cured. Not only striking workers but also white-collar employees had to be disciplined.[23]

The banking and business communities felt that they needed to immobilize their workers to prevent their escape to Canada. Some employers sought to restrain their workers physically, hiring detectives to follow them and ensure that they did not run off. Others put their employees on rotating duties in an attempt to prevent embezzlements from occurring in the first place. The humor magazine *Judge* imagined yet another solution. The cover for June 20, 1885, which was captioned "How to Make Bank Cashiers Honest," showed a bank teller shackled to his station with multiple locks and a heavy chain. The teller is literally immobilized at his desk in an exaggerated depiction of exactly what his superiors wanted. Moreover, in addition to physical restraint, it also was necessary to hold back the swelling aspirations of white-collar workers. Boodlers not only endangered the stability of financial markets but also challenged the class boundaries of the capitalist system. Ordinary clerks were not supposed to rapidly accumulate vast fortunes; they were expected to slowly, patiently work their way up over time. Getting rich quick was not a proper American dream.[24]

Rather than looking inward for systemic flaws in the financial system, the business community blamed the rash of embezzlements on an external threat: the international border. Elites found it easier to blame the crime wave on the ease of escape to Canada than to question the economic or social status quo. The promise of asylum just over the Canadian line "constantly holds out a temptation that is often too strong for even tried and trusted men," stated an editorial in the *Chicago Tribune*, looking at the issue from an employer's perspective. Washburn took a practical stance: "Probably some would take the risk under any circumstances," he reasoned. "But is it not likely that many would be deterred from committing crime if they knew that detection would surely lead to the penitentiary, but who now feel that, if the worst comes to worst, they have only to cross the border to escape punishment?" The border encouraged embezzlements because it eliminated the risk of getting caught.[25]

Although their interests differed, representatives of capital and religion diagnosed the embezzlement epidemic in similar ways. Moral reformers, too, were in a panic about the boodlers. The *Independent*, a liberal religious weekly from New York, warned readers that the Canadian border presented an evil temptation to men who might otherwise be upstanding citizens. Reverend Henry A. Riley, writing in the pages of *Zion's Herald*, agreed. Repeating the theme of the elimination of risk, he reflected: "Embezzlement is the great financial crime of the century, yet a defaulter who leaves New York twelve hours ahead of the officers of the law is absolutely safe if he takes a train for Canada. What a temptation to crime this certainty of exemption from punishment produces."[26]

The temptation of the Canadian border drove the plot of short stories, dime novels, and literary works by authors such as William Dean Howells and Theodore Dreiser. In Dreiser's *Sister Carrie*, the long moral decline of the character of George Hurstwood begins when he steals money from his employer's safe and runs off with his lover, Carrie, to Canada. This episode was based on the actual experiences of Dreiser's sister, Emma, who eloped in 1886 with a Chicago clerk who had just taken $3,500 from his employer's vault. Hurstwood is not a hardened criminal; he does not plan this crime ahead of time. Rather, he finds the safe open by chance, and even then hesitates to take the money—until he discovers that he and Carrie can safely reach Canada before his employers begin their pursuit. The facility of crossing the border is the deciding factor for Hurstwood as he succumbs to temptation.[27]

Part of the border's allure derived from its proximity. Fugitives could reach the Canadian line from the major American commercial centers in only a few hours. The *Independent* called 6:30 P.M. the most dangerous hour of the day, as that was the time the train for Montreal departed from New York City. "The paying teller of any of the large banks could by that train convey himself to Canada, with a million or two of the bank's funds," the author imagined. And his trip could not be easier or more comfortable. After taking an early dinner, the boodler would enjoy an undisturbed sleep in his Pullman car and reach Montreal in time for breakfast. In Chicago, the hour was half past eight, and the line was the Michigan Central. Though the timetables varied, the results were the same. Banker George H. Adams lamented: "It is now known to every office boy . . . that in a single night he may forever distance pursuit; when the time of detection is near, the bank teller knows he may close the bank at the usual hour, and be in Canada long before the hour of opening on the next morning."[28]

Modern transportation also alleviated the sense of psychological distance from home. An editorial in the *Boston Globe* wondered whether Americans in Canada ever felt homesick. "The nearness of the shores of Canada has been a temptation to crime," the author claimed. "The exile there felt that he was not far from his own land; only a narrow river or an imaginary line separated him from it." Many boodlers received regular visits from friends and family who lived in the United States. In a single month in the summer of 1884, John Chester Eno was visited in Quebec by his brother, sister, assorted in-laws, and close friend James F. Pierce, a state senator from New York. Boodlers stayed current with events in the United States; they read American newspapers, chatted with American tourists, and debated American politics. Occasionally, they surreptitiously sneaked across the border for a quick trip to visit a sick family member in the United States.[29]

While improved transportation generated a feeling of proximity between the United States and Canada, the limits to extradition fostered a sense of distance. Legally, the boodlers were as safe in Canada as if they had traveled to the farthest reaches of the globe. The U.S.-Canadian border produced a paradoxical sensation of being both near and far, of transparency and impermeability. American fugitives, along with their loot, could cross with ease, but American law could not. These circumstances were eminently frustrating to those who remained powerless on the southern side of the border.

Two editorial cartoons in the humor magazine *Puck* demonstrate this sense of the border's simultaneous proximity and distance. On the cover for June 17, 1885, entitled "Canada as 'Mother Mandelbaum,'" editor and illustrator Joseph Keppler highlighted the inability of American law to get hold of the boodler by drawing the border as a fence. Canada, serving as gatekeeper, only lets the ruffians in; she refuses to admit Uncle Sam, the upright constable. Yet the fence that confines Uncle Sam on the U.S. side is frustratingly low: he can clearly see the fleeing boodler on the Canadian side, flaunting his freedom with the tip of a hat, as well as the mansions of other famous boodlers. Fredericka "Mother" Mandelbaum, one of the few female boodlers, was an infamous "fence," or receiver of stolen goods. In Keppler's cartoon, Canada acts as a fence in a double sense. She is an obstacle to free passage, and she also receives the illicit boodlers as well as their stolen money. In an article accompanying this illustration, Keppler explained, "When the strong arm of the United States law reaches out after the thieves, Canada leans gently over the boundary line and says: 'I have them and you can't get them.'"[30]

The concept of a fence at the border was purely metaphorical. On the actual borderline, there were no physical impediments. In the 1880s, passengers on trains and ferries could cross without hindrance; neither passports nor identification documents nor physical examinations were required. A customs agent on the Canadian side inspected luggage looking for dutiable goods; however, the 1891 *Canadian Guide-Book* assured travelers that "the search is not severe if the traveler shows a disposition to facilitate it." Moreover, bags full of cash may have looked suspicious, but they were not dutiable.[31]

While Keppler focused on the powerlessness of law to cross the border, cartoonist Frederick Burr Opper emphasized the ease with which fugitive persons and capital could escape across the international line. Instead of an impassable fence, Opper depicted the border as a mere scratch on the ground, an invisible line rather than a physical obstacle. The light-footed boodler, with his oversized carpetbag, jumps gracefully from the United States into Canada. Unlike Keppler, who merely criticized Canada for offering an asylum, Opper accused the Dominion of actively aiding and encouraging boodlers, undoubtedly to profit from their "stolen money." The words on the sign mock Matthew 11:28: "Then Jesus said, 'Come all ye who are weary and heavy-laden, and I will give you rest.'" Canada, instead, beckons those who are "wary" of law enforcement and "heavy-laden" with loot. Meanwhile, American law is still foiled. A barely discernible detective in the upper right corner stands with his feet fixed on the U.S. side, altogether ignored by the boodler and

Canada as "Mother Mandelbaum": The U.S.-Canadian border as an impenetrable fence, preventing American law enforcers from pursuing fugitives who crossed northward. Joseph Keppler, *Puck*, June 17, 1885. Library of Congress, Prints and Photographs Division.

"The Helping Hand": Canada helps the boodler across the border. The boundary line is merely a scratch on the ground, presenting no obstacle to the crossing of American crooks and capital. Frederick Burr Opper, *Puck*, August 12, 1884. Library of Congress, Prints and Photographs Division.

powerless to halt his escape into Canada. The boodler may find the border ethereal, but it still obstructs the detective. The inability of U.S. law to penetrate the Canadian border was all the more frustrating because of the ease with which U.S. capital flowed across.[32]

The boodlers' loot was not the only U.S. capital flowing northward during the 1880s. American investments in Canada multiplied in the last decades of the nineteenth century, especially in railroads, mining, and logging. American corporations like Singer, General Electric, and Westinghouse constructed plants in Canada; Western Union and Bell Telephone operated through Canadian subsidiaries; and Standard Oil bought up rivals in the Canadian petroleum market.

Corporations also lobbied to knock down tariff walls and open up freer trade. Using the same metaphor as frustrated law enforcers, Erastus Wiman, an advocate of commercial union between the United States and Canada, condemned the customs line between the neighboring countries as "a barbed wire fence."[33]

For American companies interested in freeing up capital flows across the border, drawing a distinction between their legitimate and the boodlers' illegitimate capital was critical. But from the Canadian perspective, this difference was not always so clear-cut. Some of the boodlers invested in Canadian business ventures and even ended up on the boards of Canadian corporations. John Chester Eno invested heavily in Quebec's Lower Laurentian Railway, which eventually became part of the trans-Canada route, and served as the company's treasurer from 1891 to 1895. (Though entrusting its finances to a known embezzler might seem improbable, the company owed its life to Eno, who convinced his wealthy friends in New York to buy stock in the venture.) John Keenan, another American exile, invested in mining and real estate around Montreal. In a joke printed in *Life* magazine, a teacher asks, "What is the capital of Canada?" and a student answers, "The money taken there by United States financiers and boodlers." In many ways, the boodlers' loot was simply one more form of American capital helping to build Canada; once across the border, the authorized and unauthorized flows were both legal tender.[34]

The inability to differentiate between legal and illegal capital derailed one of the earliest attempts by the American Surety Company to trap the boodlers. The insurance company called for the fugitives' arrest under a Canadian law that prohibited transporting stolen property into the Dominion. This law previously had been used to target Métis and native peoples who conducted raiding expeditions across the border. Unlike a branded cow or a clearly recognizable horse, however, fungible U.S. greenbacks could not be readily distinguished from each other. American Surety ultimately found the Canadian statute unhelpful "because it relates only to *the identical* property stolen, and there is no identity in money; hence, strictly legal proof that the fleeing thief has brought into Canada the precise property stolen can rarely be produced."[35]

While capitalists grumbled that the border seemed to convert bad money into good, religious reformers complained that fugitives were no longer considered criminals once they crossed into Canada. *Puck* poked fun at the idea of a border-crossing baptism cleansing boodlers of their sins, joking that "the waters of the St. Lawrence . . . wash the embezzler as white as snow." Yet there was another parallel that reformers almost never cited, most likely out of fear of eliciting sympathy: the fugitive slave. Crossing the Canadian border into a new sovereign jurisdiction had once changed the legal status of African Americans as well, from slaves to free people. Most boodlers were white; African Americans generally lacked access to large pools of employers' money and were often restricted in their ability to travel. However, at least one boodler was of Chinese origin: Chu Fong, a cashier in New York's Chinatown.[36]

The boodlers' urge to get rich quick suggested the same sort of moral failing attributed to gamblers in the late nineteenth century. In fact, religious publications explicitly named the boodler a species of gambler. Among the places where the *Christian Union* stated the "sin of gambling" could be found was "in the defalcations, embezzlements, violations of trusts, that fill the ranks of the American colony in Canada." For decades, moralists had preached that the only path to success and happiness was via the virtues of hard work, thrift, prudence, and abstention. Games of chance and risk, trying to get much for little, led to misery and ruin. The border seemed to subvert this moral order by eliminating the element of risk. The legal loophole in the extradition treaty eliminated the fear of punishment, which in turn encouraged vice.[37]

Reformers also feared that the popular press made boodlers appear attractive and appealing, an alternative model of how to achieve wealth and happiness. Tabloids made a business of sensationalizing the boodlers and dramatizing their supposedly lavish lifestyles. A new genre of crime reporting was born, which embellished the everyday lives of fugitives long after their initial misdeeds. Previously, the media's focus had been the crime itself. Embezzlement was a one-time story; the theft, not the thief, was the news. But by 1885, yellow journalists began to keep readers posted on the whereabouts, lifestyles, and financial conditions of American defaulters living in

Canada. These lengthy features typically filled an entire page, bore enormous headlines, and profiled the exploits of upward of a dozen individual boodlers.[38]

John Chester Eno, for example, kept making headlines long after Judge Caron denied his extradition. Reporters trailed him in Canada, wiring home news of his every move. "Mr. Eno is enjoying a fine time in Quebec, and is well pleased with his treatments in that quaint old city on the mountain side," reported the *New York World*, and it was clear why. During the next few months, readers discovered that Eno had moved into the best country house in Quebec, won a gold medal in a billiards tournament, owned the finest horses and sleigh in town, and brought his wife to a society ball "glittering in diamonds."[39]

From these articles, the boodler became classified as a type. The yellow press portrayed boodlers as nonchalant and fabulously wealthy, "enjoying themselves as inclination and purse permit." They reportedly resided together in "boodler colonies" and enjoyed active social lives. "In Montreal," claimed the *Boston Daily Globe*, "boodlers may be seen in stores driving fashionable turnouts, at the theatres, on the principal thoroughfares, in the fashionable gambling dens of St. Lawrence, Main and St. James streets. They are mostly club men, dine and spend their evenings with the upper ton of society at fashionable establishments, and are often seen at balls given by leaders of society." In these stories, exile in Canada seemed a privilege rather than a sacrifice. Eno professed to "like the people better, and feel better" in Quebec than in New York. Abner Benyon, formerly of the Pacific National Bank of Boston, claimed that he had never enjoyed better health. The attraction of Canada could appear so threatening that, when *Century Illustrated Magazine* published a standard travel feature entitled "Canada as a Winter Resort" in February 1886, a reader replied with an irate letter accusing the magazine of encouraging embezzlements.[40]

Much of what the papers reported was erroneous. The boodlers were spread out across Canada, and few of them socialized together. They were a diverse lot, ranging in status from former bank presidents to the lowest-level clerks and cashiers. Many were practically broke, having fled the United States after losing company funds rather than embezzling money to bring with them. Nevertheless, as a composite figure in the popular press, the quintessential boodler was characterized above all by his transgression of class boundaries.

Thanks to this breach of status, the boodler took on a sympathetic, almost heroic quality in the popular press. While the sensationalized stories never actually praised the boodlers' crimes, neither did they condemn them. Boodlers were no worse than the capitalists they stole from. "Some of the millionaires of our current census obtained their fortunes by means scarcely, if any, more reputable than that resorted to by the embezzler who rifles the safe which he is paid to guard," commented *Frank Leslie's Illustrated Newspaper*. Jokes about the clever boodler turning the tables on his boss were ubiquitous. The *Life* magazine cartoon "A Financier" exemplified this portrayal of the boodler as a witty trickster. A bank president insists that his cashier accumulate a fortune before marrying his daughter. The cashier promises to have one before evening, "and—by the way—you will have no objection to the ceremony taking place in Canada?"[41]

The romanticized boodler challenged a social order in which a handful of capitalists wielded immense wealth and power, and middling managers found their dreams of "getting up the ladder" nearly impossible to achieve. By the end of the nineteenth century, middle-class Americans defined success as an "unceasing increase" of money, deal making, and prestige. Failure was signified not only by calamity or collapse but also by stasis and stagnation. A life of averageness and inertia was considered a loss of freedom, a confinement "not in a damp, dark prison but in a dull, dead office." The boodler protested his dead-end job and inability to move up in the capitalist workplace by actively fashioning a new life with all the trappings of success. A Robin Hood among robber barons, he subverted the established economic and political order by stealing from the rich. The words commonly used to describe Canada's relationship to the boodler—refuge, asylum, freedom, liberty— underscored a sense of liberation. He lived out the American dream of becoming a self-made man—but to do so, he had to go to Canada.[42]

An 1886 anecdote demonstrated that some members of the working class looked on the boodlers with a sense of solidarity. On the train to Montreal, a *New York Times* reporter realized that the railroad porters mistook him for a boodler. Describing his journey in the third person, he wrote:

> When he is received on board the train by the conductor and porter he knows that he is an object of interest, and that they feel like conspirators in permitting him to shake the dust of New-York City from his feet. They take every possible occasion to say something cheerful to him when the train is in motion, and seem anxious to keep him fully posted about the country through which the train is speedily being drawn. When he reaches the border line between the United States and Canada they break out into a laugh which seems to say, "Well, he's all right now."

Many train porters at this time were African American, though the *New York Times* article did not specify whether that one was. Possibly the porter saw the train as a parallel to the legendary Underground Railroad that helped fugitive slaves escape to Canada.[43]

Bankers and moral reformers desperately felt the need to combat the positive image of the boodler. They attempted to devise an alternate narrative that centered not on the outer trappings of boodlers' high living, but on their loneliness, regret, and inner spiritual desolation. In January 1886, the *New York Evangelist* began printing its own updates about American fugitives in Canada: "Silas E. Cheek of Clinton, Mo., having embezzled a large sum from the bank of which he was cashier, has gone to Canada, leaving this schedule of assets for his creditors: 'I am a thief and a scoundrel, knave and a liar.'" Other stories focused on the victims of embezzlements, not the capitalists but the suffering widows and orphans whose savings were lost. The American Surety Company released a report in 1887 claiming that boodler jokes lowered public morals by "familiarizing our maturing youth with flippant treatment of the subject of crime." Others challenged the appeal of crossing the border. The normally humorous columnist Bill Nye took a somber turn when writing about an American he met in Canada who described himself as "the man without a country. People think I am over here having a good time with the large sum of money I am supposed to have. I am not having a good time."[44]

In the end, however, reshaping the boodlers' image was only a partial fix. To deter future embezzlements, bankers and moral reformers realized that it was necessary to locate, capture, and discipline boodlers. The unrestrained mobility that fugitives enjoyed needed to be contained. Yet there were numerous, sometimes contradictory theories of how to control international border crossings. The boodlers had to be apprehended, but the method for catching them was still unresolved.

❋

There were many potential responses to the problem of international mobility, and extradition law was not necessarily the most effective. Banks and companies often hired private agents, particularly detectives from the Pinkerton Agency, to pursue fugitives. By doing this, they circumvented both a reliance on the state to act and the obligation to respect Canadian sovereignty. The various attempts to stop the boodlers can be grouped into two categories. One solution was to prevent them from crossing the border into Canada in the first place—in other words, to make the border more like a fence, restricting fugitives' movement across the line. The other solution was to reach the long arm of the law across the border—to weaken the legal significance of the border, thus making it easier for American law enforcement to reach to the other side.

The most commonly suggested solution to the boodler crisis was to amend the extradition treaty, but this was far from simple or speedy. It meant entering the sluggish realm of international relations: months or even years of diplomatic negotiations followed by lengthy debates in the British Parliament and U.S. Senate that were often inflamed by party politics. Moreover, extradition was not the most pressing diplomatic issue when it came to Canada. Throughout the 1880s, the United States and Britain argued over American rights to use Canadian fishing grounds, and in 1886, the United States seized Canadian ships in the Bering Sea in a dispute over the lucrative seal fur trade.[45]

After two years of negotiations, an amended extradition treaty was finally drafted in June 1886. The Phelps-Rosebery Treaty—named after Edward John Phelps, the U.S. envoy to Britain, and Lord Rosebery, the British foreign secretary—added four new extraditable crimes: manslaughter, burglary, embezzlement, and "malicious injuries to property whereby the life of any person shall be endangered." This last offense turned the otherwise uncontroversial document into a firestorm. It obviously targeted members of two radical Irish nationalist organizations operating from the United States, the Fenian Brotherhood and the Clan na Gael. These groups periodically made raids into England and Canada, attacking government buildings with dynamite as a tactic to pressure Britain to withdraw from Ireland. Both Democratic and Republican senators feared alienating the Irish vote, and they managed to delay consideration of the Phelps-Rosebery Treaty for nearly three years. The treaty's most vocal opponents portrayed it as a devil's bargain. "I wouldn't give up one decent Irishman to England for a hundred boodle Aldermen!" declared Virginia senator Harrison Riddleberger. On February 1, 1889, the Senate finally rejected the treaty by a vote of fifteen to thirty-eight.[46]

This situation was unacceptable for the banks, businesses, and insurance companies that had a financial stake in stopping the boodlers. At its annual meetings in 1885, 1886, and 1887, the American Bankers Association passed a resolution formally calling for an amendment to the extradition treaty. The vice president of the American Surety Company, which insured the largest banks in New York against defalcations by their employees, appeared before the Senate Committee on Foreign Relations in January 1889. Urging treaty revision, H. D. Lyman listed fifty-three embezzlers who took a total of $3,840,570 to Canada during the Senate's first year of delay on the Phelps-Rosebery Treaty.[47]

Rather than waiting for the Senate to act, these interested parties turned to private methods of law enforcement to stem the unauthorized flow of capital across the border. Many hired private detective agencies to track down embezzlers, retrieve their money, and set an example to deter employees in the future. The American Bankers Association even contracted the Pinkerton National Detective Agency to handle all cases involving its member banks.[48]

Ideally, detectives would apprehend embezzlers before they crossed into Canada. The arrest of Clasen Graham in 1885 demonstrated the system working at its best. Graham, a clerk for the oil brokers Spencer Trask and Company in New York City, was bonded by his company for his honesty. A detective hired by the insurance company to periodically monitor employees noticed that Graham was staying out late and spending more money than his salary justified. He began to observe Graham more closely, and one evening caught sight of him boarding the train for Montreal. The detective immediately telegraphed the insurance company that he also was getting on the train and would look for orders at the first stop in Springfield, Massachusetts. The insurers notified Spencer Trask and Company, who only then figured out that Graham had embezzled $20,000. Word was wired to Springfield, where the detective arrested Graham. Only four hours had elapsed between Graham's misdeed and his arrest; the speed of modern technology could work in the detective's favor as well as the boodler's.[49]

But pursuits did not always proceed this smoothly. The Pinkertons specialized in catching career criminals who struck multiple times, like train robbers, sneak thieves, and counterfeiters. The agency collected thousands of photographs of known criminals, called the Rogues' Gallery. Yet the identification of past criminals was practically useless when it came to stopping embezzlers, who generally had clean criminal records and sometimes acted out of spur-of-the-moment impulses. Pinkerton himself lamented that "in the case of embezzlers without criminal records, and who were not under suspicion of surveillance, it was practically impossible to intercept the fugitive between the time of his starting for and reaching Canada."[50]

Detectives began to think up new and more aggressive tactics to prevent boodlers from crossing into Canada, essentially amounting to a makeshift form of border patrol. The official U.S. Border Patrol was not created until 1924, nearly forty years later; these local constables and private detectives were improvising a new type of border policing. They stationed themselves at the most popular border crossing points and monitored Canada-bound trains, searching for suspicious-looking people. The Detroit–Windsor ferry depot was observed particularly closely, and the routes out of Chicago were patrolled so heavily that Illinois state attorney Julius Grinnell boasted: "[Boodlers] can't get away from here. The road to Canada is not wide enough . . . to travel without bumping up against one or two detectives." The strategy was simply to observe a passenger's appearance and demeanor. Some detectives claimed that they could recognize a fugitive from justice at sight, leading the St. Louis Globe-Democrat to wonder just what "the precise facial characteristics of a boodler" were. It was not uncommon for detectives to accost an innocent man.[51]

American detectives did not confine their efforts to the U.S. side; they also breached the border in their pursuits. Technically, it was acceptable under international law for a detective to follow a boodler across the Canadian boundary, but making arrests in Canada and conveying a prisoner back to the United States were violations of Canadian sovereignty. Yet Canadian sovereignty itself was an ambiguous concept, given that Great Britain still controlled its foreign affairs. Following the letter if not the spirit of international practice, American detectives set up patrols in Windsor, Ontario, hoping to seize boodlers before they stepped off incoming ferries and trains onto Canadian soil. They also tracked boodlers down at their Canadian residences and bullied them into handing over whatever stolen money remained. In novels such as William Dean Howells's The Quality of Mercy and Theodore Dreiser's Sister Carrie, American detectives track embezzlers into Canada and provoke sufficient guilt to get them to return to the United States. Without overstepping their legal bounds, these detectives made life in Canada uncomfortable, a constant reminder to the boodler that he was a fugitive and his life in Canada was based on a crime. Pinkerton agents continued to follow John Chester Eno in eight-hour shifts for months, even after it was determined that he could not be extradited. For different reasons, both detectives and yellow journalists tracked Eno's every move.[52]

At other times, American detectives more closely skirted the line of sovereignty. One strategy, pioneered by Allan Pinkerton, was known as "procurement"—using trickery to lure a boodler across the border and arresting him as soon as he stepped foot in the United States. Detectives generally employed one of three tactics, alterations of the methods that the Pinkertons used to infiltrate labor unions. The first involved befriending a boodler, often claiming to be a fellow fugitive. Soon the detective would invite his new friend on a fishing or boating expedition on the Niagara River or one of the Great Lakes, and would row him over to the American side. The second strategy involved a more complicated ruse. The boodler would be hired for a phony job and given an important assignment in a border town. When he arrived, a detective posing as a driver would offer to take him to the boss's office, just a little farther away. Former bank clerk Albert Lange fell for this ploy, allowing a detective to drive him from St. Armand, Quebec, to St. Albans, Vermont. The third strategy was the simplest and the most common. A detective would hire an attractive woman to seduce the boodler and draw him across the border. Sometimes the woman would invite the boodler on a boat or train ride. If he lived in a border town, she might offer an invitation to her room just across the line.[53]

Although hiring a procurer was expensive, the cost was worthwhile. Detective James L. Brown followed Indiana bank clerk William Schreiber to Windsor, Ontario, "secured the services of a beautiful woman with whom Schreiber was known to be smitten," and arrested him when she lured him to Detroit. Brown sent the First National Bank of Columbus a bill for $37,000. "This is costly service," pointed out one editorial, "but when a man has gone to Canada with $100,000 or more of a company's money the company does not draw its purse strings very tight in making expenditures for his capture, not only to recover the money stolen, but to prevent peculation by its other employees, through the force of the moral influence arrest and punishment never fails to exert." Procurers were able to bypass Canadian law enforcers—something state actors would not have been able to do—but they still respected the border as a jurisdictional boundary. They did not lay a hand on the fugitive until his feet touched U.S. soil.[54]

Other detectives, however, utterly disregarded the border as a line of sovereignty. Some were so brazen as to kidnap a boodler and forcibly return him to the United States. One of the first kidnap cases to receive extensive scrutiny was the abduction of Lawrence Brainerd in September 1885. The year before, Brainerd had embezzled several thousand dollars from the St. Albans Savings Bank and fled to Winnipeg with his wife. A detective from the Boston agency of Wiggins and Wood tracked Brainerd down and befriended him, claiming also to be a "crook who had skipped across the line." They were met by two of the detective's associates while duck hunting on the prairie. Telling Brainerd that they would take him "by fair means or foul," the three men overpowered the fugitive, bound him, and drove him across the American border, sixty miles away.[55]

In some cases, local Canadian law enforcers cooperated with American detectives, looking the other way or even providing assistance when coercive tactics were used. Many Canadians wanted to be rid of the boodlers, whom they viewed as a corrupting influence. "It is a great nuisance to us to be made the receptacle for all your runaway defaulters and embezzlers," Sir John A. Macdonald, the Canadian prime minister, told an American correspondent in 1887. "You may rest assured that the Canadian people are not anxious to harbor these men." A close relationship formed between A. P. Sherwood, head of the Dominion police, and William Pinkerton, who took over the agency after his father Allan's death in 1884. The two of them kept up a regular correspondence and often called on each other for help in locating wanted persons. F. S. Hussey, head of the British Columbia police, also had a good working relationship with P. K. Ahern, who ran the Pinkertons' Seattle office.[56]

But cooperation broke down when local authorities with fierce territorial pride got involved. On discovering Brainerd's abduction, outraged Winnipeg officials unsuccessfully tried to intercept his kidnappers before they crossed the border. Calling the capture a violation of Canadian sovereignty, they threatened to take legal action to enforce Brainerd's return to Canada and secure the arrest of the detectives involved. "The people of the Dominion are not prepared to submit, nor will they submit . . . to an outrage upon their hospitality and an insult to themselves such as they have been subjected to in this kidnapping affair," vowed an editorial in the *Manitoba Daily Free Press*. But before objectors could make any legal headway, Brainerd escaped from American custody and returned to

Canada. His case, nevertheless, brought to the foreground the issue of the legality of the detectives' actions. Dueling editorials in American newspapers revealed a highly contested split opinion about whether kidnapping was justified. The *Independent* called the kidnapping "an outrage, in plain violation of international law," while the *Chicago Daily Tribune* defended the abduction.[57]

The threat of abduction had a chilling effect on boodlers. "They dare not walk out alone at night for fear of being seized from behind, bound, gagged and whirled away toward Sing Sing," the *Washington Post* reported. After a series of kidnap attempts, anxious boodlers made a point to stay away from the border, or moved to towns farther north. More of them began to disguise their identities. Rumors circulated that some detectives were blackmailing boodlers, asking up to $1,000 to protect the "quaking fugitives" from kidnappers.[58]

In one sense, American detectives reinforced the reification of the border as an absolute jurisdictional divide. The boodlers had taken advantage of the sovereignty inscribed in the border to escape punishment; now, law enforcers used it toward the opposite end. If boodlers were safe the moment they stepped foot into Canada, they were also trapped as soon as they touched U.S. soil, whether or not by their own volition. At the same time, though, the border was being broken down as an absolute line of authority. Kidnappings meant that boodlers were vulnerable even on Canadian soil; the border no longer protected them. They had to move increasingly farther into Canada, or beyond, to feel safe, creating a buffer zone that symbolically pushed the border outward. As nonstate actors, detectives also broke down the divide by working on both sides of the line.

Not all Americans felt comfortable with the idea of private detectives breaching Canadian sovereignty. Some newspaper editorials proposed an alternative method of approaching the border. Instead of making it easier for law enforcers to traverse, they proposed solutions that made it harder for fugitives to cross. Invoking the detectives who patrolled Canada-bound trains and the Detroit–Windsor ferry, an 1887 editorial in the *St. Louis Globe-Democrat* called for even more stringent monitoring of the border. It proposed that travelers be required to show identification and submit to questioning before receiving permission to cross, and asked: "Would it be unconstitutional to take [such] precautions at stations on the Canadian frontier, at any rate until extradition is a little less of a sham than it is now?"[59]

Throughout much of the nineteenth century, most Americans took freedom of movement for granted. The proposals for dealing with the boodlers anticipated the gatekeeping regime that would soon arise at the U.S.-Mexican and U.S.-Canadian borders. In the wake of the Chinese Exclusion Act of 1882, the problem of Chinese "leaking" into the United States was just beginning to be seen as a national crisis in the late 1880s. During the next decades, the United States would turn to more aggressive monitoring tactics at both its borders. This method of controlling the flow of people across the border was proposed, developed, and familiarized to Americans during the era of the boodler.[60]

✳

The cross-border actions of the Pinkertons and other private detectives had a chilling effect. While nonstate actors may have slowed the flow to Canada, however, it took an act of state before the boodler phenomenon was finally declared dead. By the end of the 1880s, embezzlers were starting to flee to places other than Canada, and in 1890 a new U.S.-British extradition treaty was finally ratified. Nevertheless, a subsequent rise in embezzlement rates verified that the problem was not the Canadian border; it was the continued inability of the law to keep pace with ever-expanding mobility. When Canada ceased to offer a safe haven, fugitives simply reached farther out to find asylum. U.S. law, it seemed, could not truly be effective unless it covered the entire globe.[61]

Canadians were disappointed by the U.S. Senate's rejection of the Phelps-Rosebery Treaty in February 1889. Despite Americans' frequent accusations that Canada encouraged the boodlers and welcomed their money, moralistic Canadian politicians began campaigning on an antiboodler platform, pledging to expel the American exiles from Canadian soil. Richard Chapman Weldon, a Conservative member of Parliament and well-known jurist, introduced a bill before the House of Commons the following month. The Weldon

Extradition Bill called for Canada to unilaterally surrender all fugitives whose extradition was not provided for under existing treaties. Weldon hoped to bypass the pitfalls of international diplomacy and solve the boodler problem by statute rather than treaty. Explaining his rationale in penning the bill, he told Parliament:

> I, as well as every respectable man in the Dominion, am suffering from the facility with which a thief, or blackmailer, or briber, or embezzler can find a refuge here. I go to a hotel, and the chances are that my name on the register is preceded by that of some well-known American boodler or defaulter. In the dining-room the chances are that I am put at the same table with this thief. I ride beside him on railroad cars; he sits in the gallery of this house and mixes with my family and friends. . . . He is a social Pariah, a national disgrace, a menace to our institutions, and a temptation to our clerks, our business-men, our cashiers, our bank officials, and our children to do wrong and live in luxury on the other side of the line, safe from pursuit and punishment.

Like American religious reformers, Weldon challenged the notion that the international border altered the fugitives' legal status. Instead, he argued that boodlers were still criminals even after they entered Canada, and ought to be treated as such. He also expressed a viewpoint that often would be voiced in the future: that Americans were corrupting Canadian life.[62]

Weldon's motives were entangled in party politics. The Conservative Party had been mired in corruption scandals for more than a decade. In fact, in Canada, the word "boodler" referred to Tory politicians as well as American fugitives. The *Toronto Globe* ran a regular column called "Watch the Boodlers," which reported incidents of bribery and corruption among Conservative members of Parliament, and listed the prime minister, Sir John A. Macdonald, as the nation's top "boodler in chief." The Weldon Bill gave the Conservatives a chance to reinvent themselves as moralists by speaking out against American vice, and to distance themselves from corruption by portraying the menace as coming from south of the border.

Liberal newspapers pointed out the hypocrisy of a Conservative leading the charge against corruption.[63]

Until that point, the boodlers had never formed the tight-knit community that the yellow press depicted, but now they finally lived up to their reputation. John Chester Eno and John Keenan led the crusade against the Weldon Bill. The two of them journeyed across the Dominion, soliciting contributions from fellow boodlers, and amassed a fund of nearly $100,000. They hired a lawyer to challenge the bill's legality, and then proceeded to Ottawa to lobby members of Parliament. Their lobbying efforts, many American newspapers surmised, merely amounted to the offering of bribes.[64]

Public opinion was divided over whether Canada should continue to shelter boodlers. When the bill went up for debate in the House of Commons, the disagreement was less along party lines than geographical ones. The members of Parliament who supported the boodlers hailed from the locales that had profited most from their influx of money. Delegates from Montreal and Toronto—cities where many boodlers settled and invested—testified to personal acquaintances for whom the Weldon Bill would create an "extreme hardship." "On the faith of our laws a man comes to this country believing that he will find an asylum here," explained M. P. Joseph Lavergne of Quebec. "He settles down and becomes a good citizen. . . . His family becomes connected very often with respectable families; and it would be most unfair, it would be an infringement of acquired rights, for a person from a foreign country to come and accomplish his arrest and his extradition." In contrast to Weldon, Lavergne depicted the border as a redemptive force that reformed fugitives; indeed, receiving a fresh start transformed them into the most illustrious of citizens.[65]

The boodlers and Weldon each won a half victory. On April 23, the House of Commons passed the bill, but the Quebec delegates managed to eliminate the clause that would have made the statute retroactive. Those Americans already in Canada were safe, but future fugitives would not receive asylum. The Extradition Act's true force was in its message, however, as it was never actually implemented. England barred its execution, claiming that it constituted foreign policy and therefore overstepped the authority of the Canadian Parliament.[66]

The next year, U.S. secretary of state James Blaine presented yet another extradition convention to Congress, and this time the Senate approved it almost immediately. The ten new offenses in the treaty included embezzlement, but none of them targeted dynamiters. Irish American groups expressed their wholehearted approval. Negotiated under a new presidential administration, as well as a newly appointed British envoy to the United States, the 1890 treaty suggested the dawning of an era of cooperation and understanding in U.S.-British diplomacy.[67]

At first, the new treaty appeared to solve the boodler problem. On November 18, 1890, Charles Pscherhofer of New York became the first person extradited from Canada to the United States on charges of embezzlement. During the next year, four more accused embezzlers were extradited. Within a year, stories about Canada-bound boodlers had vanished from the papers. By 1895, the *New York Times* observed that "people hereabout have almost forgotten by this time the flock of New-York 'boodlers' that fled to Montreal about ten years ago."[68]

Nevertheless, the rate of embezzlements in the United States continued to increase steadily during the 1890s. In 1889, the last full year before the new extradition treaty was implemented, reported embezzlements added up to $8,600,000. By 1893, they had more than doubled, totaling $19,932,692. Examining the statistics, an 1891 editorial in the *Washington Post* praised the end of the mass exodus to Canada, but questioned whether the 1890 extradition treaty truly could be called a success: "The reform that will remove the temptation to get rich in a hurry will be the most effective that can be adopted; but, unfortunately, it has not yet been discovered." The increasing crime rates convinced reformers that the problem had not been Canada per se, but the breadth and flexibility of new types of mobility. During the next two decades, American fugitives continued to flee to international asylums, particularly Honduras, Costa Rica, Brazil, and other stops along the steamship route down the Atlantic coast of Central and South America.[69]

An extradition treaty had been an acceptable solution with Britain, a great power with the resources to apprehend American fugitives. Extradition was a bilateral solution with reciprocal obligations, enabling cross-border law enforcement while at the same time maintaining a respect for each nation's sovereign boundaries. But when dealing with smaller and weaker countries, the United States turned to more unilateral and informal solutions. As American agents extended the reach of their policing even farther beyond the nation's borders, they began to breach lines of sovereignty and utilize more violent tactics in order to get their man.

2

Detectives without Borders

*I*ₙ 1891, John Bassett Moore published *A Treatise on Extradition and Interstate Rendition*, a two-volume, 1,556-page opus that for decades remained the preeminent source on extradition. Moore had just spent six years handling extradition cases in the State Department, first as a law clerk, then as third assistant secretary of state, and would go on to have a long and distinguished career as an international lawyer, law professor, and diplomat. His *Treatise* delved into case precedents, parsed treaty language, and explained domestic and foreign legal codes. But this magisterial work gave no sense of how rendition worked on the ground. The recovery of fugitives, for Moore, occurred in courtrooms and foreign ministries.[1]

Yet extradition treaties were simply hypothetical unless they could be enforced. The mere presence of a treaty was hardly tantamount to apprehending a criminal; fugitives first had to be discovered, identified, and caught. Treaties were pledges of cooperation at the highest levels of government, but they depended on ground-level structures of law enforcement. The diplomat needed the detective.

The realities of rendition at the turn of the twentieth century often looked little like the highly structured procedures that Moore described in his *Treatise*. Rendition means the transfer of a criminal suspect from one jurisdiction to another. Extradition, a set of legal procedures governed by treaty and statute, was simply one form of rendition. Other methods for bringing back fugitives included abduction or informal surrender outside the terms of a treaty, practices sometimes called "irregular rendition." The phrase is a misnomer, though: "irregular" forms of rendition were as common in the late nineteenth century as "regular" extradition.[2]

During the 1880s and 1890s, American law enforcers vastly expanded their reach into foreign countries through such "irregular" means. They particularly did so in Latin America, a region where the United States frequently rehearsed new imperial strategies first. Detectives brought fugitives back to the United States without going through a tribunal, and sometimes by force. Rather than observing the formal channels of extradition, they employed informal tactics that often bypassed any diplomatic or judicial supervision. Crossing lines of sovereignty, they began to go in and take people instead of waiting for states to hand them over.[3]

The 1886 Supreme Court case of *Ker v. Illinois* was critical in giving these detectives wide latitude to operate with impunity across borders. The precedent set by that case—that international kidnappings do not violate U.S. law—has been used in the twentieth and twenty-first centuries to justify international abductions by the Federal Bureau of Investigation (FBI), the Drug Enforcement Administration (DEA), and the Central Intelligence Agency (CIA). Dozens of law review articles have analyzed the modern implications of the case, but none has explored its nineteenth-century context in depth. The full story of a fugitive named Frederick Ker, abducted from Peru by a Pinkerton detective named Henry Julian, illuminates the central role of private capital in developing on-the-ground practices for retrieving fugitives.[4]

Moore's account put the state at the center of the action; however, in reality, nonstate actors like the Pinkertons operated with little oversight by the State Department. At a time when federal and municipal law enforcement in the United States was weak, private detectives were the most effective means of pursuing fugitives who crossed borders. Their paying clients determined their agendas, and most often these patrons were banks and corporations that wanted to recover stolen funds from embezzling employees. The profit motive, rather than Moore's legal principles, governed the expansion of international rendition at the end of the nineteenth century. International manhunts were driven not by the law of nations but by the bottom line.

These cross-border chases sent an important message about the Gilded Age economic order. The Pinkertons' clients considered embezzlement so dangerous that they sometimes lost money financing international pursuits in order to set the example that fleeing thieves and embezzlers could not get away with their crimes. Banks and companies desperately needed clerks, cashiers, and other employees to believe that stealing was too risky: no matter how far they ran, they would be caught. Thus, the Pinkertons were hired to discipline a white-collar labor force. Corporate executives might have amassed their fortunes in ways that were hardly more honest or honorable, but they had the law on their side. Supporting this vision of the difference between licit and illicit capital accumulation, court decisions like *Ker v. Illinois* gave the green light to private detectives' improvisational but effective tactics for ensuring that money stayed in its "proper" place.

The Pinkertons may have been nonstate actors, but in many ways they collapsed the distinction between corporate capitalist power and formal governmental power. Max Weber defined the state as having a monopoly on legitimate violence, but the Pinkertons practiced legitimate violence too. They forcibly kidnapped fugitives, and the courts allowed them to do so with impunity. Moreover, their mission was intimately tied to the state: they pursued people who broke laws legislated by the government, bringing them back to the United States to stand trial in state or federal courts. They sometimes traveled as quasi-state agents, supplied with official state documents like extradition warrants or bringing their captives back on U.S. naval ships. And, of course, the Pinkertons were hired by the same corporations that heavily influenced the U.S. government. Private detective agencies like the Pinkertons were essentially state-sanctioned nonstate actors who enjoyed many of the benefits of the state but were not held to the same restrictions or accountability. After the Pinkertons kidnapped Frederick Ker, they opened the door for other law enforcers—both rental cops and real cops—to turn to abduction as a legitimate rendition tactic.[5]

❋

On January 23, 1883, a week after Frederick Ker left on vacation, the Chicago banking firm of Preston, Kean, and Company received the letter in the mail. "I am not able to return to my post," Ker wrote, "in consequence of some disastrous speculations." Ker held what partner Samuel Kean called "a sort of general position," filling in for absent clerks, assisting the cashier, and often doing the general book-keeping. In his letter, Ker listed the funds he had taken from the bank, totaling $55,000, but pleaded with his employers not to look for him. The money was all gone, he explained, and "I have very little left except my almost worn-out frame and mind." However, the end of the note took a more threatening turn. Ker claimed he was safe in a distant place and all would be well if there were no attempt to expose him. But "if you decide to give the details of this affair to the public," he warned, his friends would spread rumors that would cause a run on the bank and "have the effect of finishing the bank's existence."[6]

The letter did not intimidate the bankers; it only angered them. Immediately, they sought an indictment from a grand jury. Next, they called on the Pinkerton National Detective Agency. "I never saw a man more determined to bring a rascal to justice than these gentlemen," Chicago superintendent William Pinkerton later told reporters. "They absolutely put no limit on us. We could have chartered steamers or anything else, and they would never have murmured." In the end, the *Chicago Tribune* estimated, the firm spent "in the neighborhood of $10,000" in its pursuit of Ker.[7]

As soon as the detective agency accepted Preston, Kean, and Company's case, the Pinkerton machine kicked into action. Technologies such as international telegraphs and photography enabled the detectives to carry out far more extensive searches than they had been able to conduct even twenty years earlier. The agency telegraphed Ker's description to chiefs of police from Maine to California and in the principal cities of Canada, with the order to arrest him at once, "regardless of consequences." In case Ker had traveled east to take a steamship to a foreign country, founder and president Allan Pinkerton directed his New York and Philadelphia agencies to search the passenger lists of vessels that had recently sailed and to inspect every one about to sail. The agency even sent a man under-cover to take a room at the West Side boardinghouse where Ker had lived, hoping for some clue as to where he might have fled.[8]

Neither municipal police departments nor other detective agencies could have carried out so wide a search. Pinkerton's was able to call on hundreds of agents around the country at a moment's notice. The agency employed a daily force of 2,000 and professed that it could call on reserves of 30,000—more than the entire standing army of the United States. While this claim may have been inflated, Pinkerton's nevertheless had more resources than even the most well-equipped police departments. Unlike the New York Police Department, which also searched for Ker, Pinkerton's could put enough men out on the New York docks to interview every sailor who passed through.[9]

After nearly a month of diligent searching, a Pinkerton operative in New York finally got a lead: an officer on the steamship *City of Para* confirmed that he had taken a man resembling Ker to Panama. The passenger who matched Ker's description had traveled under the name Alfred Perrott, but it did not take long to verify that he was indeed the wanted man. He had given the officer his coat, remarking "that he would not need it, as he was going to a warm climate." In the loop underneath the collar of the jacket was clearly written the name Frederick Ker.[10]

The *City of Para* was part of the fleet owned by the Pacific Mail Steamship Company, which transported not only the mail but also cargo and passengers from New York to points west. The trip from New York to the port of Aspinwall, Panama, took nine days, then one more to cross the isthmus via railroad. From there, the company operated routes north to San Francisco and even as far as Alaska; south to Peru and Chile; and, from San Francisco, west to Yokohama, Hong Kong, and Shanghai. Ker might have escaped to any of these destinations. His potential flight path mapped onto the far-reaching routes of capital that marked American trade and investment.[11]

The Pinkerton Agency now called on its international networks. Within days, thanks to operatives already on the ground in Panama, the Chicago office learned that Ker had boarded a ship headed for Peru three weeks earlier. A report from one hotel even claimed that Ker, now going by the name Warren Start, represented himself as a Pinkerton agent. "The effrontery and impudence of this young man . . . gave an added zest to my desires to effect his capture," seethed Allan Pinkerton, writing about the case a year later.[12]

Pinkerton chose Henry Julian to follow Ker's trail. The twenty-eight-year-old had worked closely with the agency's president for several years, assisting in operations that required particular shrewdness and caution. He spoke French fluently and, usefully, could understand conversations in Spanish. Moreover, he was inconspicuous. Newspapers agreed that Julian looked "about as much unlike the traditional, smuggling detective as one could imagine." The *Chicago Tribune* described Julian as "a small, black-bearded gentleman, whom one would hardly take for a detective," while the *New York Herald* likened him to "a very bright young Episcopalian minister." Julian departed for Peru on February 20, exactly a month behind Ker.[13]

The Pinkertons were an example of a private police: a nonstate, profit-seeking organization that filled a void in governmental law enforcement. Before the Bureau of Investigation (later renamed the FBI) was created in 1908, the Pinkerton National Detective Agency was the closest thing the United States had to a national police force, able to coordinate operations across borders. Its motto was "We Never Sleep," printed underneath a large, glaring eye—a slogan that some believe gave rise to the term *private eye*. (The other common story is that the term is short for private investigator, or private "i.") If a fugitive escaped across a state boundary, hiring a Pinkerton was the most effective way to catch him. If a fugitive escaped across an international boundary, it was practically the only way to catch him.[14]

Although these detectives were not representatives of the state, they wielded a quasi-police power that included the ability to make arrests. But they also acted in ways that official police departments could not, thanks to their highly coordinated network of offices around the United States, as well as their willingness to employ techniques of questionable legality. Sometimes their actions were blatant violations of the law, but more often they acted in a gray area that had not yet been designated as legal or illegal—what might be called the extralegal realm.[15]

The Pinkertons had a long history as agents of capital. Founded by Allan Pinkerton in 1850, the agency was routinely hired to provide background checks, infiltrate unions, and break strikes, most infamously during the Homestead Strike of 1892. They hunted down jewel thieves, railroad bandits, and union leaders such as "Big Bill" Haywood from the Industrial Workers of the World (IWW). Catching embezzlers like Ker was simply one more service rendered on behalf of banks and corporations. The agency charged a fixed rate per detective, affordable only to those with substantial means. In the Ker case, each man cost between six and twelve dollars per day, plus expenses, depending on the agent's experience. For especially difficult or delicate cases, the charge was even higher. The detectives drew the line at only one thing: searching for evidence of adultery. Founder Allan Pinkerton refused to let his agency take divorce cases.[16]

The Pinkerton Agency was involved in cross-border work from its earliest days. Working on behalf of the Union during the Civil War, Allan Pinkerton sent his men across the lines, posing as Confederate soldiers, to obtain military intelligence. In their first international arrest, the Pinkertons caught two of the notorious Midwestern train robbers known as the Reno Brothers Gang in Windsor, Ontario, in 1868. Soon the agency was operating throughout North America. During his twenty-two-year career, Pinkerton detective Charles A. Siringo took assignments from British Columbia to Mexico City. The agency's first major transatlantic triumph came in 1873, when it cracked a forgery ring that had counterfeited more than one million pounds in Bank of England notes. The Pinkertons and Scotland Yard together apprehended members of the ring in London, New York, and Havana, in one of the most far-reaching criminal investigations to date.[17]

In Europe, centralized federal police forces performed the work of chasing fugitives, both nationally and internationally. The model for police bureaus around Europe was France's Sûreté Nationale, founded by criminologist Eugène François Vidocq in 1812. Vidocq was inspired by Napoleon's centralization of the French gendarmerie into a single Ministry of Police, devoted specifically to protecting the security of the state. In 1832, he also helped to redesign Great Britain's Metropolitan Police, better known by the name of its administrative headquarters: Scotland Yard. By the end of the century,

Scotland Yard employed more than 13,000 officers, all operating under a single head. Because of the proximity of European countries, police forces developed a tradition of cooperation, sharing information, and coordinating international pursuits. Most of the European cooperative efforts were aimed at immobilizing common threats to the state—such as the anarchist movement—rather than at petty criminals.[18]

By contrast, nineteenth-century Americans opposed a formal, centralized police precisely because they associated it with the autocratic, repressive political regimes of Europe. L. C. Baker, former head of the U.S. Secret Service, wrote in 1867 that a federal police bureau was "contrary to the spirit of our republican institutions." Monarchs feared the people and constantly kept watch for popular uprisings, he explained, but in the United States there was no such danger because the people governed. The idea of a federal police came before Congress in 1870, when the Department of Justice was created, but it was swiftly voted down.[19]

The few federal law enforcement agencies that existed before the FBI's creation in 1908 were limited in scope and ability. There was the U.S. Customs Service, formed in 1789 to uphold tariff laws; the Post Office Inspectors; and the Secret Service, created in the Treasury Department in 1865 to combat counterfeiting. The only group with an explicitly international role was the U.S. Marshals Service, which had the authority to go to foreign countries to bring back fugitives from justice. In practice, though, its efforts beyond U.S. soil focused almost exclusively on the bordering nations of Mexico and Canada. Along the Mexican border, deputy marshals tracked and captured suspects—especially those that brought in rewards—but they rarely carried out these activities beyond the borderlands region. They lacked the resources, and often the incentive, to engage in more-distant chases.[20]

During the 1860s and 1870s, the U.S. Marshals' two biggest international arrests were more a matter of luck than keen detective skills. John Surratt, accused of conspiracy in the assassination of President Lincoln, escaped to Canada and then sailed to England under an assumed name. For a year and a half, American authorities had no trace of him. The break in the case came when an old acquaintance of Surratt's recognized him serving in the papal guard in Vatican City. A short chase later, he was caught in Alexandria, Egypt, in November 1866, and extradited to the United States. The other major international capture was that of William M. "Boss" Tweed in 1876. In 1873, Tweed was convicted of fraud and imprisoned, but he escaped to Cuba where he boarded a ship to Spain. He was caught when a Spanish customs officer who spoke no English recognized him based on a cartoon by illustrator Thomas Nast.[21]

Municipal police forces also struggled to carry out international work effectively. The first public detective branches were created in Boston in 1846, New York in 1857, Philadelphia in 1859, and Chicago in 1861, but were plagued in their early years by corruption scandals. Despite their growing professionalization at the end of the century, these detective forces still had trouble carrying out faraway investigations. They ran into jurisdictional problems; outside of a circumscribed area, their badges had no force. They also suffered from limited resources and a lack of connections to foreign law enforcement agencies. When alleged bank wrecker Gideon Marsh escaped the country in 1891, Philadelphia police simply gave up the chase. Detective Frank A. O'Brien explained that "it would take considerable diplomacy and no little money" to bring the fugitive back to Philadelphia, so, in effect, he was beyond their reach. The most effective transnational public detective force took shape after Thomas Byrnes was appointed chief of New York City's Detective Bureau in 1880. Inspired by the Pinkerton practice, Byrnes built a book of photographs of more than 7,000 known criminals, European as well as American, which he also called the "Rogues' Gallery."[22]

The Pinkertons had advantages in cross-border work that state actors lacked. They had offices in all of the major cities of the United States, as well as in Canada and Mexico, and by 1890 had opened branches in Europe. As soon as they received the description of a suspect, they could telegraph it to their operatives around the world in a matter of minutes. While traveling around Europe in pursuit of transnational criminals, the Pinkertons developed contacts and friendships with foreign police agencies. Founder Allan Pinkerton and his sons Robert and William frequently exchanged correspondence with the heads of police in Canada, Great Britain, and France.

They shared an informal pool of information about suspects, creating what one later observer called "a crude but effective Victorian Age Interpol."[23]

The agency became so well known abroad that some Europeans conflated the name Pinkerton with all American police. In Giacomo Puccini's 1904 opera *Madama Butterfly*, the Japanese protagonist marries an American naval lieutenant named Benjamin Franklin Pinkerton—a name meant to epitomize Americanism. But while the Pinkertons may have symbolized American power, they did not take their orders from the State Department. They acted in the interest of their paying clients, which might include foreign banks, companies, and even governments.[24]

The clients determined whom the Pinkertons pursued, and these clients were most often banks, insurance companies, and railroads that wanted to retrieve stolen funds from thieves and embezzlers. As a result, far-flung chases usually involved crimes against property, not crimes against the person. This was reflected in the extradition records for the years 1883 through 1899. Of the 296 requests that the United States made to foreign countries, often at the behest of private agencies, 77 percent were for financial crimes (embezzlement and forgery), while only 20 percent were for violent crimes (murder, attempted murder, and rape). A killer was far more likely to find refuge abroad than an embezzler. If Ker had taken a life rather than taking $55,000, he might have lived the rest of his days undisturbed in South America. Instead, he became an object lesson in the depth of a scorned bank's pockets, and the lengths to which the Pinkertons would go for a paying client.[25]

❋

Armed with Ker's photo and a sample of his handwriting, Henry Julian discovered his man among the expatriate community in Lima. Posing as a foreign investor, he took a room in Ker's hotel and befriended him. For the next month, the two were inseparable: together they played billiards, smoked cigars, attended the opera, studied Spanish, took walks on the plaza, and admired what one newspaper called "the limpid eyes of the Lima beauties."[26]

Julian was biding his time, waiting for the proper extradition papers to arrive from the State Department. The United States and

Photograph of fugitive Frederick Ker, carried by Pinkerton detectives.
National Archives and Records Administration, College Park, Maryland.

Peru had concluded an extradition treaty in 1874, and this was the
fourth time it was invoked. The delay was not the only problem,
though. For the previous four years, Peru and Chile had been engaged in a dispute over ownership of the mineral-rich Atacama
Desert region, in a conflict known as the War of the Pacific. In early
1883, when Ker and Julian were in Lima, Chilean troops occupied

the capital, and the Peruvian government had moved to the city of Arequipa, 600 miles to the south. The United States had no extradition treaty with Chile. Julian either needed to go to Arequipa to instigate formal extradition proceedings, or he had to bring Ker home without them. He decided on the latter. With the informal consent of General Patricio Lynch, the Chilean commander in Lima, Julian arrested Ker and took him back to the United States.[27]

Newspapers around the United States celebrated Ker's capture and cast Julian as a hero. The *San Francisco Chronicle* asserted that "the arrest is certainly a very flattering testimonial of Detective Julian," and the *New York Herald* agreed that "his energy, sagacity, coolness and pluck merits much praise from all who are interested in bringing these too numerous defaulters to justice." Regarding the rumor that there was a $10,000 reward for Ker's capture, the *Herald* declared that Julian "certainly deserves it, having periled his own life in the adventure."[28]

This was the first time that the Pinkertons brought back a fugitive from so far away, and the agency made the most of the publicity. Before Ker even reached Chicago, William Pinkerton issued a lengthy press statement, printed verbatim in newspapers. On July 16, the day after Ker's arrival in Chicago, both Julian and Pinkerton superintendent Frank Warner, who accompanied the men from San Francisco, gave interviews to the press. The story got the most circulation a few months later, when the agency published *A Double Life and the Detectives*, a "true crime" novel about its detectives' most exciting pursuits. Allan Pinkerton (or his ghost writer) used the Ker case as the basis for a chapter entitled "From the Bank to the Prison." Although he altered the names slightly—Frederick Ker became Frank Curran and Henry Julian became Henry Judson—the details of Julian's pursuit and Ker's capture were otherwise nearly identical.[29]

All of these accounts glossed over a pivotal event in the story, the moment when Julian actually took custody of Ker. But Ker's lawyer, C. Stuart Beattie, wanted to make sure that the issue was not overlooked. Speaking to a *Chicago Tribune* reporter, Beattie demanded that the public know the truth: Ker "was not extradited when taken from Peru. He was kidnapped."[30]

During Ker's trial in Chicago three months later, both sides agreed on the events of April 3, 1883. In the middle of his Spanish lesson, a dozen local men stormed into Ker's hotel room. Under Julian's supervision, the men forcibly transported him to Callao Harbor, where the U.S. naval ship *Essex* was docked. Ker never stood before any court or tribunal to determine whether he should be extradited, and Julian never presented his extradition papers to any Peruvian authority. For more than three months, Julian kept Ker prisoner—first, while the *Essex* sat at Callao for two weeks; then, as it sailed to Honolulu; and, finally, as a second ship, the *City of Sidney*, made the journey from Honolulu to San Francisco. When the captive demanded a lawyer, his requests were ignored. When he asked for consular representation—Ker had been born in Canada, and thus was a British citizen—he was rebuffed again. On July 9, the ship reached San Francisco, where police were waiting on the docks to arrest Ker and bring him back to Chicago to stand trial.[31]

Ker did not proclaim his innocence; instead, his defense hinged on challenging the validity of his arrest. When prisoners were unlawfully detained, courts could issue a writ of habeas corpus (Latin for "you shall have the body") to order their release. Ker's lawyers petitioned for the writ, first in the Criminal Court of Cook County, then in the Supreme Court of Illinois, and finally, three years later, before the U.S. Supreme Court. They argued that Julian, "without any warrant or authority whatsoever from the government of Peru, or any officer or diplomatic agent thereof, forcibly assaulted, arrested, and imprisoned this defendant."[32]

Ker's lawyers were Robert Hervey and C. Stuart Beattie, two respected figures in the Chicago legal community who had known the defendant before his arrest. Hervey, a native-born Scotsman, was one of the founding members of the Chicago Bar Association. He was renowned for his gentlemanly demeanor and dramatic courtroom gesticulations: in his *Sketches and Notices of the Chicago Bar*, Franc Bangs Wilkie described how Hervey "buttons his coat across his well-shaped chest, closes his eyes as if in a rhapsody, thrusts one hand into his bosom, and gracefully emphasizes with the other." Beattie, though less well known, was a skilled trial lawyer. This was his first time arguing before the U.S. Supreme Court, but not his last.[33]

Their argument centered on the fact that Ker had not been formally extradited. In the extradition process, there were certain procedural steps that needed to be followed, including a formal identification and the presentation of evidence of guilt. Ker should have had the opportunity to consult a lawyer and present his case before a Peruvian tribunal. But none of this had occurred. He had been brought back to the United States "without due process of law," his attorneys argued. If Ker possessed certain rights under the formal extradition process, how could he lose those rights simply because his captors decided to ignore the rules? "Now as this treaty inhibits the right to extradite—to deliver up to justice—lawfully, without obeying these provisions," they reasoned, "it necessarily inhibits the right to kidnap—to deliver up to justice—unlawfully, without obeying these provisions."[34]

Ker's attorneys insisted that Julian was bound to follow the terms of the treaty and did not have the option of deviating from it. A treaty was not a suggestion: according to article 4 of the Constitution, it was the "supreme law of the land," with the same force as any act passed by Congress. But Julian had behaved as if the treaty and its terms were discretionary. "Is this treaty a law to be enforced by the courts," the lawyers rhetorically asked, "or simply an international compact, to be obeyed or waived at pleasure, by the contracting parties?" If formal extradition was optional, what was the point of having a treaty at all? Hervey and Beattie argued that the treaty gave Ker a "right of asylum"—outside of its terms, he could not be touched.[35]

On December 6, 1886, the Supreme Court handed down its decision: it denied Ker's habeas corpus petition and upheld the trial court's sentence of ten years. The court rejected Ker's argument that he had been denied due process of law. The Fourteenth Amendment had no validity on Ker's arrest in Peru, wrote Justice Samuel Freeman Miller. Ker could not claim violation of his rights under the Constitution for acts that occurred abroad. The court also denied that formal extradition was the only way to bring a fugitive back from a foreign country. Miller did not go as far as to endorse Julian's behavior; he recognized that this was "a clear case of kidnapping." However, Julian's bad acts were not reason enough to release Ker without a trial. For the purpose of the proceedings, they were but "mere irregularities in the manner in which he [was] brought into the custody of the law."[36]

Miller, a critic of corporate power, did not write his decision out of sympathy for the Pinkertons' clients. Nor did he intend for his decision to sanction international abduction. Criticizing Julian's behavior, the judge even suggested some remedies that Ker might seek against Julian in the Peruvian courts, such as bringing suit for trespass and false imprisonment. The key, however, was that this could only be done under the laws of Peru. Miller subscribed to the idea of strict territoriality: a nation's laws applied exclusively on that nation's territory. Since the kidnapping took place in Peru, only Peruvian law was relevant; U.S. law did not start to apply to Ker until his feet touched American soil.[37]

As a result, the means by which Ker entered the country were irrelevant. If he was physically located on American soil, even unwillingly, he was subject to arrest and prosecution. The irregular manner of his rendition did not affect his status in court, as the Constitution did not extend extraterritorially. There were no consequences for bypassing the formal extradition process and instead violently seizing him—a decision that implicitly if inadvertently sanctioned abduction. Peru might choose to prosecute Julian for kidnapping if it could get its hands on him, but the United States would turn a blind eye to his tactics.

On the same day as the *Ker* decision, the Supreme Court handed down another opinion about extradition, with a seemingly opposite message about the necessity of following strict rules. The case of *United States v. Rauscher* involved William Rauscher, the second mate of the American ship *J. F. Chapman*, who had killed a member of the crew. The United States extradited him from Great Britain on the sole charge of murder, but the American prosecutor later wanted to add the charge of inflicting cruel and unusual punishment. Justice Miller ruled that it would be a violation of the extradition treaty to try Rauscher for any additional offense. Since the treaty was the "supreme law of the land," the second charge must be dropped.[38]

Justice Miller distinguished the two cases by pointing out their fundamental difference: Rauscher had been formally extradited, while Ker had not. The key was that even though Julian held extradition papers, "the treaty was not called into operation, was not relied upon, was not made the pretext of arrest." The treaty triggered certain rights and protections for Rauscher, but "it is quite a different case when the plaintiff in error comes to this country in the manner in which [Ker] was brought here, *clothed with no rights* which a proceeding under the treaty could have given him, and *no duty which this country owes to Peru or to him* under the treaty." By sidestepping the extradition treaty, Julian had effectively stripped Ker of any legal protections.[39]

There was another difference between the two cases: Ker had been abducted by a private detective, while Rauscher had been brought back by representatives of the state. Were state agents limited by constitutional constraints in ways that nonstate actors were not? Justice Miller could have distinguished the two cases on those grounds, but he opted not to draw a distinction between the rendition capabilities of private versus governmental actors. This left the door open for state agents to invoke *Ker* to excuse extraterritorial abductions in the future. In the twentieth century, the *Ker* decision permitted state-sponsored kidnapping, while its nineteenth-century context helped to give private detectives the latitude to fill in the void left by weak state law enforcement.

The rule upheld by the Supreme Court was called *male captus, bene detentus*, a Latin phrase meaning "wrongly captured, properly detained." The *Ker* case established that U.S. courts would give actors like the Pinkertons broad discretion to use whatever tactics they wanted to reach into foreign countries and bring back fugitives. Previously, international borders had constrained policing, but now they actually facilitated it because they gave law enforcers more power to act outside the country than within it. The laws and constitutional constraints that restrained police at home—such as the Fourth Amendment's restrictions on search and seizure, and the Fourteenth Amendment's requirement of due process—did not hold back American agents operating abroad.

✳

Ker v. Illinois would have broad implications in the future, as it permitted the Pinkertons and other detectives to regularize tactics of irregular rendition. After *Ker*, American agents started to go into foreign countries even in the absence of an extradition treaty or permission from the local government. Banks, corporations, and insurance companies hired detectives to find thieves and corrupt employees and bring them back to the United States. Knowing that there were no domestic consequences for their actions abroad, private detectives devised tactics that were much more flexible than those of the State Department. The legal improvisation practiced by the Pinkertons in "getting their man" could be seen as parallel to the sort of extemporaneous violence practiced by vigilantes in the West or lynch mobs in the South. All were part of a larger late-nineteenth-century moment of impromptu, improvisational, and privatized law enforcement that seized culprits at will.[40]

The State Department's policy in the 1890s was straightforward: it would only pursue extradition when there was a treaty in place. Under U.S. law, the United States could only hand a fugitive to a foreign country under the terms of a treaty, and as John Bassett Moore explained in his 1890 *Treatise*, "since the government of the United States does not grant extradition in the absence of a treaty, it refrains from demanding it under the same circumstances." In his capacity as assistant secretary of state, Moore applied that principle the same year, in the case of Major E. A. Burke, a former treasurer of Louisiana who fled to Honduras with state funds. Because Honduras had no extradition treaty with the United States, Moore refused to demand Burke's surrender.[41]

Private detectives, however, were not constrained by the State Department's rules, as they had discovered in *Ker*. During the 1890s, they frequently bypassed the formal extradition process and brought fugitives back from countries that lacked treaties with the United States. In 1890, the Pinkerton National Detective Agency made headlines when Robert Pinkerton himself traveled to Honduras to bring back Edward Sturgis Crawford, who had taken $41,000 from the American Exchange Bank in New York. Occurring just months after Assistant Secretary Moore refused to pursue Major Burke's extradition, the *New Orleans Daily Picayune* noted the inconsistency of the situation. Burke "is in Honduras whence Crawford was brought. Then why not Burke?" it asked. The difference was that the Louisiana authorities went through governmental channels, whereas the American Exchange Bank hired private detectives to bring Crawford back.[42]

Detectives created their own diplomacy, carrying out negotiations directly with foreign governments. In 1894, Pinkerton superintendent W. F. Forsee appealed personally to Guatemalan president José María Barrios to hand over Joseph J. Hahn without going through any type of a hearing or judicial process. After Barrios consented, Forsee complimented him as "the most Americanized man in Guatemala." The State Department was not completely absent from this transaction, but its role was limited to the mere formality of authorizing Forsee to act in the capacity of a U.S. marshal.[43]

Perhaps most famously, the American Bankers Association hired the Pinkertons to catch Robert Leroy Parker and Harry Longabaugh—better known as Butch Cassidy and the Sundance Kid—in South America in 1903. The hunt for the infamous bank and train robbers demonstrated the Pinkertons' international networks, the flexibility and informality of their methods, and the centrality of money as a motivating factor in the pursuit of international fugitives.

The Pinkertons had been on the trail of the "Wild Bunch" for years when Butch, Sundance, and Sundance's girlfriend Etta Place fled to Argentina. Pinkerton operative Frank Dimaio had just finished an assignment in Brazil, and he immediately turned his attention to the two ringleaders of the Wild Bunch. He printed a circular in Spanish with descriptions and photos of the fugitives. American vice consul George Newbury recognized the trio and informed the Pinkerton Agency that they were residing on a sheep ranch in the Cholila Valley. Although he lacked the proper extradition papers, Dimaio rounded up a posse to catch the outlaws. However, the rainy season rendered their ranch inaccessible, and the trio escaped before Dimaio could capture them. The Pinkertons offered to continue the search for Butch and Sundance, which they estimated at $5,000, but neither the railroad companies nor the American Bankers Association were willing to continue financing the hunt. After all, if brought back to the United States, the robbers might escape and again threaten U.S. banks and railroads—thus, it was preferable that they

NOMBRE........................George Parker
ALIAS........."Butch" Cassidy [a] George
    Cassidy; [a] Ingerfield.
NACIONALIDAD ....Americano
OCUPACIÓN.............Vaquero, tratante
OCUPACIÓN CRIMINAL......Ladrón de
    bancos y asaltador de caminos, ladrón
    de ganado y caballos.
EDAD....................36 años [en 1901]
ESTATURA.............5 pies 9 pulgadas
PESO.......................................165
CONSTITUCIÓN......................Regular
TEZ...Clara
COLOR DEL PELO.................Blondo
OJOS.......................................Azules
BIGOTE....................Leonado, si lo usa
OBSERVACIONES.—Tiene dos cicatri-
    ces en la nuca ; cicatriz pequeña de-
    bajo del ojo izquierdo, pequeño lunar
    en la pantorrilla. "Butch" Cassidy
    es conocido como un criminal princi-
    palmente en Wyoming, Utah, Idaho,
    Colorado y Nevada, y ha cumplido
    sentencia en el presidio del Estado de
    Wyoming en Laramie por robo, pero
    fué perdonado el 19 de Enero de 1896.

GEORGE PARKER.
Primer retrato tomado el 15 de Julio de 1894.

GEORGE PARKER.
Ultimo retrato tomado el 21 de Noviembre de 1900.

Wanted poster circulated in Argentina for Robert Leroy Parker, also called George Parker, but better known as Butch Cassidy. Pinkerton National Detective Agency Papers, Library of Congress, Manuscript Division.

remain far away in South America. With no funding, the Pinkertons abandoned the search. After a crime spree that crisscrossed the Andes, the desperados known as *"los Bandidos Yanquís"* were reportedly killed by the Bolivian army in a shootout in 1909.[44]

New private detective agencies ventured into international law enforcement, though none came close to the Pinkertons' size and scope until the William J. Burns International Detective Agency was founded in 1909. Thiel's Detective Service Company, a competing agency started by a former Pinkerton employee, had its most celebrated international success in the capture of Christopher A. Larrabee in 1896. Larrabee's disappearance from Chicago with $25,000 of his employer's money garnered particular press attention for two reasons: he was the nephew of the ex-governor of Iowa, and he reportedly committed the crime for the benefit of "a West Side woman of much beauty and many alluring qualities." The pursuit took more than a year, and according to one account, inspectors and detectives hunted him in twenty-five states. Thiel's agent finally traced him to Monterrey, Mexico, where he was selling fish in a town market. Detectives lured him onto U.S. soil and arrested him. Trickery and fraud, like kidnapping, were not grounds for dismissal in the United States, thanks to *Ker v. Illinois*.[45]

The Pinkerton National Detective Agency had many imitators, but the most blatant impersonator was called Pinkerton and Company, United States Detective Agency. (Ironically, despite the domestic bent to the two agencies' names, they both operated internationally.) Its founder, Matt W. Pinkerton, bore no relation to the family that started the original agency, but his distinctive name gave him a leg up in the detective business. In the case of *Pinkerton v. Pinkerton*, which languished in the Chicago courts for nearly a decade, Robert and William Pinkerton sought an injunction to prevent Matt from using the Pinkerton name in the title of his agency. The suit was finally rendered moot when Matt Pinkerton's firm folded during World War I.[46]

Private detectives could cause diplomatic headaches for the State Department. The Mexican foreign minister objected to Secretary of State James Blaine in 1891, when Matt Pinkerton "extradited" an accused railroad thief named T. J. Latner by seizing him in Nuevo Laredo, Mexico, and then forcibly transporting him across the border to Laredo, Texas. Charles W. Zaremba, director of the American and Mexican Investment Company, assisted Pinkerton in the seizure. Mexican officials went on to imprison Zaremba for participation in the capture, which a judge from Nuevo Laredo deemed a kidnapping. But from the point of view of U.S. courts, Pinkerton and Zaremba had done nothing wrong. In Texas, police custody over Latner was just as secure as if he had been formally extradited.[47]

The *Ker* legacy also affected the right of individual bounty hunters to abduct suspects from foreign countries. In the 1869 case of *Reese v. United States*, the Supreme Court had ruled that the authority of bounty hunters and bail bondsmen stopped at the international border. Once a bondsman posted bail, the bounty hunter "may at any time arrest [the defendant] upon the recognizance and surrender him to the court, and, to the extent necessary to accomplish this, may restrain him of his liberty. *This power of arrest can only be exercised within the territory of the United States.*" Technically, *Ker* did not increase the legal rights of bounty hunters, but in effect it did. Even though bounty hunters still lacked authority to operate internationally, there would be no consequences within the United States if they crossed borders.[48]

Private detectives and bounty hunters regularly bypassed formal extradition, but this did not render extradition treaties irrelevant. For the sake of maintaining good relations with foreign police departments and governments, extradition was still the preferred method of bringing fugitives back to the United States. During the 1890s, the State Department made an average of twenty extradition requests per year, often on behalf of the Pinkertons and other private actors. Detectives extradited if possible, but turned to informal methods of rendition when necessary.

※

Standing on a prime piece of real estate at the intersection of Broadway and Wall Street, the American Surety Building was the tallest edifice in New York City when it was completed in 1896. At 312 feet and twenty-one stories, the structure surpassed the spire of Trinity Church, which had previously dominated the skyline of Lower Manhattan. *Munsey's Magazine* called the American Surety Building "nothing more or less than a tower," but within a few years, another word would commonly be used to describe this new type of steel-skeletoned giant: skyscraper. Looming above Wall Street, it reminded potential fraudsters of the far-reaching gaze and the tremendous financial resources of the company whose name it bore.[49]

The American Surety Company was the first U.S. firm to offer insurance against the dishonesty of employees. It was founded in 1884 by Richard Allison Elmer, who, as assistant postmaster general under the Garfield administration, earned a reputation for eliminating corruption, mismanagement, and waste. Just as fire or life insurance provided a safety cushion in case of calamity, American Surety reimbursed companies if their employees stole from them. Not only private employees but also executors, administrators, guardians, trustees, and, later, public employees paid a bond to the insurance company, usually as a condition of employment. In exchange, American Surety promised to pay an indemnity to the employer if that employee mismanaged or embezzled company money. Known as surety or fidelity insurance, this model was so successful that within a decade a dozen more surety companies went into the business of insuring the honesty of American employees.

The most prominent were the Fidelity and Deposit Company of Maryland, the National Surety Company, and the United States Fidelity and Guaranty Company.[50]

The surety companies' business model hinged on the ability to find fleeing employees, no matter where in the world they went. Insurance providers faced large liabilities if fugitives ran off to countries where embezzled funds could not be retrieved. They staked their professional reputations on the surveillance of employees, not only in the workplace but during their leisure time as well. If anyone dared to steal the money and run, the surety companies vowed, he would be tracked down and brought back. While extradition agreements smoothed the process, it was critical to these agencies to be able to recover fugitives even without a treaty. The *Ker* decision allowed these businesses to thrive.

Louis Armstrong Hilliard, the former cashier of the *Chicago Tribune*, could attest to the surety company's reach. Hilliard had embezzled $15,000 from his employer, but American Surety held the ultimate financial responsibility for his crime. In September 1893, the company sent thousands of circulars "to chiefs of police in the United States, Canada, Mexico, and Europe, to Postmasters, government officials, tourist agencies, and United States Consuls . . . from Siberia to the Cape of Good Hope." At the top of the circular was a photogravure image of Hilliard, followed by a description of the wanted man in four languages. The campaign worked: two months later, a U.S. consul in Spain reported that Hilliard had been apprehended in Seville and most of the stolen funds recovered.[51]

The ability to retrieve fugitives was so integral to their livelihood that some surety companies even employed their own staff of detectives. American Surety was the first firm to maintain its own detective corps, which received press attention for catching fugitives in Canada, Mexico, South America, and Europe. In May 1893, the *Indicator: A National Journal of Insurance* carried an article entitled "American Surety Company as a Detective," describing some of the company's captures in the United States, England, and Latin America. "Men who contemplate becoming defaulters would do well to avoid securing indemnity bonds in the American Surety Company," the article began, "for they are all but certain to be caught eventually. The company has some twenty expert inspectors in its employ and defaulters are hunted down relentlessly and with a persistence which is pretty certain to result in their apprehension no matter where they flee to." By 1896, American Surety had a staff of twenty-four inspectors, including two stationed in Mexico City. A decade later, all of the major surety companies employed staffs of "man-hunters."[52]

Insurers were willing to go to extreme lengths to catch a fugitive. Sometimes this meant losing money to gain reputation. Charles E. Schick, the secretary of Illinois Surety of Chicago, wrote a widely reprinted article that essentially served as a lengthy advertisement on behalf of the surety companies. Emphasizing that they would stop at nothing to pursue a fugitive, he vowed:

> The defalcation may amount to $50. The chase may begin in Chicago, extend to San Francisco, into Mexico, thence to South America, across a continent to Rio Janeiro, on to New Orleans, to Kansas City, thence to New York, up into Manitoba, back to Buffalo, to New York again, then London, Paris, Madrid, St. Petersburg—it makes no difference. The loss was $50. The chase may cost $5,000. But in the end the man will be caught.[53]

The capture of Augustus Kerr (no relation to Frederick) in October 1892 affirmed this seemingly hyperbolic claim. American Surety detective Joel W. Bowman chased the Kansas City clerk, charged with stealing $25,000, through Canada, France, Norway, Sweden, Denmark, Germany, and Italy before finally capturing him in Liverpool, England.[54]

The most celebrated American Surety detective was Captain Charles E. Henry, a former U.S. marshal and postal inspector who received national attention when he retrieved two American embezzlers from Brazil in 1893. Henry initially set out in pursuit of Harpin A. Botsford, accused of embezzling $20,000 from a Cleveland lumber firm. On the steamship to South America, Henry became suspicious of a fellow American passenger. Wiring the company on his arrival in Brazil, he discovered that the man was Albert A. Cadwallader, a former bank president from Superior, Wisconsin, who had defrauded bank investors out of at least $100,000. When Henry arrived back in New York in April 1893, four months after he had departed, American newspapers marveled at the detective who set off for one fugitive and came back with two.[55]

This case confirmed to surety companies that pursuing fugitives as far as South America was worth their while. When Henry arrived in Brazil bearing only a photograph of Botsford and a sample of his handwriting, the U.S. minister in Rio de Janeiro skeptically called the mission "a needle in a haymow job." (Ironically, the handwriting sample came from a note that Botsford left his employers, in which he taunted: "Your purse is not long enough to catch me.") Henry's manhunt ended up costing more than $5,000, but it was money well spent. Nearly all the funds that Botsford took were recovered, including money he had invested in a Brazilian coffee *fazenda* (farm). Cadwallader turned out to be an even more lucrative catch for American Surety; he had been bonded by them for $18,000.[56]

Henry reaffirmed that it was possible to bring men back from a country that lacked an extradition treaty with the United States. In previous attempts to retrieve American fugitives from Brazil, extradition agents came home empty-handed. The captain of the steamship that took Henry and his two prisoners to New York joked that "he had brought down criminals escaping from our country, but he had never taken any of them back."[57]

Henry's biggest challenge was to win the assent of the Brazilian government, so he looked for ways around it. Brazilian officials offered to surrender Botsford voluntarily if the United States promised to do the same in the future; Henry, however, was under strict orders not to promise reciprocity. In Cadwallader's case, moreover, he lacked all of the proper diplomatic papers to request his surrender. "The Brazilian authorities are very particular on this point involving personal liberty," Henry complained. At Cadwallader's trial in the United States a few months later, Henry testified that formal extradition had not been used. Instead, he tricked Cadwallader into getting onto a steamship departing for the United States through an elaborate ruse involving a yellow fever scare. This tactic worked so well that Henry tried it again the next year, when the Costa Rican government similarly refused to let him bring home fugitive Robert Huntington due to the lack of an extradition treaty.[58]

Whether a representative of the American Surety Company or a Pinkerton operative, private detectives concerned with profits normalized "irregular" rendition in the last decades of the nineteenth century. What started off as legal improvisation—doing whatever it took to get their man—became, in effect, a legitimate way of conducting business. When the Supreme Court affirmed that kidnappings, ruses, and other deviations from formal extradition would not affect a court's ability to exercise jurisdiction over an individual, it effectively created a new business model for private detective agencies and surety companies. While the State Department continued to negotiate more treaties, those with the means to fund their own international manhunts hammered out their own norms, which were not dependent on two nations reaching an accord.

The American courts were not alone in upholding the principle of *male captus, bene detentus*. Great Britain had an even longer tradition of permitting extraterritorial abductions. The 1886 *Ker* opinion, in fact, cited the 1829 case of *Ex parte Scott* as a precedent. Fugitive Susanna Scott, wanted in England for perjury, was apprehended in Belgium and brought back to her homeland by an English police officer. Although her arrest violated Belgian law, Lord Chief Justice Tenterden held that "the court would not divest itself of jurisdiction." Acts that occurred in a foreign country were irrelevant. Scott could bring action against the police officer for wrongful arrest, but for the sake of her perjury charge, the court would not consider the circumstances under which she came to find herself on English soil. The English courts affirmed the *Scott* decision in *Regina v. Sattler* in 1858 and *Ex parte Elliott* in 1949. However, an 1890 Scottish case set a limit to the rule established by *Scott:* courts might consider how the defendant returned to the country when there was "substantial infringement of right." Although this phrase was not defined, the Scottish court nevertheless acknowledged the potential for abuse of power in the late nineteenth century, while American courts did not do so until 1974.[59]

British newspapers likewise reported spectacular international captures, though not with the same frequency as their American counterparts. Perhaps the most dramatic story was the abduction of swindler Jabez Spencer Balfour from Salta, Argentina, in 1895. Detective Frank Froest of Scotland Yard commissioned a private train, forced Balfour onto it, transported him to Buenos Aires, put him on a ship, and took him back to England. Froest returned home a hero, as well as Scotland Yard's go-to man for international chases. "When the long arm of Scotland Yard has to be extended to the far parts of the earth, it is Mr. Frank Froest who . . . journeys across continents," one story bragged. However, while accounts of irregular rendition were common among American detectives, Froest's capture of Balfour was big news in Britain precisely because it was not so ordinary.[60]

No matter how often the Pinkertons called themselves "America's Scotland Yard," there was a difference between a Pinkerton operative like Henry Julian and a Scotland Yard detective like Frank Froest. Froest was an agent of the British government rather than a private detective for hire, and this both empowered and circumscribed him. On the one hand, because he was not dependent on private clients to pay his salary, Froest could go after a wider range of malefactors than a Pinkerton agent could. He could pursue murderers as well as thieves across borders. On the other hand, as an official agent of the state, Froest was more likely to be perceived as a challenge to a foreign government's sovereignty. The Pinkertons could cross borders with much greater latitude because they were private rather than government investigators. Thus, stories of American private eyes informally taking custody of a fugitive were common, while tales of Scotland Yard detectives circumventing an extradition treaty were less frequent. Moreover, Scotland Yard often did not need to circumvent a treaty at all: many of its great "international" captures occurred within the British Empire, where extradition was not necessary. Sensational intraimperial captures included the recovery of the Jameson Raiders from South Africa in 1896 and the arrest of wife killer Dr. Hawley Harvey Crippin in Canada in 1910.[61]

Canadian courts also invoked the principle of *male captus, bene detentus*. The 1905 case of *The King v. Walton* initially looked like a model example of transnational police cooperation. A Buffalo, New York, police officer received a telegram from Toronto stating that "a man named A. R. Walton . . . is wanted here in Toronto, secure him if possible." Two American officers arrested Walton and took him to the police station in Buffalo, where he was searched and held until Detective Mackie of the Toronto police force arrived for him. However, Walton was transferred into Mackie's custody and brought to Canada without being taken before any judicial authority. In language similar to that of *Ker*—and, indeed, citing both *Ker* and *Scott*—Justice Osler of the Court of Appeal for Ontario observed: "We cannot enquire into the circumstances under which he was brought into this country. . . . If he is found in this country charged with a crime committed against its laws, it is the duty of our courts to take care that he is amenable to justice." Other commonwealth countries such as Australia, New Zealand, and South Africa abided by the same principle, at least until the late twentieth century. Israel, too, cited the *Scott* and *Ker* cases after Mossad agents kidnapped Adolf Eichmann from Argentina in 1960.[62]

Paradoxically, the Supreme Court's decision in *Ker* furthered the power of law enforcement by limiting the reach of law. Initially, international boundaries had thwarted law enforcement, preventing continued pursuit. *Ker v. Illinois* gave detectives the means to circumvent these borders. Since law enforcers abroad were not held to the same constitutional standards as at home, they had more tools at their disposal when they operated internationally. A kidnapping that would have been illegal in the United States was accepted by the courts if it took place abroad. The Supreme Court addressed a similar issue a few years later, in the Insular Cases of 1901 to 1905, which asked whether the Constitution followed the flag into territorial possessions. These cases affirmed that lesser degrees of American sovereignty—and thus fewer constitutional restrictions—could actually mean more power. Likewise, the George W. Bush administration used the same logic when it claimed that the U.S. Navy base at Guantánamo Bay was not U.S. territory—and therefore, it argued, the U.S. Constitution did not hold sway there.[63]

The Pinkerton Agency still exists today, but its name has been changed to Pinkerton Consulting and Investigations and it functions primarily as a security consulting firm. Once the embodiment of American power, it was bought by the Swedish conglomerate Securitas AB in 1999. Yet its legacy in cross-border policing endures. The *male captus, bene detentus* rule has been repealed in Britain and other commonwealth countries, but it perseveres in the United States. In recent decades, American lawyers have cited the *Ker* decision to justify everything from the kidnapping of drug traffickers in Mexico to the post-9/11 practice of extraordinary rendition. More than one hundred years later, the day of the marauding Pinkerton detectives may be no more, but their legacy is still going strong.[64]

3

An Empire of Justice

I N HIS 1904 Annual Message to Congress, President Theodore Roosevelt laid out the position that would come to be known as the Roosevelt Corollary to the Monroe Doctrine. Justifying the use of U.S. intervention to compel Latin American nations to comply with debt obligations, Roosevelt likened the United States' role in the Western Hemisphere to that of a policeman. In "flagrant cases of . . . wrongdoing or impotence," the president explained, the United States had not only the right but also the responsibility to act as an "international police power."[1]

Roosevelt may have announced a new foreign policy position, but his description of the United States as an international law enforcer invoked a familiar image. During the previous decade, Americans had envisioned themselves policing the hemisphere, and even the globe, through the aggressive pursuit of fugitives who fled the United States. "The world is a small place, and growing smaller every year for the man who flees arrest in the United States," boasted a 1903 article in the magazine *American Lawyer*. At the turn of the twentieth century, Americans imagined a world in which U.S. law could reach beyond the nation's borders—indeed, anywhere on the globe.[2]

According to politicians, popular newspapers, and middlebrow fiction, American law extended its reach internationally not through force or coercion but instead through a mightier instrument: the extradition treaty. Although in reality, detectives often operated outside of treaty terms, these international compacts still remained important. Tactics like abduction ran the risk of alienating foreign governments, so formal extradition was always the preferred means of rendition, at least from the point of view of the State Department. Moreover, extradition treaties carried a symbolic significance, marking a measure of international status in the community of nations. They were not merely a technicality noticed only by lawyers and diplomats. Newspapers and public speakers at the turn of the century celebrated the expansion of extradition, commending new treaties as a source of national pride.

Extradition agreements were part of a widespread nineteenth-century vogue for treaty making, from postal conventions to trade reciprocity agreements. Worldwide, the incidence of treaty making increased almost sevenfold between 1800 and 1900. Put another way, the negotiation of a new international treaty went from being something that occurred twice a month to something that happened about every other day. The unprecedented growth in the number of treaties reflected changes in the diplomatic and legal culture, as the nineteenth century witnessed a movement toward a more contractual and codified way of conducting international relations. Although Europeans led the practice, this was not just an intra-European phenomenon; the network of treaties extended globally. Great Britain was the most prolific treaty maker (many of these were colonial treaties with local rulers), but the United States also was quite active, signing ten to twenty treaties per decade for most of the nineteenth century.[3]

In keeping with this trend, the number of American extradition treaties increased exponentially each decade. In 1870, the United States had extradition agreements with only fourteen countries; by the turn of the century, that number had more than doubled. Between 1900 and 1909 alone, the United States signed twenty-seven new extradition treaties. Newspapers commented whenever the United States signed a new extradition agreement; even a compact with the tiny Orange Free State (an independent Boer republic in southern Africa) received widespread media coverage. Likewise, the topic of extradition received a disproportionate amount of attention relative to the number of actual cases. On average, between 1890 and 1909, the United States requested the extradition of twenty-four people per year. Yet during the same period, newspaper articles about extradition numbered in the thousands. In his Annual Messages to Congress in 1898, 1899, and 1900, President McKinley brought up extradition twelve separate times, and President Roosevelt spoke about it at length in his 1903 address. Prominent writers such as Richard Harding Davis and O. Henry put extradition at the center of their works of fiction.[4]

Public attention to extradition peaked in the years just after 1898, at a time when Americans fiercely debated the question of territorial empire. Anti-imperialists claimed that the United States betrayed its democratic principles by acquiring colonies. Yet extradition offered another model for America's relationship with the rest of the world—one that celebrated the expansion of U.S. influence as a victory for civilization, law, and order, yet grounded it in supposedly reciprocal and voluntary treaties. Rather than taking over more territory, the United States would continue to expand power beyond its borders through law.[5]

Extradition allowed Americans to imagine themselves in a triumphant international role, expansionist in its reach and global in its scope, without the controversy of formal empire. "It is almost impossible now for a man to commit even the smallest kind of crime in the United States and find a country of refuge from which he cannot be extradited," bragged an 1899 article in the *New York Tribune*. This was an exaggeration, but it constituted a powerful myth. Through international law enforcement, the United States could extend its influence beyond its borders in a manner that was less contentious than formal empire but still affirmed a far-reaching vision of the nation's role in the world. This was an empire not of territory but of justice, and it showed that there would be a new kind of international power, the power of law, in the new century.[6]

✻

In December 1899, a prominent New Orleans lawyer reflected on the nation's progress during the past century. One of the most incredible facts of modern life, he marveled, was that "there is no longer any spot on the globe where our fugitives from justice are safe from extradition." He recalled: "When I first began to practice law, an American criminal of retiring disposition had a wide range of choice in the matter of foreign residence. Spain, Turkey, Algiers, Japan, Holland, Chile, Ecuador, the Philippines, Cuba, and all of Central America except British Honduras guaranteed security to assorted brands of fugitives." Yet, over the course of three decades, the circle of countries where a fugitive from the United States could safely flee steadily contracted, and "one by one the different countries entered into mutual treaties and put up the bars." Just as American markets spread across the globe, seemingly without bounds, so too did American justice. "The man with a warrant goes wheresoever he lists," he boasted.[7]

The New Orleans lawyer promoted an idealized image of a world where there was nowhere to hide from U.S. law. This vision was exaggerated; for one thing, the United States did not actually have treaties with all of the countries that he listed. Moreover, even though extradition was a two-way process, the media rarely focused on the ability of other countries to retrieve fugitives from the United States. Rather, popular accounts highlighted the projection of American power outward into foreign lands. With rhetoric that celebrated the extension of policing beyond U.S. borders, commentators like the New Orleans lawyer presented a new way of imagining the world— as a single American jurisdiction, where borders presented no obstacle to the policeman in hot pursuit. Periodicals regularly printed articles boasting about the reach of American justice, with headlines such as "The World Too Small for Criminals," "Criminal Never Safe Anywhere," and "World Holds Absolutely No Safe Haven." Such texts familiarized Americans with the idea of the United States as policeman, with both the capability and responsibility to spread justice around the globe. It was an empire predicated not on conquering territory but on spreading law.[8]

In the early 1890s, the image of a world with nowhere to hide was a future aspiration rather than a fait accompli. Thomas Edison, who was experimenting with wireless communications, prophesized to the *Washington Post* that his efforts might one day benefit international policing. An 1890 article in *Youth's Companion* praised the ongoing modernization of American detective work when it declared: "This world is getting too small to hold certain kinds of bad people." The author conceded that "the system is not yet perfected," but optimistically concluded that "the time is not distant when the chief of police in New York or Boston will be able to arrest a man in Australia just as easily, quickly, and cheaply as if he were in the next street."[9]

By the end of the decade, many believed that such a day had arrived. After 1898, a new confidence allowed Americans to picture their policemen reaching across borders, just as they had reached out and taken territorial possessions in Puerto Rico and the Philippines. This was a nationalism grounded in the country's international stature, and it found fertile soil in the law. In international law, the United States might not simply be the equal of the European powers, but even their superior.[10]

After 1898, the number of articles repeating the "nowhere to hide" rhetoric multiplied. Between December 1899 and April 1900, dozens of newspapers nationwide reprinted the New Orleans lawyer's remarks. He was not alone in extolling extradition as a great national accomplishment. A columnist in the *Washington Post* and *New York Tribune*, who identified himself simply as an "Ex-Attaché," associated the growth of extradition law with the rise of the United States as a world power. Writing in July 1899, he pointed out that the United States had signed more extradition treaties than any other country, including the previous leaders, Great Britain and France. Even British jurist Sir Edward Clarke conceded that in the matter of extradition, the American law was "better than that of any country in the world." If extradition was equated with the spread of justice, then the fact that the United States was at the forefront of this policy helped define America's role in relation to the rest of the world: as the conveyers of law and order.[11]

The 1899 capture of embezzler Thomas J. Hunter showed just how far the long arm of U.S. law could reach. The former auditor of the Atlanta and West Point Railway, Hunter made national news when Pinkerton detectives found the Georgia native living in Tangier, Morocco. Newspapers were transfixed by the image of Uncle Sam's law enforcers carrying out their mission in the land of the sultan, home of heathens and harems. The *Atlanta Constitution* published an account of District Attorney W. P. Hill's 10,000-mile trip to recover Hunter, accompanied by an illustration of the lawyer smoking a hookah with a fez atop his head. If American law could reach such a distant and exotic place, where couldn't it go?[12]

Popular fiction affirmed the message that the long arm of American law could reach around the world. In the 1900 detective novel *The Head of Pasht* by lawyer-author Willis Boyd Allen, a thief steals valuable Egyptian artifacts from a collector in New York, including the titular carving of the goddess Pasht. Discovering his man in Cairo, an American detective successfully secures extradition papers for the fugitive's return. Part of what made the novel exciting was that the thief was brought back from a place as exotic and distant as Egypt. In one scene, a group of men discuss how a criminal can no longer flee the United States and evade capture. One of them explains that even if the criminal managed to board a steamship, a telegraph cable dispatch would reach the destination days before his arrival. He continues, saying that extradition law covers nearly the entire globe. One member of the group expresses surprise: "What! . . . Can a man be arrested in Rome, Cape Town, or Cairo and be carried back to America?" "He can, and frequently is," confidently replies one of his companions.[13]

The claim that American detectives could catch a fugitive anywhere in the world was, in part, a celebration of national technology and intelligence, but it was also a sentiment with an imperial logic. While European countries extended their global influence by taking over territory, the United States would expand power beyond its borders through the spread of markets and law. Extradition, explained historian and political economist William Gammell, allowed the United States "to stretch forth its arm across national boundaries, over dividing rivers and mountains, beyond the ocean itself." In this vision, extradition was not a mutual agreement between two sovereign nations engaging in a bilateral exchange of prisoners, but a way of expanding American power outward, beyond its borders.[14]

Some portrayed the expansion of extradition as part of a "white man's burden" to spread civilization and progress to peoples around the globe. "International extradition covers the habitable earth with law," declared University of Chicago president Harry Pratt Judson, in a commencement address entitled "The Progress of the World."

A 1903 editorial in the *Washington Post* opined that "when notorious criminals can find shelter from the law," such countries "must still be in an undeveloped and primitive condition. It ought to be impossible for fugitives to live openly in Christendom at this stage of the world's progress." Civilization meant letting American agents in to collect their prisoners.[15]

The logic was circular: extradition helped civilize a country, yet the United States would only sign extradition treaties with nations that it already deemed civilized. This meant that the United States lacked extradition with most Asian and Middle Eastern countries. In 1886, the United States recognized Japan as part of the community of civilized nations after a decade of political, social, economic, and legal reforms, including the adoption of a constitutional government with an elected parliament and a system of Western-style courts. It marked this occasion by ratifying an extradition treaty, the first that any Western country signed with an Asian nation. However, the following year, when China's minister in Washington proposed an extradition agreement, the State Department refused, replying that "owing to the totally opposite systems of criminal procedure in the respective countries, an extradition convention between the United States and China is impracticable."[16]

The United States celebrated "law" as a civilizing force, but at the same moment claimed to exist above or outside the law of others. Like Britain, France, and other European powers, it practiced extraterritorial jurisdiction in countries deemed "uncivilized," such as China, Korea, and the Ottoman Empire. Under the system of extraterritoriality, U.S. citizens in those lands were not subject to local laws. Instead, the United States was responsible for its own subjects, who were held accountable to U.S. ministers and consuls. Extraterritorial jurisdiction was meant to aid American trade and commerce, but it also made the capture of fugitives easier. Rather than recovering fugitives through extradition, U.S. consuls unilaterally took custody of Americans accused of crime. For example, when Thomas J. Hunter was found in Morocco, the United States had no extradition treaty to turn to, as the African nation was considered insufficiently civilized to enter into such a compact. Instead, under the rules of extraterritoriality, Hunter was taken into custody by the U.S. consul and handed over to the Atlanta district attorney without going through any Moroccan tribunal.[17]

Americans were not the only ones who espoused the "nowhere to hide" rhetoric; the British also articulated a similar refrain. By the turn of the twentieth century, Great Britain and the United States led the world in the number of extradition treaties. The *Pall Mall Gazette*, a London newspaper, printed in language identical to that of American periodicals that there was "a growing lack of places for criminals to go to." However, rather than emphasizing the power of extradition law, the article attributed the improvements in policing to the telegraph, the press, and the skill of Scotland Yard's detectives. (Despite its nationalist bent, it also acknowledged that "American detectives have a most extraordinary knack of finding any criminal they choose.") Great Britain's empire of justice was grounded in technology and manpower; the United States' was based, at least in the minds of Americans, on the power of law. This made sense, as many fugitives from England fled to other parts of the British Empire, and Great Britain did not need extradition treaties within its imperial territory. Because U.S. law did not govern as large a geographical swath, it was more essential for the United States to have extradition agreements with other nations.[18]

Popular culture not only normalized the extension of American power beyond U.S. borders but also valorized it, portraying extradition law as an incontrovertible instrument for good. Who could object to the goals of extradition—putting dangerous fugitives behind bars and protecting society? Unlike territorial empire, the empire of justice seemed to expand uncontested. Even Americans who were anti-imperialist or isolationist shared the vision of their nation sending out detectives and apprehending fugitives on the other side of the world. When it came to law enforcement, so the popular press depicted, everyone imagined a global role for the United States.

Yet, in truth, this empire of justice did meet with resistance from within the United States. Turn-of-the-century newspapers may have portrayed a universal faith in the impartial, noninvasive, and civilizing power of U.S. law. But plenty of American dissidents at this time—from union leaders to suffrage activists to the black press—openly questioned whether U.S. laws were really so just. Extradition law, too, had its critics. When the United States ratified an extradition treaty with Russia in 1893, public protests ensued. Russian immigrants insisted that, under the czar's iron hand, no one extradited to that land could possibly receive a fair trial. Moreover, they argued, the treaty surely would be used as a weapon to retrieve and punish political opponents of the czar. By signing an extradition treaty, the United States seemed to give its stamp of approval to Russia's unjust criminal justice system.[19]

The Russian protesters had a point. Extradition treaties were bilateral documents with reciprocal commitments. If extradition opened up the entire world to American law enforcement, then it also opened up America to foreign law enforcers. But champions of the "nowhere to hide" rhetoric rarely considered the flip side of the extradition treaty. For those who believed that American law ought to extend around the globe, extradition was a door that swung in only one direction.

❉

In 1899, the *Chicago Record* carried a series of South American travel columns penned by William Eleroy Curtis, director of the first International Conference of American States, the precursor to the Pan-American Union and ultimately the Organization of American States. For Curtis, creating a world with nowhere to hide from U.S. law was not just a matter of national pride but an economic imperative. His September 26 column carried the alarming headline, "American Crooks in Chile," and directly tied the absence of an extradition agreement to the poor American presence in the Chilean market. But Curtis's report also contained good news: almost all of the Latin American countries were currently in treaty negotiations with the United States. An outspoken champion of the "nowhere to hide" rhetoric, Curtis pushed the message that spreading American law was an urgent necessity. His goal was nothing less than a common extradition regime uniting the entire Western Hemisphere under the legal guidance of the United States—a Monroe Doctrine of law.[20]

After the amended treaty of 1890 closed off Canada as a refuge, American embezzlers began to seek asylums to the south. "Central

America is still open to receive gentlemen who have to leave Uncle Sam's country in a hurry," quipped the *American Lawyer.* An article in the *Chicago Tribune* explained why, even after the Canadian refuge was shut, embezzlement rates continued to rise in the United States: "Some of the doors of safety have been closed, but not all. There is no further immunity in the Northern asylums, but the Southern are still open and inviting the thieves. It is easy to get to South America, though a longer route than the old one to Canada." As U.S. investment in Latin America increased, so too did the number of escape routes, which mapped onto the paths of U.S. capital. Fugitives often hopped the banana steamers that shuttled between New Orleans and Honduras, or fled on the commercial lines that traveled down the coasts of Brazil and Argentina.[21]

Historically, the United States had been reluctant to enter into an extradition agreement with any country south of Mexico. This stemmed from the State Department's belief that, because there were so many revolutions, the United States would be bombarded with requests for people who might have committed political crimes. In the 1870s, the United States concluded extradition agreements with El Salvador and Peru as part of more general treaties on amity, commerce, navigation, and consular privileges. It also signed one with Nicaragua, part of a popular route between the Atlantic and Pacific coasts, where thousands of Americans passed through each year. In 1888, the United States ratified a treaty with Colombia, likely for the same reason, as Colombia controlled the isthmus of Panama at that time. Until the late 1890s, however, these were the only extradition agreements that the United States had with any countries in Central or South America. By contrast, the United States had treaties with almost every European country by 1890.[22]

The growth of extradition law in the Americas aided the expansion of U.S. foreign investment. For business interests, it was important to be able to legally control employees abroad. U.S. companies were reluctant to expand or invest abroad if the home office could not punish agents who abused their authority or misused the firm's assets. Extradition allowed U.S. firms to bring these misbehaving agents back to domestic courts for prosecution. Weeding out fugitives also helped improve the reputation and international standing of Americans abroad, so as to better compete with European economic powers like Britain.[23]

William Eleroy Curtis promoted trade between the United States and Latin America with an evangelical passion. He championed a commercial union with the United States at the helm, declaring that "the manifest destiny of the United States is to dominate the American hemisphere . . . by the influence of example and by commercial relations." Advocating the construction of an intercontinental railway that stretched all the way from Chicago to Buenos Aires, he spoke ardently about the common destiny of the Americas. "The Creator intended there should be an exchange of products between the American continents," he declared. "He distributed their natural resources so that their population can live in prosperity and contentment without an ounce of European or Asiatic merchandise."[24]

A journalist by profession, Curtis was managing editor of the *Chicago Inter-Ocean* in 1884, when he resigned to join a commission sent out by President Arthur "to ascertain the best methods of promoting the political and commercial relations between the United States and the other American republics." With this commission, Curtis visited every Central and South American country and familiarized himself with their resources, industries, commerce, and politics. Considered a leading expert in Latin American affairs (even if his knowledge was fairly superficial), he was named the first director of the Bureau of American Republics in 1889 and served as chief of the Latin American department for the World's Colombian Exposition in Chicago in 1893.[25]

Curtis warned that the presence of American fugitives in Latin America hurt trade by sullying the overseas standing of the United States. He worried that the Latin American countries would turn to Europe as an example—and a trading partner—if the United States had a reputation for corruption and criminality. "Unfortunately, the greater part of our citizens who have made South America an abiding-place have not been such as to inspire the people of that continent with a high regard for the character, or an admiration for the conduct and culture, of the North American," Curtis cautioned in an 1889 article in the *North American Review*. "The lack of extradition treaties has tempted certain types of our population to seek asylums south of the Caribbean Sea, and at the expense of our national reputation." Fugitive criminals were not the ambassadors he wanted representing the United States.[26]

As an example of a place where potentially lucrative trade and investment opportunities were damaged, Curtis pointed to Argentina, a country that provided a larger market to Europe than to the United States. He estimated that at least 50 of the 300 Americans living in Buenos Aires were prominent financial fugitives, whose presence in Argentina was directly related to the lack of an extradition treaty. In January 1893, the American minister in Buenos Aires reported seeing Philadelphia forger Gideon Marsh casually strolling down the street, and noted the arrival into town of notorious swindler Thomas "Bunco" O'Brien and his sidekick "Doc" Minchin. "Buenos Ayres has been the favorite resort of this enterprising but undesirable class," Curtis remarked, "and when an American traveler goes there he is promptly reminded of broken banks, famous forgeries, and sensational defalcations, which were at one time familiar to him through the newspaper reports."[27]

The fugitive who upset Curtis the most was Boston forger Ezra Winslow, who lived in Buenos Aires under the name of D. Warren Lowe. On the surface, Winslow seemed to be an ideal American representative: he was the editor of the daily *Buenos Ayres Herald* and taught Sunday school in the Methodist church. But his true identity was a thinly veiled secret. In his book *The Capitals of Spanish America*, Curtis mentioned Winslow/Lowe by name, setting him in contrast to another Boston man: Samuel B. Hale, a prominent merchant and capitalist (who was not wanted by the police) and an example of the kind of American who gave the United States a good name abroad. If there was any question about whether Winslow had reformed his ways, it was eliminated in 1886, when Argentine police arrested him for real estate fraud and bankruptcy. When Winslow appealed for assistance, the American consul turned him down, commenting in a letter to the State Department that the fugitive was "now seared with the touch of crime, without a country and without citizenship, an object of commiseration as well as abhorrence, he has voluntarily placed himself in the perpetual durance of outlawry." Curtis certainly would have approved. Even though Winslow was technically still a United States citizen, his status as a fugitive negated the privilege of consular representation.[28]

In 1890, as executive director of the first International Conference of American States, Curtis created a Committee on Extradition to examine the issue on a hemispheric scale. Delegates representing thirteen countries in North and South America attended the convention, which was held in Washington, D.C. Proposed by U.S. Secretary of State James G. Blaine, it had the stated goal of promoting peace and commercial relations among the countries of the Western Hemisphere. In its final report, the Committee on Extradition suggested the creation of a broad, multilateral treaty and presented the draft of a potential text. More immediately, however, it recommended that each of the Latin American republics individually conclude treaties of extradition with the United States.[29]

Shortly after the finish of the conference, an editorial in the *New York Tribune* called for the State Department to follow up on the committee's recommendations. It was particularly important to negotiate extradition treaties with every Latin American country, the anonymous author (most likely Curtis) argued, given the special relationship the United States had with the rest of the Western Hemisphere under the Monroe Doctrine. "With no other quarter of Christendom have the extradition arrangements of the United States been so incomplete and unsatisfactory as with South America," the author asserted. This had repercussions both at home and abroad. "Not only are the ends of justice sacrificed by the facility with which murderers and embezzlers have escaped the legal penalties for their misdeeds," the author argued, "but American interests have suffered from the sorry reputation of refugees from justice." Here was the real problem: not the evasion of justice, but the detriment to American commercial interests.[30]

In the decade after the conference, the State Department repeatedly instructed its diplomats in Central and South America to solicit extradition treaties. One by one, during the next few years, the United States affirmed Curtis's vision and succeeded in ratifying extradition treaties with Latin American countries: Argentina in 1896, Brazil in 1897, a revised treaty with Peru in 1899, Chile in

1900, Guatemala in 1903, the newly independent nations of Cuba and Panama in 1904, and Uruguay in 1905.[31]

Just as the Monroe Doctrine declared the Americas part of the U.S. sphere of influence, so too did Curtis imagine the entire hemisphere united under a common extradition regime with the United States at the helm. When the State Department ratified an extradition treaty with Honduras in 1912 (the year after Curtis's death), politicians and newspapers declared his vision fully realized: there was no country left in the Western Hemisphere, they asserted, where a fugitive could hide from U.S. law. (This was technically incorrect; Costa Rica still had not signed an extradition treaty with the United States.) The *Washington Post* announced that the "last avenue of escape in North and South America was effectively closed" and the hemisphere was now unified against criminality. The *Boston Globe* described it as an "extradition chain" that linked all the countries of the Americas and stated: "Those who flee justice in the United States will hereafter find no place on the Western Hemisphere safe from extradition." The next day, it joked: "Now, will you be good!"[32]

When the United States signed an extradition treaty with Honduras, it already had sent troops to Latin America and the Caribbean fifteen times during the previous decade in the name of hemispheric unity and stability. Using the tactics known as gunboat diplomacy and dollar diplomacy, the United States used its military and economic power to mold the countries of Latin America into places conducive to U.S. investment. But it was not only through troops and dollars but also through statutes and laws that the United States shaped the hemisphere. In the short term, extradition resulted in the apprehension of an individual suspect, but in the long run, as Curtis spent his career arguing, it furthered the larger goal of creating a Western Hemisphere friendly to the financial goals of the United States.[33]

✳

William Eleroy Curtis and Joseph Wingate Folk shared a common vision of a world covered by American extradition law, but they came at this ideal from different directions. Curtis's concerns were international; he took little interest in domestic crime, instead championing extradition out of a desire to further American trade and investment abroad. "Holy Joe" Folk's crusade, in contrast, was to clean up corruption in American cities; he paid scant attention to international affairs. These two agendas—the expansion of foreign markets and Progressive reform—converged in the campaign to expand the reach of extradition at the turn of the twentieth century.

Sixty-two nations and almost every state in the Union participated in the Louisiana Purchase Exposition of 1904, better known as the St. Louis World's Fair. But according to Frank G. Tyrrell, the pastor of St. Louis's Central Christian Church, the true highlight was found outside the fairgrounds, in the campaign against municipal corruption led by Circuit Attorney Folk. "This magnificent spectacle of a free and sovereign people rising in their might and purging their government from the last taint of corruption is," he wrote, "*the grandest exhibit* to be seen in connection with the great World's Fair."[34]

Three years earlier, Folk ran for office on a pledge to clean up public graft, and the next year the crusader took on his first major case: a bribery scheme in which a streetcar company, Suburban Railway, paid off members of the St. Louis Municipal Assembly. After convincing two aldermen to turn state's evidence, Folk obtained warrants for the arrest of seven men accused of giving and taking bribes. Dubbed by newspapers the "St. Louis Boodlers," they had the potential to bring down political boss Edward Butler, the notorious symbol of the corruption controlling city government.[35]

At that time, St. Louis was the fourth-largest city in the United States, and Folk's municipal cleanup campaign helped generate discussion about the health of the American polity in general. In October 1902, *McClure's* published an article by Claude Wetmore and Lincoln Steffens entitled "Tweed Days in St. Louis," which introduced the nation to Folk and the St. Louis Boodlers. Steffens continued to champion the St. Louis circuit attorney in his muckraking classic *The Shame of the Cities*. Folk realized an important truth, Steffens emphasized: that bribery and corruption were not simply one-time offenses; they were systemic and threatened the existence of democratic government. "The great truth I tried to make plain was that which Mr. Folk insists so constantly upon,"

Steffens wrote, "that the effect of [bribery] is literally to change the form of our government from one that is representative of the people to an oligarchy, representative of special interests."[36]

Before the Suburban Railway trials began, however, four of the defendants fled the country. John K. Murrell and Charles Kratz both forfeited their bonds and went to Mexico; Daniel J. Kelly fled to Canada; and Ellis Wainwright, who was vacationing in Europe when the indictments were issued, stayed in France. The loss of Murrell and Kratz was particularly devastating to Folk, as they were the only ones who could name all of the politicians who had received shares of the bribe money. As long as those two remained out of the country, the case against the St. Louis Boodlers was shaky.[37]

At this point, Folk's campaign moved to Washington, D.C. In addition to the immediate goal of trying to retrieve the fugitives, Folk had a larger mission: to make bribery a universally extraditable offense. With the cooperation of Missouri senator Francis M. Cockrell, Folk successfully lobbied Secretary of State John Hay to negotiate an amendment adding bribery to the extradition treaty with Mexico. The new agreement was ratified in June 1903, but because it was not retroactive, it was of no immediate help in the Murrell-Kratz case.[38]

Folk helped change the terms of the national discussion about urban corruption. He pushed the message that achieving the domestic goal of cleaning up cities required taking international action. An October 1903 editorial in the *New York Tribune* recognized this connection:

> The world is becoming small, and even the remotest outposts of civilization are now accessible and habitable as refuges for criminals who have the means to live in luxury. The bribe giver and the bribe taker both belong to the globe trotting class of fugitives from justice, and it can easily be inferred from the history of the last few years—as now uncovered not only in the St. Louis indictments, but in the graver Federal Postoffice scandals—that unless the loopholes of escape are stopped we shall be in danger of losing in distant havens of refuge a whole brood of "grafters" of the Kratz, Maders and Machen stamp.[39]

Folk even drew President Theodore Roosevelt to his cause. Although Murrell voluntarily returned to the United States in late 1902, the case was still at an impasse unless Folk could somehow force Kratz's return. Determined to bring him to justice, Folk continued to press his case in correspondence with Secretary of State Hay throughout the summer and fall of 1903. Finally, in October 1903, Roosevelt invited Folk to the White House, apparently at the urging of Lincoln Steffens, who was eager to get the two reformers together. The apocryphal story is that, on being told of Folk's protracted efforts to secure the return of the St. Louis Boodlers, the president jumped up, slapped the desk with his hand, and exclaimed: "By Jove, we will get them!"[40]

Two months later, the president championed Folk's cause in his Annual Message to Congress. "It should be the policy of the United States," Roosevelt declared, "to leave no place on earth where a corrupt man fleeing from this country can rest in peace." Roosevelt made no secret that Folk had inspired this remark. His proclamation was a paraphrase of a line in one of Folk's own speeches: "If the present program is carried out, and there seems to be no reason why it should not be, there will not be a civilized country on earth where boodlers fleeing from the United States can rest in peace." The *Baltimore Sun* even ran one of Folk's speeches side by side with the relevant portion of Roosevelt's address to show their similarities.[41]

Roosevelt's 1903 Annual Message to Congress justified international policing in terms of its domestic benefits. Acknowledging the interconnectedness between the United States and the rest of the world, he argued that the only way to protect law and order at home was to eliminate safe havens abroad. "As long as public plunderers when detected can find a haven of refuge in any foreign land and avoid punishment," he warned, "just so long encouragement is given them to continue their practices." He concluded, "If we fail to do all that in us lies to stamp out corruption we cannot escape our share of responsibility for the guilt."[42]

Roosevelt explained the expanding reach of American law enforcement as merely a domestic affair, a matter of maintaining law and order at home, very different from a formal expansion of power over territory. His declaration was a statement of action, tied up with various policies that he wanted to implement to pursue and catch fugitives. It was also a statement of vision, a way of seeing the world in which the long arm of American law reached around the globe. But culturally, this power was largely rendered invisible. Roosevelt and Folk legitimized cross-border policing as a matter of national criminal justice; reaching out beyond the borders of the United States was a project with domestic aims, not international or imperialist ones. The assumption that the goals of the law were universal values—stability, tranquility, justice—allowed the denial of any sort of bullying or coercion, and deflected potential accusations that the United States was trying to build a bigger empire.

The story of the St. Louis Boodlers had a mixed ending. Roosevelt ordered the State Department to demand the extradition of Kratz, promising reciprocity with Mexico under similar circumstances (an assurance that, as a judicial matter, neither the State Department nor Roosevelt had the power to make). Kratz was arrested in Guadalajara, and after a final futile attempt to escape extradition, was brought back to St. Louis in January 1904 to stand trial. In explaining his prolonged flight from the law, Kratz testified that he had fled to Mexico only to wait for an opportunity for an unprejudiced hearing. In the end, after getting a change of venue to Butler, Missouri, the jury acquitted him. Despite this defeat, the boodle investigations established Folk's reputation as an enemy of public corruption and party machines and triggered a groundswell of public support that elevated him to the governor's office later that year. Folk left his legacy in extradition law as well: bribery also was added to the U.S.-British agreement in 1905, and was subsequently included as an extraditable offense in every new U.S. treaty.[43]

❋

Popular culture reinforced the message that the spread of extradition law was an urgent necessity. The ideal was a world with nowhere to hide, but works of journalism and fiction exposed the places where it was still possible for an outlaw to take cover. "Under no condition / is extradition / allowed in Callao," went a popular rhyme, referring to the Peruvian port. Countries that lacked extradition treaties with the United States gained infamy as common destinations for fugitives. These "rogues' colonies" captured the imagination of journalists, novelists, and playwrights, who portrayed them as chaotic, dangerous, and in need of the civilizing power of American law.[44]

Media accounts played on anxieties about a world with places to hide, depicting such spots as dens of evil. In 1897, *New York World* reporter John Langdon Heaton wrote a widely reprinted article about American fugitives living in Morocco, in which he sensationally dubbed the port of Tangier the "Wickedest City in the World." A few years later, a *San Francisco Chronicle* article nicknamed Tegucigalpa, Honduras, the "City of the Men Afraid to Die" after the writer's assertion that the sinful American fugitives living there "should have killed themselves, by all rules of shame."[45]

Richard Harding Davis, one of the best-known American writers of the turn of the century, set some of his most widely read works of journalism, travel writing, and fiction in these extradition-free zones. "The Exiles," a short story originally published in *Harper's* in May 1894, and later the title work in his best-selling collection, took place in a colony of American fugitives living in Tangier, Morocco. "The Exiles" was inspired by a conversation that Davis once had with the victims of an embezzler who had fled beyond extradition to Brazil. Davis jokingly asked the victims if they would like him to go down there and bring back the money, an idea that became the germ for his story. His hit 1904 play (and later a 1915 film) *The Dictator* followed Brooke Travers, a New York yachtsman who accidentally pushes a cabman off the docks in an argument over the fare. Leaving him for dead, Travers grabs the first ship to San Manana, a fictional Central American republic with no extradition to the United States. Davis's San Manana is a land of chaos and anarchy. "In this country you can't look as far into the future as lunch," an American expat advises Travers. "What with assassinations, revolutions, yellow fever . . . you're lucky to live till after breakfast." The existence of these rogues' colonies, Davis's work affirmed, made the world a more dangerous and unstable place.[46]

William Sydney Porter, who later became famous under his pen name O. Henry, claimed firsthand experience with a rogues' colony. After the young bank clerk was indicted for embezzlement in Texas in 1896, he fled to Honduras. A year later, on receiving the news that his wife was dying, he returned home to stand trial. He published his first short stories while serving his jail sentence. Henry's 1904 novel *Cabbages and Kings*, set in the fictional Central American country of Anchuria, was based on his impressions of Honduras during his exile there. Among the American colony are various U.S. fugitives from justice. "I recall two exiled bank presidents," his protagonist Frank Goodwin tells a newcomer, "one army paymaster under a cloud, a couple of manslayers, and a widow—arsenic, I believe was the suspicion in her case." Henry coined a new phrase in his novel to describe this land without law and order: a "banana republic." One character remarks: "At that time we had a treaty with about every foreign country except Belgium and that banana republic, Anchuria."[47]

In these stories, countries without extradition treaties were uncivilized and lawless. These were the places, Davis wrote, where "we can learn . . . just how far a man of cultivation lapses into barbarism when he associates with savages." For Henry, the lack of an extradition treaty was a sign that the country of Anchuria lacked the niceties of civilization. Goodwin describes the port town of Coralio as a place where "there are no afternoon teas, no hand-organs, no department stores—and there is no extradition treaty." The narrator of Davis's "The Exiles" depicts Morocco as having "no law and no religion and no relations nor newspapers to poke into what you do nor how you live." Lawless, in this context, simply meant that U.S. law could not be enforced there. Morocco, like other countries where American fugitives congregated, did have laws—in this case, determined by the sultan and enacted by local officials. However, if there was no extradition, these authors considered a place as having no law at all.[48]

Davis's most successful novel, *Soldiers of Fortune* (1897), glorified the expansion of American influence into these supposedly lawless foreign lands. A celebration of the United States' budding imperial power, it narrates the adventures of two Americans living in Olancho, a fictional Latin American republic. Robert Clay works as a mining engineer and occasional mercenary, while Hope Langham is the daughter of a rich American industrialist. When a coup, planned by corrupt politicians and generals, threatens the American-owned Valencia Mining Company, Clay organizes his workers and the handful of Americans visiting the mine into a countercoup force. Written on the eve of U.S. intervention in Cuba, *Soldiers of Fortune* casts the young American as the dashing hero who brings order and stability to a land of political and economic disarray.[49]

Although these works of fiction and journalism exposed the rogues' colonies of the world, they still upheld the "nowhere to hide" theme. Fugitives in these stories, quite simply, do not get away with it. Sometimes detectives catch them, despite the lack of a treaty. In Henry's *Cabbages and Kings*, the absconding president of the Republic Insurance Company successfully gains sanctuary in Anchuria, but ends up committing suicide. In many works, including Davis's *The Dictator*, the fleeing fugitive turns out to be innocent of his alleged crime. Thus, even though popular fiction revealed places where U.S. extradition law did not reach, it ultimately supported the notion that, in the long run, there was nowhere for the guilty to hide.

The idea that there was nowhere to hide from American justice was a myth: U.S. extradition treaties never covered the entire globe. Yet the U.S. government often pretended that the long-arm vision was fact, putting a great deal of effort into papering over weaknesses in that ideal. The State Department, Congress, and even the Supreme Court covered up the cracks in the "nowhere to hide" image, either through obfuscation, legislation, or the invention of legal fictions that would allow extradition to extend even farther than treaties legitimately allowed.

To the dismay of State Department officials, newspapers and almanacs frequently published lists of which countries had—and did not have—extradition treaties with the United States. The 1903 edition of *The American Almanac, Year-Book, Cyclopaedia and Atlas* printed a detailed chart of treaties and extraditable crimes, as well as a list of the countries with which the United States had no extradition treaty. Newspapers also published lists of "safe" countries in response to readers' questions. During his nearly four decades at the State Department, from 1886 to 1924, Assistant Secretary of State

THE EXTRADITION OF CRIMINALS.
(Compiled for The American Almanac from "Treaties in Force, 1899," and subsequent treaties provided for this purpose by the State Department.)

Country	Murder and Attempts	Arson	Robbery	Burglary (f)	Larceny	Obtaining Money by Deceit	Embezzlement	Counterfeiting	Having Counterfeiters' Tools	Forgery	Fraud	Criminal Assault or Abduction	Bigamy	Procuring Criminal Operation	Mayhem	Perjury	Destruction or Obstruction of Railroads	Crimes at Sea	Crimes Against the Laws on Slavery	Other Crimes
Argentine R.	Yes	Yes	Yes	Yes	Yes*	No	Yes†	Yes	No	Yes	Yes*	Yes	No	No	No	Yes	Yes	Yes	Yes	—
Austria-Hungary	Yes	Yes	Yes	No	No	No	Yes	Yes	No	Yes	No	No	No	No	No	No	No	Yes	No	—
Baden	Yes	Yes	Yes	No	No	No	Yes(g)	Yes	No	Yes	No	No	No	No	No	No	No	Yes	No	—
Bavaria	Yes	Yes	Yes	No	No	No	Yes(g)	Yes	No	Yes	No	No	No	No	No	No	No	Yes	No	—
Belgium	Yes	Yes	Yes	Yes	Yes	Yes	Yes	Yes	No	Yes	No	Yes	Yes	No	No	Yes	Yes	Yes	No	(e)
Bolivia	Yes	Yes	Yes	Yes	No	No	Yes†	Yes	No	Yes*	Yes	No	No	No	No	Yes	Yes	Yes	Yes	(b)
Chili	Yes	Yes	Yes	Yes	No	No	Yes†	Yes	No	Yes	No	No	No	No	No	Yes	Yes	Yes	Yes	(b)
Columbia	Yes	Yes	Yes	Yes	No	No	Yes	Yes	No	Yes	No	Yes‡	No	No	No	Yes	Yes	Yes	Yes	—
Denmark	Yes	Yes	Yes	Yes	No	No	Yes	Yes	No	Yes*	No	Yes	No	No	No	Yes	Yes	Yes	Yes	(b)
Ecuador	Yes	Yes	Yes	Yes	No	No	Yes(g)	Yes	No	Yes	No	No	No	No	No	No	No	Yes	No	—
France	Yes	Yes	Yes	Yes	No	No	Yes	Yes	No	Yes	No	Yes‡	No	No	No	No	No	No	No	—
Germany‖																				
Gt. Britain	Yes	Yes	Yes	Yes	No	No	Yes	Yes	No	Yes	Yes	Yes§	No	No	No	Yes	No	Yes	Yes	(a b)
Hayti	Yes	Yes	Yes	No	No	No	Yes	Yes	No	Yes	No	No	No	No	No	No	No	Yes	No	—
Italy	Yes	Yes	Yes	No	No	No	Yes	Yes	No	Yes	No	Yes‡	No	No	No	No	No	Yes	No	(c)
Japan	Yes	Yes	Yes	No	No	Yes(g)	Yes	Yes	No	Yes	No	Yes‡	No	No	No	No	No	Yes	No	—
Luxemburg	Yes	Yes	Yes	No	No	No	Yes	Yes	No	Yes	No	Yes	No	Yes	No	Yes	Yes	Yes	No	(a d)
Mexico	Yes	Yes	Yes	Yes	Yes	Yes	Yes	Yes	Yes	Yes	Yes	Yes§	Yes	No	Yes	No	Yes	Yes	No	(a d)
Netherland	Yes	Yes	Yes	Yes	Yes	Yes	Yes	Yes	No	Yes	No	Yes§	Yes	No	No	Yes	Yes	Yes	No	(b d)
Nicaragua	Yes	Yes	Yes	No	No	Yes	Yes	Yes	No	Yes	No	Yes§	Yes	No	No	Yes	Yes	Yes	Yes	(b)
Norway	Yes	Yes	Yes	Yes	No	No	Yes	Yes	No	Yes	No	No	No	No	No	No	No	Yes	No	—
Peru	Yes	Yes	Yes	Yes	No	No	Yes	Yes	No	Yes*	Yes	No	No	No	No	No	Yes	Yes	Yes	(b)
Prussia	Yes	Yes	Yes	No	No	No	Yes(g)	Yes	No	Yes	No	No	No	No	No	No	No	Yes	No	—
Russia	Yes	Yes	Yes	Yes†	No	No	Yes	Yes	No	Yes	No	No	No	No	No	Yes	Yes	Yes	Yes	(b)
Salvador	Yes	Yes	Yes	Yes	No	No	Yes	Yes	No	Yes	No	Yes§	No	No	No	Yes	Yes	Yes	No	(b)
Servia	Yes	Yes	Yes	Yes	No	No	Yes	Yes	No	Yes	Yes(a c)*	No	No	No	No	Yes	Yes	Yes	Yes	(b)
Spain	Yes	Yes	Yes	Yes	No	No	Yes	Yes	No	Yes	No	Yes‡	No	No	No	No	No	Yes	No	(c)
Sweden	Yes	Yes	Yes	Yes	No	No	Yes	Yes	No	Yes	No	No	No	No	No	No	No	Yes	No	(b)
Switzerland	Yes	Yes	Yes	Yes	No	No	Yes	Yes	No	Yes	No	Yes§	Yes	Yes	No	No	No	Yes	No	(b)
Turkey	Yes	Yes	Yes	Yes	No	No	Yes	Yes	No	Yes	No	Yes‡	No	No	No	No	No	Yes	No	—

The nations with which the United States now has no treaties of extradition are Brazil, Bulgaria, China, Costa Rica, Dominican Republic, Egypt, Greece, Guatemala, Honduras, Korea, Morocco, Paraguay, Persia, Portugal, Roumania, Siam, Uruguay and Venezuela.

Notes: *Property of value of $200. †In excess of $200. ‡Covers criminal assault only. §Includes kidnapping and child stealing. ‖The treaty with Prussia applies to other German states. (a) Receiving goods known to have been dishonorably obtained an extraditable crime. (b) Participation is extraditable. (c) Also kidnapping of minors or adults. (d) Attempts to commit crimes covered by the treaty are also extraditable. (e) Attempts upon the life of a ruler, whatever the purpose of the assault, not to be regarded as a political crime. (f) Most nations include shop or office breaking. (g) Only embezzlement of public moneys.

Extradition chart, outlining which crimes were extraditable and where. To the chagrin of the State Department, these charts were commonly available in almanacs. *The American Almanac, Year-Book, Cyclopaedia and Atlas*, 1903.

Alvey Adee vigorously discouraged the publication of such lists. When civilians consulted the State Department with queries about the extradition status of certain countries, Assistant Solicitor Frederick Van Dyne sent evasive replies and recorded the name of the inquirer.[50]

The State Department also tried to hide the content of extradition treaties so that the public would not know which offenses were—and were not—covered. When Octavia F. Rogan, a librarian at the Texas State Library, asked for a copy of the treaty between the United States and Costa Rica, the State Department turned down her request. In a flurry of notes about Rogan's application, Gaillard Hunt of the Division of Publications objected: "She isn't a murderess. . . . Now, why on earth can't she have this treaty? Are we trying to conceal a law? We can't. It has been publicly proclaimed. Everybody is entitled to see it." But a solicitor for the State Department responded emphatically: "*We do not* send libraries copies of extradition treaties."[51]

The most alarming—and absurd—crack in the system was Cuba. After 1898, when the United States ruled Cuba through a provisional government for four years, hundreds of American civil servants relocated to Havana. One of them, Charles F. W. Neely, was arrested in Rochester, New York, in May 1900, for embezzling between $150,000 and $200,000 from the Cuban Post Office. (He was caught, in part, because of his extravagant style of dress, which included buying $30 underwear and wearing thousands of dollars of diamonds.) Because Neely committed his crimes in Havana, the law said he should be tried there. But if Cuba were an independent country—as American officials claimed it was—then Neely could only be handed over via formal extradition. However, no extradition treaty existed between the United States and Cuba, and because there was no Cuban government in place, there was no one with the authority to negotiate such an agreement.[52]

Frustratingly, this also meant that American fugitives in Cuba might not be recoverable, even though the United States occupied the island. One journalist contemplated this scenario:

> What foreign country is the safest hiding place for a criminal from the United States? Morocco, Persia, Central Africa, Siam, Thibet, thousands of miles away? Not at all. . . . The man about to flee doesn't have to seek the uttermost ends of the earth to escape arrest and extradition. Just a ninety-mile jaunt—less than the distance from New York to Philadelphia—and he is as immune from arrest by anybody as if he were surrounded by a wall of ice at the North Pole. . . . And this haven of refuge? Cuba.[53]

In June 1900, in response to the Neely dilemma, Congress passed a bill permitting extradition without a treaty in cases involving territories controlled by the United States. In the past, the courts had ruled that international extradition was permissible only if there was an extradition treaty in place, whereas interstate extradition needed no special authorization. Neely's extradition case brought up a fundamental question for the nascent empire: Should the territories occupied by the United States be treated more like separate countries or separate states?[54]

The constitutionality of the June 1900 act came before the Supreme Court the following December, in the case of *Neely v. Henkel*. The case asked, first, whether Congress had the authority to order extradition without a treaty. Second—and most sensational—was the question of Cuba's status. Should it be considered a territory controlled by the United States, as Puerto Rico and the Philippines clearly were? Or was Cuba a separate country, as authorities insisted, even though it was being governed by the United States? Finally, the case asked whether the Sixth Amendment's requirement of trial by jury applied in Cuba while it was under U.S. occupation. Following Spain's civil law tradition, Cuban courts had no juries; judges alone decided criminal cases. Neely's case involved one of the first judicial articulations of a question that had been a major issue in the election of 1900: Does the Constitution follow the flag?[55]

On January 14, 1901, the Supreme Court handed down its decision, penned by Justice John Marshall Harlan. It ruled that the law was constitutional; extradition could be mandated by an act of Congress. The court held that Cuba was neither an independent country nor part of the United States, but fell into a new category: a foreign territory held in trust. Finally, as a foreign territory, the Bill of Rights did not apply, so Neely could be tried without a jury. Therefore, the court concluded that Neely should be extradited to Cuba to stand trial.

Neely v. Henkel was part of a series of decisions known as the Insular Cases, in which the Supreme Court ruled on the constitutional relationship between the United States and the territorial acquisitions that it gained in the Spanish-American War. The week after the court heard the arguments for *Neely*, it also heard cases involving Puerto Rico and the Philippines. A few weeks later, it would hear *Downes v. Bidwell*, the most famous of the cases that asked whether the Constitution followed the flag. In *Downes*, the Supreme Court defined unincorporated territories like Puerto Rico as "foreign in a domestic sense," a space where the U.S. Constitution only applied selectively.[56]

The *Neely* decision was unique among the Insular Cases in a number of ways. Most obviously, it was the only case to involve Cuba. Spain had surrendered Cuba to the United States after the war, but had not "ceded" it, as it had Puerto Rico, the Philippines, and Guam. In fact, because Cuba was not a formal U.S. territory, some scholars do not consider *Neely* to be one of the true Insular Cases. Additionally, the Supreme Court's decision was unanimous, whereas it was bitterly divided in most of the Insular Cases. Justice Harlan's decision stood at odds with his other opinions, such as his dissent in *Downes* a few months later. There, he firmly asserted that the Constitution followed the flag and applied in territories held by the United States. It is possible that in *Neely* the court handed down a results-based decision—given the size of the embezzlement scandal, the justices may have felt pressured to extradite Neely and came up with a rationale for doing so.[57]

Neely v. Henkel was the link between extradition and formal empire, and it illustrated how the U.S. empire operated through the creation of exceptions and exceptional spaces. To govern the empire, the United States had to be able to punish people who committed crimes. In other words, there needed to be extradition. But extradition only occurred between sovereign nations, and interstate rendition only occurred between states. What about spaces that were neither sovereign nations nor states? The Supreme Court shored up gaps in extradition by creating new legal fictions, like the category of "foreign territory held in trust." The ambiguity of this classification allowed the government to treat Cuba like a domestic space when it came to extraditing Neely without a treaty, and a foreign space when it came to trying him without a jury. Through the manipulation of legal categories, the Supreme Court transformed a case that seemed to challenge the "nowhere to hide" ideal into one that validated it.

※

Far from being an arcane matter of international law, extradition prevailed in the American popular media in the 1890s and early 1900s.

As a stand-in for empire, it allowed Americans to envision and take pride in extending their country's international reach, but in a context that was less controversial than formal territorial conquest. Just as Americans spread their power and influence globally through nonterritorial means like markets, so too did they do it through law. The Open Door Notes of 1899 pressured foreign markets to accept U.S. goods and investments, and extradition, similarly, opened up other countries to American detectives and warrants.

When Paul Stensland, the former president of the Milwaukee Avenue State Bank of Chicago, was apprehended in Tangier in 1906, the local consul noted the similarity to the arrest of Thomas Hunter seven years earlier. Both were accused of embezzlement, both tried to hide in Morocco, and both were located with the aid of newspapers. Hadn't Stensland learned his lesson, the *Chicago Tribune* wondered? Didn't the Hunter case teach him that "nowhere in the world can [fugitives] find safety from the avenging hand of justice"? The *Tribune*'s headline—"Criminal Never Safe Anywhere"—was both a warning and a boast, but also a statement of wishful thinking. For lurking behind all the "nowhere to hide" rhetoric, there was still an unaddressed issue, one whose articulation would call into question the proclaimed greatness of the nation. For every Hunter or Stensland who was caught and whose story was trumpeted by newspapers, how many silently got away?[58]

4

Extradition Havens

AT FREDERICK T. MOORE's hearing in Santiago in January 1900, his lawyer presented not just one but four reasons why Chile should not extradite his client to the United States. First, sheltering the accused embezzler could be financially advantageous: Moore had already started investing in mines in the Valparaíso region. The lawyer pointed to the precedent set by Chile four decades earlier, when it protected an American embezzler named Henry Meiggs, "and every one knew . . . how beneficial to his adopted country that gentleman remained to the present day." Second, Moore was the ideal immigrant, prepared to live an honest life in Chile. The lawyer identified yet another American fugitive, William Bushnell, who "works and lives honorably, just as my client desires to do." Third, Moore's lawyer argued that his client had not really committed a crime at all. "In the case of Moore we have not an ordinary matter of appropriation of the money of others," he claimed, "for my client meant simply . . . to purchase mines and other property and to return, not retain, the money of his employers." Finally, and most fundamentally, Chile did not yet have an extradition treaty with the United States; it would not sign one until later that year. Therefore, the South American country was under no international legal obligation to hand Moore over. At least one of these rationales convinced the Chilean Supreme Court, which decided in Moore's favor and set him free.[1]

As the practice of extradition spread globally, the United States actively solicited treaties with every Latin American nation, but some deliberately rebuffed the State Department's advances. Argentina and Chile did not ratify treaties until 1900, Honduras held off until 1912, and Costa Rica refused to sign an extradition treaty with the United States until 1923—nearly three decades after most other Latin American nations. The arguments on Moore's behalf went to the heart of why some countries chose to reject extradition and shelter fugitives: for the sake of economic development and to assert national sovereignty. Fugitives were both a resource and a form of resistance to the growing U.S. influence in the region.[2]

Richard Harding Davis portrayed extradition havens as irrational and lawless, but there were actually sound economic reasons why a nation might choose to protect fugitives. American fugitives often brought valuable investment capital to countries that desperately needed it. They were responsible for building major railroad lines in Chile and Peru, developing copper mines in Honduras, and establishing banana plantations in Costa Rica. "Fugitive philanthropists" such as Henry Meiggs in Chile and E. A. Burke in Honduras made such a significant financial impact in their host countries that they were celebrated as national heroes. Refusing to extradite was a way of protecting these investments and attracting new funds for development.

Another motivation for resisting extradition was racial: U.S. and European fugitives could contribute to the whitening of local populations. Countries like Argentina and Costa Rica, obsessed with the racial composition of their body politic, welcomed all white immigrants regardless of their criminal pasts. Ironically, at a moment when nativists in the United States were bemoaning newly arrived immigrants as threats to the republic's racial purity and public safety, individuals in Latin America could countenance criminal immigrants as a racially elevating force.

Shielding fugitives also was a deliberate way of standing up to the United States and its efforts to extend its influence across the hemisphere. Extradition havens challenged the American vision of a world where there was nowhere to hide, in an era when the United States invoked the Monroe Doctrine and then the Roosevelt Corollary to assert itself more aggressively in the Western Hemisphere. Offering asylum was a way for a country to declare its own version of what it wanted its nation to be—whether that meant objecting to the death penalty, defending its own definitions of criminality, or simply refusing to sign the document that the United States wanted.[3]

The signing of an extradition treaty, however, did not necessarily represent outright acquiescence. In some instances, certainly, it was a register of U.S. domination, but there also existed a complex host of reasons why nations chose to sign on the dotted line. A country might agree to the terms of an extradition accord in order to secure benefits for itself, achieve a measure of international status, and in other ways resist U.S. hegemony from within rather than without. Japan, for example, empowered itself by buying into and ultimately reproducing the world order that initially sought to control it, and it celebrated its newfound status as a "civilized" nation by signing an extradition treaty with the United States in 1886. Central and South American nations made similar calculations. The decision to extradite could be just as strategic as the determination not to do so.

Chile, Honduras, Argentina, and Costa Rica each had different reasons for opting to shelter fugitives. For Chile and Honduras, it was mostly for financial gain; for Argentina, attracting immigrants; and for Costa Rica, to assert sovereignty. These extradition havens differed from a spot like Tangier, a crowded international port where fugitives notoriously congregated. Morocco lacked an extradition treaty because the United States considered it insufficiently civilized to enter into such compacts. In contrast, the United States put pressure on Latin American havens to hand over fugitives, ideally with an extradition treaty in place, and if necessary, without one.

The first American fugitive to make his mark in Latin America was Henry Meiggs, a San Francisco real estate speculator who fled to Chile in 1854. Within a decade, he was the most renowned railroad builder on the continent. Meiggs offered an alternate model for how Latin American countries could obtain funds for investment and infrastructure, demonstrating just how profitable sheltering fugitives could be. He built a country up rather than bringing it down.

Meiggs's original plan had been to develop the North Beach section of San Francisco, but he needed money. Forging the signature of the mayor and city comptroller on municipal promissory notes, he embezzled at least $250,000 and possibly as much as $800,000. When he feared he was about to be caught, he stole another $10,000 of gold and fled the country. Using this capital, Meiggs became a successful railroad builder in his adopted country of Chile, constructing a highly traveled line between Santiago and Valparaíso. In 1868, the *"rey del ferrocarril"* (railroad king) moved on to Peru, where he received exorbitant subsidies from the government to build railway lines between the port of Callao and the silver mines of the Andes. At the time of his death in 1877, he was in the process of constructing a railroad system in Costa Rica on behalf of U.S. coffee and banana exporters. The project was completed by his nephew, Minor C. Keith, the shipping magnate who later became vice president of the United Fruit Company.[4]

Unlike later fugitives, who strategically chose where to seek refuge, Meiggs ended up in Chile largely by chance. Writer Samuel Curtis Upham learned the details of the getaway from Captain Jacob Cousins, master of the bark *America*, the privately commissioned ship on which Meiggs made his escape. When asked for his destination, Meiggs replied that he would sail wherever the captain pleased. He was an expatriate afloat with no particular place to go. They stopped in Tahiti for thirteen days (leaving just before the newspapers arrived from San Francisco with the news of Meiggs's flight), proceeded to Pitcairn Island in the South Pacific, and then on to Talcahuano, Chile.[5]

Chile initially balked at offering Meiggs asylum. In May 1855, the governor of California wrote to the U.S. minister in Santiago, instructing him to request Meiggs's extradition. Although there was no extradition treaty between the United States and Chile, the Chilean Supreme Court ordered that Meiggs be handed over as an act of goodwill toward the United States. However, thanks to the skill of his lawyers—and the depth of his pockets—Meiggs managed to evade surrender. Watt Stewart, Meiggs's biographer, quipped: "It seems safe to say that Sr. [Antonio] Varas [of the Chilean foreign ministry], some six years later, thanked his lucky stars that Henry Meiggs was still in Chile and not rusting in a California prison."[6]

Although Meiggs was a fugitive, Chileans came to treat him like a hero. At times, his luster seemed larger than life. On the Day of the Immaculate Conception, 1863, a fire broke out during a crowded service in Santiago's Church of La Campaña. Henry Meiggs was among those who came to the rescue and helped drag victims out of the flames. An article in the newspaper *El Mercurio* paid tribute to the North Americans who risked their lives in the inferno, and particularly singled out Meiggs as a Good Samaritan. "The conduct of Mr. Meiggs, especially towards the working and needy classes, is too well known to require us to refer to it here as a eulogism," the author praised. An eyewitness described Meiggs and others "on that terrible night, with grief upon their countenances, their clothing torn and soaked with water. . . . We are assured that Mr. Meiggs caused himself to be wet through on purpose, so as to enter into the midst of the flames. This is not humanity only, it is heroism." The article may have been hyperbolic, but it was a significant tribute to someone who almost had been extradited eight years earlier.[7]

Peru also courted Meiggs and considered itself a beneficiary of his gifts. In 1870, Alvin P. Hovey, the U.S. minister in Lima, reported to the State Department that "no American on this coast is more popular"—or more powerful—than Meiggs. His investments in that country were far-reaching: railroads, real estate, guano, and mining. One of the major railroad lines that he constructed went from the southern port of Mollendo to Arequipa, Peru's second-largest city, and ended in Cuzco, the old Inca capital. Another connected Callao, the port of Lima, to the silver mining region of Huancayo, and was critical in opening up the exploitation of copper and base metals in the Andes. Meiggs also bought up large guano reserves in Peru and Bolivia. He even took a stab at city planning, constructing a seven-mile-long park between the old and new sections of Lima. In a series of books on the great men of Peruvian history, published in the 1960s, the two foreigners featured were Alexander von Humboldt and "Enrique" Meiggs.[8]

Meiggs blurred the line between legal and illegal capital flows. His "illicit" capital helped build the infrastructure that supported "legitimate" American investments like mining and guano in South America and banana exporting in Central America. This symbiosis was recognized in the United States, where Meiggs's reputation was rehabilitated later in his life, though he was never able to return home

for fear of being arrested. After his death in 1877, American obitu-
aries downplayed Meiggs's crimes and celebrated him as a pioneer
who had opened up Latin America to U.S. investment. The *New York
Times* predicted that "men, overlooking the stain upon the projec-
tor's early career, will pause to marvel at the audacity which has
evoked such a mighty work from the apathy of a petty South American Republic." His unbridled ambition, the article suggested, caused
both the lows and the highs of his career. Ultimately, it concluded,
Latin America was better off for providing the fugitive Meiggs with
an asylum, as "none but a man of Anglo-Saxon race could have
achieved such a career."[9]

Meiggs showed Latin American governments that sheltering an
outlaw could be profitable. Other countries tried to get their own
Meiggs—a fugitive investor who brought along significant capital to
benefit their economy and development. The nation that tried hardest
to attract fugitive funds was Honduras.

❋

If fleeing to Canada was a catchphrase in the 1880s, by the end of
the century, it was replaced by Honduras. In 1900, the *New Orleans
Daily Picayune* called Honduras "a perfect paradise for men who have
committed any crime . . . where the officials of the government protect all thieves that come to them." For almost two decades, Honduras rejected American overtures for an extradition treaty. For
Honduras—the poorest Central American country, saddled with foreign debt—fugitives were a source of national income. Starting in
the late 1880s, successive regimes knowingly sheltered fugitives who
sought asylum in the republic. This policy was even enshrined in
Honduras's 1894 Constitution, which declared: *"La República de Honduras es un asilo sagrado para toda persona que se refugie en su territorio"*
(The Republic of Honduras is a sacred asylum for all persons who
take refuge in its territory).[10]

By the end of the 1870s, Honduras was deeply in debt. Liberal
president Marco Aurelio Soto, hoping to thrust his country into the
modern capitalist world, had negotiated loans in British and French
financial markets to build an "Interoceanic Railroad" that would
connect the Atlantic and Pacific coasts. The plan was to use revenue

from the economic development of the Pacific coast to recoup the massive foreign debt. But the project failed completely; only a few miles of track were built before the money ran out due to corruption and an economic crisis. (The railroad would remain unbuilt for decades—in 1918, it still reached only thirty miles inland.) In 1888, one observer calculated the debt to Britain at £12 million, noting that "at prevailing land values, Honduras could not repay such a debt by selling its entire national territory."[11]

But it could provide a home to Major Edward A. Burke, the former state treasurer of Louisiana. Burke had served as the director general of the World's Exposition at New Orleans in 1884, where he met Luis Bográn, the president of Honduras. In 1886, Bográn granted Burke two valuable mining concessions along the Jalan and the Guayape Rivers in exchange for his pledge to help build an industrial school in Tegucigalpa. While Burke was in London in December 1889, raising money for his Central American investments, the news broke that he had taken nearly $400,000 of bonds belonging to the Louisiana State Agricultural Society. Before the extradition papers went through to Great Britain, Burke fled to Honduras.[12]

Burke was doubly safe: he had the personal protection of President Bográn, and Honduras had no extradition treaty with the United States. The *Chicago Tribune* predicted that "in his new home he will be a big man." Because Burke was well provided with money, valuable concessions, and the backing of a number of big English capitalists, "he is likely to play an important part in Central America, like [fellow fugitives] Meiggs and Winslow in South America." The *New York Tribune* imagined an idyllic life for the fugitive, strolling down tropical streets on moonlit nights, spending time in charming mountain resorts, and being entertained at the Presidential Palace. "Amid these beautiful scenes and the life of official favor and patronage," it envisioned, "he forgets the indictments awaiting his presence in Louisiana."[13]

These conjectures were not far off. A socially prominent figure, Burke managed to navigate the perilous terrain of Honduran politics. Burke developed close relationships with successive leaders (or bought them off), and even attended the wedding of one president's daughter. In 1890, he purchased half of the mineral-rich Apamul

zone, and two years later corresponded with future president Policarpo Bonilla about developing silver mines. During the next three
decades, he invested heavily in real estate, mining, and infrastructure, particularly the Honduras Interoceanic Railway and the
National Railway of Honduras. He also helped attract additional
dollars, advising potential American investors who visited the
country. As one of the nation's most prominent residents, Burke was
the representative who greeted Charles Lindbergh's plane in January
1928, when Lindbergh landed in Tegucigalpa as part of his Hemispheric Goodwill Tour. Burke remained a U.S. citizen his entire life,
but on his death at the age of eighty-nine, he bequeathed half of his
fortune to the government of Honduras, grateful for the asylum it
had provided for nearly forty years.[14]

The Honduran media reported Burke's death with the same degree of respect and gravitas that it reserved for the highest digni-
taries. "The death of Major Burke has caused deep sorrow throughout
the Republic," reported the magazine *Renacimiento*. "He was loved
and appreciated by all." In an editorial in the Tegucigalpa paper *El
Democrata*, J. M. Callejas vowed that "we Hondurans will hold on to
his memory as *the greatest foreigner who has ever pitched his tent on our
promised land*." The newspaper *El Cronista* reported that throngs of
people flocked to the Hotel Ritz, where Burke died, to pay their
respects.[15]

The Honduran government made no secret that it was protecting
fugitives such as Burke. In 1910, the United States and Honduras
came closer than ever before to signing an extradition treaty. However, Luis Lazo, the Honduran minister in Washington, wanted a
specific provision in the treaty pledging "that the Government of the
United States . . . will not now or hereafter request the Government
of Honduras to surrender Major E. A. Burke for crimes now charged
against him in the state of Louisiana." A major stumbling block in
negotiations was the question of whether the treaty would be retroactive. The United States wanted to cast the net as widely as possible,
while Honduras was unwilling to sacrifice valuable immigrants who
already had made a home there.[16]

Other fugitives, though less prominent than Burke, also were
useful additions to Honduran society. Dr. Gustav Adolph Walther,

a naturalized American from Germany, became the director of Te-gucigalpa's Hospital General and helped construct a health clinic in the capital. Later generations fondly remembered him for intro-ducing the first Christmas tree to Honduras. But the story of his arrival in Central America was less heartwarming. He fled Chicago in September 1902, after an indictment based on "a serious charge" made by the parents of ten-year-old Ethel Berkland. A resident of Tegucigalpa wrote to Police Chief O'Neil that Walther was living there, but was in the good graces of the president and had his protection. Chicago police tried, but failed to find a way to arrest him.[17]

Though law enforcers at home were anxious to bring fugitives back, American investors in Honduras were not as bothered by their presence. Some fugitives worked for American-owned companies that did business in Central America. Samuel E. Clark, an absconding postmaster from Alabama, worked for the United Fruit Company, and Fred J. Owens, wanted for forgery in St. Louis, worked with the chief engineer for Samuel Zemurray's Cuyamel Fruit Company. The most visible fugitive working for an American-based interest was Dan Coughlin. Accused of jury bribing in Chicago, Coughlin moved to Puerto Cortés, where he went by the name Jim Davis. He became the right-hand man of J. W. Grace, one of the three brothers who formed W. R. Grace and Company, the powerful mercantilists whose investments spread across Latin America. (Among W. R. Grace's many endeavors, it provided Henry Meiggs with most of his supplies when he built his railroads in Peru.) E. M. Stella, a wholesale banana dealer who lived next door to Coughlin for three years, told the *Chicago Tribune* that "Capt. Grace seemed to think a great deal of Davis—I mean Coughlin—and trusted him with the complete su-pervision of the big things he was doing in Honduras. . . . Coughlin alone supervised the raising of the whole town of Puerto Cortez. The town was raised to the level of the railroad to make it more healthy. He also built a big road in the interior for the government. He was a strictly sober fellow, well behaved, and well liked."[18]

Despite their exile, many fugitives remained loyal to the United States. Burke staunchly supported American expansionist ambitions, both economic and territorial. He played an advisory role, often

sending unsolicited pieces of advice to the State Department via
the U.S. consul in Tegucigalpa. Invoking the Monroe Doctrine, he
strongly advocated Honduras coming under the orbit—even the direct control—of the United States. In 1898, when an attempted Central American Union foundered, Burke suggested that the United
States sweep in and take Honduras. "As the people [of Honduras] had
accepted a Statehood in a weak Union," he explained, "it appeared
timely to suggest application for Statehood in a Union which had become a World Power." (Presumably, this suggestion ran contrary to
Burke's self-interest, as he would need to find a new asylum if Honduras came under the political control of the United States.) Burke
continued to pledge his support for American intervention in Honduras well into the twentieth century.[19]

Burke was, in some ways, the ideal immigrant: a captive colonist
who had no choice but to invest his dollars in Honduran ventures.
But his primary allegiance remained with the country that wanted
to prosecute him, and with its economic interests. Burke's mixed
loyalties were typical of asylum seekers. Their continued links to
American foreign investment meant that, ironically, the United
States gained economic advantages when countries like Honduras refused to extradite. In this sense, offering an asylum was not an act
of aggression toward the United States—it achieved goals that were
very much in keeping with the interests of American businesses.

*

The most infamous fugitive funds that Honduras welcomed, however, came not from an individual but from a lottery. After moral reformers shut down the Louisiana State Lottery, Honduras provided
it with a new home, allowing it to continue operations from Honduran soil, for a price. As with fugitive criminals, Honduras welcomed capital that was illicit in the United States and weathered
similar accusations that it encouraged crime and immorality by providing a shelter.

By the end of the nineteenth century, moral reformers succeeded
in shutting down all official lotteries within the United States. The
largest, the Louisiana State Lottery, was popularly called the "Golden
Octopus" because it seemed to get its tentacles into every home. In

1890, Congress made it a federal offense to use the mail for lottery advertisements, effectively shutting down state lotteries, but the Louisiana State Lottery managed to hang on for another three years. Opponents of the lottery banded together to denounce it as immoral, and when the lottery's charter expired on December 31, 1893, the Louisiana State Legislature voted not to renew it.[20]

Rather than shutting down operations, the managers of the Louisiana State Lottery moved their venture to Honduras. In exchange for $20,000 per year and 20 percent of the lottery's profits, the Honduran government granted the fugitive lottery a charter to operate in the country. Renamed the Honduras National Lottery, the operation relocated to Puerto Cortés, a Caribbean port town that was a mere 900 miles from New Orleans. According to Richard Harding Davis, who traveled to Puerto Cortés in 1895 to write about the lottery for *Harper's Weekly*, Honduras was not the first country that the lottery approached. Its operators initially contacted Mexico, but President Porfirio Díaz asked for too much money, worried that it would compete with Mexico's own national lottery. Colombia and Nicaragua also turned the lottery down. Honduras, however, was not so demanding.[21]

Despite the new name of the lottery, few of its operations actually took place in Honduras. Florida law banned state lotteries, but not foreign ones, so the lottery's managers established headquarters in Tampa, where they received payments for tickets. Once a month, they sent all the lottery tickets to Puerto Cortés. The only part of the venture that actually took place in Honduras was the drawing.[22]

Honduras's willingness to provide the lottery with a home angered the moral reformers who had worked so hard to ban lotteries within the United States. The evangelical press was outraged by the existence of the Honduras National Lottery. The religious weekly *Outlook* repeated a common refrain: to protect the morals of Americans, it was necessary to reach beyond the borders of the nation to control what was happening in Honduras. "It is to the glory of this Nation that each of its commonwealths severally expelled lotteries from its borders," *Outlook* declared. "It is now the National duty to prevent our citizens from being plundered from beyond our borders." It called for the State Department to put pressure on the "supposedly friendly" Honduras to "prevent its harboring criminals openly engaged in the violation of our laws."[23]

At a time when revenue was scarce, the lottery was a reliable source of income for Honduras, and successive regimes allowed it to stay. Journalist Frederick Palmer, who traveled through Central America in 1908, estimated that the annual income to the Honduran government was $100,000. This was shortly after the lottery shut down, and Palmer noted how much its loss hurt the Honduran economy. (In 1907, the Secret Service raided the U.S. offices of the lottery's printers and distributers, resulting in more than fifty arrests, nearly $300,000 in fines, and the downfall of the operation.)[24]

By the first decade of the twentieth century, Honduras had developed the characteristics associated with a banana republic: dependence on foreigners, a one-crop economy, and endemic corruption. When political instability threatened American economic interests in the country, the United States directly intervened, sending in gunboats in 1903, 1907, 1911, and 1912. The State Department stopped short of forcing an extradition treaty on Honduras, but it did become more aggressive in demanding fugitives. In 1908, the Honduran Foreign Ministry, declaring itself "very desirous of pleasing the [State] Department," handed over William Adler, former president of the State National Bank at New Orleans. The same year, despite the lack of a treaty, it also surrendered four men who had hijacked the steamship *Goldsboro* and its cargo from New York, planning to start a colony near Puerto Cortés. When one of the defendants, Francis Bailey, tried to appeal to the Honduran Supreme Court for protection, the Foreign Ministry intercepted his telegrams.[25]

Despite the State Department's sustained pressure, an extradition treaty with Honduras did not come easily. The two nations negotiated a treaty in 1909, but the Honduran government suddenly and unexpectedly rescinded it. The recalcitrant Honduran Congress was not afraid of defying the United States; in 1911, it overwhelmingly voted down a loan contract with J. P. Morgan, arranged by the State Department, denouncing it as an assault on national sovereignty and independence. Later in 1911, banana king Samuel Zemurray and

American mercenary Lee Christmas organized a revolutionary uprising to install a regime friendlier to investors' interests. The next year, President Bonilla's government ratified an extradition treaty.[26]

The 1912 treaty reflected a shift in priorities: pleasing the State Department was now more important than attracting fugitive funds. Although individuals like Burke continued to receive sanctuary, Honduras began to extradite American fugitives—even those with deep pockets—on a regular basis. Within a few years, it lost its reputation as the go-to spot for wrongdoers. This was the legal side to dollar diplomacy: Honduras still depended on dollars coming from the United States, only now they had to be those dollars that the State Department wanted them to take.

✳

In addition to supplying foreign capital, the fugitives themselves could be a resource for countries that were trying to attract immigrants of European, and especially Anglo-Saxon, origin. Countries like Argentina and Costa Rica did not mind if immigrants arrived with criminal pasts, as long as they were of the right color.[27]

Increasing immigration was a pressing public policy issue in Argentina. A group of liberal politicians known as the Generation of 1880 strove for Argentina to catch up to the wealthier, more "modern" nations of Europe, the United States, and Canada. Part of their plan for achieving this was to stimulate mass immigration from Europe. Late nineteenth-century Argentine scientists subscribed to theories of racial hierarchies and Nordic and Anglo-Saxon superiority, and Argentine progressives sought to bring in immigrants who would "whiten" the country. One of the central fictions of their new national identity was the idea of a European-based and unified race, one that left out the native peoples of Argentina and those of African heritage.[28]

Liberal political theorist Juan Bautista Alberdi wanted to form an industrial Argentina by bringing in Europeans with discipline and responsible work habits. Education was not enough: Argentina needed European blood. "If we were to take the ragged homeless from Chile, our gauchos, the half-breeds from Bolivia—the basic elements of our masses—and let them experience all the transformations of our best system of instruction," he claimed, "we would not in one hundred years have made any of them into an English laborer who works, spends, and lives in a dignified and comfortable manner." In the interest of breeding a stronger national race, Alberdi proposed an aggressive immigration policy that would alter the cultural and ethnic profile of the Argentine population. "Europe will bring us its fresh spirit, its work habits, and its civilized ways with the immigrants it sends us," he declared. Many of Alberdi's suggestions were incorporated into the Constitution of 1853.[29]

In his annual message at the opening of the Argentine Congress in 1882, President Julio Argentino Rocas also emphasized the importance of attracting more settlers of European origin. Discussing the status of immigration over the past year, he reported that there had been 32,817 new arrivals—a disappointing number, which was "feeble when compared to the advantages that the country offers." Fortunately, many of these newcomers arrived with enough money to make a start without assistance from the state. However, other New World countries such as Mexico, Brazil, and the United States competed with Argentina to welcome the "vivifying stream" of European immigrants. In order to draw in more of these settlers, President Rocas proposed, Argentina must "speedily make some sacrifice to secure them" by lowering the passage rates and making it easier to obtain land. Immigrants were indispensable for building up infrastructure and promoting the national project, he argued, and Argentines should use "every means in our reach" to attract them.[30]

Until the 1890s, Argentina had an open-door immigration policy, which included wiping the slate clean for persons of European origin who were accused of crimes in their home countries. In 1876, President Nicolás Avellaneda repeated a common refrain: that emigrating to Argentina turned bad men good. In response to a request by Italy for a group of fugitives living in Buenos Aires, the president reportedly replied: "We mean to give these men asylum, because this country has the rare faculty of converting many European criminals into good citizens." Fugitives from around Europe—Great Britain, Italy, Spain, Germany, Belgium—joined other immigrants in Buenos Aires or settled as farmers in Argentina's interior. The *Buenos Ayres Standard*, an English-language newspaper edited by British expatriates, observed in 1892 that "the criminal class, especially of

Southern Europe, have come to regard Argentina as 'a happy hunting-ground.' "[31]

Americans reported that Buenos Aires was a haven for fugitives from the United States as well. In one of his volumes on *The History of Nations*, Henry Cabot Lodge described the Argentine capital as a "city [of] refuge of those under the ban of law," and prominent travel writer Frank G. Carpenter quipped that "Buenos Aires has more men living under assumed names than any city in the world." Carpenter told a humorous anecdote, typical of the stereotype of foreigners in Buenos Aires:

> A year or so ago, it is said that four Americans were chatting together in one of the cafés of Buenos Aires, when three of the crowd for some reason began to jeer at the fourth. He grew angry and said: "Well, gentlemen, you may sneer at me if you please, but I want you to understand that there is at least one county in the United States that I dare go back to without fear of the sheriff. I know none of you can say as much."[32]

By the turn of the century, however, Argentine officials ended the open-door policy and began implementing restrictions to keep out undesirable immigrants. Immigration accelerated at the end of the century; by 1890, it had reached nearly 300,000 annually. Around the same time, Juan Vucetich, a Buenos Aires police official known for pioneering the use of fingerprinting, presented extensive statistics documenting the rise of crime rates in the crowded cities. In his 1892 book *Las causas del delito (The Causes of Crime)*, Antonio Dellapiane argued that immigrants were largely responsible for this rise in urban crime. He identified immigrants as carriers of contagion—not only of communicable diseases but also of moral depravity and destabilizing political ideas. In 1899, legislator Miguel Cané called for more restrictive laws against those immigrants "thrown from Europe who expulses them like a poison threatening its organism." Three years later, the national legislature debated putting restrictions on entry, modeled after those of the United States, to filter out "dangerous types" such as convicts, prostitutes, the mentally ill, and anarchists. Argentines had lost faith in immigration's redeeming power.[33]

The adoption of extradition treaties was part of the broader effort to restrict the immigration of undesirables. During the 1890s, Argentina began surrendering accused criminals to their home countries. Argentina and Italy signed an extradition agreement in 1886, which was ratified four years later. In 1892, Argentina handed over a man named Winkelmann to Germany, and two fugitives each to Belgium and Spain. An extradition treaty with Great Britain went into effect at the end of 1893. Finally, after having made diplomatic overtures to the Argentine Foreign Ministry since 1887, the United States signed a treaty with Argentina in 1896, which went into effect in 1900. The first person extradited to the United States was William Hoeppner, accused of forgery and larceny in New York, in 1901. During the next two decades, Argentina extradited seventeen more Americans. The South American nation was no longer the fugitive's "happy hunting ground."[34]

Well into the twentieth century, Costa Rica also took advantage of its status as an extradition haven to stimulate immigration. In September 1911, under instructions from the State Department, U.S. consul Gustavus L. Monroe approached Manuel Castro Quesada, the minister of foreign affairs, with a draft of a possible extradition treaty between the two nations. Castro Quesada responded "that his Government would not sign the treaty; that there are several Americans in Costa Rica who have committed crimes in the United States but who now make excellent citizens for this country." In his correspondence back to Washington, Monroe insisted that "I urged the acceptance of the treaty as far as I could, but he seemed indifferent."[35]

In defense of this position, former Costa Rican president Cleto González Víquez delivered a defiant statement outlining the reasons why Costa Rica should resist pressure from the United States to sign an extradition treaty. The weightiest reason for refusing such a treaty, González claimed, was the simple fact that Costa Rica needed more immigrants. It did not matter if they had a criminal past, as "Costa Rica, a country of a small population, is greatly interested in attracting immigrants and any nation in our circumstance is not, and should not be, so scrupulous concerning the life and antecedents of those who come and settle on its soil."[36]

As in Argentina, the immigrants that González wanted to attract were white settlers of European origin, not indigenous emigrants or the West Indian workers that the fruit companies brought to work on banana plantations. Costa Rican elites propagated the idea that whiteness was part of the national self-identity, particularly in contrast to neighboring countries. Therefore, it was essential that immigrants were of European origin. When Henry Meiggs began construction of his rail line from the Central Valley to the Caribbean coast in 1871, President Tomás Miguel Guardia advised him, wishfully, that German, Belgian, and Swiss workers would be particularly welcomed.[37]

During the following decades, as the fruit companies brought in more West Indian workers of African descent, Costa Rican elites reached a state of panic. In response to a 1927 census that showed that West Indians were the largest immigrant group, Dr. Clodomiro Picado, one of Costa Rica's most important scientists, declared that "Our Blood Is Blackening! And if we continue like this, it will not be a nugget of gold that comes out of the crucible, but rather a piece of charcoal." He hoped that "perhaps there is still time to rescue our European patrimony" and bring Costa Rica back to its racial makeup of a century earlier, when, he claimed, the population had been 75 percent European. But to do this, it was necessary to bring in immigrants of the right color.[38]

In his manifesto against extradition, González pointed out the hypocrisy of the U.S. request. Back in the early nineteenth century, when the United States needed more immigrants, it too had rejected extradition. "The United States themselves, who today would like to have a treaty of extradition with every nation, at one time were not very particular as to the class of immigrants, nor were very inclined to agree to the surrender of the delinquents who landed on their shores," González remarked. "And they were right," he continued. "To be eager to see that every crime receives its penalty may be very laudable, but among nations, high ideals of justice and universal order are sometimes surmounted by interest and selfishness." In the future, he speculated, the Central American nations would reach a point in their development where they no longer needed immigrants, and at that time would solicit treaties of extradition.

"Meanwhile," however, "they would not be very wise if, consciously, they were to put such a drawback in the way of their development and expansion."[39]

Argentina and Costa Rica took divergent paths: While Argentina began extraditing fugitives by the end of the nineteenth century, Costa Rica continued to welcome white immigrants regardless of their criminal pasts. This difference in policy arose, in part, because of elite Costa Ricans' fears of West Indian newcomers. While Argentines blamed European undesirables for crime and the degradation of society, in Costa Rica there was another immigrant group on whom to place the blame. Europeans and Euro-Americans, even those with criminal backgrounds, remained the "good" immigrants in contrast to the dark-skinned West Indians.

❊

Extradition treaties were ambiguous documents. Different countries disagreed as to what exactly constituted a crime and what was a reasonable sentence. An act that carried a twenty-year jail term in one country might only warrant ten in another, and might not even be a crime in a third. The severity of U.S. punishments—especially the death penalty—seemed particularly draconian to Latin Americans. A number of countries, including Costa Rica and Brazil, refused to even consider an extradition treaty with the United States if capital punishment were a possibility.

In Argentina, for example, the standards of punishment in Europe and the United States seemed excessive and even unjust. The editors of the *Buenos Ayres Standard* complained about the laxity of criminal justice in their adopted land, lamenting the "very mild form of punishment which it is customary to impose in this country on murderers, swindlers, robbers, forgers &c." A convicted murderer who might be executed in England or the United States, for instance, might only be jailed in Argentina. The punishment for forgery or embezzlement was five to ten years in Europe, but "this seems to Argentine jurisconsultants an extreme severity." Many Argentines felt sympathy for Jabez Spencer Balfour, a British member of Parliament and financial tycoon who sought refuge in Argentina after being accused of fraud. President Luis Sáenz Peña, himself a former judge on the Supreme Court of the province of Buenos Aires, found it "unfair to condemn an ex-member of Parliament, like the fugitive Balfour, to a convict prison, for an offense which is viewed with extreme clemency in the River Plate."[40]

Laws conflicted from country to country; sometimes a felony in one jurisdiction was not a crime in another. The disparities between national laws became a central issue in the 1893 case of Francis Henry Weeks, a New York lawyer who took refuge in Costa Rica after losing nearly a million dollars of his clients' trust funds. Although there was no extradition treaty, the U.S. State Department nevertheless petitioned Costa Rica for Weeks's surrender. The resulting judicial hearing about whether Weeks should be handed over was a huge spectacle, followed closely by the media in both countries. Weeks spared no expense, hiring the best legal counsel in the country, with eminent lawyer Mauro Fernández leading the team.[41]

At the center of Weeks's case was the claim that the acts deemed illegal in the United States were not criminal in Costa Rica. What prosecutors called theft in New York was not necessarily theft elsewhere. According to Harrison R. Williams, the U.S. consul in San José, Weeks's lawyers were "industriously working up sympathy by declaring Weeks' position very little more than that of a bankrupt." Fernández argued that there was "no criminality"; Weeks was "merely unfortunate in [his] investments." Fernández further claimed that U.S. laws were excessively harsh and that Costa Rica should not collude with them. "In the United States such a 'mistake' as his is looked upon more severely than in other nations," he contended. "It is a crime only in that he invested the trust funds in the West instead of New York, thus being criminal only by New York Statutes."[42]

After a month of legal wrangling, the court ruled against Weeks, demanding his surrender to American authorities. The Costa Rican newspaper *El Diario de Comercio* protested: "Weeks is no criminal. He has been unfortunate in the management of funds—no more." At stake were not just competing definitions of criminality, but the very issue of Costa Rican sovereignty. The newspaper suggested that

President Rodríguez merely was trying to please the United States by handing Weeks over. "What right has been accorded to our Government to place a foreigner in rigorous detention out of mere regard for external influences?" it asked. "The people of Costa Rica will see with indignation the surrender of Weeks to the authorities of New York."[43]

Hoping to avoid another Weeks incident, the State Department and the president of Costa Rica each invited negotiations for an extradition treaty. In his Annual Message to Congress in December 1893, President Grover Cleveland praised Costa Rica for having "lately testified its friendliness" by handing Weeks over. He felt so certain that the two countries would come to an agreement, he announced that "the formation of a treaty with that country to meet recurring cases of this kind will soon be accomplished."[44]

But the negotiations fell apart in 1894 over the issue of the death penalty. Costa Rica was one of the first Latin American countries to abolish capital punishment, and it refused to enter into any treaty unless the pact expressly guaranteed that defendants would not be executed. The State Department could not make such a promise: most defendants would be tried in state courts, not federal ones, and decisions about punishment were the prerogative of the states. If the State Department agreed to take the death penalty off the table, it would be illegitimately usurping the states' power. When the United States and Costa Rica finally signed an extradition agreement in 1923, it contained an addendum promising that the State Department would not ask for the extradition of anyone who might be subject to the death penalty in his or her jurisdiction.[45]

The death penalty was the most controversial issue in negotiations with other countries as well. Several Latin American countries abolished capital punishment in the late nineteenth and early twentieth centuries: Venezuela (1863), Costa Rica (1877), Brazil (1882), Panama (1903), Ecuador (1906), Uruguay (1907), and Colombia (1910). The question of the death penalty obstructed extradition treaties even though murder and treason, the only crimes punishable by death in most places, were relatively rare extradition offenses. American jurist and politician William Beach Lawrence had doubts about the future of the entire system of international extradition, suggesting that its "death-blow" could come from the abolition of the death penalty in some countries but not in others.[46]

As in Costa Rica, Brazil's negotiations with the United States came to a standstill over the issue of the death penalty. In 1911, the Brazilian legislature passed a law that rescinded all of Brazil's existing extradition treaties as of July 1913, including the 1897 compact with the United States. Any future treaty, it instructed, must guarantee that sentences of death or corporal punishment be commuted to imprisonment. According to a State Department memo, Brazil's attitude toward the death penalty caused "not a little apprehension regarding this question of extradition." Another memo elaborated: "In this state of facts the probabilities are that it would be extremely difficult, if not impossible, to obtain extradition of any person committing murder, or other crime punishable by death, from the foreign country to which he fled, if there was within our treaty with that country a provision similar to that contemplated by Brazil."[47]

After Brazil rescinded its treaty, there was no extradition with the United States until 1961. During those fifty years, Brazil became famous as a haven for fugitives. In the 1952 thriller *The Steel Trap*, a bank officer played by Joseph Cotten decides to rob his own bank and head to a country without extradition. A monologue early in the film reveals a remarkably detailed if incomplete knowledge about extradition law:

> I checked every country in Europe and the British Empire, Mexico and Central America, and in South America. All had extradition treaties. I had a notation to look up a Brazilian amendment. It was the last possibility. . . . And there it was! In 1913, for some unaccountable reason, Brazil revoked her extradition treaty. So there actually was a country without extradition! . . . This was the turning point in my thinking; the idea had now become an obsession.[48]

In the cases of both Costa Rica and Brazil, the problem was not solved until the United States budged and agreed to take the death penalty off the table. These countries were in a position of power because the United States needed the treaty more. In the standoff between strong and relatively weaker nations, the smaller country held out; it was the United States that flinched.

✳

By the end of the century, as American detectives and State Department officials demanded the return of increasingly more fugitives, these pressures gave rise to new forms of resistance. Choosing to give asylum to a fugitive was a way of asserting sovereignty over one's territory. Refusing to extradite symbolically pushed back against the military and economic dominance of the United States. Sometimes there was no immediate gain for sheltering a fugitive, except simply to make the point of challenging American power.

Among the various issues at stake in the 1893 Weeks case, the question of sovereignty loomed largest. Because the hearing occurred just a few months before Costa Rica's presidential election, the rhetoric surrounding the case was particularly politically charged: the standing president, José Rodríguez, supported handing Weeks over to the United States, while Weeks's lawyers were associated with the opposition. Using the language of sovereignty and resistance to American hegemony, they made their case for Weeks while appealing to a sense of nationalism. The Weeks trial also took place three months after José Martí visited San José, which may have added to the vehemence of their expression.[49]

In his arguments on behalf of Weeks, Mauro Fernández emphasized that Costa Rica did not need to conform to the wishes of the United States to be a civilized nation. Citing international legal precedent, he pointed out that some of the most quintessentially "civilized" nations—including Great Britain and the United States—refused to extradite in the absence of a treaty. Fernández insisted that Costa Rica act according to the standards of international law, not according to the demands of the United States. "If Costa Rica is going to act internationally in accordance with the law of nations, following the example of the most civilized countries," he argued, "it is absolutely impossible to agree to the extradition, and in the name of justice, we must deny it." Legal scholars agreed that there was no duty to extradite: it was a choice, a prerogative, a sovereign decision.[50]

Some journalists equated the demand for Weeks's extradition with more pernicious forms of bullying and coercion by the United States. An October 1893 article in *La Prensa Libre* invoked the United States' most visible act of imperialism to date: the Mexican War of 1846–1848. It asked, rhetorically: "Does there exist a treaty of extradition between this country and the nation which implanted in America the right of might with its conquest of half Mexico?" Echoing the anti-imperialist language of José Martí, the editorialist went on to accuse "the colossus of the North" of invading the rights of Costa Rica. The author wrote of the "boastful pretentions" of Secretary of State James G. Blaine, who had issued the formal request for Weeks. "Our road is clear," the article concluded. "Let us concede to the American Government whatever it is entitled to—but nothing more."[51]

The final decision to surrender Weeks sparked widespread public controversy. U.S. consul Harrison R. Williams reported that "the opposition to the Government have seized upon this as a political weapon" and "being the first extradition granted by this Government it has, of course, excited a great amount of discussion." While he insisted that he still felt "a very friendly feeling evinced toward the United States," many Costa Rican newspapers expressed a different sentiment. The newspaper *El Heraldo de Costa Rica* reported "invectives against the Yankees." But, it pointed out, this was a no-win situation: if Costa Rica opted not to hand people over to the United States, it would be giving "a naturalization card to all the scoundrels in its territory."[52]

Less than two months after Weeks's surrender, detective C. E. Henry of the American Surety Company got the tip that Robert G. H. Huntington, the absconding secretary of Chicago's House Building and Loan Association, was also in Costa Rica. The easy part was finding him: Within a half hour of landing at the Atlantic port of Limón, Henry located his man. The tricky part was getting him out of the country. Consul Williams felt that it would "probably [be] a difficult matter to secure [Huntington's] extradition so close upon Weeks' case," due to "the opposition to the extradition of Weeks and the excitement thereby occasioned." The Weeks case had "left some bitterness behind."[53]

This time, less than a month before the presidential election, extraditing Huntington was too politically risky. Candidate Rafael Yglesias Castro, a minister in President Rodríguez's cabinet, was trying to curry the favor of the public. "It is well known that a large number of people in this country are opposed to extradition on general principles," Consul Williams explained to the State Department. "Extradition treaties have been repeatedly defeated in Congress." Henry was frustrated by the "excuses and delays" of the Costa Rican government: "They are afraid to act till after the election February 5th," he wrote home. In the end, Huntington never made it back to the United States. He died of yellow fever in Limón on February 1, four days before the election. Rather than bringing home his man in glory, Detective Henry was stuck making the funeral arrangements.[54]

More than a decade later, Cleto González continued the refrain that an extradition treaty with the United States would impinge on Costa Rica's sovereignty. Although it was supposedly an agreement with mutual and equal obligations, the ex-president questioned what Costa Rica would get out of such a treaty and how bilateral it really would be. To sign the treaty would be "to put Costa Rica in a police role" *(un papel de gendarmes)* in service of the United States. "For every hundred criminals claimed by the Government of a populous nation, we might request the extradition of one and that one we would not be very likely to claim," González predicted. "What sense is there then in agreeing to a treaty that does not benefit us in the least and which will bring responsibilities and difficulties?" In short, he did not want Costa Rica to do the dirty work for the United States. With the ease of movement between the U.S.-occupied Panama Canal Zone and Limón, Costa Rica might be called on to pursue hundreds of suspected offenders.[55]

Refusing to extradite was a way for a country to proclaim that its own best interests were not necessarily the same at those of the United States. It was, in short, a form of resistance to U.S. dominance in Latin America. Moreover, the fact that countries like Costa Rica were able to frustrate the United States by refusing to extradite shows that U.S. hegemony in the region was not absolute. Extradition was one area in which there was some flexibility for Latin

American countries to assert sovereignty by standing up to the colossus of the North.

✳

Later in the twentieth century, South American countries sheltered
more infamous fugitives. After World War II, Argentina took in
hundreds, perhaps thousands, of ex-Nazis and Nazi collaborators, including members of Hitler's inner circle. Adolf Eichmann was living
in a suburb of Buenos Aires when members of the Israeli Mossad captured him in 1960, and Dr. Josef Mengele moved between Argentina, Paraguay, and Brazil until his death in 1979. Notwithstanding
legends of Vatican involvement and illicit caches of gold, strongman
leaders like Argentina's Juan Perón and Paraguay's Alfredo Stroessner
welcomed these fugitives out of sympathy for the Axis powers and
admiration for European fascism.[56]

Financial fugitives continued to find homes in Latin America, as
well. In 1973, Robert Vesco, accused of securities fraud in the United
States, donated $2.1 million to a company owned by Costa Rican
president José Figueres. In return, Figueres passed a law, commonly
called the "Vesco Law," guaranteeing that Costa Rica would not extradite the fugitive. Five years later, when a different presidential
administration repealed the law, Barbados, Nicaragua, Antigua, and
Cuba all welcomed Vesco, who was reportedly worth $200 million.
Like the earlier extradition havens, these post-1945 asylums existed
for two reasons: to assert national sovereignty and for financial gain.[57]

In the late nineteenth and early twentieth centuries, Latin American countries had learned that they could use sanctuary as a political
tool. Safe havens were a resource that they could offer. These asylums were an example of weaker states using the tools at their disposal to stand up to stronger states. At a time when the United States
was dictating economic policies, these countries could resist complete domination by refusing to concede to the United States in other
ways.

Yet if attracting investment capital was one aim of these nonextra-
diting nations and resisting U.S. domination was another, those two
goals sometimes worked at cross-purposes. Fugitives brought investment dollars with them, but often ultimately served as intermediaries

between their host country and American corporations. As American businesses took root in foreign countries, the likelihood that the United States would intervene in the affairs of those nations to protect national interests also increased (as did indeed happen in Honduras). The State Department and the War Department were largely appendages of American enterprise; therefore, a country that welcomed a fugitive's financial "services" was likely inviting eventual American penetration. To refuse extradition but welcome criminal capital was in some ways a poor resistance tactic, given that fugitives appeared to attract the sort of businesses that increased the likelihood of formal U.S. intervention, management, or even military occupation.

Moreover, as Cleto González pointed out, rather than defying the United States, these countries were acting just like their northern neighbor, which had long called itself a nation of asylum. As the United States pressured other countries to adopt extradition treaties and hand over fugitives, it grappled with its own identity as a haven and a place for immigrants to start anew. Asylum was a complicated word, alternately a denunciation and a tribute, depending on who was being sheltered and where.

5

Asylum No More

*I*N MIDAFTERNOON on July 24, 1899, U.S. marshal George L. Sie-brecht stepped into the El Paso County Jail, extradition warrant in hand. A few minutes later, he emerged with two companions: the deputy sheriff and a prisoner, a golden-haired woman of about forty. While policemen tried to disperse the gathering crowds of news-paper reporters, the three stepped into a carriage parked behind the jail and proceeded south toward the Santa Fe Street Bridge, which spanned the Rio Grande between El Paso, Texas, and Ciudad Juárez, Chihuahua. As they approached the bridge, the prisoner unfolded a cloth bundle in her lap, revealing an American flag. Throwing the stars and stripes around her shoulders, the woman turned back to face El Paso as the carriage stopped at the bridge's midpoint. Even after she was handed over to Mexican authorities, she refused to part with the flag, pulling it over her head as she entered her cell in the Juárez jail.[1]

This was not the first time that Mattie Rich's name made head-lines. For the previous two months, newspapers nationwide had closely followed her case, and five months later President William McKinley would even mention her in his Annual Message to Con-gress. As the first U.S. citizen ever formally extradited to a foreign country—sent to Mexico to stand trial for the murder of her husband—Rich set a legal precedent that sparked widespread con-troversy in her time. Many of Rich's countrymen believed that the surrender of a white U.S. citizen to the Mexican government was a betrayal of American principles.[2]

However, the extension of power over fugitives, and the spaces that harbored them, was not only a matter of the United States reaching into foreign countries. Extradition was a bilateral, reciprocal process, and other countries demanded fugitives too. Americans applauded when their own detectives brought criminals back from abroad, but their reactions were more complicated when other nations requested fugitives seeking shelter in the United States. While most Americans agreed that foreign criminals posed a threat to society, they were divided over the question of whether citizens like Rich should be surrendered to foreign governments. The Rich case tested Americans' beliefs about the purpose and proper target of acts like extradition, as well as the power of the state to grant or deny sanctuary.

In the early 1800s, Americans preferred to think of their country as a nation of asylum. Extradition was so contentious an issue that it was effectively suspended, for aliens as well as citizens. But over the course of the nineteenth century, as the United States ratified more extradition agreements, it began to hand over people who had previously been protected within its own borders. By 1900, the United States had one of the most expansive extradition policies in the world, surrendering dozens of people per year to be tried in foreign courts. In under a century, the United States moved from refusing to extradite anyone, to handing over foreigners but not citizens, to finally surrendering citizens like Mattie Rich as well.[3]

The change over time was dramatic, and it can best be understood by thinking of extradition not only as a matter of international relations but also as a form of crime control. Just as immigration and deportation laws excluded foreign felons from the United States, so too did extradition purge the country of "undesirable" convicts. The more Americans perceived border-crossing criminals as a threat to society, the greater their willingness to abandon the asylum ideal and extradite fugitives—even U.S. citizens—to foreign governments. The United States may have formally adopted the policy of extradition in the name of international diplomacy, but Americans accepted it for the sake of domestic law and order.

❋

In 1883, Emma Lazarus composed "The New Colossus," an ode to the United States as a refuge for the world's oppressed. Yet among the groups who were not invited into America's welcoming fold were foreigners who had been convicted of crimes. During the second half of the nineteenth century, Americans loosened their commitment to the idea of their country as a safe haven for all. This was reflected in both immigration restrictions and extradition laws. However, one group of lawbreakers—U.S. citizens—received absolute protection from extradition through the end of the century. When the Mattie Rich case broke in 1899, Americans were increasingly qualifying the notion of their nation as an asylum, yet remnants of this view still persisted when it came to the protection of citizens within U.S. borders.[4]

Mattie Rich's extradition marked a drastic change from U.S. policy a half century earlier. For nearly the first seventy years of the nation's existence, the founding myth of the United States as a land of asylum had deterred any extradition at all. As Thomas Paine implored in *Common Sense*, "O! receive the fugitive, and prepare in time an asylum for mankind." Although the United States was never the idealized asylum that some Americans envisioned, the nation did resist extradition at a time when many European countries were routinely signing such treaties with each other. Not only did Americans cling to the idea that their land was a refuge but they also looked on most foreign judicial systems with suspicion.[5]

Between 1776 and 1843, the United States handed over only one person to a foreign nation, and that case was so controversial that international extradition seemed a doomed policy. The Jay Treaty of 1794 contained the young republic's first extradition agreement, a provision between the United States and Great Britain calling for the mutual surrender of murderers and forgers. In 1799, Britain demanded the extradition of seaman Thomas Nash, accused of taking part in a mutiny and killing several officers aboard the British ship *Hermione*. The sailor, however, insisted that he was an American citizen named Jonathan Robbins and had been impressed onto the *Hermione*; therefore, he had a right to secure his escape. At the urging of President John Adams, Judge Thomas Bee ordered Robbins's surrender to Britain pursuant to the terms of the Jay Treaty. Robbins was subsequently taken to Jamaica and, to the horror of many Americans, summarily court-martialed, convicted, and hanged. Democratic-Republicans seized on the incident to attack the Federalist president, and the Robbins affair contributed to Adams's defeat to Thomas Jefferson in the presidential election the next year. Indeed, Robbins's surrender sparked so much outrage that the United States let the extradition provision lapse in 1807 and did not enter into another such agreement for the next thirty-five years.[6]

As improvements in transportation made it easier for fugitives to gain impunity simply by crossing borders, however, the parameters of America's "asylum for mankind" narrowed. With thousands of miles of international boundary on either side, it was a practical law enforcement necessity to come to some agreement about how to exchange fugitives. In fact, in an effort to keep the peace, border states attempted to extradite on their own. In 1839, Governor Silas Jennison of Vermont ordered George Holmes, a resident of Quebec, arrested and sent back to Canada to be tried for murder. The U.S. Supreme Court chastised him for this, ruling in *Holmes v. Jennison* that extradition, as a matter of foreign relations, was the exclusive power of the federal government; a state governor had no authority to unilaterally hand over fugitives to a foreign country. Three years later, after decades of abstaining from surrendering fugitives, the United States finally signed an extradition agreement: Article 10 of the Webster-Ashburton Treaty with Britain. Its first extradition treaty with Mexico was ratified in 1861. By 1899, the year of Mattie Rich's surrender, the United States was party to extradition treaties with thirty-four nations, mainly in Europe and the Americas.[7]

The first person extradited from the United States under the Webster-Ashburton Treaty, in August 1843, foreshadowed the Mattie Rich case fifty-six years later. Like Rich, Scotswoman Christina Gilmour was accused of murdering her husband and then departing for the United States. Her lawyer tried to block her extradition by claiming insanity, calling his client a "daft Scotch lassie." He also attacked the very practice of extradition as unconstitutional, specifically violating the Fourth and Fifth Amendments. On both fronts, he was rebuffed. A district court judge in New York found sufficient evidence of both sanity and guilt, and Attorney General John Nelson wrote a vigorous opinion defending the constitutionality of the extradition process. Gilmour was subsequently surrendered to Britain.

However, unlike the earlier Robbins case or the later Rich case, few voices spoke out against Gilmour's extradition.[8]

In fact, there was surprisingly little controversy surrounding the decision to start surrendering foreign criminals. Americans debated the status of fugitive slaves under extradition treaties, whether to hand over military deserters, and how to protect political offenders. They did not put up a fuss, however, when common criminals were extradited. Newspaper editorials about the first few extraditions from the United States in the mid-1840s simply wondered how the process would move forward: Did witnesses need to cross the Atlantic to testify at an extradition hearing? Would other countries reciprocate? Those international incidents that did cause a stir called for asylum for a fellow countryman but did not take issue with the practice of extradition. In 1852, for example, Irish protesters in New York held rallies and crowded the courtroom in opposition to the extradition of Thomas Kaine. Yet a disturbance like Kaine's was the exception; few early international extradition cases caused this much uproar.[9]

It would be inaccurate, however, to say that antebellum Americans did not care about extradition matters. They did pay close attention to them, but the extradition that felt more relevant was interstate rather than international. The U.S. Constitution effectively created one of the largest extradition zones in the world, binding all of the states with the pledge to return fugitives to each other. Article 4, section 2—also known as the Extradition Clause—provided that a person "charged in any state with treason, felony, or other crime, who shall flee from justice" must be sent back "on demand of the executive authority of the state from which he fled . . . to the state having jurisdiction of the crime." Supplementing the Extradition Clause, the Fugitive Slave Act of 1793 mandated that authorities in free states return escaped slaves to their Southern masters.[10]

This immense extradition zone did not always operate smoothly, especially when it came to matters involving slavery. Many Northern states tried to circumvent the Fugitive Slave Act of 1793, and the Supreme Court greatly weakened it in the 1842 case of *Prigg v. Pennsylvania*, where it ruled that states did not have to offer aid in the hunting or recapturing of slaves. This led to the stricter and hugely controversial Fugitive Slave Act of 1850, which penalized officials who did not arrest an alleged runaway slave. Cases like that of Shadrach Minkins in 1851 and Anthony Burns in 1854 galvanized the nation, as proslavery and abolitionist forces squared off over whether these escaped slaves would be returned from freedom in the North to bondage in the South.[11]

In the antebellum United States, therefore, the question of whether Massachusetts would surrender an escaped slave to Virginia was a far more pressing issue than whether the United States would hand over a fugitive criminal to France. In fact, many Americans still believed that with the North American continent so isolated the United States did not have to worry about issues like international extradition. To some extent, they were correct: through the 1850s and 1860s, the United States received only two to five extradition requests per year, mainly from Britain, France, and Prussia.[12]

But international extradition grew at a rapid rate after the Civil War. By the 1880s, the United States regularly handed more than twenty people per year to foreign countries. In part, the decision to start surrendering more fugitives to foreign governments was a diplomatic necessity. Though American detectives did not necessarily need a treaty to bring back fugitives from foreign countries, it certainly made the process easier and smoother if there was a treaty in place. According to the reciprocal nature of extradition treaties, this meant that the United States needed to start handing people over too, if it hoped to continue receiving its own fugitives.[13]

The growth of extradition in the late nineteenth century was not just a matter of reciprocity; it also helped achieve a goal that was very much in keeping with the evolving politics of border control. At a time when Americans grew ever more concerned about the criminal character of immigrants, extradition helped rid the body politic of lawbreakers. Studies of immigration and deportation law have documented the erosion of American asylum, yet such works rarely if ever mention extradition. This oversight is easy to understand, as extradition cases went through a different administrative apparatus than immigration ones. Moreover, the numbers were far from equivalent: annually, extradition cases only numbered in the dozens, while the United States turned away or deported thousands. Yet while today's scholars may have missed the connection, nineteenth-century Americans recognized extradition as complementary to immigration restriction and deportation. Like deportation, extradition "rids the country of refuge of undesirable persons," explained John Bassett Moore, the U.S. assistant secretary of state, in 1890.[14]

As immigration law expanded, extradition grew as well. Opposition to the immigration of criminals went back to colonial times; in 1751, Benjamin Franklin famously suggested shipping rattlesnakes across the Atlantic in return for all the convicts England was sending to America. During the antebellum years, when states regulated the admission of foreigners, New York and other states with major ports of entry passed laws excluding newcomers with criminal records. Extradition, in a sense, was simply a way of removing those lawbreakers who had gotten past inspection. The Page Act of 1875, the first restrictive immigration law passed by Congress, banned the entry of three groups of "undesirable" foreigners: forced laborers from Asia, prostitutes, and convicts. While the first two categories largely targeted émigrés from China, the ban on convicts affected immigration more widely, and reflected just how dangerous and pressing a threat Americans considered foreign felons. During the same decade as the Page Act, the United States ratified nine new extradition treaties also targeting foreign criminals. The expansion of extradition supplemented the gatekeeping impulse that gave rise to immigration restrictions and deportation orders.[15]

As the United States began to hand fugitives over to foreign governments on a regular basis, it insisted on certain safeguards. True to the "nation of asylum" ideal, it would not surrender political offenders. It insisted that there could be no extradition in the absence of a treaty (this was violated once, in 1864, in the case of slave trader José Agustín Arguelles, who was surrendered to Cuba despite the lack of a treaty with Spain), and that people could only be tried for the offense for which they were extradited (called the rule of specialty). Finally, at least through the end of the nineteenth century, the United States did not extradite its own citizens. In *Elements of International Law,* one of the most influential law books of the nineteenth century, American jurist and diplomat Henry Wheaton espoused the principle that "a State should never authorize the extradition of its own citizens or subjects." When it came to extradition, citizens were off-limits.[16]

The nonextradition of citizens was not a characteristic unique to the United States; most countries refused to extradite nationals. John Bassett Moore affirmed in 1891 that "the preponderant practice of nations at the present day is to decline to deliver up their citizens." The Italian Penal Code of 1890, for instance, expressly provided that "the extradition of a citizen is not permitted." There was one difference, though. As a civil law country, Italy—as well as most European and Latin American nations—would prosecute a citizen at home for an offense committed abroad. In contrast, the United States, as a common-law country, adhered to a policy of strict territoriality, in which U.S. courts would only try crimes committed in that jurisdiction—that is, on U.S. soil. Great Britain, also a common-law country, had the same strict adherence to the policy of territorial jurisdiction, although it could try someone for a crime committed anywhere in its empire. Thus, some citizens were safer on their home soil than others, and U.S. citizens were among the safest of all.[17]

There were exceptions to the policy that citizens found absolute refuge on U.S. soil. Naturalized citizens were still vulnerable to denaturalization and deportation, as happened to Emma Goldman and approximately 22,000 others between 1907 and 1973. Women who married foreigners were likewise stripped of their U.S. citizenship and left vulnerable. The Expatriation Acts of 1868 and 1907 set forth numerous ways that Americans, both foreign- and native-born, could lose their citizenship; these ranged from pledging allegiance to another state to deserting the military. There were even reports that, as early as the 1850s, American and British authorities quietly extradited their own citizens to each other.[18]

American officials generally opposed the policy of protecting citizens, but they had trouble bringing European governments to their side. As early as 1846, Secretary of State James Buchanan pointed to the massive amount of immigration to the United States and argued: "A treaty of extradition would be of comparatively little value, if such of these foreigners as shall commit crimes in this country should be excluded from its operation, in case they were able to escape to their own country." Negotiations with Switzerland broke down when the U.S. Senate refused to ratify an extradition treaty that, at the insistence of the Swiss, exempted citizens. For the same reason, negotiations broke down with Belgium in 1868. However, the United States yielded in several cases and allowed for the immunity of citizens from extradition, as the alternative was no treaty at all. Agreements with Austria-Hungary and Prussia, for example, explicitly stated that citizens or subjects could not be extradited. Other treaties simply said that neither country was "bound to deliver" its nationals, essentially ensuring no extradition of citizens.[19]

Prominent turn-of-the-century jurist John Bassett Moore opposed the exemption of citizens from extradition for the simple reason that crimes were best prosecuted in the place where they were committed. The refusal to extradite citizens, he believed, rested on "sentimental considerations" and "an exaggerated notion of the protection which is due by a state to its subjects." Moore concluded that "there appears to be no valid reason why the system of extradition, which is intended to avert a failure of justice, should not be extended to citizens." Other eminent American jurists of the late nineteenth century, such as Francis Wharton and Samuel T. Spear, agreed that citizens ought to be extradited.[20]

Nevertheless, when it was asked to extradite citizens, the U.S. government refused. This policy was affirmed in the 1884 case of Alexander Trimble, a native-born American citizen who robbed a Mexican National train near Nuevo Laredo, Mexico, then fled to the northern side of the Rio Grande. In the course of the robbery, a fireman was killed and the engineer severely injured. San Antonio judge J. C. Russell was on the verge of extraditing Trimble to Mexico when the State Department stepped in. Secretary of State Frederick Frelinghuysen telegrammed Texas governor John Ireland, commanding him "under no circumstances" to deliver an American citizen to foreign authorities. Trimble was subsequently released and went unpunished.[21]

Trimble was safe not because asylum was an inherent right of citizenship, but because the president lacked the legal authority to act without express permission in the treaty. Frelinghuysen pinpointed the sixth article of the extradition treaty with Mexico: "Neither of the contracting parties shall be bound to deliver up its own citizens under the stipulations of this treaty." This phrase appeared in fourteen other extradition treaties to which the United States was a party. Citing various legal scholars, Frelinghuysen concluded that the treaty conferred on the president no affirmative power to surrender an American citizen: "I understand the treaty with Mexico as reading thus: The President shall be bound to surrender any person guilty of crime, unless such person is a citizen of the United States." Extradition was not a plenary power, like regulating immigration and deportation. Absent the explicit authorization in a treaty, the executive did not have the power to extradite citizens. Seven years later, in *Ex parte McCabe*, the U.S. district court in Texas gave judicial affirmation to the principle that the United States could not extradite citizens unless the power was explicitly granted to the president in a treaty—and in the case of Mexico, it was not.[22]

The United States responded to this void in presidential authority in the next extradition treaty that it negotiated after the Trimble case, with Japan. The U.S.-Japanese Treaty of 1886 was notable for a number of reasons. First, it was the only extradition treaty that a Western nation had ever signed with an Asian country. Second, it was the first to take into account modern technologies, allowing requests for provisional arrest and extradition to be sent via telegraph. Finally, it explicitly provided for the extradition of citizens. The treaty read: "Neither of the contracting parties shall be bound to deliver up its own citizens or subjects under the stipulations of this convention, *but they shall have the power to deliver them up* if in their discretion it be deemed proper to do so." The United States had the upper hand in negotiating the Japanese treaty; most European countries would not have accepted such a clause. However, extraditing citizens was not a pressing issue with Japan. Sixteen years would pass before the citizenship clause in the Japanese treaty was actually invoked.[23]

The nonextradition of citizens was becoming a significant problem in relations with Mexico, though. Preventing crime became an imperative as American entrepreneurs increasingly invested in the borderlands region. Sonora and Chihuahua on the Mexican side, and West Texas and the Arizona Territory on the U.S. side offered American capitalists potentially rich opportunities in railroad construction, ranching, and mining. However, as American investment in the U.S.-Mexico border region increased in the last decades of the nineteenth century, cross-border banditry and violence threatened the stability of these ventures. For borderland investors, it was important to ensure that property rights were secure and lawbreakers punished, regardless of their nationality. The border could no longer serve as a shield protecting outlaws and raiders who committed depredations on one side of the line, then escaped to their home soil.

Borderland investors began to petition the federal government for a change, arguing that the inability to extradite citizens was hurting investment in the region. In 1884, in response to Trimble's release and lack of punishment, William Jackson Palmer, president of the American-financed Mexican National Railroad, speculated to Secretary of State Frelinghuysen that the policy of nonextradition of nationals would hamper railway construction in the borderlands: "If robbers and murderers can avoid punishment and feel safe by simply *escaping across the borders of the Rio Grande* either way, then travel is safe neither in Mexico nor in Texas, and the singular spectacle will be presented of a few border ruffians standing between trade and peaceful communication of 60,000,000 of industrious and law abiding people." For the sake of protecting investments, the citizenship of an offender was irrelevant; what mattered was only that he could be punished.[24]

Another problem with the nonextradition of nationals was that it was not always so easy to determine who nationals were. Extradition's alien-citizen binary had begun to break down. "Asylum on one's home soil" sounded good in theory, but in practice, determining one's "home soil" was tricky, especially as it implied one home soil that mapped neatly onto the political and legal boundaries of a nation-state. This created particular difficulties in the U.S.-Mexico border region. In an era before standardized birth certificates, it could be difficult to determine birthplace, and with it, legal citizenship. In 1893, Francisco Benavides and Prudencio Gonzalez were

arrested near San Antonio, Texas, accused of leading the San Ygnacio
Raid in Mexico. Neither Benavides nor Gonzalez spoke English, but
at their extradition hearings, they invoked asylum as American citizens, born in Texas. Their hearings turned into a procession of long-
lost childhood friends testifying where they went to school, priests
producing baptismal certificates, election officials pulling up voting
records, and old men trying to remember where their fathers lived
in 1845. For those who lived their lives on both sides of the border,
transnationality either allowed them to manipulate the rules by
alternately claiming either citizenship, or disempowered them by
letting them prove neither.[25]

   In the Trimble, Benavides, and dozens of other cases, fugitives
who damaged American property and American interests in Mexico
were getting off scot-free just because they were (or claimed to
be) U.S. citizens. Likewise, the United States could not get its hands
on Mexican citizens who committed crimes in the United States.
Texas governor John Ireland made repeated pleas to the secretary of
state to amend the Mexican treaty, claiming: "Since it has become
known that neither Mexico nor the United States will surrender one
of their own citizens to be taken to the other government to be tried
for crime, the people on the right bank of the Rio Grande have
become emboldened, and they stand on Mexican soil covered with
the blood of our women and children and their booty in sight of
our people." One of the most frustrating cases involved Chester Rowe,
an Iowan embezzler who fled to Mexico and promptly bought
property there. Under Mexican law, this made him a naturalized
Mexican citizen. Therefore, to the exasperation of the State Department, Mexico would not extradite Rowe, though it did try him
for the embezzlement and sentence him to twelve years in prison.
Since Mexico would prosecute and punish its citizens for crimes
committed outside its territory, whereas the United States would
not, the people truly "getting away with it" were Americans sheltered
in the United States. Borderland capitalists and Texas politicians furi-
ously petitioned the U.S. and Mexican governments to change the
treaty.[26]

   Finally, in 1899, the United States and Mexico signed a revised
treaty, explicitly allowing for the extradition of citizens. According
to article 4 of the new treaty, "neither of the contracting parties shall

be bound to deliver up its own citizens under the stipulations of this convention, but the executive authority of each shall have the power to deliver them up, if, in his discretion, it be deemed proper to do so." In other words, the U.S. president was now expressly granted the power to extradite citizens to Mexico, and the presidents of each country had the prerogative of deciding whether or not to turn citizens over to the neighboring nation to stand trial. The new treaty was meant to eradicate the ambiguities and impunities that let destroyers of American property, like Trimble, go free. It also was meant to eliminate show trials like those of Benavides and Gonzalez, since extradition no longer required a determination of citizenship. Asylum was still possible, but it was now a matter of case-by-case discretion.[27]

Initially, the new treaty did not receive much attention in the American press. While most major newspapers printed a short notice about it, they did not mention the provision that allowed for the extradition of citizens. Only borderland papers like the *Arizona Republican* referenced the citizenship clause, and even these periodicals did not elaborate or editorialize about it. It seemed, at first, that the extradition of citizens would go unnoticed. No one anticipated the firestorm that would arise when the United States actually tested the new clause. The country was divided over the surrender of Mattie Rich, and the public storm revealed different assumptions about whether Americans had a right of asylum on their home soil. When it came to fugitives like Rich, was it the state's responsibility to protect the individual citizen or to safeguard the body politic?[28]

Mattie Howard and John Rich met in 1893 at the World's Columbian Exhibition, better known as the Chicago World's Fair. At that time, Mattie ran a boardinghouse in her native Chicago, though previously she had performed in various local circuses and even competed as a female boxer, proudly claiming the title of "Lady Pugilist Champion of Illinois." John, from an affluent banking family in Iowa, had run away from home at age seventeen, seeking adventure in the West. The couple married later that year in Las Cruces, New Mexico, before moving to El Paso, Texas, and then across the border to Mexico.[29]

The Texas-Chihuahua border region where the Riches spent most
of the 1890s was characterized by its vibrant cross-border traffic.
People, goods, and capital constantly moved across the international
border in both directions, largely unimpeded by governmental bar-
riers. Identity documents were not yet required to cross the border,
though an outbreak of smallpox in 1898 prompted the Texas Board
of Health to demand that every person crossing into El Paso present a certificate of vaccination. While the 1882 Chinese Exclusion
Act prohibited laborers of Chinese origin from entering the United
States, no such restrictions applied to Mexicans. A steady stream
of Mexican immigrants looking for work in railroad construction,
mining, or ranches entered the United States via El Paso during the
1890s. Many planned to stay in the United States only temporarily,
or they periodically returned to Mexico to visit their families.[30]

The flow of labor moved in both directions: Americans also mi-
grated to Mexico in search of work, especially during the cycles of
economic recession in the last three decades of the nineteenth
century. As Americans living in Juárez at the turn of the twentieth
century, the Riches had plenty of company. Though the most visible Americans in Mexico were the capitalists who invested in mining,
transportation, and ranches, workingmen like John Rich also were
lured by economic opportunities south of the border, taking jobs
with the U.S.-owned railroads or providing necessary services to the
American "colonies" in railroad and mining centers. In late 1893, the
Riches moved to Torreón, a railroad junction in the border state of
Coahuila, where John found work as an agent for the recently completed Mexican Central Railroad. The next year, he took a job in the
office of the auditor of the Sierra Madre Railroad in Ciudad Juárez.
In a Mexican twist on the American dream, he soon saved up enough
money to go into business for himself, buying up half of Juárez's
International Grocery and running the Mexican Central eating
house.[31]

On the morning of April 27, 1899, in Ciudad Juárez, Mrs. Mattie
Rich called for a doctor. Dr. Jesús Aguirre found Mattie in her husband's bedroom, tending to a gunshot wound to his abdomen. When
asked who had shot him, John Rich responded vaguely, saying that
"it was an accident, and that he didn't know how it happened."

Dr. Aguirre recommended that Rich be taken to the state-of-the-art Hotel Dieu Hospital, across the river in El Paso. Physicians initially diagnosed a full recovery, and the *El Paso Daily Times* reported that "J. D. Rich has a large number of friends on both sides of the river who will be pleased to hear that his wound is doing nicely and that his condition shows a marked improvement." Already a suspect, Mattie was prohibited from entering her husband's sickroom, but she refused to leave the hospital and even figured out a way to climb onto a window ledge to watch him. On the night of April 30, however, John's health took a turn for the worse. He died the next afternoon in his hospital room in Hotel Dieu, his wife anxiously waiting outside.[32]

The timing of John Rich's death was not fortuitous for Mattie. Normally, an affair like theirs would not receive extensive international attention. However, three days before John was shot, the new extradition treaty between the United States and Mexico went into effect, and both Washington and Mexico City were looking for a test case.

It was hardly surprising that Mexico City jumped at the opportunity to test the new treaty. During his thirty-five-year dictatorship, Mexican president Porfirio Díaz not only attempted to transform Mexico into a modern bureaucratic state but also put a great deal of effort into projecting an image of cosmopolitanism and modernity to the outside world. At the 1889 Universal Exposition in Paris, Mexico constructed its largest and most expensive World's Fair exhibit ever, with displays presenting the nation as liberal, democratic, rational, and industrialized. In particular, Díaz sought to attract foreign investment by constructing an image of Mexico as a land of justice, order, and the rule of law. In a combination of public performance and political repression, Díaz reorganized Mexico City's law enforcement in the late 1870s to create a larger, better-equipped, and more professional force modeled after those in the United States and Europe. Díaz's corps of advisers, known as *cientí-ficos*, also turned to the study of criminology in an attempt to systematically construct social order. A strict extradition policy was consistent with the law-and-order image that Díaz was trying to promote internationally.[33]

Acting under instructions from Mexico City, Francisco Mallan, the Mexican consul in El Paso, filed a request for Mattie Rich's preliminary arrest on May 4, just three days after John Rich's death. Two weeks later, Mexican ambassador Manuel de Aspíroz followed up with a formal request to U.S. secretary of state John Hay for Rich's extradition. From the start, the Mexican authorities made it clear that Mattie Rich would be merely a test case for the new treaty. A Mexican official told the *El Paso Daily Times* that "the Mexican government made a strong fight for Mrs. Rich's extradition because our government wanted to test the new treaty. It was not a desire to get possession of Mrs. Rich, but our government wanted an American interpretation of the provisions of the treaty."[34]

El Paso's law enforcers did not hesitate to comply. Hours after a local judge issued an arrest warrant on May 2, Constable W. J. Ten Eyck arrested Rich outside the Chicago Hotel in El Paso, despite her loud protestations of innocence. The next step was an extradition hearing to determine whether sufficient evidence of Rich's guilt existed. If a prima facie case could be made, Mexico's extradition papers would be forwarded to Washington for a final decision. Rich waited nearly two months in the El Paso County Jail for her extradition hearing to begin. When it finally got under way on June 27, she confidently pled not guilty.

Rich's confidence was not unfounded. The evidence against her was largely circumstantial; the most damning item, John Rich's dying statement that his wife shot him, was largely discredited by doctors who testified that he was not rational in his final hours. Her lawyers had a hard time explaining away her compelling motive for murdering her husband, though. On cross-examination, Rich admitted that the couple had quarreled just hours before the shooting. Reluctantly, Rich told the court: "It happened this way. At about 7 or 7:30 o'clock that evening I saw my husband walking on the railroad track with a woman known on this side as Blanche Chapman. She had her dress thrown over her head. I went up to her and punched her face, gave her two black eyes." Rich insisted that she and her husband then went home and resolved their differences. Nevertheless, on July 5, Judge F. B. Sexton, United States commissioner for Western Texas, delivered the verdict that sufficient evidence existed for Rich to stand

MRS. MATTIE C. H. RICH
Who is now being examined in extradition proceedings on account of alleged murder in Juarez, Mexico.

Sketch of Mattie Rich, the first American extradited to a foreign country. *El Paso Daily Herald*, June 28, 1899.

trial for homicide. The decision about whether or not she would be extradited to Mexico now lay in President McKinley's hands.[35]

As Mattie Rich waited for the decision from Washington, her case became a cause célèbre. Many Americans vehemently objected to the idea of Mattie Rich being extradited. According to an Associated Press report, thousands of telegrams and letters streamed into the White House, "some almost hysterical in the strength of their protests against the extradition of the woman." Her defenders rarely mentioned the possibility of her innocence; most assumed that she had indeed shot her husband. Instead, their objections focused on the injustice of surrendering someone who was an American citizen—and a woman, no less—and handing her over to Mexico, whose judicial and penal systems were seen as deficient.[36]

The idea of forcibly removing Mattie Rich—a citizen—from the United States violated cultural assumptions about who could justifiably be excluded from the nation. Those who protested Rich's extradition believed that American nationals had an absolute right of asylum on U.S. soil. They often expressed their opposition to the extradition of a citizen in visceral terms. One newspaper editorial maintained that "the demands of the law cannot rob of its *unnaturalness* the action of the United States in turning its own citizen over to a foreign country." According to this logic, citizenship trumped the language of the treaty. Even if giving her up was technically legal, it was a "terrible and incredible" betrayal of American principles. The government may have had the legal authority, but it did not have the moral authority to extradite Mattie Rich.[37]

Rich's whiteness was central to the assumption that she belonged in the nation. Even though she resided in Mexico, no one asked Rich for proof of her U.S. citizenship: her Anglo-Saxon name, unaccented English, "broad, north country face," and "loose locks of . . . yellow hair" were confirmation enough. It was not always "unnatural" for the United States to turn nonwhites over to a foreign country. Dozens of Chinese were deported each year from El Paso, where Rich's extradition hearing was held, and Mexican nationals were frequently extradited on request by their home government. The difference, in Rich's case, was that her whiteness marked her as a recognized—and protected—American citizen. Plus, as *Washington Post* correspondent Olive Ennis Hite pointed out, Mattie Rich's family had made sacrifices for the country. "Her father was a soldier of the civil war," Hite wrote, "and let us not forget that, if it should be that the doors of a Mexican jail shall close upon her."[38]

Newspapers often emphasized Rich's gender, tapping into cultural assumptions that women represented the domestic sphere and that their defense was analogous to the protection of the nation. "The case of Mrs. Rich has attracted wide attention," reported the *Los Angeles Times*, sparking "protest[s] against the extradition of an American citizen. . . . The fact that in this case the citizen is a woman has greatly intensified the objection to the procedure." In her own testimony during her extradition hearing, Rich emphasized her gendered role as wife in the domestic sphere of the home. Many newspapers printed the rumor, which turned out to be false, that Rich was six months pregnant.[39]

Hite painted a picture of Rich as a typical damsel in distress, appealing to her male readers to protect Rich: "She, broken mind and body, sits in her cell awaiting the summons to a fate which may be death, or worse." The reference to a fate worse than death, while a cliché, also had sexual undertones: Rich, a white woman, would be surrendered to brutish, dark-skinned men. The imagery was reminiscent of the propaganda used to whip up support for the Spanish-American War the year before. Cuba was invariably portrayed as a helpless maiden, brutalized by the Spanish and in need of rescue by the United States. Mattie Rich's case also evoked memories of Lizzie Borden's sensational trial six years earlier. Both involved women accused of murdering a family member, and both were highly visible in the national media. Most notably, in both cases, the defense appealed to public sympathy by invoking imagery of pure, moral womanhood.[40]

Other objections focused on the fact that Rich would not be handed over to just any foreign country, but to Mexico. Numerous articles reported the popular sentiment that "it would be an act of barbarism to place an American woman at the mercy of the Mexican law and officialdom." Mexico was portrayed as an uncivilized land lacking law and order, where an American could not possibly receive a fair trial. In contrast to the general lack of attention paid to foreigners who were extradited, there was an almost morbid fascination with imagining what might happen to Rich in Mexico. "If Mattie Rich goes to Mexican justice," warned one journalist cryptically, "may God help her, for . . . all men know what that means to an American." Dreaded even more than the Mexican criminal justice system were Mexican prisons, commonly referred to as dungeons. Rich herself propagated this image of Mexican jails, telling reporters: "I will never go back to Juarez; I will never be taken to a Mexican dungeon." Objecting to the sentiment in El Paso that Rich ought to be extradited, O. W. Johnson wrote to the *El Paso Daily Times:*

I wish to ask of the people of El Paso if any of them know what life in a Mexican prison is. Several years ago I was sentenced to serve fifteen years in one of those Mexican dungeons, and I wish to say God pity any one who is so unfortunate as to get a sentence of even a day in one of those hells on earth. . . . I say now may God watch over and protect Mrs. Rich, and in case she is found guilty, may death more merciful than the Mexicans release her from their power.[41]

The dominant view in the national media was that Mattie Rich, as a citizen, had a right to asylum in the United States. Yet there was another chorus of voices that argued just the opposite, strongly insisting that the state not only had the power but also the responsibility to hand Rich over to Mexico. These people saw Rich not as a fellow citizen deserving of protection, but as an undesirable deviant who threatened to pollute the body politic. Proextradition crusaders insisted that it was important to punish criminals like Rich and remove them from society—citizens or not—as their presence in American towns and cities threatened the domestic order.

Most of the proextradition voices came from Texas, particularly El Paso, where Mattie Rich was being held. The sentiment among Texans that Rich should be extradited was so strong that Governor Joseph D. Sayers wired Washington recommending that Rich be sent to stand trial in Mexico. The *El Paso Daily Herald* bluntly proclaimed: "There can be no doubt that Mrs. Rich ought to be brought back to Mexico and tried for the murder of her husband." Indeed, El Paso journalists came down so hard on Rich—and seemed to affect local public opinion so much—that she despairingly remarked: "If I die, it will be through the newspapers."[42]

For El Pasoans, granting Mattie Rich asylum meant embracing her as part of their local community. Given that the penniless Rich could not afford to return to her native Chicago, nor could she go back to Juárez, the residents of El Paso likely feared that, if freed, she would remain in their city. Between the time of John's death and Mattie's arrest, an El Paso paper reported that "Mrs. Rich is still on this side of the river, and shows no disposition to return to Juarez." Even if the United States chose not to extradite Rich, she could never again return to Mexico, where the warrant for her arrest would remain valid. If Rich were not somehow removed from the El Paso community, she threatened to become part of it.[43]

El Pasoans knew what to expect if Rich stayed in town. In her habits as well as her background, Mattie Rich was hardly a paragon of respectable femininity. In an era when child rearing was the predominant social role for women, Mattie Rich had not borne any children in six years of marriage. Physically, Rich was neither dainty nor delicate: "At the county jail Mrs. Rich amuses herself occasionally by athletic exercises and the exhibition of feats of strength. Her muscles are like chilled steel and she can floor an ordinary man with perfect ease, by one stroke." Given that Rich was accused of killing her husband, these demonstrations must have caused El Paso's male residents unease.[44]

Newspaper articles frequently mentioned Mattie Rich's drinking habits, a detail that would not have been lost on moral reformers, who sought to shut down El Paso's saloons. "Mrs. Rich was addicted to the use of intoxicants and under the influence of alcohol often became violent and aggressive. When she came to this city as a yellow haired bride almost her first act was to get drunk at a party," the *El Paso Herald* reminded readers. Rich's alibi for the night of her husband's shooting, in fact, was that she was out drinking at the Moctezuma Saloon in Juárez. Reporters observed that "drinking beer at a saloon was not an exception" for Rich, as she was "fond of looking upon the wine when it sparkles." Moreover, even in the El Paso County Jail, Rich was falling in with the wrong crowd. She and her cell mate, a prostitute named Mamie Freeman, "frolic[ked] around like kittens" and were known to ask visitors "to send up a bucket of beer and . . . a few matches to light their cigarettes."[45]

Reports of Rich's behavior resonated with El Paso's moral reformers, who actively combated the town's "Sin City" reputation by trying to clean up vice and crime. Beginning in the late 1890s, and picking up steam around the turn of the century, reform organizations such as the Law and Order League, the Women's Christian Temperance Union, and the Citizens' League applied pressure on the city government to erase destabilizing "dens of vice"—brothels, saloons, dance halls, and casinos—from the El Paso landscape. Many of El Paso's trends were common to Progressive "moral uplift" campaigns nationwide. Reformers frequently represented vice and deviance as a social evil and a moral contagion. Such behavior was often criminalized, leading to the segregation of social deviants in mental institutions, vice zones, prisons, or reformatories designed for social "rehabilitation." Such legislation rarely eradicated vice, though. Instead, in a phenomenon called the scatter syndrome, many purveyors of vice simply left towns where their behavior was criminalized and relocated in another city where the local vice district remained open.[46]

El Paso's location on the border gave the scatter syndrome a new twist. Prostitution had flourished in El Paso, as in many other western frontier towns, since the arrival of the railroad in the early 1880s. City ordinances not only confined prostitutes but also slowly pushed them into Mexico. During the 1890s, many moved to Ciudad Juárez, where prostitution was legal, to avoid arrest or fines. When prostitution and dance halls were finally abolished in El Paso in 1904, the majority of women who worked in these establishments also relocated across the river, where their former clients could easily visit them. Defiant signs nailed to boarded-up brothel doors read: "We are spending our money in Juarez." Saloons and casinos similarly reopened across the border when targeted by moralistic legislation.[47]

Mattie Rich violated local conceptions of proper feminine behavior in a manner similar to other transgressive women, such as prostitutes, who were regularly pushed over the border into Mexico. In El Paso, where the symbolic boundaries between social inclusion and exclusion were literally mapped onto the borders of the nation, belonging was not determined only by birthplace or racial status but also by one's adherence to prescribed behaviors. For many residents of El Paso, there was nothing "unnatural" about Mattie Rich's extradition. Rather, according to their assumptions about who could be expelled from the body politic, it made sense that she would be turned over to Mexico. In her rejection of middle-class standards of decorum, Rich seemed to have more in common with the prostitutes or saloon keepers marked for social expulsion.

Though Mattie Rich was never explicitly called a prostitute, local newspapers maligned her moral character in similar terms. In contrast to the national press, which often portrayed John Rich as an abusive and philandering drunk, the El Paso papers deemed him a "worthy young man" who "had many friends in this city and in Juarez." Articles frequently pointed out that Rich came from "an excellent family" and that "Rich's father and uncle are both bankers at

Fort Dodge and quite prominent." In contrast, as a former boxer and circus performer, Mattie Rich "had lived a vicious life with low vicious people." "According to her own testimony," one article confirmed, "Mrs. Rich, when a child, cast her lot with a class of people proverbially vicious and immoral, and she is what those people made her." She was "an extremely jealous woman, with an ungovernable temper who made Mr. Rich's life very unhappy." Like the prostitutes who seduced the respectable men of El Paso, Mattie, the flashy temptress, caused the innocent John's downfall. One journalist imagined their first encounter: "Rich's widow was formerly an attaché of a circus and rode bareback horses around the ring in all the glory of pink tights, gauzy skirts and spangles. It was while she was thus engaged that he met her and became infatuated." Another article bluntly called Mattie "a matrimonial mistake."[48]

Some El Pasoans expressed the belief that Rich was insane and ought to be placed in a mental institution, despite the fact that she exhibited no clear signs of dementia or delusions. Doctors in the late nineteenth century frequently ascribed psychological character defects such as hysteria onto women who did not conform to the family and gender-role socialization demanded of them. In Rich's case, the result was the same whether she was incarcerated or institutionalized: she would be prevented from reentering El Paso society. She would be contained.[49]

Although the McKinley administration wished to establish a precedent with Mexico for the surrender of citizens, it also sought, according to Secretary of State Hay, "to avert, as far as possible, any occasion for popular agitation and arousing a sentiment hostile to the execution of this clause of the treaty." Nevertheless, on July 15, 1899, President McKinley announced his decision: Mattie Rich would be extradited. Later that day, the State Department issued a formal warrant for the delivery of Rich to the Mexican authorities. Nine days afterward, American flag wrapped around her, Mattie Rich was transferred into Mexican custody on the midpoint of the international bridge. Many national periodicals lamented the surrender; El Paso newspapers cheered it.[50]

President McKinley's verdict had implications that extended far beyond the Mexican borderlands. In 1899, the year of Rich's extradition, the United States was taking on many new subjects—in the Philippines, Puerto Rico, and Hawaii—whose rights, privileges, and citizenship status were ambiguous. One might expect a more rigid alien-citizen distinction to emerge at this time. Yet, for the state, ambiguity—rather than clarity—was power. Clear-cut categories meant rigid rules, rights, and protections. On the local, national, and international levels, the state could assert its power more flexibly by abandoning the binary alien-citizen distinction in favor of a blanket discretionary power over anyone in its jurisdiction. This included the ability to extradite any person, without the need to determine a definitive nationality.

The debate over Mattie Rich's fate revealed a fundamental disagreement over the power of the state to remove its citizens. Was asylum a right afforded to all American citizens, or a privilege that the government could take away in the name of public safety and order? Those who opposed Rich's extradition adhered to a viewpoint reminiscent of the Jonathan Robbins affair: it was preferable to let a guilty citizen go free than to turn her over to a foreign nation. Yet the opposing opinion won out, both in the individual case of Mattie Rich and in the future of American extradition. The El Paso stance in support of expanded extradition went national, as Progressive reformers emphasized the dangers of criminal offenders roaming the American streets freely. Going forward, the federal government would exercise the power to remove criminal citizens as well as aliens.

❊

In the early years of the twentieth century, the American public came to accept and even support the authority of the government to extradite citizens. After Mattie Rich's surrender, the United States continued to extradite citizens—just to Mexico at first, and then to other nations as well, even if reciprocity was not an option. However, the clouds of controversy had blown over. Subsequent cases received much less attention in the press and did not prompt the sorts of frenetic objections that had marked the Rich hearing. By 1910, when the extradition of a citizen once again sparked political debate, an overwhelming number of Americans actively advocated the surrender of citizens from the United States for offenses committed abroad.

Americans' acceptance of the extradition of citizens occurred alongside a growing fear of crime and a concern about urban disorder. Just as El Paso's reforming elite pushed for Mattie Rich's removal to Mexico, so too did Progressives around the country worry about criminals and social deviants within the body politic. Extraditing citizens, Americans came to realize, was the only way that offenders could be held accountable for serious crimes committed abroad. A 1911 editorial by the American Society of International Law warned: "If not surrendered for punishment, they will then escape all punishment. It is thus not a mere extradition agreement which breaks down, but the whole theory of social protection so far as universality and certainty of punishment are concerned." The presence of these criminal citizens in American towns and cities threatened domestic law and order, as they could very well strike again at home. Lawbreakers needed to be rehabilitated or disciplined, yet legally this could only occur in the jurisdiction where the crime was committed. Thus, it was necessary to enlarge the authority of the state, to endow it with the power to extradite citizens in the name of protecting the social welfare. The alternative—that they escaped penalty altogether—was dangerous and unacceptable.[51]

Though social reformers often associated immigrants with criminal activity, the Progressive campaign against crime and vice targeted domestic as well as foreign bodies. The assassination of President McKinley by anarchist—and U.S. citizen—Leon Czolgosz in 1901 demonstrated that native-born Americans could be among the most serious threats to society. Like Czolgosz, Americans who broke the law in foreign countries were criminals first and fellow citizens second. In addition, the state was taking on a tremendous coercive power over the bodies of people marked as delinquent. Juvenile courts, for example, could remove a child from the home simply for "bad associations." Likewise, extradition judges could remove a citizen from the country on a mere prima facie demonstration of guilt.[52]

Moreover, at a time when the word of professional experts carried substantial weight, the nation's most prominent international legal scholar advocated the extradition of citizens. In his widely referenced *Digest of International Law*, published in 1906, John Bassett Moore decisively stated: "The only mode in which the ends of justice can be completely satisfied is by the extradition of fugitives, without regard to their nationality, for trial at the place where their crime was committed." A 1910 *New York Times* article presented the protection of citizens as an antiquated and outdated policy, while the extradition of citizens was more modern, more forward-thinking. The article identified Henry Wheaton and others who opposed the extradition of nationals as "the older authorities," while it lauded Moore, then a professor at Columbia, as "the recognized authority on the subject."[53]

A series of cases in the early years of the twentieth century reflected the emerging consensus on the extradition of citizens. Eight months after Mattie Rich's surrender, the United States extradited another citizen to Mexico. Like Rich, Blas Aguirre was wanted for murder in Mexico, accused of killing saloon keeper Juan José Escajeda and then retreating into the United States. Aguirre stood before F. B. Sexton, the same United States commissioner as Rich, at his extradition hearing in El Paso. However, this case attracted little national attention, even though it had diplomatic significance, as Aguirre faced the death penalty in Mexico. (According to Mexican law, Rich had been exempt from capital punishment because she was a woman.) Aguirre was even more of a liminal citizen than Rich. He spoke no English and was, according to the *El Paso Daily Herald*, "a typical Mexican"—with the caveat that he had been born just over the line in Texas.[54]

After his surrender to the authorities in Ciudad Juárez in April 1900, Aguirre was, indeed, sentenced to be shot. American newspapers reported that this was the first time a U.S. citizen was sentenced to death in Mexico, yet they expressed no sense of injustice. The *St. Louis Post-Dispatch* printed a full-page story on Aguirre's execution, entitled "First American Doomed to Die by Mexican Law," complete with an image of a scowling bandit in a sombrero. The author, identified only as a special correspondent in Ciudad Juárez, called Aguirre's death "well-merited." The article continued, "Aguirre has long been known as a bandit and his death will put an end to one of the most troublesome bands of outlaws with which the border police have had to deal." Although Aguirre was a U.S. citizen, the story emphasized his foreignness—in his dress, his name, his mother tongue, and his banditry—thus making his extradition more palatable to Americans.[55]

Likewise, there was no public outrage regarding the third American extradited to Mexico, another ethnic Mexican. Sabas (also known as Samuel) Baca was part of a gang responsible for a particularly atrocious offense, which the *El Paso Daily Herald* called "one of the most fiendish crimes ever committed in northern Mexico." In July 1900, Baca and several others crossed the Rio Grande into Mexico and burglarized a store belonging to an old man. They tortured the store owner, searing his feet and hands with hot coals and mutilating him with a knife, until he told the robbers where he had hidden his life savings of $1,200. After taking the money, the gang bound and gagged the storekeeper, then repeatedly raped his young wife. They then left the occupants of the store for dead. Baca's extradition in April 1901 received more attention than Aguirre's, due to the sensationally savage nature of his crime. The *Atlanta Constitution* deemed his offense "one of the most brutal crimes known in the annals of the border" and the *Cincinnati Enquirer* called it an "atrocious crime . . . one of the most brutal crimes on record." Again, there was no sense of indignation in American newspapers when Baca was executed on June 14, 1901. The *San Francisco Chronicle* bluntly described the scene: "Blindfolded, bound hand and foot, with his face to a thick stone wall, Sabas Baca, an American citizen, died before a squad of Mexican soldiers at Chihuahua, Mexico, Tuesday morning."[56]

Aguirre and Baca were both ethnic Mexicans who had committed particularly violent crimes. The next few people extradited to Mexico were Anglos who had committed financial crimes, yet there was no particular sympathy or outrage for them either. John Krug, accused of stealing $10,000 from the Wells Fargo Express Company in Escalón, Mexico, and apprehended in New Orleans, was actually a German citizen, although the Associated Press mistakenly reported that he was an American and that error was reprinted in newspaper articles throughout the country. Krug put up a particularly fierce fight against his extradition, but was nonetheless surrendered by a U.S. marshal at the midpoint of the international bridge in August 1901. George Deering Reed was accused of embezzling $16,000 from his employer in Oaxaca. He fought his extradition from the United States not on the grounds that he was citizen, but on a technicality— because Mexico had not filed the correct paperwork within forty days of his arrest, as required by the treaty. Although a New Jersey district court ordered Reed's release, he was rearrested after the proper paperwork arrived from Mexico and subsequently extradited in 1907. The press coverage on both cases lacked any editorializing about the injustice of their surrenders. The extradition of American citizens was becoming commonplace.[57]

Mexico, in contrast, was less forthcoming about extraditing its citizens. In January 1900, the United States requested the extradition of Mexican national Leonardo Gonzales, wanted for murder in Texas. The Mexican government denied the request; however, it insisted that the refusal was due to a lack of evidence, not because of Gonzales's nationality. In 1903, Mexico again refused to extradite a citizen, Francisco Guerra, wanted for rape in El Paso. Yet after irritated correspondence from the State Department, it finally extradited Mexican national Teofilo Campos in 1904, followed by Alberto Cabrera in 1907 and Teodosio Jimenez and Juan de Dios Rodriguez in 1909, among others.[58]

Meanwhile, the United States was handing over citizens on a regular basis, surrendering between three and five people per year to its neighbor to the south. The United States did not deliver its citizens only to Mexico, though. U.S. citizen Francis Mayer, accused of forging and uttering a debenture bond of the Yokohama Steam Laundry Company, was extradited to Japan in 1902. Japan reciprocated in 1908, when it sent Japanese national Yoshitaro Abe to Hawaii to stand trial for forgery.[59]

The prospect of extraditing an American citizen became a national sensation one more time in the early years of the twentieth century. In terms of the sheer number of news stories, the case of Porter Charlton, stretching from 1910 to 1913, was even bigger than that of Mattie Rich. But in the Charlton case, the tables were turned: most people were shocked and horrified at the idea of this U.S. citizen *not* being extradited.

Porter and Mary Scott Castle Charlton went missing in June 1910 while honeymooning in Italy. Mary was a divorcée and a failed actress in her early forties, while Porter was a young bank clerk half her age. Mary's bruised and beaten body was found by fishermen in the middle of Lake Como, stuffed in a trunk. Initially, search parties dragged the lake looking for the vanished Porter, afraid he had met the same fate. However, Porter Charlton turned up a few weeks later on a German steamship heading to New York. Met by police on his arrival, he confessed to murdering his wife. "We were ideally happy," he admitted in an interview, "but we quarreled and I went mad with rage."[60]

Since American courts solely recognized territorial jurisdiction, Charlton could be punished for the crime only in Italy. Yet it was uncertain whether or not the United States would extradite him. For one thing, the killer came from an influential family. His father, Paul, was a federal judge in Puerto Rico and a Yale classmate of President Taft. The Charlton family put its sizable resources behind the protection of Porter, hiring a team of eminent psychologists to diagnose him as insane. Moreover, Italian authorities made it clear that even if Charlton were handed over, they would not reciprocate and extradite Italian citizens. There was no room for negotiation: Italian law firmly prohibited the extradition of nationals. Charlton's lawyers took his writ of habeas corpus all the way to the Supreme Court, arguing that the lack of reciprocity nullified the extradition treaty. In addition, the treaty merely called for the delivery of "persons" charged with specified crimes; it did not explicitly allow for the extradition of citizens the way the Mexican and Japanese treaties did. According to the logic that had saved Alexander Trimble, Charlton should go free.[61]

Publicly, there was little sympathy for Charlton, the "wife-slayer," in the United States. According to editorials, "sound public sentiment" supported Charlton's extradition; anything else would be a "miscarriage of justice." Many Americans were horrified at the idea that, if extradition to Italy did not work out, Charlton would be freed and go unpunished for "uxoricide"—an obscure term used by the newspapers, meaning the murder of one's wife. Prominent lawyer Frederic Coudert speculated that it might be possible to try Charlton in a U.S. court if he had planned his crime in New York. But mostly, Americans simply wanted his extradition to Italy. "If the United States declines to surrender Porter Charlton," explained a veteran diplomat writing in the *New York Times*, "it practically endows him with immunity for the singularly atrocious and brutal murder which he had confessed to have committed in Italy." *New York Tribune* reader J. Raymond Gimbernat wrote to the paper: "It would be an outrageous thing, in my opinion, if he were to escape trial for the murder with which he is charged."[62]

The same newspapers that had protested Mattie Rich's extradition eleven years earlier now insisted that, in the name of justice, extraditing citizens was the only proper course of action. The *Boston Globe*, in an article tantalizingly entitled "How a Murderer May Escape," leaned on the authority of experts: "The best legal authorities contend that the only mode in which the ends of justice can be completely satisfied is by extradition of fugitives without regard to their nationality." The *Chicago Tribune* similarly contended that the non-extradition of citizens "is a principle so contrary to the interests of public justice . . . that it should be eliminated from the relations of civilized states." In contrast to the outrage expressed during the Rich case, extraditing citizens was now a mark of civilization and judicial advancement.[63]

In the decision of *Charlton v. Kelly*, handed down in 1913, the Supreme Court ruled that Charlton could be extradited. The opinion first stated that a lack of reciprocity did not void the Italian extradition treaty. It also ruled that the treaty language, which called for the extradition of "persons," included citizens. This decision was applauded in the American press as "sound in principle and right as a precedent." The editorial board of the *American Journal of International Law* celebrated that "we have avoided the unpleasant spectacle of an atrocious crime, confessed to, yet absolutely unpunished. The reign of justice is nobler than the law of tit for tat." When Charlton was finally extradited to Italy in August 1913, American newspapers cheered that justice had been served.[64]

In extraditing Porter Charlton, the United States went above and beyond what was required by the Italian extradition treaty—a far cry from "asylum for mankind." The State Department had the prerogative of denying Charlton's extradition, even after the Supreme Court's ruling, due to the lack of reciprocity on the part of the Italian government. But it chose to extradite him anyway. Moreover, the decision in *Charlton v. Kelly* contradicted the earlier opinions in the Trimble and McCabe cases. There, the courts and the State Department had insisted that the president had no power to extradite nationals unless given explicit permission in the treaty. Now, the Supreme Court broadened the federal power to extradite by interpreting the word "persons" to include citizens, even when there was no express authorization to extradite them.

In just more than a decade, Americans had gone from vehemently opposing Mattie Rich's extradition to enthusiastically supporting Porter Charlton's. Of course, there were significant differences in the two cases. The fact that Rich was a woman added to the sympathy for her. Moreover, although both were accused of killing their spouses, Rich's seemed more like a justifiable crime of passion. John Rich had been a philanderer and possibly a drunk, giving Mattie some grounds for shooting him. In contrast, Charlton's misdeed appeared to have been planned out and was particularly brutal—an autopsy revealed that Mary Charlton still had been alive when the trunk was dropped into Lake Como. Additionally, the two were extradited to different countries. Many Americans viewed Mexico as semibarbaric, while Italy, as a European nation, was "a highly civilized country" whose "courts can be trusted to mete out substantial justice." Finally, journalist Will Irwin hypothesized in 1911 that Americans were fascinated with the Charlton case because the killer was "rich and connected." Irwin hinted that there was a bit of public schadenfreude at seeing someone of the "upper class" punished for a typically "lower" crime.[65]

Perhaps the most significant difference, though, was that many Americans had become accustomed to the idea of citizens being extradited. Espousing the Progressive principle of empowering the state to reform society, they accepted that the government had the capacity to hand over their fellow citizens, and even applauded this as a victory for justice. A 1910 article in *Outlook* magazine entitled "A Menace of Crime" elaborated on two reasons why this was the case. First, in the name of public welfare, it was necessary for the United

States to surrender nationals. The idea that Charlton might go unpunished was "inimical to the very safety of society." Second, the extradition of citizens was a sign of judicial progress and civilization. If Charlton were not extradited, then "two great nations have left themselves in a condition which only barbarous and uncivilized countries are supposed to maintain." The fact that the United States handed over citizens was no longer a flaw, as it had appeared in the Mattie Rich case; instead, it was a source of pride, a sign of American judicial superiority.[66]

While extradition may have served diplomatic ends, the surrender of fugitives was not simply a concession to foreign powers. Evolving ideas about criminality altered the international extradition regime. As Americans' fears of crime and social instability grew, so too did their willingness to extradite, first aliens and then citizens. Once an "asylum for mankind," the United States surrendered dozens of people each year by the 1920s. An increase in immigration, the spread of capital across borders, and a desire for crime control made it important to Americans that fugitives no longer be able to find asylum in the United States.

✳

Following a trial in Ciudad Juárez in January of 1900, Mattie Rich was found guilty of the murder of her husband and sentenced to fourteen years in prison. Three and a half years later, the Supreme Court of Chihuahua reversed her conviction. Charles E. Wesche, the U.S. vice consul in Ciudad Juárez, did not explain the grounds of this decision when he reported to the State Department on July 29, 1903, that "Mrs. Rich is again a free woman." Although Rich had spent years appealing her case, she was unprepared for freedom. She initially refused to leave her Chihuahua City prison cell, complaining, "I have nowhere else to go." A month later, she showed up in Ciudad Juárez, where she told a reporter that she was planning a trip to Mexico City. Mattie Rich's paper trail then stops. There is no record of her in the 1910 U.S. Federal Census, under either her married or her maiden name. Perhaps she remarried, or perhaps she remained in Mexico. If she chose not to return to the United States, it would not be surprising, for as she sat in her Juárez cell in late 1899 awaiting her trial, she turned to verse as an outlet for her feelings of hurt and betrayal toward the nation that had sacrificed her. One of her poems read:

> I wrap the flag around me
> For it drives away my tears
> Whenever I recall the day
> That my country gave me clean away.[67]

6

Camouflaged Extradition

WHEN THE U.S. commissioner at San Antonio ruled that Juan José Arredondo would not be extradited to Mexico, the revolutionary leader seemed to be in the clear. In September 1906, Arredondo had led sixty men in a raid on the town of Jiménez in the Mexican state of Coahuila. Later that year, when he was captured near Del Rio, Texas, the Mexican government demanded his extradition on the charges of arson, robbery, and murder. Arredondo's extradition hearing was one of the longest and most expensive on record; more than 200 witnesses came in from Mexico to testify. He admitted that he had seized the Jiménez customs house and town treasury, and had attacked federal troops who tried to stop his men. But he insisted that he should not be handed over to the Mexican government because his acts were political in nature, directed against the dictatorial regime of President Porfirio Díaz.[1]

Arredondo's defense invoked a fundamental principle of American extradition law: those accused of political crimes received asylum. Generally, under extradition treaties, two countries agreed to hand fugitives over to each other for certain specified crimes after a showing of sufficient evidence. But there was an important exception to this—the United States would not surrender anyone whose extradition was demanded on political grounds, or who had committed a crime of a political nature.[2]

Although Arredondo succeeded in convincing U.S. Commissioner Neill that his acts were political—and that he was therefore exempt from extradition—his celebration was premature. Outside the courthouse, immigration agents from the Department of Commerce and Labor were waiting to immediately rearrest him, this time with an eye toward his deportation. Arredondo was a convict in Mexico, and thus had violated U.S. immigration law by entering the United States. If he were deported, Mexican police would be waiting to apprehend him the moment he crossed the border. Technically, it was not an extradition, but the result would be exactly the same. When he appeared before an immigration board, his lawyer demanded to know whether the deportation effort was "another subterfuge to remand Arredondo back to Mexico in spite of law." Clearly it was, and the immigration board ultimately agreed to let Arredondo remain in the United States.[3]

The effort to deport Arredondo may have failed, but many other insurgents were not so lucky. Whereas the United States had once been a refuge for all types of revolutionists, by the turn of the twentieth century, it had begun to close its doors as an asylum. In a panic over the idea of alien agitators importing radical violence, Americans struggled with the question of which foreigners deserved sanctuary. Extradition was one means of expelling radicals, but increasingly, deportation was another way to achieve the same result. In fact, deportation was an even more powerful tool than extradition: it occurred behind closed doors, involved fewer due process rights, and sidestepped the issue of the political offense exception.

By the time of Arredondo's case, dozens of widely publicized American extradition hearings had centered on the question of how to define a political crime. Like Arredondo's, these proceedings were not just about the fate of one person but also a larger verdict on the question of asylum in the late nineteenth and early twentieth centuries. Between the bombing at Haymarket in 1886, the assassination of President McKinley by an anarchist in 1901, and the increasingly militant labor movements of the early twentieth century, Americans struggled to classify and control new types of public violence performed in the name of a larger movement. In the early 1800s, a youthful nation had proclaimed itself a refuge for political insurgents of all stripes, but by the end of the century, amid heightened fears of foreign terror, Americans loosened their practice of protecting individuals. Public debates about extradition provided a transition, as the United States left behind the idealism of an earlier age and came to treat asylum as something more limited and exclusive.

Arredondo's case also illustrated a shift in state power. During the nineteenth century, questions of asylum and expulsion were decided exclusively by judges or U.S. commissioners who were granted a quasi-judicial authority. But with the rise of the Bureau of Immigration's administrative capacity, deportation became a more powerful mechanism for expelling anarchists and radicals. When extradition was impossible, impractical, or simply inconvenient, deportation could be used to achieve the same ends. By the 1910s, the federal government relied on immigration laws and summary hearings to expel alien agitators. As deportation replaced extradition, the administrative power of the executive branch expanded at the expense of the judiciary.

Debates about the political crimes exception often raged concerning three turn-of-the-century revolutionary movements: Irish nationalists advocating separation from Great Britain, Russian opponents of Czar Nicholas II, and Mexican challengers to longstanding president Porfirio Díaz. Historians have generally treated American responses to each of these groups separately, along ethnic lines. However, bringing them together through the lens of extradition shows how Americans grappled with the idea of political crimes and asylum on a more abstract level, by trying to devise a consistent standard that would apply to all groups. Making sense of public violence was not just a matter of judging individual messages but also of trying to fit them into broader taxonomies of classification.[4]

The political offense exception was grounded in a tradition of American asylum and support for foreign revolutionaries, yet its parameters were vague and contested. Were the "political crimes" in the treaties limited to defined wars fought by uniformed soldiers, or could they extend beyond the traditional setting of the battlefield? Late nineteenth-century anarchists and other radicals took their bloodshed onto the city streets, waging indiscriminate attacks against civilians in the name of social transformation. Should these crimes be deemed political and therefore protected? Or were they senseless acts of terror and thus extraditable?

The idea of protecting political offenders went back to the days of the American Revolution, when the founders maintained that citizens had the natural, inalienable right to overthrow tyrannical regimes. This principle was enshrined in the Declaration of Independence, which proclaimed that whenever a government deprived its people of life, liberty, and the pursuit of happiness, "it is the Right of the People to alter or to abolish it, and to institute new Government." In the name of political asylum, the United States pledged to shelter foreign revolutionaries from regimes that sought their persecution. In fact, distrusting foreign judiciaries in general, the United States extradited only a single person during its first sixty-five years.[5]

Yet by the mid-nineteenth century, the facility of international travel—and escape—made a world without extradition increasingly unfeasible. An 1843 treaty with France balanced concerns about law and order with the tradition of asylum. It listed murder, arson, and various other crimes as extraditable, but included the stipulation that the treaty "shall not be applied in any manner . . . to any crime or offense of a purely political character." Extradition was made palatable to a hesitant American public by designating a category of people—political offenders—who could not be surrendered.[6]

During the next few decades, an exception for offenses of a political character became boilerplate in U.S. extradition agreements. The treaties with France (1843), Mexico (1861), and Peru (1870) included the word "purely"; all others simply specified "crimes or offenses of a political character." Yet the meaning of the word "political" was never defined in any of these treaties. Surely, acts like treason and sedition were political, but it was unclear how far the exception could—or should—be stretched.[7]

For much of the nineteenth century, the vagueness of the treaties was unproblematic and the protections afforded under the political offense exception went uncontested. In 1848, a wave of revolutions swept Western and Central Europe; after these uprisings failed, many insurgents sought asylum in the United States. These exiles matched certain romantic notions held by Americans about how a revolutionary looked. Like the Founding Fathers, most were Anglo-Saxon and middle class, fighting to overthrow oppressive monarchies and implement liberal reforms. Many of these "Forty-Eighters" became prominent and respected U.S. citizens. German revolutionary Carl Schurz was elected to the U.S. Senate in 1869 and later served in President Hayes's cabinet.[8]

Louis Kossuth, the leader of Hungary's struggle for independence, exemplified the authority, austerity, and principle that mid-nineteenth-century Americans associated with political revolution. When the Austrian and Russian governments attempted to extradite Kossuth from Turkey in 1849, the American press denounced the idea of handing him over. Secretary of State William A. Marcy affirmed that there existed a moral duty to protect revolutionaries like Kossuth; extraditing him, he wrote in 1853, would be "an act meriting the reprobation of mankind."[9]

But by the early 1880s, new groups of people claimed the label of revolutionary, many of whom did not resemble the freedom fighters of 1776 or 1848. Whereas past revolutionaries had been men of principle and restraint, anarchists challenged the very idea of structure, order, and authority. Dynamite, invented in 1866, elevated violence to a new level. Attacks were no longer confined to defined military battles; now even civilians were vulnerable targets. Radicals like Mikhail Bakunin and Johann Most advocated "propaganda by the deed"—the use of indiscriminate acts of violence against people seen as threats to the working class, meant to symbolize a larger structural assault.[10]

Americans initially believed this violence was contained in Europe, but during the depression of the 1880s, it hit home. Labor strikes and upheavals across the country culminated in 1886, when Chicago police clashed violently with militant anarchists and labor movement protesters in Haymarket Square. The popular press pinned the blame on foreigners, and Americans fearfully wondered whether their sanctuary for the oppressed threatened domestic safety and security. Meanwhile, foreign governments sought to set an example by punishing exiled insurgents. Britain wanted to extradite Irish Republicans from the United States, and czarist Russia hoped to send its opponents to Siberia. The line between political offense and ordinary crime had once seemed obvious, even intuitive; now the ambiguity of the definition became apparent.

Should foreign fugitives receive immunity from prosecution simply because they claimed to be acting politically? One uncertainty arose when Americans felt sympathy for the motives of violent actors but revulsion toward their tactics. Irish nationalism received a large amount of public support in the United States, but groups like the Fenian Brotherhood and the Clan na Gael used dynamite to incite fear in the English. A series of bombings of public buildings in January 1885—including the Tower of London and the House of Commons—were even plotted on American soil. In the July 1885 issue of the *North American Review*, three prominent men of letters debated whether dynamite crimes were beyond the pale of sanctioned behavior. Even those who agreed with the Irish nationalists' cause could not condone their violent tactics. In spite of admirable motives, "it is incompatible with the safety of society that a political end should be sought by such means," wrote James B. Angell, president of the University of Michigan.[11]

A wave of assassinations targeting heads of state in Europe and the United States also cast a shadow on the notion that every politically motivated crime ought to be protected. Assassination hit particularly close to home after the murders of President Lincoln in 1865 and President Garfield in 1881. When Russia's czar Alexander II was assassinated by a nihilist in 1881, the U.S. Senate immediately passed a resolution "unit[ing] its voice with that of all civilized peoples in denouncing assassination as a means of redress for any grievance." During the 1890s, Americans expressed grief and horror when Italian anarchists assassinated both French president Marie François Sadi Carnot and Empress Elisabeth of Austria-Hungary.[12]

Even acts that looked like ordinary theft or banditry could arguably have a political motive. When the delegates of the Pan-American Conference of 1890 attempted to define political crimes, a representative from the Republic of Colombia expressed the difficulties in distinguishing political offenses from commonplace ones. "In the revolutions, as we conduct them in our country, the common offenses are necessarily mixed up with the political," he stated. If a revolutionist needed horses, saddles, or arms, he would not go to a public market; instead, he would take them from the first pasture or shop he could find. "This is called robbery everywhere, and is a common offense in time of peace," the delegate explained, "but in time of war it is a circumstance closely allied to the manner of waging it." Acts of theft, arson, and even murder could not be judged in isolation. They needed to be contextualized within the larger society, to assess their political nature.[13]

Among Irish and Russian immigrant communities, there was widespread sympathy and support for their own revolutionary movements, and appeasing these ethnic groups often took priority in Congress. Although the 1886 Haymarket Affair sparked widespread fears about foreign anarchism, Congress rejected five bills during the next decade that would ban the immigration of anarchists and nihilists. No one wished to protect anarchists, but some congressmen feared that the law might be used against their constituents' compatriots. In 1898, despite the urging of U.S. attorney James M. Beck, the United States did not send a delegate to an international antianarchism conference in Rome. "The fear that the word 'anarchist' might be construed to include political offenders prevented the United States from taking any part," Beck complained. Not until 1903, after the assassination of President McKinley, did Congress finally pass a bill prohibiting the immigration of anarchists.[14]

Extradition cases, as judicial matters, were supposed to be decided neutrally, apart from the pressures of ethnic lobbies. An 1892 editorial in the *San Francisco Chronicle* called on the courts to sort out different types of violence, insisting that extradition must not be simply a matter of which cause the public supported. Most Americans would not mind if a Russian nihilist killed the czar, it remarked, but then hypothetically posed the assassination of Queen Victoria by a Fenian, or the killing of the U.S. president by an anarchist. "As a matter of simple justice," the author ruminated, "what is the practical difference between the three cases?" There needed to be a consistent standard for determining which crimes were political, no matter where or by whom they were committed.[15]

The debates over extradition and the political offense exception helped usher an end to revolutionary enthusiasm in an age of violence and global mobility. Americans began to feel that sanctuary was something that needed to be doled out selectively, not offered to all. It was in this context that judges presiding over extradition hearings faced the challenge of creating a test that would separate protected actions from extraditable crimes. Expelling foreign revolutionaries while simultaneously clinging to the symbol of the nation as asylum required the invention of distinctions between certain ambiguous categories: political versus nonpolitical offenses, domestic versus foreign conflicts, legitimate versus criminal acts of violence.

During the 1890s, judges and legal scholars attempted to create tests that would clearly draw the line between political and nonpolitical crimes. The purpose of these tests was to bring order, rationality, and understanding to acts of foreign violence, even if it meant oversimplifying their motives. Americans looked to the courts to sort out which foreigners were sympathetic and deserved asylum, and which were dangerous and ought to be expelled.

The most effective standards were those that drew a stark line corresponding to public notions of morality or revulsion. The treaty provision known as the *attentat* clause (from the French word for murder attempt) offered one unambiguous standard; it stated that persons charged with assassinating heads of state could not claim protection under the political offense exception. The *attentat* clause was first codified in the 1856 extradition agreement between Belgium and France, and was included in every U.S. treaty after the assassination of President Garfield in 1881.[16]

British courts offered another firm line that was quickly adopted by their American counterparts—excluding anarchists from political protection. Like the United States, Great Britain wrestled with how to defend political freedom in an age of violent revolution. In 1892, French anarchist Théodole Meunier sought political asylum in London after throwing a bomb into a crowded Parisian café. The Queen's Bench rejected his plea. Anarchists could not be political actors, it ruled, because they did not advocate a specific regime change; instead, they sought the overthrow of all government. Ordering that Meunier be sent back to France to stand trial, the court concluded that "the party of anarchy . . . is the enemy of all."[17]

These stark lines made cases involving assassins or anarchists easy for extradition judges to decide and for the public to accept. But they also oversimplified social movements, conflating what it meant to be political under the treaty with what it meant to have a political message. Assassination, arguably, was the most political of acts—an aggressive attempt to remove a head of state. And although anarchists rejected the political process, they directed their deeds at the ruling class. But by framing extradition decisions in black-and-white terms, judges sent the message that crimes that did not fall under the political offense exception were devoid of any political content. Extradition decisions established the logic that an act outside the bounds of legal protection was also outside the bounds of morality.

Most extradition cases were not as simple for judges—or as morally comprehensible to the public—as those involving assassins and anarchists. Rather than making decisions on an individual basis, the courts tried to devise abstract rules for more complex cases. A British court formulated one of the most influential standards in 1891, when it decided to protect Angelo Castioni, who killed a Swiss politician during a local uprising. Fugitives were not to be extradited, it ruled, "if [their] crimes were incidental to and formed a part of political disturbances." American courts adopted the reasoning of *In re Castioni* in a standard that legal scholars dubbed the uprising test: If an act formed part of a political protest, revolt, or uprising, it was protected.[18]

The uprising test was applied in U.S. courts in the case of General Antonio Ezeta, the former commander in chief of El Salvador. During a civil war in 1894, Ezeta and his men summarily executed soldiers who refused to defend the regime, and publicly mutilated the corpses of suspected rebels. When it became clear that his government would be overthrown, Ezeta cleaned out the vault of the International Bank of Salvador and Nicaragua (calling it a "forced loan") and escaped the country aboard a U.S. naval ship. The new Salvadorian regime requested Ezeta's extradition on the counts of murder, attempted murder, and robbery.

Judge William M. Morrow of the U.S. district court in San Francisco ruled that, under the uprising test, Ezeta's crimes were political and therefore protected. Morrow was clearly torn by his decision, acknowledging the deplorable nature of Ezeta's acts. "Crimes may have been committed . . . of the most atrocious and inhuman character," he wrote in his opinion; nevertheless, "I have no authority, in this examination, to determine what acts are within the rules of civilized warfare, and what are not." Ezeta's political position and the timing of his acts—during a coup d'état—were the decisive factors.[19]

Judge Morrow may have felt uneasy about the outcome of the uprising test, but the public accepted it. As a former military dictator, Ezeta was hardly the liberal revolutionary once envisioned in the political offense exception. But his asylum did not threaten American institutions; his violence was contained in Central America. All of the major American newspapers applauded the clear logic of the *Ezeta* decision (although the *Washington Post* joked that Salvador could expect "another revolution in sixty to ninety days"). John Bassett Moore held up Morrow's logic as a model application of the uprising test.[20]

In practice, the uprising test left open difficult interpretive questions: How was a judge to determine what constituted a political disturbance? Were all acts committed during an uprising protected, even if their motives were not political? By focusing on the external context, the uprising test was supposed to eliminate subjective assessments of a defendant's motive or intent. But when political and ordinary crimes appeared indistinguishable, the courts still had to rely on testimony about the perpetrator's mental state.

One ambiguous case involved the San Ygnacio raiders, a gang that attacked a northern Mexican military camp in 1892. At first glance, the men appeared to be ordinary bandits. They seized the garrison's horses, saddles, and arms; then, leaving, they set the barracks on fire. But when the gang's leaders were apprehended in Texas, they argued that their actions had actually been political, carried out in opposition to Mexican dictator Porfirio Díaz. Were they, as one editorial's headline asked, "Insurgents or Cutthroats?"[21]

The San Ygnacio case demonstrated the subjectivity and unpredictability of the uprising test: given the same set of facts, two judges came to opposite conclusions. The extradition commissioner in San Antonio ruled that the attack was clearly for personal, not political, gain. Even though nothing prevented the raiders from advancing into Mexico, he reasoned, they instead chose to retreat with their spoils into Texas. On appeal, however, the circuit court ruled that the defendants should not be extradited. Had the movement succeeded in overthrowing the Mexican government, Judge Thomas Maxey wrote, "a doubt would scarcely be entertained that it was political in its character. . . . Disaster and defeat do not change the legal complexion of the act." The case reached the U.S. Supreme Court in 1896, but rather than offering another evaluation of the raid, the court decided that the original decision was binding; the political nature of an event was a point of fact that could not be appealed.[22]

When rulings varied so clearly from judge to judge, they began to lose legitimacy. The public looked to the courts expectantly, hoping for them to organize violence into clear categories, but judges could not draw a stable line between political and nonpolitical crimes. An editorial in the *Washington Post* called for "consistency in extradition," criticizing decisions that applied more lenient standards to Russian fugitives than to Mexican ones. "If we are going into the business of furnishing asylum to every vicious criminal that chooses to give a poetic name to his deviltry," it railed, "upon what principle can we surrender Benavides [the leader of the San Ygnacio raiders]?" Judicial inconsistency was causing headaches in the State Department as well. The Mexican minister to Washington, Matías Romero, paid multiple visits to Secretary of State Walter Gresham to rehash the San Ygnacio rulings. Gresham first sent Romero a letter describing why the offenses were political, then backtracked and explained why they were not.[23]

Nevertheless, through the end of the nineteenth century, there were no major challenges to the court's authority in extradition cases. But when President McKinley was assassinated, all of that changed. The assassination of President McKinley by anarchist Leon Czolgosz in September 1901 sparked alarm about foreign violence invading the nation. Although Czolgosz was a native-born citizen, his name sounded suspiciously alien, and he openly admitted his intellectual debt to foreign-born radicals such as Emma Goldman and Alexander Berkman. In a flurry of panic, Americans demanded that immigration restrictions be tightened. In 1903, after consideration for almost sixteen years, Congress finally passed the Anarchist Exclusion Act.[24]

In the decade following McKinley's assassination, extradition cases reached new heights of public attention and debate. While judicial inconsistency had been tolerated in the 1890s, it was now criticized as leniency. Many Americans felt that they could no longer passively allow judges to decide who was to be protected and who was to be extradited. The courts' decisions were too contradictory, and they doled out asylum too arbitrarily. One prominent New York attorney, Frederic Coudert, publicly argued that judges should no longer be allowed to rule on the political offense exception. Instead, the State Department could provide the necessary consistency that individual judges lacked. "The Department of State is equipped to decide such questions, and it should decide them," Coudert stated at the 1909 meeting of the American Society of International Law. "One judge in one place might consider revolution to be rife in a certain country and another judge some place else might consider that country to be peaceful." The question of whether violent foreigners should be allowed to live freely in the United States was too important to leave up to the individual caprices of extradition judges.[25]

Protests over judicial inconsistency and leniency reached fevered heights in 1903 regarding the extradition case of James Lynchehaun. For many, this case confirmed that judges were far too inclusive in offering political protection. The Irishman was accused of attacking his landlady, with whom he had had a failed love affair. According to police, Lynchehaun scaled the wall of her farm, set fire to her house, and then attacked her as she came outside. In the course of the struggle, he bit off her nose, crushed her right eye, and mutilated her genitalia. But when Pinkerton detectives hired by the British government located the fugitive in Indianapolis, he insisted that he had been acting politically, reclaiming Irish land from an English Protestant.[26]

Lynchehaun's extradition hearing received so much public attention that, in Ireland, it was even mentioned in a folk ballad (perhaps the only one ever to include the phrase "extradition law" in its lyrics):

> Some years ago here in Mayo, we had a great outrage;
> A lady's place in Achill was almost set ablaze.
> The Lady too was cruelly used and taken was the man,

> To Castlebar Jail they did repair and bring brave
> Lynchehaun.
>
> If you heard the murmuring on every barrack wall:
> "Surely we will capture him, if he's not gone abroad.
> And even then, we'll have him still by extradition law,
> And surely we will chain him down for fear he'd climb
> the wall."[27]

When Judge Charles Moores decided to grant Lynchehaun asylum in the United States, the ruling immediately caused a backlash. Even Irish Americans believed that Lynchehaun's crime was unspeakably vile and his defense flimsy. The defendant testified that he had acted on behalf of the Irish National Land League, yet he could only produce evidence that he had attended one meeting. Witnesses who swore to his long history of activism were widely believed to be offering perjured testimony. Michael Davitt, the head of the Irish Land League, chose to distance himself and his organization from Lynchehaun. Though Irish Americans formed defense committees that rallied to Lynchehaun's aid, they supported the fugitive not because they believed his story, but for the larger cause he claimed to represent.[28]

The decision to shelter Lynchehaun confirmed that extradition rulings did not occur in a geopolitical bubble: they could adversely affect diplomatic relations. The British Foreign Office warned that the case jeopardized the system of extradition, as there was nothing to stop future fugitives from making similar excuses. "If every man who spoke at a public meeting where a political question was being discussed could commit crime and shield himself under the defense that it was a political offense," one British memorandum criticized, "it would not be long before all criminals would be political speakers." The British press also was incensed by the Lynchehaun decision. The *London Globe* threatened that "Americans will have no cause for complaint if the [Lynchehaun] result throws out of gear the whole machinery of extradition between the United States and Great Britain." It invoked the assassination of President McKinley two years earlier, warning that "the next assassin of a president will plead Commissioner Moores' judgment with irresistible force if he escapes across the Canadian line."[29]

The Lynchehaun case exposed the problems in leaving extradition decisions up to judges. After his release, State Department officials tried to smooth diplomatic relations with Britain by directing the case to the Bureau of Immigration. As a convicted felon, Lynchehaun was subject to deportation for violation of the immigration laws. U.S. immigration inspectors worked in conjunction with private detectives hired by the British government to search for Lynchehaun, who disappeared after his extradition hearing, but they were unable to locate him.[30]

During the 1890s, Americans had looked to the courts for consensus, but after McKinley's assassination, the political offense exception divided the public. During the next few years, two factions vied to define who should receive protection as a political actor. One group, concerned with the threat that radicals posed to American society, demanded that the category of protected persons be narrowed. They hearkened back to the pre-1880s notion of the liberal revolutionary, contending that only a select few should be considered political offenders under the treaties. Another group, sympathetic to Russian and Mexican dissidents, wanted to expand the scope of American asylum. Protection should be extended not only to those who could prove they had acted politically, they argued, but also to those who would not receive a fair trial after extradition.

The debate over a new judicial standard came to a head in 1908, in two highly publicized cases involving Russian radicals. Both Jan Pouren and Christian Rudowitz were members of a socialist labor party that opposed the czarist regime. Pouren burned down a vodka factory in St. Petersburg, protesting a vodka tax that the czar had levied to generate revenue. Rudowitz murdered a family of three in the Baltic village of Benin, claiming they were spies. Though the cases were unrelated, the Russian consuls in New York and Chicago demanded the extraditions within months of each other, and the American press often treated the two cases as one. For people like Pouren and Rudowitz, the definition of the word "political" was a matter of more than mere semantics; it was the difference between asylum in the United States and exile in Siberia.[31]

The counsel for the Russian government, Frederic Coudert, became the spokesman for a narrower, more exclusive extradition standard. Coudert combined an attention to legal detail with an appeal to public morality. Pouren and Rudowitz were precisely the sort of terrorists who should not be protected under the political offense exception, he contended, as their wanton destruction of life and property were the antithesis of American morals and civilized debate. Asylum was not a right but a privilege that should distributed sparingly.

Coudert argued that common sense and public morality should govern the political offense exception. While judges struggled to draw a line between political and nonpolitical offenses, the average American instinctively knew the difference between noble and repellant acts of violence. He claimed that "the man in the street would recoil in horror" at the suggestion that Pouren and Rudowitz were as deserving of asylum as a Lafayette or a Carl Schurz. "The spontaneous differentiation which the universal instinct of every civilized community would make between such cases, may not as yet correspond to any legal distinction," he criticized.[32]

Coudert accused judges of mistaken priorities: rather than protecting political offenders, they ought to concern themselves with the security of American society. Giving protection to anyone who demonstrated a political intent was absurd, he argued, when radical aliens so clearly threatened public safety. The United States had gone too far in allowing judges, with their myopic focus on legal codes, to determine the bounds of asylum. "Are we to be slaves to mere legalism," Coudert asked, "or will we try to fulfill the real purpose of extradition, viz.: remove from this country those persons whose brutal and hideous conduct, whatever its ultimate causes may have been, make them dangerous and unfit members of our society?"[33]

On the opposing side, Pouren and Rudowitz received a tremendous amount of support from Americans on the left. Their cases gained the attention of reformers and Progressives around the country who objected to the idea that an American judge might perform the dirty work of the Russian czar. Jane Addams established a fund in Rudowitz's defense, and four prominent lawyers, including

Clarence Darrow, offered to represent both defendants free of charge. The most relentless lobbying for their release came from a group called the Political Refugee Defense League, which circulated petitions, handed out pamphlets, and organized mass rallies on behalf of the two Russians. According to one report, more than 2,500 people attended a November 1908 meeting at Chicago's Seventh Regiment armory.[34]

The Political Refugee Defense League argued that, rather than scrupulously analyzing their crimes, the court ought to consider what kind of justice would be meted to Pouren and Rudowitz if they were extradited. Russian-born attorney Isaac C. Hourwich, himself wanted for political crimes against the czar, described the Russian judicial system as backward and barbaric, where enemies of the state were tried in closed-off chambers without benefit of counsel. Extradition to czarist Russia, Hourwich argued, was equivalent to a death sentence. "Shall We Return the Fugitive to the Torture Chamber?" cried one petition.[35]

The Political Refugee Defense League latched on to an emotionally resonant rhetorical device: comparing the extradition treaty with Russia to the Fugitive Slave Law of 1850. Just as the Fugitive Slave Law demanded that Northerners return runaway slaves to the South, so too did extradition with Russia deliver the persecuted into the hands of their oppressors. Extradition with Russia "imposes on the entire nation the role of slave-catcher at the bidding of a foreign despotism," one petition asserted. Protecting Russian dissidents was, it implied, a way for Americans to make up for the crime of slavery, proving themselves the friends of freedom and enemies of subjugation.[36]

There was another factor to consider in the 1908 battle over Pouren and Rudowitz: electoral politics. In both cases, Coudert won the court battle; judges decided that the crimes of the two men did not fall under the political crimes exception, and that therefore they should be extradited. But the Political Refugee Defense League understood that the executive, not the judiciary, had the final say. Pouren's extradition was scheduled for September 1908, two months before the 1908 presidential election, and Theodore Roosevelt's handpicked successor, William Howard Taft, was in a close race.

Pouren's supporters took advantage of this timing. In public speeches and addresses, they emphasized that "the American nation is on trial on November 3rd. That must be impressed on every voter." The pressure worked: at the last minute, Secretary of State Elihu Root intervened to stop the extradition of the Russians.[37]

The old tests for determining a political offense could no longer hold, and there was no consensus on what should replace it. But the Pouren and Rudowitz cases made one thing clear: the State Department was willing to intervene in extradition cases, and in the future, the executive would continue to assert its strength over the judiciary. The power to grant or deny asylum had once belonged exclusively to judicial authorities, but as the administrative capacity of the executive grew, deportation developed into a more powerful means of expelling foreigners.

✻

The shift from extradition to deportation occurred alongside the rise of U.S. immigration law. Before the 1880s, the federal government did not exercise the power to deport, for the simple reason that there were not yet any immigration statutes to enforce. Extradition was the only way to expel aliens deemed undesirable or dangerous to American society. However, starting with the Page Act of 1875, immigration restrictions offered new ways of keeping aliens out: refusal to admit and deportation. Between 1882 and 1924, Congress passed successive restrictions prohibiting new categories of aliens from entering the United States—Chinese laborers (1882); "idiots, lunatics, convicts, and persons likely to become a public charge" (1882); "polygamists, persons convicted of crimes involving moral turpitude, and those suffering a loathsome or contagious disease" (1891); epileptics, the insane, professional beggars, anarchists, and prostitutes (1903); the illiterate (1917); and all persons of Asiatic origin (1924).[38]

As federal immigration law expanded, so too did the administrative capacity to enforce it. The Immigration Act of 1882 empowered the secretary of the Treasury to administer immigration laws, thus shifting the duty to regulate immigration from the individual states to the federal government. The Immigration Act of 1891 established the first bureaucracy, creating an Office of Immigration within the Treasury Department. In 1903, Congress transferred responsibility for the administration of immigration laws to the newly created Department of Commerce and Labor. During the next decade, as its duties grew, the Bureau of Immigration ballooned in size. By 1911, Ellis Island alone employed a force of 523; its administrative boards heard up to 100 immigration cases a day.[39]

The system of deportation was so expansive, State Department official John Bassett Moore realized, that it could be used to achieve the same ends as extradition. At the 1893 World's Congress of Jurisprudence and Law Reform in Chicago, Moore proposed using an administrative rather than a judicial process to return suspected criminals to their home countries. U.S. immigration laws barred the entry of convicts, he pointed out, so that anyone convicted of a crime in a foreign country could be summarily sent back to the country from which he came. Moore explained:

> It is . . . worthy of notice that the immigration laws of the United States require the return to the country from which they came, of all non-political convicts. Though this measure is not in the nature of an extradition treaty, the execution of which another government may require, its full significance, as affecting the subject of extradition, has, perhaps, hardly been appreciated. With such a provision in our statutes, it is difficult to set a limit to the extent to which the system of extradition may logically be carried.[40]

Moore was an unlikely figure to criticize the practice of extradition. As a law clerk in the State Department from 1885 to 1886, then as assistant secretary of state, he oversaw all international extradition cases that passed through Washington. In his two-volume *Treatise*, published in 1891, Moore lauded extradition as a triumph of common sense and justice, replacing romantic notions of asylum and outdated prejudices against foreign judiciaries. But Moore's perspective in the State Department also left him with an understanding of its practical setbacks. Extradition proceedings were slow and costly, judges' decisions were unpredictable and inconsistent, and refusals to extradite could have diplomatic repercussions. Precisely because of his strong support for the principles of extradition, Moore railed against the pitfalls that held up its timely and reliable execution.[41]

Immigration cases were heard in a summary administrative hearing, not a judicial trial, and were therefore a faster and cheaper way to remove foreigners from the country. In the Immigration Act of 1893, Congress established Boards of Special Inquiry to decide matters of alien admissibility. The hearings held by these boards lacked many of the procedural guarantees that a defendant would receive in an extradition hearing before a U.S. commissioner, and thus resulted in speedier and more predictable decisions. Proceedings were not open to the public. Aliens had no legal right to an attorney, or to subpoena witnesses and evidence on their behalf. Deportation decisions were made by a panel of three inspectors who had wide discretion to interpret the law. There was no judicial review of their decisions; appeals could be made only to the secretary of the Treasury (and later, of Commerce and Labor), whose decision was final.[42]

The ambiguous language of U.S. immigration law gave officials wide discretion to send accused criminals back to their home countries, even if they claimed to have acted politically. An alien could be deported for committing a crime of "moral turpitude"—a category that was broad enough to include almost any felony. Or he could be sent back on the grounds that he was "likely to become a public charge." This label originally referred to paupers dependent on charity, but immigration officials stretched the label so far as to make it practically meaningless. The very fact that someone was wanted for a crime in a foreign country was evidence that he might end up a "public charge" in an American jail.[43]

In the late 1890s, the United States and Great Britain began to experiment with immigration law as a way to bypass formal extradition. In 1896, time was running out to file the proper extradition papers for Henry Arthur Barfield, a postmaster wanted for embezzlement in London. Instead of dealing with warrants and depositions, the British undersecretary of state telegraphed its consul in Boston, who in turn informed the immigration commissioner that the fugitive would be arriving by steamship three days later. When immigration inspectors at Boston Harbor located Barfield, they confiscated the stolen money he had with him; then, calling him a pauper, deported him back to England on the same ship on which he had come. When it arrived in Liverpool, British authorities were waiting on the dock to arrest him. The end result was a de facto extradition, but the parties had avoided the difficulty and expense of a judicial hearing.[44]

During the next decades, such schemes became common practice with Britain, particularly in cases involving Canada. The deportations went in both directions; fugitives from justice were also returned to the United States on the charge of illegal entry. Charles Lanctot, the deputy attorney general of Quebec, believed that "deportation when it may be secured is preferable to extradition," as it was "a more expeditious and less expensive proceeding." Mexico, too, both received deportees and deported fugitives wanted in the United States. Article 33 of the Mexican Constitution of 1917 gave the chief executive the power to expel any "pernicious foreigner"—a vague category that was not subject to any judicial review. The term "thirty-three" was coined to designate the fate of any foreigner expelled in such a manner.[45]

Later scholars acknowledged the irregularity of "disguised extradition," as some called it, and debated its legality. In *Fong Yue Ting v. U.S.* (1893), one of the Supreme Court's Chinese exclusion cases, the majority stated that "the order of deportation is not a punishment for a crime." Taking this as a starting point, political scientist Alona Evans explained how disguised extradition was tantamount to punishment. "The decision to extradite an alleged offender is a serious matter," she affirmed, "for the liberty and possibly the life of the accused is at stake." Deportation eliminated the procedures that safeguarded the apprehension and delivering up of accused offenders, established in the Extradition Act of 1848. These included the identification of the accused, the production of warrants of arrest and depositions, and the weighing of evidence submitted.[46]

Disguised extradition elevated the role of the executive at the expense of the judiciary. Through the 1880s, the expulsion of aliens primarily had been an issue of extradition; now, it was a matter of deportation. Before they even had a chance to reach the courts, the

Bureau of Immigration seized cases once decided by federal judges. This course of action was undertaken with the full sanction of the State Department. In a 1911 paper entitled "The Difficulties of Extradition," Moore, the former assistant secretary of state, asserted that "no reason can be given why, if the fugitive from justice is called an immigrant, he is returned upon the fact of his conviction, while, if the immigrant is called a fugitive from justice, the question of his guilt should be re-examined." Green H. Hackworth, a legal adviser to the State Department, affirmed that "requests are sometimes made by governments for the deportation by other governments of fugitives from justice," and such persons were usually deported.[47]

Perhaps most significant, deportation cases generally sidestepped political and diplomatic headaches. In contrast to the huge protests surrounding the Lynchehaun, Pouren, and Rudowitz extradition cases, deportation hearings occurred behind closed doors, away from public scrutiny. Extradition still clashed with idealistic visions of the nation as asylum, while immigration laws had widespread support, even though the result was the same. "Call our statute an immigration law, its enforcement is commended and arouses no suspicion," Moore remarked. "Call it an extradition law, and large opportunities are afforded to evade and defeat it." Deportation was particularly helpful when it came to bypassing the political offense exception. Not only did it sidestep the public spectacle but it also eliminated the risk that an unpredictable judge might refuse to extradite.[48]

The U.S. and British governments collaborated to deport Irish Republicans who might claim political protection. After James Lynchehaun's extradition was denied in 1903, the State Department tried to get him deported to smooth relations with Britain. In the 1908 case of Irishman Michael Byrne, the British Foreign Office preemptively instructed its consul in New York to go directly to the U.S. immigration authorities rather than initiate extradition proceedings. It did not matter that his offense, stealing cattle, was seemingly apolitical. Even when the alleged crime had nothing to do with politics, any Irishman might claim political persecution and amass the weight of the Irish-American community behind him. Into the 1980s, in fact, the United States continued to use deportation as a substitute for extradition in the cases of Irish Republican Army (IRA) members wanted by Britain.[49]

In the years leading up to the Mexican Revolution of 1910–1920, the United States and Mexico collaborated to deport rebels who might otherwise be shielded by the political offense exception. The United States had plenty of reasons to support Porfirio Díaz, the longtime dictator of Mexico. Above all, Díaz welcomed American investments, which grew rapidly in Mexico in the 1890s. Revolutionary violence threatened these interests, however, and even risked spilling across the border. As a sign of support for the Díaz regime, the U.S. government began apprehending rebel leaders living in the United States. Among the targeted were the Flores Magón brothers—Ricardo, Enrique, and Jesús—who printed the anarchist newspaper *Regeneración* and led the revolutionary Partido Liberal Mexicano from St. Louis. Ricardo Flores Magón was arrested in 1907 for violating the U.S. neutrality laws, and spent the next fifteen years in and out of American prisons. Although he was never deported, he was effectively immobilized.[50]

The Department of Commerce and Labor did not consider itself bound by judicial rulings. It regularly issued warrants for deportation even after extradition was denied, as in the case of Juan José Arredondo, or while an extradition hearing was in process. When the Mexican government realized it would lose the extradition case against Antonio Villareal, a radical journalist and a close associate of the Flores Magón brothers, it simply contacted the Bureau of Immigration. During his extradition hearing in El Paso in 1906, Villareal attracted a great deal of local public support. Fearing that his offenses (murder and "inciting rebellion against the government") would be deemed political, the Mexican consul informed the Bureau of Immigration that Villareal had once served a term in prison. As a felon, he was considered unfit to enter the United States and subject to deportation. Officials of the State Department, the Department of Justice, and the Department of Commerce and Labor formed a united front: all agreed that Villareal should be deported, even though he would be arrested for treason as soon as he stepped foot across the border. "This action will avoid legal tangles which might result from the attempt to decide whether the taking of army ammunition was really a criminal or political offense," commented the *Washington Post.*[51]

By the end of the 1910s, judges had lost much of their authority to determine questions of political asylum. The role of extradition hearings was largely limited to procedural questions, such as whether enough evidence existed to make a prima facie case. The real power had instead shifted to the executive. As the administrative capacity of the Bureau of Immigration grew, deportation became a more powerful mechanism for expelling radicals. Deportation may have made the exchange of fugitives more streamlined and predictable, as John Bassett Moore had hoped, but it also meant fewer legal protections, due process rights, and transparency. Rather than taking place in a courtroom, immigration officials now decided the fate of political offenders out of sight.

For two decades, Americans had grappled openly with the question of where to draw the line between political acts and crimes of terror. The shift from extradition to deportation shut down these public debates. Between November 1919 and January 1920, Attorney General A. Mitchell Palmer ordered the arrest and deportation of more than 500 foreign-born radicals living in the United States. The Palmer Raids displayed the unprecedented and largely unchecked ability of the Department of Justice to orchestrate the mass expulsion of aliens. After two decades of "disguised extradition," deportation had become the familiar means of removing foreign radicals from the United States. Whereas Americans once had wrestled with the question of whether politically minded aliens should be protected or expelled, they now had come to accept that the process was not supposed to be transparent, and was predetermined. The Palmer Raids marked the end of an era when Americans had grappled with the idea that contemporary violence was meant to be contemplated, not automatically condemned.

7

From the Pinkertons to the FBI

BELLE CASSIDY, the granddaughter of detective Allan Pinkerton, reminisced about her famous ancestor in the pages of *Colorado Magazine* in January 1952. She recounted how he had worked as a Union spy during the Civil War, thwarted an assassination attempt on President Lincoln, and founded the famous detective agency. Her grandfather, Cassidy boasted, "was known as the first 'F.B.I. man.'"[1]

Cassidy, of course, was mistaken. Allan Pinkerton could not have been called "the first FBI man" during his lifetime for one simple reason: the Federal Bureau of Investigation (FBI) was founded in 1908, twenty-four years after his death. Yet, during the 1950s and 1960s, the moniker stuck. Mrs. Jeanette Gustin wrote to the Pinkerton Agency in 1968, narrating the research she had conducted on the family. Allan Pinkerton first gained his fame, she claimed, by uncovering a mid-nineteenth-century counterfeiting ring. Repeating Cassidy's anachronism, she continued: "He then reported it to the Government and because of this was called, either jokingly or seriously, 'The first FBI man.'"[2]

In the context of the mid-twentieth century, the nickname made sense. By that time, the FBI had largely taken over the sorts of investigations that the Pinkertons had dominated the century before. In what might be called a "deprivatization" of policing, authority shifted from the private Pinkertons to the public FBI and other federal agencies. This trend only accelerated after J. Edgar Hoover became director of the bureau in 1924. As journalist Murray Kempner put it in 1971, "The replacement of Allan Pinkerton, dealer in detectives for Wealth during the late nineteenth century, by J. Edgar Hoover, supervisor of detectives for Commonwealth, must be the only episode in our social history to realize Marx's prescription for the transformation of capitalistic private property into socialized property." Kempner was certainly trying to goad the notoriously anticommunist Hoover, but he also put his finger on a very real change in the distribution of power.[3]

This shift in power was part of a broader centralization of state authority during the Progressive and New Deal eras. The rise of the FBI during the 1920s and 1930s was yet another incarnation of the same centralizing impulse embodied by the Progressive reformers of the early twentieth century, the state expansion of the war years, and the emerging New Deal apparatus. The FBI matured during a time of widespread alarm about violent crime, and this fear produced strong support for a federal solution. Outlaws like Bonnie and Clyde or John Dillinger exploited the limited jurisdiction of local and state police by fleeing across city, county, and state boundaries. As Claire Bond Potter argues, "the confrontations between the G-man and the bandit, the Bureau of Investigation and the gang, became arenas for articulating nationalist narratives about the benefits of an interventionist state."[4]

Calling Allan Pinkerton "the first FBI man" made explicit the direct connections between the Pinkerton National Detective Agency and the Federal Bureau of Investigation. Pinkerton biographer Frank Morn claimed that Allan Pinkerton had pioneered many of the devices used by J. Edgar Hoover. "Much of what Hoover had done for the public and the police," he wrote, "had been done earlier by Allan Pinkerton and his two sons." For example, the Pinkertons had been the first to collect fingerprints and photographs of known criminals in a compendium called the Rogues' Gallery. In 1924, the FBI created a national identification center to centralize these records, a venture that had been proposed by William Pinkerton back in the 1890s. Hoover followed in the Pinkerton tradition of creating ties with both national and international police departments, and both Pinkerton and Hoover glamorized and mythologized their personal and organizational successes in the media and popular novels. Perhaps most significant, both used violence and intimidation to staunch labor radicalism. As Kempner put it, "Hoover found the tablets already engraved; no further exercise was demanded of him except some tracery at the edges."[5]

The FBI also took over one more Pinkerton practice: the international manhunt. Nowadays, wrote A. W. Parsons in 1950, it was not the Pinkertons but the FBI that was "likely to be chasing a bank-breaker across three continents." Indeed, the FBI was likely to chase not only bank breakers, but also bootleggers, gangsters, and murderers. Unlike the Pinkertons, who focused mostly on financial crimes, the FBI had a wider mandate. Instead of simply pursuing a profit, the FBI measured its successes in terms of how many "public enemies" it captured. Because it went after more varied types of fugitives, the deprivatization of policing resulted in an extended reach for the long arm of American law. Any federal crime fell under the purview of the FBI, and the list of federal crimes grew longer every year. Although municipal police departments were professionalizing in the early twentieth century, they engaged less often in international manhunts. In the 1920s, the New York Police Department even instituted a rule forbidding its officers from traveling abroad on official investigations.[6]

Despite the wider mandate, the shift from private to public policing was marked more by continuity than change. In many ways, the international manhunts carried out by the early FBI resembled those conducted by the Pinkertons and other private agencies decades before. The FBI employed many of the same on-the-ground tactics that private agencies had used in the late nineteenth and early twentieth centuries. While the FBI had the benefit of new technologies, many basic strategies were largely unchanged. The FBI also utilized the same sorts of legal rationales as the Pinkertons, particularly in its reliance on the *Ker v. Illinois* precedent to justify international abductions and other forms of irregular rendition. Although the FBI was concerned with reducing public violence, like the Pinkertons it was fundamentally committed to protecting private property. Additionally, the FBI drew on the same type of popular rhetoric as earlier detectives, normalizing the idea that there ought to be—and indeed was—nowhere in the world where a fugitive could hide from American justice.

✻

The decline of the Pinkertons began in July 1892, when manager Henry Clay Frick hired the agency to put down a burgeoning strike at Andrew Carnegie's steel factory in Homestead, Pennsylvania. Frick gave the detectives authority to defeat the laborers by any means necessary; the Pinkertons chose to do so with Winchester rifles. On July 6, three hundred Pinkerton agents exchanged gunfire with striking workers for nearly fourteen hours. By the end of the day, three detectives and nine workers were dead.[7]

The Homestead Strike dealt a devastating blow to the Pinkerton reputation. Friends of labor denounced the agency in the strongest terms, and the ballad "Father Was Killed by the Pinkerton Men" roused popular anger. Even those who were not sympathetic to the striking workers felt deeply disturbed by the idea of a private army that was not accountable to the people. "Governments are organized to protect life and property," declared William Jennings Bryan to Congress. "These functions should not be transferred to private individuals and hired detectives until we are ready to acknowledge government a failure." By the end of the year, both the House and Senate began formal investigations into Homestead, as well as private policing more generally.[8]

The Homestead Strike ended up costing the agency one of its biggest clients: the federal government. In March 1893, Congress passed a resolution stating "that hereafter no employee of the Pinkerton Detective Agency, or similar agency, shall be employed in any Government service or by any officer of the District of Columbia." Prior to this, the Justice Department had regularly hired the Pinkertons to carry out investigations. The ban left the Justice Department without a much-needed investigative force, eventually paving the way for the creation of the Bureau of Investigation fifteen years later.[9]

Another blow came to the Pinkertons with the establishment of the William J. Burns International Detective Agency in 1909. Frustrated with the proliferation of private detective firms, the

Pinkertons began denouncing their new rival at every opportunity. Nevertheless, within three months, Burns managed to steal the Pinkertons' biggest client, the American Bankers Association (ABA). This meant that if there were a robbery or embezzlement at any of the 11,000 member banks, the work would go to Burns rather than the Pinkertons.[10]

Despite its name, before founding his agency, William J. Burns had minimal international experience. As a Secret Service agent, he had looked abroad in one case, uncovering a forgery scheme involving Costa Rican currency. Yet, before long, he developed a knack for international investigations. One of those cases involved Joseph Holl, accused of embezzlement from an ABA bank in Portland, Oregon, in 1915. The Burns Agency, by this time, had offices in twenty-four cities, including a branch in London. Burns suspected that Holl had fled the country for Europe, and the agency's strategy was simple. It sent a photograph and description of the wanted man to local consular offices around Europe. Two months later, the American consulate general in Berlin wrote back, reporting that the local police had located a man who met Holl's description.[11]

The ABA was particularly concerned when A. B. Crouch defrauded a member bank of a considerable sum in 1916. The secretary of the ABA, Colonel Fred E. Farnsworth, personally called Burns on a daily basis to ask about progress on the investigation. The Burns Agency thought it had a lead when the American consul at Newcastle, Australia, reported that a man resembling Crouch was working as a carpet maker in Brisbane. However, the fugitive was not actually apprehended until 1929, when he was finally caught in New Zealand. The application for extradition boasted that "detectives and officers . . . have been working unceasingly for the past thirteen years to bring this man to trial."[12]

The more sensational the catch, the more business the Burns Agency took away from the Pinkertons. Burns's exploits made national news, earning him the nickname "America's Sherlock Holmes." Detective magazines printed "true crime" stories based on his investigations. Among the high-profile cases that the Burns Agency accepted were the bombing of the *Los Angeles Times* building in 1910 and the Leo Frank case (which the Pinkertons also took on) in 1913. In 1921, Burns agents traveled to Eastern Europe in pursuit of a suspected bomber who had killed thirty-eight people on Wall Street. Meanwhile, the public view of the Pinkertons soured even more when former detective Charles Siringo penned a memoir in 1915, entitled *Two Evil Isms: Pinkertonism and Anarchism*. In it, he accused the Pinkertons of bribing jurors, fixing elections, kidnapping witnesses, corrupting public officials, and causing the execution of an innocent man. The Pinkertons attempted to sue Siringo for libel; when that failed, they bought up copies of the exposé in the hopes of minimizing the number of readers. However, the public battle—not to mention the scathing title of the book—caused irreparable damage to the Pinkerton reputation.[13]

Meanwhile, an even bigger competitor to both the Pinkertons and Burns was slowly emerging: the Department of Justice's Bureau of Investigation. Established in 1908, the Bureau of Investigation was the first incarnation of today's FBI. (It would add the word "Federal" to its name in 1935.) After the 1893 ban on hiring private detectives, the Department of Justice appropriated Secret Service agents from the Treasury Department to do its investigative work, but in 1907, Congress prohibited the use of the Secret Service by other departments. This was self-serving; agents were investigating a land fraud case that implicated several congressmen. At the urging of Attorney General Charles Bonaparte, President Theodore Roosevelt created by executive order a new detective force with a staff of special agents, specifically commissioned for the Department of Justice.[14]

In its first dozen years, the fledgling Bureau of Investigation took on only a handful of international cases, limiting itself to the most sensational offenses and high-profile fugitives. An example of both was the famed boxer Jack Johnson, who escaped to Canada after being convicted of violating the Mann Act in 1913. The Mann Act, a federal law passed in 1910, made it a felony to transport across state or national boundaries "any woman or girl for the purpose of prostitution or debauchery, or for any other immoral purpose." Meant to address the hysteria over "white slavery"—the forced entry of young, middle-class girls into prostitution rings—prosecutors zealously used the Mann Act to target consensual sexual activity as well.

In Johnson's case, the "immoral purpose" was miscegenation—the African American athlete had relationships with white women, and even wed a white woman in 1912. For the next seven years, the Bureau of Investigation tracked Johnson's movements as he lived in exile with his wife, Lucille, in Europe, South America, and Mexico. He eventually surrendered to federal agents at the Mexican border in September 1920.[15]

Another high-profile case that the Bureau of Investigation undertook in its early years involved Franz von Rintelen, a German spy during World War I. He arrived in the still-neutral United States in 1915, with the mission to sabotage American ships carrying munitions and supplies to the Allies. Though he stayed in the United States for only a year, he did a fair amount of damage: he planted small "pencil bombs" on multiple American merchant ships, setting fires and causing the crew to throw munitions overboard; tried to organize strikes and slowdowns among American munitions workers; and, in a precursor to the Zimmermann Telegram, met with Mexican president Victoriano Huerta about the possibility of attacking the United States. While trying to sail back to Germany in 1916, von Rintelen was captured by British agents and held in England as a prisoner of war. The Bureau of Investigation sent a man across the Atlantic to interrogate the German saboteur, and the State Department successfully fought to get him extradited to the United States.[16]

The worlds of public and private detection collided when William J. Burns became director of the Bureau of Investigation in 1921. His tenure is remembered mainly for how it ended. In a series of events known as the Daugherty-Burns scandal, Burns ordered federal agents to investigate a congressman who was a personal enemy; refused to hand documents over to a congressional investigation; and sent men to the offices of newspapers that had portrayed the Bureau of Investigation in a negative light, in an effort to intimidate them. Due to the backlash in public opinion and in Congress, Attorney General Harlan Fiske Stone forced Burns to step down. He was the last head of the bureau before J. Edgar Hoover, who would take control of the agency after Burns's resignation in 1924, and remain director for the next half century.[17]

Yet the Burns years were also a time of real innovation, particularly in the Bureau of Investigation's willingness to take on more international manhunts. During his time as head, the bureau pursued at least fifteen international cases, involving fugitives in Canada, Mexico, Europe, and Latin America, and crimes ranging from embezzlement to car theft, liquor smuggling, and mail fraud. Perhaps Burns's most high-profile catch was Don P. Collins, known in the New York underworld as "Dapper Don," who ran a liquor-smuggling ring from the Bahamas. The Bureau of Investigation discovered the fugitive staying in a chateau in Deauville, France. Because smuggling was not included in the French extradition treaty, Collins was instead extradited on the charge of larceny.[18]

Burns brought the tactics and techniques of private detectives to the Bureau of Investigation. For example, in the case of Sid T. Mercer, he used exactly the same strategy that his firm had employed in the earlier hunt for Joseph Holl. Mercer was the former assistant cashier of the First National Bank of Moultrie, Georgia, and had disappeared in 1917 with a sizable shortage in his accounts. For five years, the case lay dormant, as it was believed that Mercer had fled to Cuba. Burns, however, revived the investigation in 1922. He sent a circular containing a description and photograph of Mercer to American consuls throughout Latin America, and his efforts paid off. Henry S. Waterman, the American consul in Costa Rica, replied with a new lead: there was a man working at the Aguacate Mine near San José who went by the name of Sanford, but Waterman was almost certain that he was actually the wanted man. Before setting up its own overseas program in the 1940s, the FBI would rely extensively on the assistance of U.S. consuls.[19]

One of the reasons why the Bureau of Investigation began chasing more international fugitives was because there were so many more federal crimes to pursue. The bureau was charged with detecting and prosecuting "crimes against the United States." Initially, this included interstate shipment of "stolen goods, contraceptives, obscene books, and prizefight films, and the transportation of liquor into dry States." During the next dozen years, Congress granted the bureau additional duties: the 1910 Mann Act, the 1914 Harrison Narcotics Act, and the 1919 Dyer Act, which forbade the transport of stolen

automobiles across state or national lines. Embezzlement, tradi-
tionally the bread and butter of the private detective agencies, became a federal crime—and thus the responsibility of the Bureau of
Investigation—in 1918. The National Bank Act targeted "any officer,
director, agent, or employee of any Federal reserve bank, or of any
member bank . . . who makes any false entry in any book, report, or
statement . . . with intent in any case to injure or to defraud." The
president or attorney general also could summon the FBI for political
reasons. For example, the bureau might be called on to target anarchists, communists, or radicals, as occurred in the 1919 deportations
of Emma Goldman and Alexander Berkman. Or it might be ordered
to arrest strikers, as happened during the Great Railroad Strike
of 1922.[20]

In 1934, the Unlawful Flight to Avoid Prosecution statute (also
known as the Fugitive Felon Act) broadened the mandate of the FBI
to an unprecedented degree, giving it control over any case in which
a suspect fled the original jurisdiction of the crime. Passed at the
height of the gangster scare, the act was part of a wider crime
control package proposed by President Franklin D. Roosevelt.
Consistent with the New Deal trend of extending federal reach, the
act authorized the FBI to step in and take over investigations from
local authorities. Specifically, the act gave the FBI primary investigative responsibility for cases of unlawful flight involving murder,
kidnapping, burglary, rape, assault with a deadly weapon, and threats
of violence. In 1936 and 1938, respectively, Rinaldo DePietro and
James W. Borton were accused of murder, generally a state crime that
would not involve the FBI. However, because both of the men fled
the country—DePietro to Chile, Borton to Cuba—the Feds took
over their cases. Other legislation that extended the jurisdiction of
the FBI included the Stolen Property Act, the Anti-Racketeering
Act, the National Firearms Act, and amendments to the National
Bank Act and the Federal Kidnapping Act.[21]

The Pinkertons were losing ground to the FBI, and this became
even more apparent with the rise of J. Edgar Hoover to the head of
the agency in 1924. A number of innovations put in place by Hoover
made the Pinkertons increasingly obsolete when it came to the international pursuit of fugitives. Hoover expanded the reach of the

FBI through innovations in technology, particularly the use of fingerprints. On taking control of the agency, one of the first things Hoover did was create the Identification Division (known as "Ident") to collect fingerprints from police departments nationwide. While the Pinkertons had pioneered the practice of collecting the fingerprints of known criminals, the FBI centralized numerous collections in its massive database. In the late 1920s, the FBI started exchanging fingerprints with Canada, and in 1932, it added twenty-two other nations. The following year, it created a corresponding civil fingerprint file for noncriminal cases. By 1946, the total reservoir of fingerprint cards had swelled to 100 million.[22]

Hoover's FBI also surpassed the Pinkertons in terms of international cooperation. Since its earliest years, the Bureau of Investigation circulated Identification Orders (IOs)—early wanted posters that included fingerprints and other details about criminal suspects on the run—throughout Canada and Europe. There also were attempts to create formal alliances between police departments for the purpose of exchanging information. The U.S.-based International Association of Chiefs of Police (IACP) organized a conference in New York in 1922, but it failed to attract much attention outside of the United States and Canada. More successful was a meeting in Vienna in 1923, where the International Criminal Police Commission (ICPC)—the precursor to Interpol—was founded. Meant to facilitate international police cooperation, the ICPC constructed a database of criminals and criminal activity around the world. The United States sent an informal delegate to the Vienna conference, and formally joined the ICPC in 1938. In 1940, the FBI opened its first Legal Attaché office in London; by the end of the decade, the bureau had similar offices, called "Legats," in Mexico City, Ottawa, Bogotá, Paris, and Panama City.[23]

By the 1930s, the Pinkerton National Detective Agency was effectively shut out of international manhunts. J. C. Meinbress, superintendent of the San Francisco office, wrote to the State Department with great deference in 1930: "If it is not asking too much, may we be advised on the following point: What are the names of the countries with which the United States has no extradition treaty?" After the State Department refused this request, Meinbress wrote back, slightly more irritated: "I may not have made it clear in my first letter as to the object of wanting the information about extradition treaties. It is not idle curiosity. We serve banks, insurance companies, and other business houses extensively, and questions of this type frequently come up. . . . It is merely to further the ends of justice that the information is desired." The State Department again refused to supply the information.[24]

Also in 1930, Allan Pinkerton II (the grandson of the founder) died, and his son Robert A. Pinkerton took over the firm. A graduate of Harvard University and Columbia Law School, Robert Pinkerton was initially reluctant to give up his job as a Wall Street stockbroker. He told a reporter that when he took over the agency, he "started from scratch." He had no experience as a detective; he had never even taken part in an investigation. All he knew about the family business was "what I heard my father discuss at home." During the next thirty-seven years, he would drastically reshape the firm and adapt it to modern conditions.[25]

During Robert Pinkerton's tenure, the focus of the agency shifted from detective work to security services. Rather than performing investigations, the guarding of property became central to its business. During World War II, Pinkerton operatives were hired to guard war supply plants. The agency also provided uniformed security forces for industrial projects and sporting events. Its biggest job was the 1964 New York World's Fair, for which the Pinkertons supplied 4,500 security personnel. In a sign of the times, the firm removed the word "detective" from its name in 1965 and changed it simply to Pinkerton's, Inc. By the time of Robert Pinkerton's death in 1967, security services made up 90 percent of the agency's business; it had grown from a $2 million operation to a $71 million a year company with 18,000 employees and branch offices in sixty-five U.S. and Canadian cities.[26]

Pinkerton's, Inc. thrived as a private security business, but the agency's place in popular culture faded when it stopped conducting private investigations. "The importance of a private detective agency may be difficult for a modern reader to understand," explained the *Illinois Central Magazine* in January 1946, "but in his day Allan Pinkerton and his agency were as well known as Edgar J. Hoover [*sic*] and the F.B.I. are today." A. W. Parsons, the American correspondent for London's *Sunday Dispatch*, elaborated on the change in situation for his readers in a 1950 article: "Today private detectives seldom track down the perpetrators of spectacular crimes, such as robbery with violence, murder, and kidnapping. Changes in federal laws, extradition treaties, and scientific methods now enable the police or F.B.I. to deal with many cases where private detectives would formerly have operated." The changing of the guard—from the Pinkertons to the FBI—was complete.[27]

✻

The mandate of private detective agencies like Pinkerton's had been simple. The paying clients decided whom they pursued, and these patrons most often were banks and big businesses. Consequently, private detectives who crossed borders most likely were chasing professional thieves or middle-management embezzlers. In contrast, the jurisdiction of the FBI encompassed anyone who committed a federal crime. Answering only to the Department of Justice, the FBI had the flexibility and the command to go after a much broader set of criminals than the Pinkertons.

Nevertheless, the FBI was largely driven by the same basic objective as the Pinkertons: the protection of private property. The fugitives who helped the FBI make a national name for itself—Bonnie and Clyde, John Dillinger—were first and foremost bank robbers. Their violent and sensational crimes received the most media attention (and did the most to consolidate the FBI's power), but in reality, it was far more common for G-men to spend their time tracking more prosaic financial fugitives. Between 1918 and 1940, nearly 25 percent of the FBI's international investigations were for violations of the National Bank Act. Embezzlement was the most common offense for the Feds to investigate, much as it had been for private detectives in earlier decades.[28]

The story of Samuel Insull, the most prominent extradition case of the 1930s, illustrates both the continuities and the changes in international investigations. On the one hand, Insull was indicted for some familiar financial offenses, including embezzlement and fraud. Yet he also was one of the nation's most eminent business magnates.

Along with Thomas Edison, he cofounded the company that became General Electric, and then went on to build up a vast web of power, utility, and transportation companies. By the end of the 1920s, his empire was worth $3 billion. In other words, Insull was the kind of person who would have *hired* the Pinkertons, not the sort of rough-neck desperado or middle manager that the Pinkertons so often pursued. By investigating Insull, the FBI signaled that it would take on a new type of "public enemy": the corrupt industrialist. In the context of the Great Depression, the financial elite was the new popular foe, and for the first time, someone who represented the interests of capital became the target of the international manhunt. The FBI was still protecting private property, only now it was looking out for those whose savings had been lost by investing in Insull's companies.[29]

Following the stock market crash of 1929, Insull became a scape-goat for the public's frustration with the financial woes of the na-tion. The collapse of his companies seemed to embody the excesses of American business. Thousands of Americans had bought millions of dollars of stocks, which were now worthless. In 1932, Insull owed $16 million more than his worth; according to one banker, he was "too broke to be bankrupt." Orson Welles later claimed that Charles Foster Kane, the protagonist of *Citizen Kane*, was partially mod-eled on Insull's rise and fall. Insull's photographs on the cover of *Time* magazine illustrated his transformation from national hero to na-tional villain. In 1929, a serene Insull beamed from the front cover; five years later, the cover revealed a dejected old man trying to hide his face from the camera.[30]

Fifteen FBI agents led a six-month investigation against Insull, providing Department of Justice attorney Dwight H. Green with "bales and bales of ammunition." In some ways, the utilities mag-nate seemed an unlikely target, as he previously had a comfortable relationship with federal law enforcement. He was widely believed to be a member of the Secret Six, a group of influential Chicago busi-nessmen who helped bring down Al Capone in 1931 and funded the legal team that brought tax evasion charges against the gangster. But the Roosevelt administration was determined to prosecute Insull. In a campaign speech in 1932, Franklin Delano Roosevelt targeted him by name, vowing to save the common man—gouged for years by the private utility companies—from "the Ishmaels and Insulls, whose hand is against every man's." Insull also was a longtime foe of Harold L. Ickes, who became secretary of the interior in 1933.[31]

Insull was in Paris when, in October 1932, he was indicted on charges of bankruptcy fraud, embezzlement, and mail fraud. Before he could be extradited, he took flight from France to Greece. The United States and Greece had negotiated an extradition treaty in 1931, but Congress had not yet ratified it. As soon as Insull chose his refuge, the Senate sped up ratification of the treaty. After a long and highly publicized hearing, the Greek courts ultimately refused to extradite, claiming that there was not enough evidence to prove Insull's guilt. As one political cartoon evocatively expressed, Americans were frustrated that the fugitive was "Insull-ated" in Greece. The refusal to surrender Insull upset Washington so much that the State Department denounced the Greek extradition treaty.[32]

The State Department used diplomatic pressure to finally get hold of Insull. With the end of Prohibition in the United States in 1933, the Greek wine and liquor interests were concerned about getting their product into the U.S. market. Afraid of souring U.S.-Greek relations, the Greek government informed Insull that his visa would not be renewed and he would have to leave the country by January 1, 1934. Insull obtained a small steamboat, the SS *Maiotis*, and began sailing to Romania. His boat stopped in the Bosporus to stock up on fuel, food, and supplies and, at the request of American authorities, was seized by Turkish police, who took Insull into custody. Although there was no extradition treaty between the United States and Turkey, Turkey voluntarily handed him over. Burton Y. Beery, the American vice consul at Istanbul, accompanied him back to the United States. When they arrived in New York, FBI agents were waiting on the dock to arrest Insull and take him back to Chicago.[33]

Insull is generally remembered for his fall and flight more than the actual outcome of his case. Tried on three separate charges, he was acquitted each time. Yet his reputation was ruined and he died penniless in a Paris metro station a few years later. The point had been made. In a sign of the times, the FBI was going to go after the financial bigwigs, not just the middle managers. There was new fed-

Insull-ated!

"Insull-ated!" Utilities magnate Samuel Insull
avoids U.S. extradition in Greece, but is eventually
extradited by Turkey. Edmund Gale, *Los Angeles
Times*, December 29, 1932. Copyright © 1932 *Los
Angeles Times*. Reprinted with permission.

eral oversight of swindlers and corporate tycoons in this post-Ponzi,
New Deal age.

Pinkerton detectives may have been a thing of the past, but their
techniques continued to influence the FBI and other law enforcement
agencies. Federal agencies eventually adopted and institutionalized
many of the tasks and tactics originated by the Pinkertons. One of
these was the willingness to set aside formal extradition treaties and
instead turn to informal methods of rendition to capture fugitives.

Legal scholar M. Cherif Bassiouni describes irregular rendition
as falling into three categories: "(1) the abduction and kidnapping of

a person in one state by agents of another state; (2) the informal surrender of a person by agents of one state to another without formal
or legal process; and (3) the use of immigration laws as a device to
directly or indirectly surrender a person or place him in a position
in which he or she can be taken into custody by the agents of another state." In the early twentieth century, the FBI and other federal agencies—including the U.S. Army, the Border Patrol, and the
Federal Bureau of Narcotics—did all three. They regularly relied on
the precedent set by the Pinkertons in *Ker v. Illinois* (1886), that
failure to adhere to formal extradition procedures did not invalidate
an international capture.[34]

Irregular rendition was the norm along the U.S.-Mexico border
during the years of the Mexican Revolution. Diplomatic relations
broke down between the United States and Mexico in 1913, after the
fall of the Francisco Madero regime. Not recognizing any legitimate
Mexican government, the United States cut off extradition with its
neighbor to the south. There would be no formal extradition between the two countries for a decade. Yet cross-border crime continued; in fact, given the chaos of the Mexican Revolution, lawlessness only increased. To maintain any semblance of the rule of law in
the borderlands, it was necessary to use tactics that were more informal to apprehend fugitives.[35]

The Punitive Expedition of 1916–1917, in which General John
J. Pershing led U.S. Army troops into Mexico in search of the revolutionary Pancho Villa, was a consequence of the breakdown of
the extradition treaty. If extradition had been in place, the United
States could have asked Mexico to hand over Villa to stand trial for
the crime of killing eighteen people in Columbus, New Mexico.
Mexico might have refused; however, the lack of any functioning
system of extradition left many Americans with the perception that
they had no choice but to breach the border and chase down Villa
and his men. A 1916 cartoon by Clifford Berryman illustrates the
limited sense of options that Americans felt they had after the Villa
attack. They could stay on their own side of the border and passively
accept the affront or they could jump the fence and take action. Extradition, or any sort of cooperation from Mexican authorities, was
not on the table.[36]

"I've Had about Enough of This": Uncle Sam leaps across the Mexican border to chase Pancho Villa. March 10, 1916. Clifford Berryman collection, National Archives and Records Administration.

Gus T. Jones, a Texas Ranger who joined the FBI's San Antonio office in 1921, negotiated a functioning system of informal rendition along the Mexican border. According to biographer George Ellis, the special agent had such a friendly relationship with his law enforcement counterparts on the Mexican side that they would frequently hand fugitives to each other without going through any formal procedures: "A fugitive would suddenly appear at a border port, be walked halfway across the international bridge by the Mexican police, and then 'welcomed' by the American police. It may have been extra-legal, but it worked." Jones himself reported to FBI Headquarters in 1923 that he had "perfected a most excellent arrangement along the border in the San Antonio district whereby we are assured the most hearty cooperation of all border Mexican authorities" in handing over American fugitives who hid in Mexico.[37]

One of Jones's victories was the capture of Joseph Baiata, handed over by Mexican authorities to the FBI in the summer of 1923, shortly before the United States resumed diplomatic relations with Mexico. Baiata, a barber turned banker who also went by the name Joseph B. Marsino, was accused of embezzling more than $220,000 of bonds from the First National Bank of Warren, Massachusetts. The FBI had spent considerable time and expense tracking Baiata and David Lamar, another fugitive, to Mexico City. But with no extradition, how could they be brought to justice? The attorney general confidentially suggested that the State Department take up the matter "with the proper representatives of the Mexican Government with the view of having these two individuals taken into custody by the Mexican authorities and deported to the United States." Ultimately, this was exactly what happened. Baiata was deported as a "pernicious foreigner" under article 33 of the Mexican Constitution and delivered to Jones himself at the Texas border. This was a quid pro quo: at the same time, the United States deported Patricio Camarena, a Mexican postmaster charged with malfeasance in office, swindling, and forgery, who escaped to the United States after breaking out of a Mexican prison. Because he was a convict, Camarena had violated U.S. immigration law by entering the country.[38]

After the formal recognition by the United States of Álvaro Obregón's government on August 31, 1923—just days after Baiata's deportation—formal extradition resumed between the United States and Mexico. The first person extradited under these newly resumed relations was Bob Bates, a bootlegger and smuggler, who killed a customs officer named Wallen at Del Rio, Texas, and escaped to the Mexican side. He was extradited on October 1, 1923. Slowly but steadily, extradition relations normalized between the two countries.[39]

Nevertheless, informal rendition—handing over fugitives without complying with the legal requirements for extradition—continued. In 1940, FBI agents were implicated in the kidnapping of Juan Barrena from Mexico. Barrena was wanted in San Francisco in connection with a Spanish prisoner swindle, an old confidence trick similar to today's Nigerian prince scam. Allegedly, Barrena told his victims that he was in correspondence with a wealthy nobleman who had been imprisoned in Spain; if the mark sent money to secure his release, he was promised a reward after the prisoner's liberation. According to Barrena's sister, two men who posed as Mexican Secret Service agents detained her brother, bound and gagged him, took him by automobile to the border, and handed him over to waiting FBI agents, who gave the Mexican abductors a reward. Although the Mexican press was adamant that "G-Men" had kidnapped Barrena, J. Edgar Hoover denied that the FBI was involved in the case. Instead, he pointed the finger at another federal agency, claiming that investigators from the Post Office Department had orchestrated the abduction. Either way, agents of the U.S. government were implicated in the act.[40]

The Mexican newspaper *Excélsior* reported that this was not the only recent incident of abduction. In Piedras Negras, a Mexican citizen named José Benavides, accused of killing his wife in Texas, was arrested pending extradition papers. Given that Mexico generally declined to extradite citizens, it looked unlikely that he would be surrendered. However, on September 12, 1940, the warden removed Benavides from his cell and delivered him to U.S. Border Patrol agents, who "extradited" him immediately. The Border Patrol agents paid the warden a reward of either $500 or $5,000, depending on the account. Benavides was eventually put to death by electric chair in San Antonio, Texas.[41]

Increasingly, the Mexican government was not willing to put up with these irregular renditions. The Secretaría de Relaciones Exteriores (Office of Foreign Relations) protested when American authorities brought fugitives across the border without adhering to the extradition treaty. In January 1934, San Antonio constable Eduardo Villareal informally arranged for his counterparts on the Mexican side to hand over Luis Lopez, a drug smuggler wanted for violation of the Harrison Narcotics Act. Lopez was taken by car to the Rio Grande, then put in a bathtub and towed across the river into United States territory (newspapers dubbed this the "bathtub kidnapping"). The government in Mexico City was outraged. It demanded that Constable Villareal and Tomas Hernandez, another San Antonio policeman, be extradited to Mexico to stand trial on the charge of kidnapping. Despite an impassioned defense of Villareal and Hernandez by the citizens of San Antonio, a U.S. commissioner ordered the two men extradited to Mexico that May.[42]

In *Ex parte Lopez* (1934), the district court in Texas heard Lopez's application for habeas corpus. The government of Mexico intervened in the judicial proceedings, claiming that Mexico's sovereignty had been violated through the abduction. It requested that Lopez be surrendered to Mexican authorities, who would hold him in custody in Mexico pending the hearing of an extradition application. However, the district court, citing *Ker v. Illinois*, dismissed Lopez's petition and rejected Mexico's request. The court's opinion conceded that "the intervention of the government of Mexico raises serious questions, involving the claimed violation of its sovereignty," but suggested that the complaint "be presented to the Executive Department of the United States," as "this court has no jurisdiction." Mexico's sovereignty may have been violated, but that was irrelevant to the case at hand.[43]

Although cases of Mexican law enforcers kidnapping fugitives from the United States were rare, those that did occur caused diplomatic ripples. Two young Americans "who appear to be but boys," Edward M. Blatt and Lawrence F. Converse, were kidnapped from El Paso and brought to a prison in Ciudad Juárez. The twenty-one-year-olds had briefly joined the revolutionary forces in Mexico and had stayed in an insurrectionist camp, but they claimed that they had abandoned the cause and were on their way home. They were standing about 500 feet from the border, on the American side, when four Mexicans accosted them. According to their account, the men took all their possessions, bound them by rope, forcibly transported them across the Rio Grande, and handed them to Mexican soldiers. They were then held incommunicado in the Juárez jail for three days and charged with sedition. They remained imprisoned for two months, but after great diplomatic pressure from the State Department, were released in April 1911.[44]

Mexico might try kidnapping, but when faced with the disapproval of the United States, it could not get away with it. In 1914, Samuel Cantú, the wealthy former mayor of Lampazos, Mexico, was lured to the international bridge in Laredo, Texas, by a decoy letter. Mexican *federales* seized him on the U.S. side and then dragged him into Mexico. He was tried quickly and sentenced to be shot, although the charges against him were never made public. Outraged Texas newspapers tried to stir up public anger; in one of its largest fonts, the *El Paso Herald* proclaimed on the top of its front page: "U.S. Soil Violated." For a few days, the Cantú kidnapping became a bona fide diplomatic dispute. Alerted by the American consul in Nuevo Laredo, the State Department demanded Cantú's immediate release and return. Secretary of State William Jennings Bryan threatened that if the demand was not complied with, the United States government "will find it necessary to consider drastic measures." The diplomatic pressure worked: four days later, Cantú was released and returned to the United States. He immediately sent telegraphs of thanks to Secretary of State Bryan and Texas governor Oscar Colquitt.[45]

Rogue Canadian officers also kidnapped fugitives from the United States, but generally had to release them once their superiors in the Canadian government found out. Although the 1905 case of *The King v. Walton* resulted in a ruling similar to *Ker*, the Canadian government preferred to avoid abductions. In 1908, Adeland Lafond was seized in Illinois, taken to Canada, and held in a Winnipeg jail. He complained to the U.S. consul, at whose request he was released by order of the attorney general of Canada and taken back to Illinois. Similarly, in September 1909, a man named Marker was abducted on the American side of the border by two men in plain clothes, one of whom alleged that he was a constable of the North West Mounted Police, and brought to Canada. After the matter was taken up with the British ambassador in Washington, he wrote to the acting U.S. secretary of state to say that Marker would be released and allowed to return to the United States, and blamed the incident on confusion about where the boundary line was.[46]

However, when American agents engaged in "informal extraditions" on the Canadian border, they did not have to release their arrestees. Charles H. Unverzagt claimed that he was abducted from Vancouver, British Colombia, on April 24, 1924. American law enforcers, he testified, forcibly took him over the border to Washington State to face charges of mail fraud. In the case of *United States v. Unverzagt*, the Ninth Circuit Court of Appeals dismissed his application for habeas corpus, once again citing *Ker v. Illinois*. The abduction did not invalidate the arrest.[47]

But the abduction could result in punishment for the offending officer. In 1931, two Federal Bureau of Narcotics agents, Sarro Vaccaro and Fred G. Mertz, were accused of kidnapping and murdering suspected drug dealers from Quebec. According to testimony, Vaccaro and Mertz crossed into Canada and bought narcotics from two dealers named Amedee Bilodeau and Robert Price. The agents succeeded in enticing Bilodeau into the United States and arrested him. Then they returned with their prisoner to the international boundary line near Calais, Vermont, with the hope of getting Price across the line. Bilodeau attempted to escape and was shot and killed by Mertz, while Price was pulled across the line by Vaccaro and taken to jail. Canada requested Vaccaro's extradition on the charge of kidnapping, and a U.S. commissioner agreed to surrender him. Canada also requested Mertz's extradition on the charge of murder, but it was denied, as it was not clear whether the killing took place in Canada or the United States.[48]

The fact that Americans were punished for carrying out irregular renditions indicated that the U.S. government did not condone the practice. In fact, the State Department actively tried to discourage any deviation from formal extradition treaties. It was particularly perturbed when Los Angeles detective Antonio Felix abducted Antonio Martinez from Baja California in 1905, plying the wanted man with alcohol until he passed out and then smuggling him across the border in a carriage. The State Department refused to give Martinez back, but extradited Detective Felix to Mexico to stand trial for kidnapping.[49]

After the advent of the Good Neighbor Policy, Franklin D. Roosevelt's administration emphasized reciprocal exchanges rather than unilateral snatches. As Secretary of State Cordell Hull stated, no nation "has the right to intervene in the internal or external affairs of another." However, although American agents like Villareal, Vaccaro, and Felix ultimately had to answer for their extralegal actions in Mexico and Canada, the arrests they made remained valid. Even if fugitives ended up in the United States by shady or duplicitous means, they would still be tried in U.S. courts of law. Whether brought in by the Pinkertons in the 1880s or federal agents in the 1930s, the *Ker v. Illinois* precedent persevered.[50]

✳

J. Edgar Hoover made his reputation waging war against some of America's most notorious gangsters in the 1920s and 1930s. The manhunts and shoot-outs are the stuff of legend, but generally they are remembered only as domestic pursuits, dragnets that stayed within the boundaries of the United States. However, searches for prominent gangsters often had an international component as well. These were fierce manhunts, and Hoover wanted to leave no stone unturned. In the mid-1930s, the FBI opened international investigations against three people labeled, at different times, "Public Enemy Number One"—John Dillinger, "Baby Face" Nelson, and Alvin Karpis. Ultimately, none of them was apprehended abroad. Yet the very presence of an international element to these high-profile chases signaled that the FBI's dominion would not stop at the borders of the United States. Similar to the Pinkertons, Hoover built the reputation of the FBI on the notion that there was nowhere in the world where a fugitive could escape American justice.

John Dillinger himself warned authorities that he planned to flee abroad. In January 1934, police in Tucson, Arizona, arrested the notorious bank robber and three members of his gang. While in custody, he freely admitted to police that his plan was to leave the country that summer for South America, where he hoped to become a rancher. Just more than a month later, after being sent to Indiana to stand trial, Dillinger escaped from jail using a gun carved out of wood. Following the sensational prison break, he stole a car and crossed state lines, giving the FBI jurisdiction to join the manhunt. For the next few months, as the FBI tried in vain to recapture him, newspapers speculated as to his whereabouts. "Is Dillinger Dead? Wounded? Or Fled U.S.?" asked the *Atlanta Daily World*. Its theory was "that Dillinger and his henchman, John Hamilton, have fled the country to a South American sanctuary to which they had previously dispatched the greater portion of their loot."[51]

Newspaper articles assured the public that the FBI could catch Dillinger anywhere in the world. A 1934 feature in the *Washington Post* pointed out that the FBI's Identification Division exchanged fingerprints with fifty-nine foreign countries. "If a badly sought criminal flees the United States," it claimed, "he is very likely to find that the police of almost any country in which he tries to hide will receive his fingerprints from Washington." Indeed, it affirmed, the public need not worry about John Dillinger escaping the United States. Dillinger's prints have been sent "round the world. . . . There is practically no large city in Europe, Asia or South America where he could not be positively identified within a few minutes."[52]

Although FBI records do not indicate a South American search for the outlaw, they do reveal a transatlantic hunt. On May 4, 1934, the FBI received intelligence that Dillinger was on the Canadian Pacific liner *Duchess of York*, headed for Scotland, Ireland, and finally England. A mysterious coded cablegram had mentioned both Dillinger's name and the name of the ship. The ship was due to arrive at its first port the next day, so FBI officials immediately got in touch with Scotland Yard. Dozens of newspaper reporters, photographers, and even cameramen met the ship at Greenock, Scotland, in the hopes of witnessing the arrest of America's "Public Enemy Number One." The ship was searched from stem to stern, and the passengers examined by immigration officials, but Dillinger was not found. Indeed, it turned out that he had never left the Midwest. Two and a half months later, on July 22, 1934, he would be shot and killed by FBI agents outside the Biograph Theater in Chicago.[53]

Later in 1934, similar reports surfaced regarding the FBI's new "Public Enemy Number One"—Lester Joseph Gillis, better known as "Baby Face" Nelson. Based on pictures in the newspapers, a resident of Havana, Cuba, reported to the American consul that she had seen Nelson in the city. The FBI promptly jumped on the lead. It sent cards containing Nelson's description, photograph, and fingerprints to Cuban authorities (Identification Order No. 1223). A local newspaper printed a reproduction of the cards and, according to the consul, it was determined that the suspected person was not Baby Face Nelson. Nevertheless, the FBI was closing in on him. Less than a month later, Nelson would be killed in a shoot-out with FBI agents in Barrington, Illinois.[54]

The last "Public Enemy Number One" to be captured (the label eventually gave way to the FBI's "Top Ten Most Wanted" list), the gangster Alvin "Creepy" Karpis, also was the target of an international manhunt. Hotel manager Nathaniel Heller was charged in a Miami court of harboring Karpis and a female companion at the Hotel Parkview in the beach resort of Varadero, Cuba, from September to December 1934. An American woman also in the area recognized Karpis from photographs and contacted the American consul in Havana, who passed the information on to the State Department and the FBI. Two FBI agents came to the hotel looking for the suspicious guest, but by that time he had departed. Purportedly under the orders of these FBI agents, Cuban authorities detained Heller (though J. Edgar Hoover claimed that they voluntarily offered to arrest him as an undesirable alien and deport him). It was only then, Heller claimed, that he discovered the guest was Karpis. Heller said that the man had gone under the name of E. M. Wagner, and that he was "just the same as any other guest at the hotel." But according to Hoover, Heller served as a go-between in Cuba for the disposal of kidnapping money from the Karpis-Barker gang. A Miami judge later dropped the charges and Heller threatened to sue the Department of Justice and Special Agents McKee and Brown.[55]

The FBI wanted to show not only that there was no place to hide from American justice but also that the United States was not safe ground for foreign fugitives. Therefore, it also spent considerable time and effort searching for fugitives from other countries who took refuge in the United States. In fact, the FBI took the responsibility of rooting out foreign criminals so seriously that, in June 1940, Assistant Secretary of State Adolf A. Berle instructed the agency "not to investigate on requests from British Consulates. Otherwise, the F.B.I. would be doing nothing else."[56]

The FBI was receptive to requests from foreign diplomats; indeed, Hoover often reported on these cases personally. In 1941, Luis Fernández, the minister of Costa Rica in Washington, was charged by his government with finding José María Sandoval Lara, convicted in Costa Rica of embezzlement *(estafa)*. "The investigation has been difficult," Fernández wrote to Secretary of State Cordell Hull in March 1941, "and for that reason I am writing to the Department, requesting the cooperation of the Department of Justice in order to be able to ascertain the place of residence of Sandoval Lara whose extradition the Government of Costa Rica proposes to request." The case was handed over to the FBI, and a month later, Hoover wrote a "Personal and Confidential" letter to the State Department to report on Sandoval's situation. A man meeting Sandoval's description had been arrested in November 1938 in New Orleans for stealing a sum of money from the desk of the Costa Rican consul there. He was then turned over to the immigration authorities. "I will be pleased to have a wanted notice posted against this man's record should the Minister of Costa Rica believe he is identical with the fugitive in whom he is interested," Hoover offered. The next month, he reported that the FBI discovered from the Bureau of Immigration and Naturalization Service that Sandoval had been deported in June 1939 on a steamship headed from New Orleans to Puerto Limón, Costa Rica. However, he somehow ended up in Bogotá, Colombia, and according to a letter, hoped to go to work for an oil company there, save some money, and return to the United States.[57]

Great Britain wanted Alexander Strakosch, alias Alexander Graham, for the crime of fraudulent conversion and obtaining money or valuable securities by false pretenses. Hoover wrote directly to the State Department to report that Strakosch was living in Brentwood, California, a suburb of Los Angeles, and promised to keep his men monitoring the fugitive's movements. In January 1939, a special agent of the FBI apprehended him. Despite Strakosch's strenuous objection that, as a German citizen, he would be held as a prisoner of war, the United States extradited him to Britain in May 1940. There was nowhere to hide internationally and there would be nowhere to hide domestically, the FBI vowed.[58]

※

Between 1936 and 1941, the La Follette Civil Liberties Committee tapped into the public discomfort with unregulated private detective agencies that bore too much power. This congressional subcommittee launched an investigation into the five biggest private detective firms in the United States. Before receiving his subpoena, Robert Pinkerton frantically destroyed incriminating company records; he also reportedly encouraged employees to lie on the stand. Still, the committee found enough evidence to declare that, as late as 1937, both the Pinkerton and Burns agencies had sent spies to infiltrate labor unions. This revelation caused an immediate backlash. As in the wake of the Homestead Strike, the public felt uncomfortable with the idea of a private army, unaccountable to the people, carrying out actions of questionable legality. By shifting the powers of investigation to a state agency, there was at least a semblance of greater accountability, responsibility, and legitimacy.[59]

Although the FBI inherited many of the practices pioneered by the Pinkertons, the two organizations were far from identical. Despite the fact that both were fundamentally committed to the protection of private property, the FBI took on a wider variety of cases than the Pinkertons. Progressive and New Deal legislation empowered the FBI to delve into a host of new federal offenses. The FBI also went after new types of offenders, specifically representatives of big business like Samuel Insull. Most significant, international investigations bore the imprimatur of the state. A branch of the government, not a private company, now served as the long arm of American law.

EPILOGUE
How Rendition Became Extraordinary

*H*ASSAN MUSTAFA OSAMA NASR, also known as Abu Omar, was an Egyptian cleric living in Milan, Italy. In February 2003, without the consent of local authorities, Central Intelligence Agency (CIA) agents seized him as he was walking to a mosque for noon prayers. They then put him on a private jet and transported him to a prison in Egypt.[1]

The Abu Omar kidnapping caused an uproar in Italy. In November 2009, an Italian court convicted twenty-three CIA agents on the charge of illegal abduction. Because they were tried in absentia, the guilty verdict was largely symbolic. One judge, Guido Salvini, condemned the violation of Italy's territorial sovereignty. "Abu Omar's kidnapping is not only illegal, for it breached Italian sovereignty," he asserted, "but it is also an ill-omened and polluting act with regard to the whole fight against terrorism." Yet abductions like Abu Omar's were not an aberration. They were a central component of the United States' strategy in the war on terror in the early twenty-first century, part of a program called extraordinary rendition.[2]

Adding the adjective "extraordinary" to rendition changes its fundamental meaning. Ordinary rendition—even by abduction—results in a trial. Suspects are taken back to the United States in order to face their day in court with the proper judicial safeguards. The defendant may appeal a ruling, apply for a writ of habeas corpus, or even be acquitted. Abductees have brought their appeals all the way to the U.S. Supreme Court. Extraordinary rendition, in contrast, rarely involves a trial. Instead, in a tactic that began under the Clinton administration and ballooned after 9/11, suspects are brought to third countries to be interrogated, often with the use of harsh and coercive techniques. Criminal charges are rare, and judicial supervision and review are absent.[3]

Despite their core differences, however, a direct line can be drawn from nineteenth- to twenty-first-century practices. Extraordinary rendition was not a policy that emerged, sui generis, after 9/11. It developed gradually, beginning with the 1886 decision in *Ker v. Illinois* and evolving through the twentieth century. *Ker* held that even when a suspect was kidnapped from another country, U.S. courts still retained jurisdiction. Over time, that precedent was stretched to defend violations of another state's territorial sovereignty and breaches of customary international law. Even though the U.S. government has shrouded its own rationales for extraordinary rendition behind the doctrine of state secrets, commentators and law professors explaining the practice have repeatedly pointed to *Ker* and subsequent cases as justification.[4]

After World War II, the *Ker* precedent was invoked repeatedly. Perhaps the most famous international kidnapping of the twentieth century—the 1960 seizure of Adolf Eichmann from Argentina by Israeli agents—was justified in court in part by invoking *Ker v. Illinois*. Not only private actors, as in *Ker*'s day, but also state agents frequently turned to the ruling to defend their actions. In 1950, Morton Sobell, an electrical engineer working for the navy, was accused of being a Soviet spy, part of Julius Rosenberg's espionage ring. Sobell and his family fled to Mexico City, where, a few weeks later, he was kidnapped by armed men, transported to the U.S. border, and handed over to the FBI. Citing *Ker*, the U.S. Court of Appeals for the Second Circuit ruled that the abduction presented no jurisdictional impediment to trial.[5]

In 1952, the Supreme Court expanded the *Ker* doctrine. The case of *Frisbie v. Collins* involved a domestic rather than an international abduction: a murder suspect was seized in Illinois and taken to Michigan to stand trial. Although this violated the Federal Kidnapping Statute, the court ruled that it did not invalidate the arrest. Judges would not question how a defendant ended up in custody. The principle of noninquiry, or *male captus, bene detentus* (wrongly captured, properly detained), from that point forward would be known in U.S. courts as the *Ker-Frisbie* doctrine, applicable to both domestic and international kidnappings.[6]

During the 1970s, however, it looked like the *Ker-Frisbie* precedent might be in trouble. The American judicial system had just gone through a "due process revolution," in which the Supreme Court vastly expanded procedural rights for accused persons. In *Mapp v. Ohio* (1961), for instance, the court ruled that evidence obtained in violation of the Fourth Amendment could not be used in state criminal prosecutions. One commentator noted the "bizarre state" of American law: the courts would not admit stolen evidence, but they would admit stolen people. In 1973, the U.S. Court of Appeals for the Second Circuit heard the case of Francisco Toscanino, an Italian citizen who was wanted in the United States on narcotics charges. Toscanino was kidnapped from his home in Uruguay, interrogated in Brazil for three weeks, and then flown to the United States. In Brazil, he claimed, U.S. agents from the Bureau of Narcotics and Dangerous Drugs had participated in questioning him under torture. Interrogators had pinched his fingers with metal pliers, flushed alcohol into his eyes and nose, forced fluids up his anal passage, and electrocuted him with wires attached to his earlobes, toes, and genitals. The U.S. government refused to confirm or deny these allegations. The court, clearly disturbed by these grievances, granted Toscanino's habeas corpus petition and released him. When a rendition "shocks the conscience," it ruled, the courts should not have jurisdiction. Acknowledging the constitutional revolution that had occurred in the previous decade, it predicted the "erosion" of the *Ker-Frisbie* doctrine. Applauded by human rights activists, the *Toscanino* decision seemed to substantially curtail judicial tolerance of international abductions.[7]

But the death knell for *Ker-Frisbie* was premature. During the next few years, courts repeatedly decided that international abductions did not meet the "shocks the conscience" standard set by *Toscanino*. In three separate cases within a few years of the *Toscanino* decision, U.S. agents kidnapped Benjamin Zuleta Herrera, Julio Juventino Lujan, and Rafael Lira from different countries in Latin America. However, in each of their cases, the courts denied habeas corpus: applying *Ker*, they ruled that the court was not divested of jurisdiction by virtue of the kidnapping. In *Lujan v. Gengler*, a more conservative Second Circuit court held that only "government conduct of the most shocking and outrageous character" would justify declining jurisdiction over someone who had been abducted. In the Lira case, the defendant claimed that he had been tortured during interrogation by members of the Chilean police before being put on a plane to the United States, but his petition was still denied. These cases set the stage for more audacious abductions in the future.[8]

The modern practice of extraordinary rendition got its start with two pieces of legislation passed in the mid-1980s that vastly expanded American jurisdiction in cases involving terrorism. The Comprehensive Crime Control Act of 1984 made it a federal crime to take an American hostage anywhere in the world. Broadening this, the Omnibus Diplomatic Security and Antiterrorism Act of 1986 made a terrorist attack against an American anywhere in the world a violation of American law. Through these pieces of legislation, the United States asserted extraterritorial jurisdiction—a crime did not need to take place on U.S. soil for it to be tried in U.S. courts. This was called the passive personality principle; jurisdiction was based on the nationality of the victim, not where the crime occurred.[9]

Still, the Reagan administration was having difficulty gaining custody over suspected terrorists: the United States lacked extradition treaties with the countries most commonly harboring terrorists, and states sometimes asserted that the suspects were not eligible for extradition since their crimes were "political." The more hawkish presidential advisers and members of Congress pushed to make abduction a more central part of America's counterterrorism strategy. Leading the charge was Republican senator Arlen Specter, a member of the Senate Judiciary Committee. Specter was not only aware of the *Ker* precedent, but made it his mission to spread knowledge of the case, even writing about *Ker v. Illinois* in an op-ed article— entitled "How to Make Terrorists Think Twice"—in the *New York Times*. Specter argued that "we should be prepared to resort to forcible seizure and arrest" and, indeed, were entitled to do so under the *Ker-Frisbie* doctrine. In January 1986—in the aftermath of the hijackings of TWA flight 847 and the cruise ship *Achille Lauro*, as well

as terrorist attacks on the Rome and Vienna airports—President
Reagan secretly authorized the CIA to kidnap criminal suspects,
what one official called a "snatch, grab, and deliver operation." Although abductions had been occurring for a century, including by
state actors, this was the first time that it became official government
policy. The next year, the CIA used this authority to lure suspected
hijacker Fawaz Younis to Cyprus and onto a yacht, where FBI agents
captured him in international waters.[10]

Ironically, at the very moment when international abduction
became official government policy, the U.S. government began
clamping down on private bounty hunters. The most prominent incident involved Sidney Jaffe, wanted for land fraud in Florida, who
was kidnapped outside his Toronto home by American bounty
hunters Timm Johnsen and Daniel Kear. The Jaffe matter caused
tensions between the United States and Canada, and in 1986, Johnsen
and Kear were extradited to Canada and convicted of kidnapping.
In an exchange of diplomatic letters between the two countries, Secretary of State George P. Shultz guaranteed that future American
bounty hunters would be similarly extradited. Whereas the Pinkertons had once pioneered the tactic of extraterritorial abduction, now
private civilians were shut out of the process. Bounty hunters would
be punished for international kidnappings, while CIA agents were
legally authorized to perform the same actions. In the nineteenth
century, international abductions had been driven by the desire to
make a profit and the need to discipline white-collar workers; now,
kidnapping was a tool of the state, used in an entirely different way.[11]

The George H. W. Bush administration took the practice of
"lifting" suspects even further, turning its attention not just to terrorism but also to the war on drugs. On December 20, 1989, more
than 24,000 American troops attacked Panama as part of Operation
Nifty Package, aimed at capturing Panamanian head of state Manuel
Noriega. Twenty-six Americans and more than 700 Panamanians,
mostly civilians, were killed. But the invasion force got its man, and
brought Noriega to Miami to stand trial for drug smuggling and
money laundering. Defense lawyers made the argument that the capture violated international law—specifically, the United Nations
charter, which obligated the United States to "refrain . . . from

the . . . use of force against the territorial integrity or political independence of any state" and the Charter of the Organization of American States, which declared that "the territory of a State is inviolable." The military invasion also violated customary international law (rules that derive from custom and practice rather than written law), which prohibited the violation of another state's sovereignty. Citing the *Ker-Frisbie* doctrine, however, the U.S. Court of Appeals for the Eleventh Circuit refused to divest the court of jurisdiction.[12]

For a brief period in the 1970s, it looked like *Ker-Frisbie* might be on the way out, but by the 1990s, the courts were invoking it to defend increasingly brazen abductions. The U.S. Supreme Court finally revisited the issue—and affirmed its commitment to *Ker-Frisbie*—in *United States v. Álvarez-Machain*, a 1992 ruling that would be cited often in the future as a justification for extraordinary rendition. The case involved the 1985 torture and murder of Enrique Camarena Salazar, a U.S. Drug Enforcement Administration (DEA) agent working in Mexico. Dr. Humberto Álvarez Machain was accused of using his medical expertise to keep Camarena alive during his torture so that he could be brutalized longer. Without the permission of the Mexican government, the DEA orchestrated the kidnapping of Álvarez from Guadalajara. Although the actual abduction was carried out mainly by former Mexican military police operating as private agents, the DEA reportedly paid them a reward as soon as Álvarez reached U.S. soil. Two lower courts granted Álvarez's habeas corpus petition, only to be overturned, six to three, by the Supreme Court. *Ker* stood; despite his abduction, the U.S. courts retained jurisdiction.[13]

Álvarez-Machain was a highly controversial decision. The Mexican government vigorously protested both the abduction and the ruling. Álvarez had been kidnapped even though, at worst, he was a relatively minor player in Camarena's murder. The evidence against him was weak; in fact, he was ultimately acquitted of the crime at trial and returned to Mexico. Unlike the unanimous decisions in *Ker* and *Frisbie*, in this case, the Supreme Court was divided. The dissent, written by Justice John Paul Stevens (and joined by Justices Souter and Blackmun), argued that the abduction violated both international law and the terms of the extradition treaty with Mexico. Justice Stevens emphasized that the government's involvement in the kidnapping made it particularly problematic, contending that "a critical flaw pervades the Court's entire opinion. It fails to differentiate between the conduct of private citizens, which does not violate any treaty obligation, and conduct expressly authorized by the Executive Branch of the Government, which unquestionably constitutes a flagrant violation of international law, and in my opinion, also constitutes a breach of our treaty obligations."[14]

The international reactions to *Álvarez-Machain* demonstrated the growing hostility of other countries to the U.S. practice of kidnapping, which they viewed as a violation of international law. A report surveying the reactions of thirty-four countries found that foreign newspapers around the globe overwhelmingly condemned the *Álvarez-Machain* decision, calling it "the law of the jungle" and a return to the principle of "might makes right." Nations that once also had adhered to the *male captus, bene detentus* rule—like Great Britain and Canada—had begun to retreat from it by the 1990s. These countries denounced *Álvarez-Machain* in the strongest terms. The House of Lords, then the highest appellate court in Britain, attacked the Supreme Court's reasoning and result as "monstrous." It continued: "To hold that the court may turn a blind eye to executive lawlessness beyond the frontiers of its own jurisdiction is . . . an insular and unacceptable view."[15]

To U.S. proponents of international kidnapping, extraordinary rendition was a logical extension of the *Álvarez-Machain* ruling. Three years after the Supreme Court decision, President Clinton signed an executive order—Presidential Decision Directive, or PDD-39—for a new policy on counterterrorism. During the early Clinton years, the United States had been shocked by two major terrorist attacks: the 1993 bombing of the World Trade Center and the 1995 Oklahoma City bombing. PDD-39 expanded the CIA's ability to render terrorists from abroad. Although it stated that "where possible and appropriate" the Departments of State and Justice would attempt to take custody of terrorists overseas "through negotiation and conclusion of new extradition treaties," it also explicitly authorized abduction. A portion of PDD-39 read:

We shall vigorously apply extraterritorial statutes to counter acts
of terrorism and apprehend terrorists outside of the United
States. When terrorists wanted for violation of U.S. law are at
large overseas, their return for prosecution should be a matter
of the highest priority. . . . If we do not receive adequate cooperation from a state that harbors a terrorist whose extradition
we are seeking, we shall take appropriate measures to induce cooperation. Return of suspects by force may be effected without
the cooperation of the host government.

One of the first international captures after PDD-39 was the 1995
seizure from Islamabad of Ramzi Yousef, accused of conspiracy in
the World Trade Center bombing and other terrorist acts. Yousef was
transported back to the United States to stand trial, and the courts
rejected his jurisdictional challenges. Mir Qazi (also spelled as Kasi
or Kansi), who attacked CIA employees outside the Langley headquarters in 1993, was captured by a joint FBI-CIA task force in Pak-
istan in 1997 and rendered back to the United States.[16]
    In some ways, PDD-39 was simply a continuation of old policies.
But there were also changes. The Clinton administration began to
render abductees not to the United States, but to third countries such
as Egypt, Jordan, and Syria. Initially, there were some safeguards:
there had to be a warrant or indictment against the suspected terrorist, and the person was not supposed to be sent to a country where
there was a likelihood of torture. By sending people to third countries, however, they lost the protections that would have been present in U.S. courts. Moreover, it was well known that interrogators
in Egypt often used torture. According to the estimate of former
CIA director George Tenet, around seventy of these renditions occurred before September 11, 2001.[17]
    The pieces were already in place for the George W. Bush admin-
istration to pick up the program. In the aftermath of 9/11, the legal
process requirement was dropped, countries with a record of torture
were selected for transfer, and "rendition to justice" became extraordinary rendition. Under the new program, the very purpose of rendition
was transformed. It was once used to obtain personal jurisdiction and
prosecute an individual, but it became an interrogation strategy

in the war on terror, a means to collect intelligence. The personnel involved also changed. Whereas in the past, the Departments of State and Justice had to approve renditions, after 9/11 the CIA was authorized to conduct those operations on its own. Instead of renditions in the dozens, they now numbered in the thousands. And, rather than prohibiting torture, there was the specific intent to bring detainees to countries with aggressive interrogation techniques. As one unnamed U.S. official succinctly put it, "We don't kick the [expletive] out of them. We send them to other countries so they can kick the [expletive] out of them." The strategies were no longer aimed at bringing a suspect into the ambit of the U.S. judicial system, but rather on keeping him out of it.[18]

Extraordinary rendition has been criticized strongly by human rights advocates, the United Nations, and other governments. But defenders of extraordinary rendition have cited both *Ker* and *Álvarez-Machain* as supporting case law, and tend to downplay the potential for torture in third countries. When Daniel Benjamin of the Brookings Institution explained extraordinary rendition in 2007, he pointed to *Álvarez-Machain* and renditions under the Clinton administration as grounds for the program. Some counterterrorism experts have argued that extraterritorial abductions do not, in fact, violate either customary or codified international law. Others have asserted that international law is irrelevant; U.S. law and legal precedents, like *Ker*, should be controlling.[19]

But nineteenth-century tools do not always serve twenty-first-century ends. Today's practice of extraordinary rendition originated in a vastly different time and place. In 1886, the year *Ker v. Illinois* was decided, police forces lacked the manpower and organization to engage in distant investigations, extradition law was relatively undeveloped, and international cooperation in crime control was virtually nonexistent. In that context, abduction by private detectives was one of the only ways to apprehend fugitives who crossed borders. Today, the options for international law enforcement are not so limited. The United States has extradition treaties with more than 100 countries, which have proven effective in getting hold of hunted fugitives. With 190 member states, Interpol reaches around the globe, facilitating the mutual exchange of information in criminal pursuits. Human rights norms that did not exist in the nineteenth century now prohibit international kidnapping. While other countries adhered to the *male captus, bene detentus* rule in the late nineteenth century, now the United States stands virtually alone among Western nations in supporting the doctrine. At the heart of extraordinary rendition is a nineteenth-century relic rather than a twenty-first-century innovation.

The *Ker* decision has been distorted over time. Originally, it excused abductions that brought suspects into the United States to stand trial. Frederick Ker eventually got his day in court, his full due process rights, and his chance to appeal all the way to the Supreme Court. But after 9/11, extraordinary rendition delivered suspected terrorists not to American courts of law, but to detention centers in third countries. Detainees were held for years without hope of a trial and were in some cases subjected to torture. Instead of private, non-state actors carrying out the abductions, twenty-first-century kidnappings were authorized and supported by the federal government, sometimes with the full force of the U.S. military behind them.

Nineteenth-century Americans imagined a world with nowhere to hide from U.S. justice. In this vision, the long arm of American law would extend its reach globally through extradition treaties and international cooperation. The reality, however, was not always so harmonious. Through abductions, deportations, and other forms of irregular rendition, the United States flexed its muscle rather than reaching out its hand. Instead of an empire of law, Americans had created an empire that claimed to be above the law.

Notes

Abbreviations

ANCR: Archivo Nacional de Costa Rica
    DRE: Documentos de Relaciones Exteriores de Costa Rica
ANH: Archivo Nacional de Honduras
FRUS: Papers Relating to the Foreign Relations of the United States
HCA: Hiram College Archives
    CEHP: C. E. Henry Papers
LAC: Library and Archives Canada
    MG: Manuscript Group
    RG: Record Group
LOC: Library of Congress
    PNDA: Pinkerton National Detective Agency Papers
LSU: Special Collections, Louisiana State University
    EAB: E. A. Burke Papers
NARA: National Archives and Records Administration
    CDF: Central Decimal Files
    RG: Record Group
    RG 59: General Records of the Department of State
NAUK: National Archives, United Kingdom
    FO: Foreign Office
    HO: Home Office
SRE: Archivo Histórico de la Secretaría de Relaciones Exteriores de México
    AEMEUA: Archivo de la Embajada Mexicana en Estados Unidos de
            América

Introduction: Crimes of Mobility

1. Jules Verne, *Around the World in Eighty Days* (London: Sampson Low, Marston, Low, & Searle, 1874), 14–18. For another analysis of this scene, see Stephen Kern, *The Culture of Time and Space, 1880–1918* (Cambridge, MA: Harvard University Press, 1983), 211–212.

2. Nellie Bly, *Around the World in Seventy-Two Days* (New York: Pictorial Weeklies, 1890).

3. *The Picturesque Tourist: A Handy Guide Round the World* (London: Hamilton, Adams, 1877), 15–16, 22; David Harvey, *The Condition of Postmodernity: An Enquiry into the Origins of Cultural Change* (Oxford: Blackwell, 1989). On the impact of new technologies in the late nineteenth century, see Emily S. Rosenberg, ed., *A World Connecting, 1870–1945* (Cambridge, MA: Belknap Press of Harvard University Press, 2012).

4. "Mr. Edison as a Prophet," *Washington Post*, October 28, 1894, 17; "Our Detectives," *Youth's Companion*, June 12, 1890, 327.

5. William Gammell, "Asylum and Extradition among Nations," in *William Gammell, LL.D.: A Biographical Sketch with Selections from His Writings*, ed. James O. Murray (Cambridge, MA: Riverside Press, 1890), 300–301.

6. John Bassett Moore, *Report on Extradition with Returns of All Cases from August 9, 1842 to January 1, 1890 and an Index* (Washington, DC: U.S. Government Printing Office, 1890), 3.

7. Cesare Lombroso, *Criminal Man*, translated and with a new introduction by Mary Gibson and Nicole Hahn Rafter, with translation assistance from Mark Seymour (1876; reprint, Durham, NC: Duke University Press, 2006); Michel Foucault, "La vérité et les formes juridiques," synopsized in Mathieu Deflem, *Policing World Society: Historical Foundations of International Police Cooperation* (New York: Oxford University Press, 2002), 95.

8. "Canada as a Refuge," *Independent*, January 12, 1888, 23 (emphasis in original). On the rise of the passport regime, see Craig Robertson, *The Passport in America: The History of a Document* (New York: Oxford University Press, 2010); John Torpey, *The Invention of the Passport: Surveillance, Citizenship, and the State* (New York: Cambridge University Press, 2000); Martin Lloyd, *The Passport: The History of Man's Most Travelled Document* (Stroud, UK: Sutton, 2003).

9. M. Cherif Bassiouni, *International Extradition: United States Law and Practice*, 5th ed. (New York: Oceana, 2007), 3; Edward Keene, "The Treaty-Making Revolution of the Nineteenth Century," *International History Review* 34 (2012): 475–500. On nineteenth-century international law, see Antony Anghie, *Imperialism, Sovereignty, and the Making of International Law* (New York: Cambridge University Press, 2005); Martti Koskenniemi, *The Gentle Civilizer of Nations: The Rise and Fall of International Law, 1870–1960* (New York: Cambridge University Press, 2002); Stephen C. Neff, *Justice among Nations: A History of International Law* (Cambridge, MA: Harvard University Press, 2014).

10. On "disguised extradition," see Paul O'Higgins, "Disguised Extradition: Deportation or Extradition?," *Cambridge Law Journal* 21 (1963): 10–13;

M. Cherif Bassiouni, "Unlawful Seizures and Irregular Rendition Devices as Alternatives to Extradition," *Vanderbilt Journal of Transnational Law* 7 (1973–1974): 25–70. On extraterritorial jurisdiction, see Teemu Ruskola, *Legal Orientalism: China, the United States, and Modern Law* (Cambridge, MA: Harvard University Press, 2013); Eileen P. Scully, *Bargaining with the State from Afar: American Citizenship in Treaty Port China, 1844–1942* (New York: Columbia University Press, 2001).

11. On the attempted extradition of fugitive slaves, see David Murray, "Hands across the Border: The Abortive Extradition of Solomon Moseby," *Canadian Review of American Studies* 30 (2000): 187–209; Alexander L. Murray, "The Extradition of Fugitive Slaves from Canada: A Re-evaluation," *Canadian Historical Review* 43 (1962): 298–314; Roman J. Zorn, "Criminal Extradition Menaces the Canadian Haven for Fugitive Slaves, 1841–1861," *Canadian Historical Review* 38 (1957): 284–294; Patrick Brode, *The Odyssey of John Anderson* (Toronto: University of Toronto Press, 1989); Paul Finkelman, "International Extradition and Fugitive Slaves: The John Anderson Case," *Brooklyn Journal of International Law* 18 (1992): 765–810.

12. Peter Andreas and Ethan Nadelmann, *Policing the Globe: Criminalization and Crime Control in International Relations* (New York: Oxford University Press, 2006), 108.

13. On the types of maps available to turn-of-the-century Americans, see Susan Schulten, *The Geographical Imagination in America, 1880–1950* (Chicago: University of Chicago Press, 2001).

14. William R. Hunt, *Front-Page Detective: William J. Burns and the Detective Profession, 1880–1930* (Bowling Green, OH: Bowling Green State University Popular Press, 1990).

15. H. C. Potter, "National Bigness or Greatness—Which?," *North American Review*, April 1, 1899, 443.

16. On the history of the Pinkerton National Detective Agency (PNDA), see James David Horan, *Pinkertons: The Detective Dynasty that Made History* (New York: Crown, 1967); Frank Morn, *The Eye that Never Sleeps: A History of the Pinkerton National Detective Agency* (Bloomington: Indiana University Press, 1982).

17. "Biographical Sketch of William A. Pinkerton," Box 14, Folder 5, PNDA, LOC. My thanks to Julie Greene for suggesting the concluding question.

18. A helpful historiographical essay on law and American empire is Clara Altman, "The International Context: An Imperial Perspective on American Legal History," in *A Companion to American Legal History*, ed. Sally E. Hadden and Alfred L. Brophy (Hoboken, NJ: Wiley-Blackwell, 2013), 543–561. Other works that examine American empire through a legal lens include Daniel S. Margolies, *Spaces of Law in American Foreign Relations: Extradition and Extraterritoriality in the Borderlands and Beyond* (Athens: University of Georgia Press, 2011); Bartholomew Sparrow, *The Insular Cases and the Emergence of American Empire* (Lawrence: University of Kansas Press, 2006); Sally Engle Merry, *Colonizing Hawai'i: The Cultural Power of Law* (Princeton, NJ: Princeton University Press, 2000); Christina Duffy Burnett, "Untied States: American

Expansion and Territorial Deannexation," *University of Chicago Law Review* 72 (2005): 797–879; Christina Duffy Burnett and Burke Marshall, eds., *Foreign in a Domestic Sense: Puerto Rico, American Expansion, and the Constitution* (Durham, NC: Duke University Press, 2001).

19. Ivan Anthony Shearer, *Extradition in International Law* (Dobbs Ferry, NY: Oceana, 1971), 12.

20. Annual Message to Congress, December 7, 1903, *FRUS 1903* (Washington, DC: U.S. Government Printing Office, 1903), xv–xvi (emphasis added).

21. George W. Bush, "Trying Detainees: Address on the Creation of Military Commissions," September 6, 2006, available at www.presidentialrhetoric .com/speeches/09.06.06.html.

22. Ker v. Illinois, 119 U.S. 436 (1886); Gregory S. McNeal and Brian J. Field, "Snatch-and-Grab Ops: Justifying Extraterritorial Abduction," *Transnational Law and Contemporary Problems* 16 (2006–2007): 491–522.

1

The Embezzlement Epidemic

1. "Scott Takes $160,000," *Boston Daily Globe*, June 3, 1885, 1; "Teller Scott's Flight," *New York Times*, June 4, 1885, 1.

2. "Two Thousand Boodlers," *Boston Daily Globe*, June 22, 1889, 3; "Epidemic of Embezzlement," *St. Louis Post-Dispatch*, May 27, 1884, 4. On the etymology of the word *boodle*, see "Boodle," *Magazine of American History*, July–December 1887, 353; "Origin of the Word 'Boodle,'" *Atlanta Constitution*, February 7, 1887, 1.

3. Great Britain granted Canada full autonomy in domestic affairs in 1867, but continued to control Canada's foreign affairs until 1926. On Britain's influence on Canadian extradition policy, see Bradley Miller, "'A Carnival of Crime on Our Border': International Law, Imperial Power, and Extradition in Canada, 1865–1883," *Canadian Historical Review* 90 (2009): 639–669.

4. On the concept of "crimes of mobility," see Lawrence Friedman, *Crime and Punishment in American History* (New York: Basic Books, 1993), 193–210. On the immense social changes during the Gilded Age, see Alan Trachtenberg, *The Incorporation of America: Culture and Society in the Gilded Age* (New York: Hill and Wang, 1982); Robert H. Wiebe, *The Search for Order, 1877–1920* (New York: Hill and Wang, 1967); Martin J. Sklar, *The Corporate Reconstruction of American Capitalism, 1890–1916: The Market, the Law, and Politics* (New York: Cambridge University Press, 1988).

5. On nineteenth-century clerks, see Brian P. Luskey, *On the Make: Clerks and the Quest for Capital in Nineteenth-Century America* (New York: New York University Press, 2010); Thomas Augst, *The Clerk's Tale: Young Men and Moral Life in Nineteenth-Century America* (Chicago: University of Chicago Press, 2003); Michael Zakim, "The Business Clerk as Social Revolutionary; or, a Labor History of the Nonproducing Classes," *Journal of the Early Republic* 26 (2006):

563–603; Michael Zakim, "Producing Capitalism: The Clerk at Work," in *Capitalism Takes Command: The Social Transformation of Nineteenth-Century America*, ed. Michael Zakim and Gary J. Kornblith (Chicago: University of Chicago Press, 2012), 223–247. On clerks and criminality, see Stephen Mihm, "Clerks, Classes, and Conflicts," *Journal of the Early Republic* 26 (2006): 605–615, esp. 613–614; Jerome P. Bjilopera, *City of Clerks: Office and Sales Workers in Philadelphia, 1870–1920* (Urbana: University of Illinois Press, 2005), 123–128.

6. Webster-Ashburton Treaty, 8 Stat. 572, T.S. 119 (1842); Charles I. Bevans, comp., *Treaties and Other International Agreements of the United States of America, 1776–1949*, vol. 12 (Washington, DC: U.S. Government Printing Office, 1968), 82–89; Edward Everett, "Biographical Memoir of the Public Life of Daniel Webster," in *The Works of Daniel Webster*, vol. 1 (Boston: Little, Brown, 1851), cxxx; Christopher H. Pyle, *Extradition, Politics, and Human Rights* (Philadelphia: Temple University Press, 2001), 70–72.

7. "A Refuge for Invalid Politicians," *New York Times*, December 22, 1871, 4; David Dudley Field, *Outlines of an International Code* (New York: Baker, Voorhis, 1876), 95.

8. Joel Prentiss Bishop, *Commentaries on the Criminal Law*, 6th ed., vol. 2 (Boston: Little, Brown, 1877), 176 (emphasis added); Olivier Zunz, *Making America Corporate, 1870–1920* (Chicago: University of Chicago Press, 1990), 126. On the origins of the common-law crime of embezzlement, see Richard J. Soderlund, "'Intended as a Terror to the Idle and Profligate': Embezzlement and the Origins of Policing in the Yorkshire Worsted Industry, c. 1750–1777," *Journal of Social History* 31 (1998): 647–669.

9. Herman Melville, "Bartleby, the Scrivener: A Story of Wall Street," originally published in *Putnam's Magazine*, November–December 1853; "Broken Banks and Lax Directors," *Century Illustrated Magazine*, March 1882, 768–777.

10. The statistics on embezzlements come from a series of 1888 articles in the *Chicago Daily Tribune*, chronicling every reported case of embezzlement in the United States between 1878 and 1888. For 1880, see "Millions Were Stolen," *Chicago Daily Tribune*, July 6, 1888, 9. For 1885, see "The Stolen Money in 1885," *Chicago Daily Tribune*, July 12, 1888, 9. On the invention of the cash register, see Stephen Van Dulke, *Inventing the 19th Century: 100 Inventions that Shaped the Victorian Age* (New York: New York University Press, 2001), 49–51.

11. *Appletons' Railway and Steam Navigation Guide* (New York: D. Appleton, 1873); *The Rand-McNally Official Railway Guide and Hand Book, for the United States and the Dominion of Canada* (New York: National Railway, 1886).

12. Peter Andreas and Ethan Nadelmann, *Policing the Globe: Criminalization and Crime Control in International Relations* (New York: Oxford University Press, 2006), 108. On informal cooperation by law enforcers along the U.S.-Mexican border during the late nineteenth century, see Samuel Truett, *Fugitive Landscapes: The Forgotten History of the U.S.-Mexico Borderlands* (New Haven, CT: Yale University Press, 2006); Rachel C. St. John, *Line in the Sand: A History of the Western U.S.-Mexico Border* (Princeton, NJ: Princeton University Press, 2011).

13. Mexico extradited fugitives charged with embezzlement to the United States at least eight times during the 1880s; Extradition Case Files, 1836–1906, Entry 857, RG 59, NARA. On Diaz's obsession with Mexico's image as a nation of law and order, see Pablo Piccato, *City of Suspects: Crime in Mexico City, 1900–1931* (Durham, NC: Duke University Press, 2001); Mauricio Tenorio-Trillo, *Mexico at the World's Fairs: Crafting a Modern Nation* (Berkeley: University of California Press, 1996). On the case of Dallas embezzler J. H. Baum, who fled to London, Ontario, see "A Cotton Swindler," *Galveston Daily News*, March 22, 1885, 6.

14. Gilbert Haven, "Canadian Methodism, Second Paper," *Christian Advocate*, October 31, 1878, 689; Charles G. D. Roberts, *The Canadian Guide-Book* (New York: D. Appleton, 1891), 2–3. On the history of the greenback, see Irwin Unger, *The Greenback Era: A Social and Political History of American Finance, 1865–1879* (Princeton, NJ: Princeton University Press, 1964).

15. Dawn Hutchins Bobryk, "The Defalcation of John Chester Eno" (master's thesis, Trinity College, 2006); Henry Clews, *Twenty Eight Years in Wall Street* (New York: Irving, 1888), 167–170.

16. Elmus Wicker, *Banking Panics of the Gilded Age* (New York: Cambridge University Press, 2000), 34–40.

17. Extradition case file of John C. Eno, Entry 857, Box 17, RG 59, NARA; Ex. P. John C. Eno, 10 Quebec L.R. 173 (1884), in *The Legal News*, ed. James Kirby (Montreal: Gazette, 1884), 7:360–361. The rule that judges could only extradite under the terms of a treaty was affirmed in The Commonwealth of Kentucky v. Smith N. Hawes, 76 Ky. (13 Bush) 697 (1878).

18. George H. Adams, "The Extradition of Eno," *Albany Law Journal*, August 23, 1884, 144–147.

19. Melville E. Stone, *Fifty Years a Journalist* (Garden City, NY: Doubleday, Page, 1921), 92–93.

20. U.S. Const., art.IV, §2.

21. "Current Topics," *Albany Law Journal*, June 14, 1884, 461.

22. "Address of Professor Albert S. Bolles on Defalcations," in *Proceedings of the Convention of the American Bankers Association, 1885*, vol. 11 (New York: ABA, 1885), 103–110.

23. Edward S. Washburn, "The American Colony in Canada," *Proceedings of the Seventeenth Annual Meeting of the National Board of Trade* (Boston: George E. Crosby, 1887), 231.

24. "How to Make Bank Cashiers Honest," *Judge*, June 20, 1885, cover.

25. "The Defaulter's Refuge," *Chicago Daily Tribune*, June 12, 1885, 4; Washburn, "American Colony," 231.

26. "Canada as a Refuge," *Independent*, January 12, 1888, 23; Henry A. Riley, "Notes of Legal Matters of General Interest," *Zion's Herald*, July 1, 1885, 202.

27. William Dean Howells, *The Quality of Mercy* (New York: Harper, 1892); Theodore Dreiser, *Sister Carrie* (New York: Doubleday, Page, 1900), chaps. 27–29. Examples of serialized and popular fiction about boodlers include: "The Strange Case of Alderman Shekel and Mr. Slide," *Puck*, July 7, 1886, 299; Luke Sharp, "Trapped," *Weekly Detroit Free Press*, August 28, 1886, 1; "Uncle Sun Up, the Born Detective: Or, Boodle vs. Bracelets," *Banner Weekly* 674 (1891).

On Emma Dreiser's experience, see Theodore Dreiser, *A Book about Myself* (New York: Boni and Liveright, 1922), 438–439.

28. "Canada as a Refuge," *Independent*, January 12, 1888, 23; George H. Adams, "Our State Department and Extradition," *American Law Review* 18 (1886): 545.

29. *Chicago Daily Tribune*, February 28, 1889, 4; "Banker Eno House Hunting," *Boston Daily Globe*, August 8, 1884, 5; "American Boodlers," *Galveston Daily News*, October 21, 1888, 1.

30. Joseph Keppler, "Canada as 'Mother Mandelbaum,'" *Puck*, July 17, 1885, 241; "Cartoons and Comments," *Puck*, June 17, 1885, 242.

31. Roberts, *Canadian Guide-Book*, 3.

32. Frederick Burr Opper, "Putting a Premium on Peculation," *Puck*, August 12, 1884, 379.

33. David M. Pletcher, *The Diplomacy of Trade and Investment: American Economic Expansion in the Hemisphere, 1865–1900* (Columbia: University of Missouri Press, 1998), 69–76; Erastus Wiman, *Commercial Union between the United States and Canada* (New York: E. Wiman, 1887), 26.

34. John C. Eno Fonds, folder 1, vol. 1, MG 29, A27, LAC; Bobryk, "Defalcation of John Chester Eno," 123; "Lower Laurentian Railway," *New York Times*, December 18, 1891, 6; "The Boodlers in Canada," *Washington Post*, January 16, 1890, 4; "Geographical Information," *Life*, November 22, 1888, 289.

35. Andrew R. Graybill, *Policing the Great Plains: Rangers, Mounties, and the North American Frontier, 1875–1910* (Lincoln: University of Nebraska Press, 2007), 53–54; Report of the American Surety Company, December 1887 (hereafter, American Surety Report, 1887), in "Canada as a Refuge," *Independent*, January 12, 1888, 23 (emphasis in original).

36. *Puck*, February 6, 1889, 389; "A Chinaman's Dark Ways: Chu Fong and a Lot of Money Gone," *New York Tribune*, December 22, 1889, 1.

37. "The Lottery Nuisance," *Christian Union*, April 4, 1889, 419. On the moral failing attributed to gamblers in the nineteenth century, see Ann Fabian, *Card Sharps and Bucket Shops: Gambling in Nineteenth-Century America* (New York: Routledge, 1999); Jackson Lears, *Something for Nothing: Luck in America* (New York: Viking, 2003).

38. On the rise of yellow journalism, especially with regards to crime reporting, see Patricia Cline Cohen, *The Murder of Helen Jewett: The Life and Death of a Prostitute in Nineteenth-Century New York* (New York: Alfred A. Knopf, 1998); David R. Spencer, *The Yellow Journalism: The Press and America's Emergence as a World Power* (Evanston, IL: Northwestern University Press, 2007); Guy Reel, *The National Police Gazette and the Making of the Modern American Man, 1879–1906* (New York: Palgrave Macmillan, 2006). For an example of a boodler profile, see "Secure in Canada," originally published in *New York World*, reprinted in *Milwaukee Sentinel*, January 12, 1885, which profiled twenty-three separate boodlers.

39. *New York World* article, reprinted as "Grant, Ward, Fish and Eno," *Raleigh Register*, July 23, 1884, 2; "Eno in Quebec," *Chicago Daily Tribune*, February 8, 1885, 14.

40. "Two Thousand Boodlers," *Boston Daily Globe*, June 22, 1889, 3; "Eno Pleased with Canada," *Chicago Daily Tribune*, March 2, 1890, 2; "The Exiles Who Are Living in Canada," *Boston Daily Globe*, January 31, 1886, 1; *Century Illustrated Magazine*, March 1885, 798.

41. "What Shall We Do with Embezzlers?," *Frank Leslie's Illustrated Newspaper*, January 14, 1882, 338; C. Broughton, "A Financier," *Life*, June 16, 1892, 371.

42. Scott A. Sandage, *Born Losers: A History of Failure in America* (Cambridge, MA: Harvard University Press, 2005), 233, 253–254. This account of the boodler as Robin Hood resembles that of the traditional social bandit, as described in Eric Hobsbawm, *Bandits* (New York: Delacorte, 1969).

43. "The Two Boodle Carriers," *New York Times*, April 11, 1886, 3.

44. "Current Events," *New York Evangelist*, January 7, 1886, 8; American Surety Report, 1887; "Bill Nye in Canada," *Boston Daily Globe*, December 8, 1889, 20.

45. Robert L. Beisner, *From the Old Diplomacy to the New, 1865–1900* (Arlington Heights, IL: Harlan Davidson, 1975), 62.

46. Joseph Patrick O'Grady, *Irish-Americans and Anglo-American Relations, 1880–1888* (New York: Arno, 1976); "That Dynamite Treaty," *Chicago Daily Tribune*, January 22, 1887, 1; *Journal of the Executive Proceedings of the Senate of the United States*, vol. 26 (Washington, DC: U.S. Government Printing Office, 1901), 446.

47. American Bankers Association, *Proceedings of the Convention of the American Bankers Association, 1885*, vol. 11 (New York: ABA, 1885), 164; *Proceedings of the Convention of the American Bankers Association, 1886*, vol. 12 (New York: ABA, 1886), 53; *Proceedings of the Convention of the American Bankers Association, 1887*, vol. 13 (New York: ABA, 1887), 141; *Senate Executive Journal*, vol. 26, January 21, 1889, 435; American Surety Report, 1887.

48. Annual reports of the Pinkerton National Detective Agency (PNDA) to the American Bankers Association, Box 21, Folder 7, PNDA, LOC.

49. "He Was Quickly Caught," *Washington Post*, October 18, 1885, 6.

50. Thomas Byrnes, *Professional Criminals of America* (New York: Cassel, 1886); "American Embezzlers: The Flight to Canada of Many Fugitives," *Galveston Daily News*, May 12, 1890, 5. On the identification of criminals, see Simon A. Cole, *Suspect Identities: A History of Fingerprinting and Criminal Identification* (Cambridge, MA: Harvard University Press, 2001).

51. "Bothering the Boodlers," *Daily Inter Ocean*, February 22, 1887, 1; *St. Louis Globe-Democrat*, February 26, 1887, 4. On the history of the U.S. Border Patrol, see Kelly Lytle Hernandez, *Migra! A History of the U.S. Border Patrol* (Berkeley: University of California Press, 2010); Joseph Nevins, *Operation Gatekeeper: The Rise of the "Illegal Alien" and the Making of the U.S.-Mexico Boundary* (New York: Taylor and Francis Group, 2002).

52. "Watching at Windsor," *Daily Inter Ocean*, July 26, 1887, 1; Howells, *Quality of Mercy*; Dreiser, *Sister Carrie*; Ledger Book 1884–1885, Box OV 7, PNDA, LOC.

53. For examples of the first strategy, see the cases of Joseph H. Wilkins, "A Detective's Sharp Work," *New York Times*, September 13, 1885, 14; William

E. Jones, "A Canadian Exile," *Rocky Mountain News*, February 14, 1889, 1; and Daniel Brown, "Notes of Cases," *Albany Law Journal*, September 4, 1886, 182. For examples of the second strategy, see the cases of Albert Lange, "Over the Line," *Atchison Daily Globe*, June 27, 1887, 3; and William P. Spear, "An Embezzler Caught," *New York Times*, February 18, 1887, 1; "Decoyed across the Canada Line," *St. Louis Globe-Democrat*, February 18, 1887, 3. For examples of the third strategy, see the cases of Bill McFadden, "A Daring Detective," *National Police Gazette*, June 3, 1882, 13; and Abner Benyon, "Bill Nye in Canada," *Boston Daily Globe*, December 8, 1889, 20.

54. "Demands a Princely Fee," *Chicago Daily Tribune*, September 23, 1891, 7; "American Embezzlers: The Flight to Canada of Many Fugitives," *Galveston Daily News*, May 12, 1890, 5.

55. "Found at Winnipeg," *New York Times*, September 8, 1885, 2; "Bold, Bad Detectives: They Kidnap and Bring Back from Canada an Ex–Bank President," *St. Louis Globe-Democrat*, September 8, 1885, 1; "Caught in Canada: American Detectives in the Role of Kidnappers," *Milwaukee Sentinel*, September 9, 1885, 3.

56. "Our Criminals in Canada," *Chicago Daily Tribune*, June 1, 1887, 5; David R. Williams, *Call in Pinkerton's: American Detectives at Work for Canada* (Toronto: Dundurn Press, 1998), 116–117. The relationship between Sherwood and Pinkerton is documented in A. P. Sherwood Letterbook, 1883–1887, vol. 3124, Royal Canadian Mounted Police Dominion Records, RG 18, LAC.

57. "An Outrage," *Manitoba Daily Free Press*, September 9, 1885, 2; *Independent*, September 17, 1885, 18; "Defaulter Brainerd Captured," *Chicago Daily Tribune*, September 10, 1885, 4.

58. "M'Garigle in Canada," *Washington Post*, August 1, 1887, 1; "Boodlers' Unhappy Lot," *Milwaukee Daily Journal*, May 24, 1886, 1.

59. *St. Louis Globe-Democrat*, February 26, 1887, 4.

60. On the idea of the right to free movement in the nineteenth century, see John Torpey, *The Invention of the Passport: Surveillance, Citizenship and the State* (New York: Cambridge University Press, 2000), esp. chap. 4. On Chinese immigration and border control, see Julian Ralph, "The Chinese Leak," *Harper's New Monthly Magazine*, March 1891, 515–525; Erika Lee, *At America's Gates: Chinese Immigration during the Exclusion Era, 1882–1943* (Chapel Hill: University of North Carolina Press, 2003), esp. chap. 5.

61. "Two Thousand Boodlers," *Boston Daily Globe*, June 22, 1889, 3.

62. Richard Chapman Weldon, speech before the Canadian House of Commons, February 27, 1889, in Canada House of Commons, *Official Report of the Debates of the House of Commons of the Dominion of Canada*, vol. 21 (Ottawa: McLean, Roger, 1886), 346–347.

63. "The Boodlers in Chief," *Toronto Globe*, February 19, 1887, 10; *Toronto Globe*, March 1, 1889, 4; *Montreal Herald*, March 6, 1889, 4.

64. "Canada's Exiles Alarmed," *New York Times*, March 7, 1889, 2; "Boodlers Combine," *Boston Daily Globe*, March 7, 1889, 8; "Boodlers Raise a Fund," *Chicago Daily Tribune*, March 9, 1889, 9; "On the Black List: The American Colony in Canada Thrown into a Panic," *Washington Post*, March 13, 1889, 4.

65. Canada House of Commons, *Official Report*, April 23, 1889, 1475.

66. "No Longer a Haven for Thieves," *Chicago Daily Tribune*, April 24, 1889, 5.

67. "After Fleeing Criminals: Extradition Treaty with England Ratified," *New York Times*, February 19, 1890, 1.

68. Extradition case file of Charles Pscherhofer, Entry 857, Boxes 30–31, RG 59, NARA; "Gossip of Gotham," *New York Times*, February 10, 1895, 16.

69. "The Embezzlement Business," *Washington Post*, March 6, 1892, 4. For a table of extradition statistics through 1893, see "Embezzlements of '93," *Chicago Daily Tribune*, December 31, 1893, 27.

2
Detectives without Borders

1. John Bassett Moore, *A Treatise on Extradition and Interstate Rendition*, 2 vols. (Boston: Boston Book, 1891).

2. On irregular rendition, see M. Cherif Bassiouni, "Unlawful Seizures and Irregular Rendition Devices as Alternatives to Extradition," *Vanderbilt Journal of Transnational Law* 7 (1973): 25–70; Melanie M. Laflin, "Kidnapped Terrorists: Bringing International Criminals to Justice through Irregular Rendition and Other Quasi-Legal Options," *Journal of Legislation* 26 (2000): 315–335.

3. On the idea of Latin America as a laboratory for empire, see William Appleman Williams, "Latin America: Laboratory of American Foreign Policy in the 1920s," *Inter-American Economic Affairs* 11 (1957): 3–30; Greg Grandin, *Empire's Workshop: Latin America, the United States, and the Rise of the New Imperialism* (New York: Metropolitan Books, 2006).

4. On the contemporary relevance of *Ker v. Illinois*, see Alan W. Clarke, *Rendition to Torture* (New Brunswick, NJ: Rutgers University Press, 2012), 77–78; Gregory S. McNeal and Brian J. Field, "Snatch-and-Grab Ops: Justifying Extraterritorial Abduction," *Transnational Law and Contemporary Problems* 16 (2007): 491–522; Abraham Abramovsky, "Extraterritorial Abductions: America's 'Catch and Snatch' Policy Run Amok," *Virginia Journal of International Law* 31 (1990–1991): 151–210; Jonathan A. Bush, "How Did We Get Here? Foreign Abduction after Alvarez-Machain," *Stanford Law Review* 45 (1993): 939–984; Charles Fairman, "Ker v. Illinois Revisited," *American Journal of International Law* 47 (1953): 678–686.

5. Max Weber, "Politics as a Vocation," in *From Max Weber: Essays in Sociology*, ed. H. H. Gerth and C. Wright Mills (New York: Routledge, 2009), 78.

6. Testimony of Samuel A. Kean, Extradition case file of Frederick Ker, Entry 857, Box 15, RG 59, NARA.

7. *Advance*, May 10, 1883, 816; "Defaulter Ker," *Chicago Tribune*, July 18, 1883, 8.

8. Allan Pinkerton, *A Double Life and the Detectives* (New York: G. W. Carleton, 1884), 188.

9. The statistic about the number of Pinkerton agents on reserve has been reprinted extensively. Its original source was probably Arthur Gordon Burgoyne, *Homestead: A Complete History of the Struggle of July, 1892* (Pittsburgh, PA: Rawsthorne Engraving and Printing, 1893).

10. Pinkerton, *Double Life*, 208.

11. George Henry Preble and John Lipton Lochhead, *A Chronological History of the Origin and Development of Steam Transportation* (Philadelphia: L. R. Hamersley, 1895), 323; John Haskell Kemble, *Hundred Years of the Pacific Mail* (Newport News, VA: Mariners' Museum, 1950).

12. Pinkerton, *Double Life*, 209.

13. Ibid., 210; "The Longest Way 'Round," *New York Herald*, September 27, 1885, 14; "Ker Has Come," *Chicago Daily Tribune*, July 17, 1883, 8.

14. On the concept of a private police, see David A. Sklansky, "The Private Police," *UCLA Law Review* 46 (1999): 1165–1288; Clifford D. Shearing, "The Relation between Public and Private Policing," in *Modern Policing*, ed. Michael Tonry and Norval Morris (Chicago: University of Chicago Press, 1992); Theodore M. Becker, "The Place of Private Police in Society: An Area of Research for the Social Sciences," *Social Problems* 21 (1974): 438–453. On the birth of the Federal Bureau of Investigation (FBI), see Richard Bach Jensen, "The United States, International Policing and the War against Anarchist Terrorism, 1900–1914," *Terrorism and Political Violence* 13 (2001): 15–46; Rhodri Jeffreys-Jones, *FBI: A History* (New Haven, CT: Yale University Press, 2007).

15. James D. Horan, *The Pinkertons: The Detective Dynasty that Made History* (New York: Crown, 1967); Robert P. Weiss, "Private Detective Agencies and Labour Discipline in the United States, 1855–1946," *Historical Journal* 29 (1986): 87–107.

16. Sigmund A. Lavine, *Allan Pinkerton: America's First Private Eye* (New York: Dodd, Mead, 1963), 21; David R. Williams, *Call in Pinkerton's: American Detectives at Work for Canada* (Toronto: Dundurn, 1998), 36. The existing histories of the Pinkertons tend to be hagiographical. These include Horan, *Pinkertons;* Frank Morn, *"The Eye that Never Sleeps": A History of the Pinkerton National Detective Agency* (Bloomington: Indiana University Press, 1982); Richard Wilmer Rowan, *The Pinkertons: A Detective Dynasty* (Boston: Little, Brown, 1931).

17. Reno Brothers Gang Case File, Box 153, Criminal Case Files, 1853–1992, PNDA, LOC; Charles A. Siringo, *Cowboy Detective: A True Story of Twenty-Two Years with a World Famous Detective Agency* (Chicago: W. B. Conkey, 1912), 33–38, 241–246, 279–285; Ethan Avram Nadelmann, *Cops across Borders: The Internationalization of U.S. Criminal Law* (University Park: Pennsylvania State University Press, 1993), 56; Rowan, *Pinkertons*, 281–289. The Bank of England case is narrated from the perspective of one fugitive in George Bidwell, *Bidwell's Travels from Wall Street to London Prison* (Hartford, CT: Bidwell, 1897).

18. On the history of European international policing, see Peter Andreas and Ethan Nadelmann, *Policing the Globe: Criminalization and Crime Control in International Relations* (New York: Oxford University Press, 2006); Mathieu Deflem, *Policing World Society: Historical Foundations of International Police Cooperation* (New York: Oxford University Press, 2002).

19. L. C. Baker, *History of the United States Secret Service* (Philadelphia: L. C. Baker, 1867), 34–35; Morn, *"Eye that Never Sleeps,"* 69; Deflem, *Policing World Society*, 87; Nadelmann, *Cops across Borders*, 16.

20. Ethan A. Nadelmann, "The Evolution of United States Involvement in the International Rendition of Fugitive Criminals," *NYU Journal of International Law and Policy* 25 (1992–1993): 860; Jacqueline Pope, *Bounty Hunters, Marshals, and Sheriffs: Forward to the Past* (Westport, CT: Praeger, 1998).

21. On Surratt, see James L. Swanson, *Manhunt: The Twelve-Day Chase for Lincoln's Killer* (New York: William Morrow, 2006). On Tweed, see John Adler, *Doomed by Cartoon: How Cartoonist Thomas Nast and the* New York Times *Brought Down Boss Tweed and His Ring of Thieves* (Garden City, NY: Morgan James, 2008).

22. Nadelmann, *Cops across Borders*, 82; "The Keystone Bank," *San Francisco Chronicle*, September 14, 1891, 2; Thomas Byrnes, *Professional Criminals of America* (New York: G. W. Dillingham, 1895).

23. On the Pinkertons' international ties, see Nadelmann, *Cops across Borders*, 56–57; Horan, *Pinkertons*, 255, 280–320. Correspondence with foreign police chiefs is in Family Directors File, 1853–1990, PNDA, LOC. On the Pinkertons' international offices, see Box 22, Branch Offices, Administrative File, 1857–1999, PNDA, LOC.

24. Giacomo Puccini, *Madama Butterfly: A Japanese Tragedy* (Milan: G. Ricordi, 1906). On the Canadian government hiring the Pinkertons, see Williams, *Call in Pinkerton's*.

25. The other 3 percent of extraditions were for crimes like perjury that did not fall into either category. These statistics were calculated from Warrants of Arrest and Extradition, 1843–1930, Entry 859, RG 59, NARA.

26. "Extradited from Peru," *New York Herald*, May 4, 1883, 7.

27. William F. Sater, *Andean Tragedy: Fighting the War of the Pacific, 1879–1884* (Lincoln: University of Nebraska Press, 2007).

28. "Tracked by Detectives," *St. Louis Globe-Democrat*, May 5, 1883, 4; "A Chicago Criminal," *San Francisco Chronicle*, July 10, 1883, 8; "Extradited from Peru," *New York Herald*, May 4, 1883, 7.

29. "Ker Has Come," *Chicago Tribune*, July 17, 1883, 8; Allan Pinkerton, "From the Bank to the Prison," in *A Double Life and the Detectives* (New York: G. W. Carleton, 1884), 176–276.

30. "On Habeas Corpus," *Chicago Tribune*, September 2, 1883, 10.

31. Transcript of Record, Frederick M. Ker v. The People of the State of Illinois, Supreme Court of the United States, October Term, 1885, 11–13.

32. Ibid., 11. On the history of the writ, or legal action, of *habeas corpus* in the common-law courts, see Paul D. Halliday, *Habeas Corpus: From England to Empire* (Cambridge, MA: Harvard University Press, 2010).

33. Franc Bangs Wilkie, *Sketches and Notices of the Chicago Bar* (Chicago: Henry A. Sumner, 1871), 19.

34. Robert Hervey and C. Stuart Beattie, Brief and Argument for Plaintiff in Error, 119 U.S. 436, October Term 1885, 22.

35. Ibid., 9.

36. Ker v. Illinois, 119 U.S. 436 (1886), 443, 440.

37. Michael A. Ross, *Justice of Shattered Dreams: Samuel Freeman Miller and the Supreme Court during the Civil War Era* (Baton Rouge: Louisiana State University Press, 2003).

38. United States v. Rauscher, 119 U.S. 407 (1886); Moore, *Treatise*, vol. 1, 233–239.

39. Ker v. Illinois, 443 (emphasis added); Moore, *Treatise*, 299–300.

40. On vigilantism, see Richard Maxwell Brown, *No Duty to Retreat: Violence and Values in American History and Society* (New York: Oxford University Press, 1991); Amy Louise Wood, *Lynching and Spectacle: Witnessing Racial Violence in America, 1890–1940* (Chapel Hill: University of North Carolina Press, 2009).

41. Moore, *Treatise*, vol. 1, 40.

42. "Why Not Burke?," *Daily Picayune*, May 7, 1890, 4. On the Crawford case, see Box 69, American Exchange Robbery, PNDA, LOC; Cleveland Moffett, "The American Exchange Bank Robbery: Stories from the Archives of the Pinkerton Detective Agency," *McClure's Magazine*, July 1895, 179–191. The Pinkertons apprehended Crawford in Honduras, but did not succeed in bringing him back. On the night before an American ship was scheduled to transport him back to the United States, Crawford escaped from the hotel room where he was being held. For weeks, detectives and soldiers searched for him, but he was never recovered. It was believed that he had escaped to Guatemala. However, a few years later, reports surfaced that Crawford was back in the United States and living in Brooklyn, running another criminal ring.

43. Extradition case file of Joseph J. Hahn, Entry 857, Box 38, RG 59, NARA; "Hahn Is Extradited," *San Francisco Chronicle*, February 12, 1894, 10.

44. Anne Meadows, *Digging Up Butch and Sundance* (New York: St. Martin's, 1994), 39–43; Richard Patterson, *Butch Cassidy: A Biography* (Lincoln: University of Nebraska Press, 1998), 198–201; Larry Pointer, *In Search of Butch Cassidy* (Norman: University of Oklahoma Press, 1977), 193–203.

45. "He Leaves in Haste," *Chicago Tribune*, March 19, 1895, 1; "Christopher A. Larrabee Captured," *Chicago Tribune*, April 11, 1896, 1.

46. On Matt Pinkerton's agency, see A. T. Andreas, *History of Chicago*, vol. 3 (Chicago: A. T. Andreas, 1886), 119. On the lawsuit, see Pinkerton v. Pinkerton, 1904–1905, Part A, Reels 9 and 10, PNDA, LOC; *Bulletin of the National Association of Credit Men*, October 15, 1912, 853.

47. Charles W. Zaremba, *The Merchants' and Tourists' Guide to Mexico* (Chicago: Althrop, 1883); "They Think Uncle Sam Is Too Slow," *Chicago Tribune*, February 2, 1891, 5; "Dr. Zaremba's Case," *Daily Inter Ocean*, February 2, 1891, 7.

48. Reese v. United States, 76 U.S. 13 (1869), 21 (emphasis added). On bounty hunters, see Andrew Berenson, "An Examination of the Rights of American Bounty Hunters to Engage in Extraterritorial Abductions in Mexico," *University of Miami Inter-American Law Review* 30 (1999): 461–488; Stuart H. Traub, "Rewards, Bounty Hunting, and Criminal Justice in the West: 1865–1900," *Western Historical Quarterly* 19 (1988): 287–301.

49. "The Tall Buildings of New York," *Munsey's Magazine*, March 1898, 837. On the history of the American Surety Building, see Sarah Bradford Landau and Carl W. Condit, *Rise of the New York Skyscraper, 1865–1913* (New Haven, CT: Yale University Press, 1996), 231–235; Gail Fenske and Deryck Holdsworth, "Corporate Identity and the New York Office Building, 1895–1915," in *The Landscape of Modernity: Essays on New York City, 1900–1940*, ed.

David Ward and Olivier Zunz (New York: Russell Sage Foundation, 1992), 129–159. On late nineteenth-century impressions of the American Surety Building, see "Insurance: The Tall Office Building," *Independent*, February 27, 1896, 24.

50. For descriptions of how fidelity insurance worked, aimed at late nineteenth-century audiences, see "To Guarantee Character," *New York Times*, July 20, 1884, 7; "Can You Give a Guarantee?," *Omaha World Herald*, June 1, 1890. On Richard Allison Elmer and the American Surety Company, see David Bigelow Parker, *A Chautauqua Boy in '61 and Afterward* (Boston: Small, Maynard, 1912), 283–285; "Sketch of Richard A. Elmer," prepared for the *Insurance Times* by Charles Nordhoff, *Hamilton Literary Magazine*, June 1888, 396–398; *Weekly Underwriter*, October 6, 1888, 165, 170; "American Surety Company," *New York Times*, May 21, 1887, 5; *Bankers Magazine*, March 1900, 419.

51. "Arrest of Hilliard," *Chicago Daily Tribune*, November 14, 1893, 2.

52. "American Surety Company as a Detective," *Indicator: A National Journal of Insurance*, May 1893, 315; "An Embezzler Captured in Canada by the American Surety Company of New-York," *New York Times*, April 15, 1887, 5; *The Insurance Year Book*, vol. 24 (New York: Spectator, 1896), 294; "Dealers in Human Honesty," *Moody's Magazine*, May 1907, 694.

53. Charles E. Schick, "Why Embezzlements Are Fewer Today than Ever," *Chicago Daily Tribune*, April 14, 1912, G4, reprinted in *San Francisco Chronicle*, April 28, 1912; "Rough Road for Embezzlers," *Washington Post*, April 21, 1912, M2; "Getting Harder to Embezzle," *Washington Post*, February 16, 1913, M5.

54. "Comes in Shackles," *Chicago Daily Tribune*, December 8, 1892, 8.

55. C. E. Henry to American Surety Company, March 1, 1893, Box 4, C. E. Henry's Notes on His Mission of Extradition to South America, December 1892–March 1893, CEHP, HCA; "He Caught Two Embezzlers," *New York Times*, March 30, 1893, 5; "Return of Fugitives: Two American Embezzlers Are Brought Back from Brazil," *Chicago Tribune*, April 2, 1893, 3; "Captain Henry's Captures," *New York Times*, April 3, 1893, 1; "He Searched Brazil for His Man," *New York Tribune*, April 3, 1893, 9; "Captain Henry's Prisoners," *Washington Post*, April 3, 1893, 1.

56. Frederick A. Henry, *Captain Henry of Geauga: A Family Chronicle* (Cleveland, OH: Gates, 1942), 438, 471; C. E. Henry to Family, January 31, 1893, Box 4, C. E. Henry's Notes.

57. Henry, *Captain Henry of Geauga*, 467.

58. Ibid., 458, 466; C. E. Henry to Wife, January 20, 1894, Box 4, Letters Written by C. E. Henry concerning Costa Rica Extradition Mission, January–November 1894, CEHP, HCA.

59. Paul Michell, "English-Speaking Justice: Evolving Responses to Transnational Forcible Abduction after Alvarez-Machain," *Cornell International Law Journal* 29 (1996): 383–500, esp. 448–451; Ex parte Susanna Scott, 9 B. & C. 446, 109 E.R. 106 (1829); Regina v. Sattler, 169 Eng. Rep. 1111 (1858); Ex parte Elliott, 1 All E.R. 373 (1949); Sinclair v. H. M. Advocate, 17 R. (Ct. of Sess.) 38 (H.C.J. 1890). In United States v. Toscanino, 500 F.2d 267 (1974), a U.S. court declined jurisdiction when the abductee had been tortured. However, in recent decades, the Toscanino decision has been largely ignored.

60. David McKie, *Jabez: The Rise and Fall of a Victorian Rogue* (London: Atlantic, 2004), 163–174; "Some Curious Criminal Cases," *American Lawyer*, January 1906, 19, reprinted in *Criminal Law Journal of India*, March 31, 1906, 86.

61. Nadelmann, *Cops across Borders*, 60. On the Jameson raiders, see Richard Harding Davis, *The Jameson Raiders vs. the Johannesburg Reformers* (New York: Robert Howard Russell, 1897). On Dr. Hawley Harvey Crippen, see Richard Gordon, *The Private Life of Doctor Crippen* (Cornwall, UK: House of Stratus, 2001).

62. The King v. Walton, 10 Can. Cr. Cas. 269, 11 O.L.R. 94 (1905), reprinted in W. J. Tremeear, ed., *Canadian Criminal Cases Annotated*, vol. 10 (Toronto: Canada Law Book, 1906), 275; Michell, "English-Speaking Justice," 451–458; Attorney-General v. Eichmann, 36 I.L.R. 5 (1961).

63. On the Insular Cases, see Bartholomew H. Sparrow, *The Insular Cases and the Emergence of American Empire* (Lawrence: University of Kansas Press, 2006); Kal Raustiala, *Does the Constitution Follow the Flag? The Evolution of Territoriality in American Law* (New York: Oxford University Press, 2009); Christina Duffy Burnett and Burke Marshall, eds., *Foreign in a Domestic Sense: Puerto Rico, American Expansion, and the Constitution* (Durham, NC: Duke University Press, 2001). On the question of Guantánamo's juridical space, see Amy Kaplan, "Where Is Guantánamo?," *American Quarterly* 57 (2005): 831–858; Karen J. Greenberg and Joshua L. Dratel, eds., *The Torture Papers: The Road to Abu Ghraib* (New York: Cambridge University Press, 2005), 29–37.

64. Official website for Pinkerton Consulting and Investigations, available at www.securitas.com/pinkerton.

3

An Empire of Justice

1. Theodore Roosevelt, "Annual Message of the President, December 6, 1904," *FRUS 1904* (Washington, DC: U.S. Government Printing Office, 1905), xli.

2. "The Criminal's Last Haven of Refuge," *American Lawyer*, August 1903, 340. On Americans' ideas about their position in the world at the turn of the twentieth century, see Frank Nincovich, *Global Dawn: The Cultural Foundations of American Internationalism, 1865–1890* (Cambridge, MA: Harvard University Press, 2009); Susan Schulten, *The Geographical Imagination in America, 1880–1950* (Chicago: University of Chicago Press, 2001).

3. Edward Keene, "The Treaty-Making Revolution of the Nineteenth Century," *International History Review* 34 (2012): 475–500.

4. Charles I. Bevans, comp., *Treaties and Other International Agreements of the United States of America, 1776–1949* (Washington, DC: U.S. Government Printing Office, 1968), vols. 5–12; "Treaty with Orange Free State: Provision for Extradition of Fugitives from this Country," *Washington Post*, December 12, 1896, 11. The average number of extraditions per year was calculated with data from Warrants of Arrest and Extradition, 1843–1930, Entry 859, RG 59, NARA. For mentions of extradition in the Annual Message to Congress, see William

McKinley, "Annual Message to Congress, December 5, 1898," *FRUS 1898* (Washington, DC: U.S. Government Printing Office, 1898), lxxix; William McKinley, "Annual Message to Congress, December 5, 1899," *FRUS 1899* (Washington, DC: U.S. Government Printing Office, 1899), xiv–xv, xxv; William McKinley, "Annual Message to Congress, December 3, 1900," *FRUS 1900* (Washington, DC: U.S. Government Printing Office, 1900), xvi–xvii, xxv–xxvi; Theodore Roosevelt, "Annual Message to Congress, December 7, 1903," *FRUS 1903* (Washington, DC: U.S. Government Printing Office, 1903), xv. On extradition in literature, see Richard Harding Davis, "The Exiles," in *The Exiles and Other Stories* (New York: Harper and Brothers, 1894); O. Henry, *Cabbages and Kings* (New York: McClure, Phillips, 1904); Richard Harding Davis, *The Dictator: A Play in Three Acts* (New York: Charles Scribner's Sons, 1906).

5. On anti-imperialism and the Anti-Imperialist League, see Robert L. Beisner, *Twelve against Empire: The Anti-Imperialists, 1898–1900* (New York: McGraw-Hill, 1968); Frank A. Nincovich, *The United States and Imperialism* (Malden, MA: Blackwell, 2001).

6. "A Network of Extradition," *New York Tribune*, January 29, 1899, 11. John Fousek's concept of "American nationalist globalism" provides an interesting comparison to the "nowhere to hide" trope. Writing about the Cold War years, Fousek argues that "public discourse continuously linked U.S. global responsibility to anticommunism and enveloped both within a framework of American national greatness." Substituting "law enforcement" for "anticommunism," Fousek could be describing the turn of the twentieth century. His emphasis on the role of the press and the broad popular consensus also parallels the turn of the century. This suggests that the "nationalist globalism" that he describes actually had its roots earlier than he acknowledges. John Fousek, *To Lead the Free World: American Nationalism and the Cultural Roots of the Cold War* (Chapel Hill: University of North Carolina Press, 2000).

7. The man is unnamed; he is referred to only as "a prominent New Orleans lawyer." This story was written for the *New Orleans Times-Democrat*, reprinted as "No City of Refuge Left," *New York Tribune*, December 31, 1899, 6; "No Place of Refuge," *Boston Daily Globe*, December 31, 1899, 30.

8. "The World Too Small for Criminals," *Los Angeles Times*, August 7, 1887, 4; "Modern Methods of Pursuit," *Atlanta Constitution*, December 22, 1899, 6; "A Growing Lack of Places for Criminals to Go," *New York Tribune*, December 30, 1900, B9; "The Criminal's Last Haven of Refuge," *American Lawyer*, August 1903, 339; "World Holds No Absolutely Safe Haven for Criminals Now," *New York Tribune*, September 9, 1906, B2; "Criminal Never Safe Anywhere," *Chicago Daily Tribune*, September 9, 1906, B3; "The Grip of Extradition," *Washington Post*, August 28, 1910, M3.

9. "Mr. Edison as a Prophet," *Washington Post*, October 28, 1894, 17; "Our Detectives," *Youth's Companion*, June 12, 1890, 327.

10. On the role of international lawyers in the emergence of the United States as a world power in the early twentieth century, see Benjamin A. Coates, "Transatlantic Advocates: American International Law and U.S. Foreign Relations, 1898–1919" (PhD diss., Columbia University, 2010).

11. Ex-Attache, "Extradition: A Modern Form of Jurisprudence that Owes Its Origin to the United States," *New York Tribune*, July 30, 1899, B7, reprinted as "Surrender of Refugees: Practice of Extradition Originated by the United States," *Washington Post*, July 30, 1899, 27; Sir Edward Clarke, *A Treatise upon the Law of Extradition* (London: Stevens and Haynes, 1888), 28. Publications that reprinted the New Orleans lawyer's remarks in the weeks following its initial publication on December 31, 1899, included "Cities of Refuge Gone: World Has Wiped the Last from the Map," *Los Angeles Times*, January 13, 1900, I7; *American Lawyer*, March 1900, 99; *Independent*, April 19, 1900, 965.

12. Extradition case file of Thomas J. Hunter, Entry 857, Box 53, RG 59, NARA; "W. P. Hill Talks of His Ten Thousand Mile Trip to Morocco and Return," *Atlanta Constitution*, January 27, 1900, 5; "Alleged Defaulter Caught," *New York Times*, December 16, 1899, 4; "Hunter Is Held," *Atlanta Constitution*, December 16, 1899, 9; "Tom Hunter Will Soon Be in Atlanta," *Atlanta Constitution*, January 24, 1900, 2; "From a Morocco Prison," *Washington Post*, January 26, 1900, 2.

13. Willis Boyd Allen, *The Head of Pasht* (New York: E. P. Dutton, 1900), 259.

14. William Gammell, "Asylum and Extradition among Nations," paper read before the Rhode Island Historical Society, March 9, 1880, in *William Gammell, LL.D.: A Biographical Sketch with Selections from His Writings*, ed. James O. Murray (Cambridge, MA: Riverside Press, 1890), 309–310.

15. "Education and Social Progress," commencement address delivered June 29, 1911, by President Harry Pratt Judson of the University of Chicago at the University of Michigan, in *The Michigan Alumnus*, July 1911, 558, 560; "Extradition Treaties," *Washington Post*, May 25, 1903, 6.

16. Senate Ex. Doc. No. 272, 50th Cong., 1st sess., 12, 16; John Bassett Moore, *A Treatise on Extradition and Interstate Rendition*, vol. 1 (Boston: Boston Book, 1891), 81–82n1.

17. On the United States and extraterritorial jurisdiction, see Teemu Ruskola, *Legal Orientalism: China, the United States, and Modern Law* (Cambridge, MA: Harvard University Press, 2013); Eileen P. Scully, *Bargaining with the State from Afar: American Citizenship in Treaty Port China, 1844–1942* (New York: Columbia University Press, 2001).

18. "The Perils of Extradition," *Pall Mall Gazette*, reprinted in *New York Tribune*, December 30, 1900, B9.

19. Russian-American National League Broadside, New York, 1893, Portfolio 239, Folder 5, Printed Ephemera Collection, LOC; "Say It Would Work Injustice," *New York Times*, February 26, 1893; "The Bear's Drag-Net," *Chicago Tribune*, March 2, 1893; "They Oppose a Treaty with Russia," *New York Tribune*, March 7, 1893.

20. William Eleroy Curtis, "American Crooks in Chile," *Chicago Record*, September 26, 1899, in William Eleroy Curtis Scrapbooks, Box 17, Vol. 87, Public Policy Papers, Department of Rare Books and Special Collections, Princeton University Library. On Curtis's Pan-Americanism, see Benjamin A. Coates, "The Pan-American Lobbyist: William Eleroy Curtis and U.S. Empire, 1884–1899," *Diplomatic History* 38 (2014): 22–48.

21. "The Criminal's Last Haven of Refuge," *American Lawyer*, August 1903, 339; "Some Causes of Embezzlement," *Chicago Daily Tribune*, December 8, 1890, 4.

22. Bevans, *Treaties and Other International Agreements*, vol. 6, 895–899 (Colombia); vol. 7, 495–498 (El Salvador); vol. 10, 347–350 (Nicaragua), 1052–1056 (Peru).

23. Thomas D. Schoonover, *The United States in Central America, 1860–1911: Episodes of Social Imperialism and Imperial Rivalry in the World System* (Durham, NC: Duke University Press, 1991), 79, 162.

24. William Eleroy Curtis, "United States to Dominate the Hemisphere," in *Today Then: America's Best Minds Look 100 Years into the Future on the Occasion of the 1893 World's Colombian Exposition*, comp. Dave Walter (Helena, MT: American and World Geographic, 1992), 87–88. This railway was a serious proposition; see "Report of the International American Conference Relative to an Intercontinental Railway Line, May 19, 1890," Senate Exec. Doc. 125, 51st Cong., 1st sess. (Washington, DC: U.S. Government Printing Office, 1890).

25. Curtis wrote about his travels with President Arthur's commission in William Eleroy Curtis, *The Capitals of Spanish America* (New York: Harper and Brothers, 1888). On Curtis's appointments, see *National Cyclopedia of American Biography*, vol. 5 (New York: James T. White, 1894), 43–44.

26. William Eleroy Curtis, "Friends in South America," *North American Review*, September 1889, 377–378.

27. John R. G. Pitkin, Legation of the United States in Buenos Aires, to John W. Foster, Secretary of State, marked "Confidential," January 16, 1893, Despatches from the United States Ministers to Argentina, 1817–1906, Microfilm Roll 25, RG 59, M69, NARA; William Eleroy Curtis, "The City of Buenos Ayres," *Chautauquan*, June 1899, 254.

28. Curtis, *Capitals of Spanish America*, 562; Hanna to Bayard, August 14, 1886, U.S. Embassy, Argentina, Despatches, 1817–1906, Microfilm Roll 21, vol. 25, RG 59, M69, NARA.

29. *Minutes of the International American Conference*, Senate Exec. Doc. 231, 51st Cong., 1st sess. (1890), 719–720. On the International Conference of American States, see David Pletcher, *The Diplomacy of Trade and Investment: American Economic Expansion in the Hemisphere, 1865–1900* (Columbia: University of Missouri Press, 1998), 24–29, 45.

30. "Extradition with Latin America," *New York Tribune*, July 17, 1890, 6.

31. Bevans, *Treaties and Other International Agreements*, vol. 5, 67–71 (Argentina), 808–813 (Brazil); vol. 10, 1074–1078 (Peru); vol. 6, 543–549 (Chile); vol. 8, 482–488 (Guatemala); vol. 6, 1134–1137 (Cuba); vol. 10, 673–677 (Panama); vol. 12, 979–983 (Uruguay).

32. Extradition treaty between the United States and Honduras, ratifications exchanged at Washington, July 10, 1912, in Bevans, *Treaties and Other International Agreements*, vol. 8, 892–897; "Last Refuge of Criminals," *Washington Post*, August 4, 1912, M4; "Last Refuge Gone," *Boston Globe*, July 12, 1912, 16; "Editorial Points," *Boston Globe*, July 13, 1912, 6.

33. Richard Grimmet, *Instances of Use of United States Armed Forces Abroad, 1798–2001* (Congressional Research Service Report for Congress, 2002), available at www.fas.org/man/crs/RL30172.pdf.

34. Frank G. Tyrrell, *Political Thuggery; or, Missouri's Battle with the Boodlers* (St. Louis, MO: Puritan, 1904), 7 (emphasis in original).

35. Steven L. Piott, *Holy Joe: Joseph W. Folk and the Missouri Idea* (Columbia: University of Missouri Press, 1997), 29–40; Louis G. Geiger, "*Joseph W. Folk v. Edward Butler*: St. Louis, 1902," *Journal of Southern History* 28 (1962): 438–449.

36. Claude H. Wetmore and Lincoln Steffens, "Tweed Days in St. Louis," *McClure's Magazine*, October 1902, 577–586; Lincoln Steffens, *The Shame of the Cities* (New York: McClure, Phillips, 1904), 17. Other works of national prominence that championed Folk and his campaign include Lincoln Steffens, "The Shamelessness of St. Louis: Something New in the History of American Municipal Democracy," *McClure's Magazine*, March 1903, 545–560; Lincoln Steffens, "Enemies of the Republic," *McClure's Magazine*, March 1904, 395–402; Claude H. Wetmore, *The Battle against Bribery: Being the Only Complete Narrative of Joseph W. Folk's Warfare on Boodlers, Including Also the Story of the Get-Rich-Quick Concerns and the Exposure of Bribery in the Missouri Legislature* (St. Louis, MO: Pan-American, 1904); Lee Meriwether, "The Reign of Boodle and the Rape of the Ballot in St. Louis," *Arena*, January 1905, 43–51.

37. Piott, *Holy Joe*, 40.

38. Supplementary Extradition Convention, signed at Mexico City June 25, 1902, entered into force April 13, 1903, in Bevans, *Treaties and Other International Agreements*, vol. 9, 918–919.

39. "Extradition for Bribery," *New York Tribune*, October 10, 1903, 6. Adolph Maders was another of the St. Louis Boodlers; August W. Machen was the superintendent of the rural free delivery system of the Post Office Department, dismissed from his post in May 1903 after accusations that he had received bribes and misused government funds.

40. Piott, *Holy Joe*, 59. Steffens confirms that Folk petitioned the president and the secretary of state in his effort to get Kratz back; Lincoln Steffens, *The Struggle for Self-Government: Being an Attempt to Trace American Political Corruption to Its Source in Six States of the United States* (New York: McClure, Phillips, 1906), 8.

41. Theodore Roosevelt, "Annual Message to Congress, December 7, 1903," *FRUS 1903* (Washington, DC: U.S. Government Printing Office, 1903), xv–xvi; "President Said to Have Used Ideas of Mr. Folk," *New York Times*, December 8, 1903, 1; "Folk Talks of Message: In Sections the President Used the Missourian's Exact Words," *Baltimore Sun*, December 10, 1903, 9.

42. Roosevelt, "Annual Message to Congress, December 7, 1903," xvi.

43. Piott, *Holy Joe*, 59–60; Supplementary Extradition Convention, signed at London, April 12, 1905, entered into force February 22, 1907, in Bevans, *Treaties and Other International Agreements*, vol. 12, 272–273.

44. Variations of this rhyme appeared in British and American works of fiction, including Robert Louis Stevenson, *The Wrecker* (1891); Andrew Lang, *The Disentanglers* (1902); P. G. Wodehouse, *The Gold Bat* (1904); and Fergus

Hume, *The Mandarin's Fan* (1904). It made more sense in the British context, as Great Britain lacked an extradition treaty with Peru into the early twentieth century.

45. John Langdon Heaton, "The Wickedest City in the World," *San Francisco Chronicle*, January 10, 1897, 6; "City of the Men Afraid to Die," *San Francisco Chronicle*, August 13, 1905, 7.

46. Davis, *The Exiles and Other Stories;* "Mr. Richard Harding Davis" (interview), *Boston Sunday Herald*, April 12, 1896, 26, cited in Arthur Lubow, *The Reporter Who Would Be King: A Biography of Richard Harding Davis* (New York: Charles Scribner's Sons, 1992), 113; Davis, *The Dictator*, 96–97. For a biography of Davis, see John Seelye, *War Games: Richard Harding Davis and the New Imperialism* (Amherst: University of Massachusetts Press, 2003).

47. Henry, *Cabbages and Kings*, 45, 160. On O. Henry's time in Honduras, see Charles Alphonso Smith, *O. Henry Biography* (New York: Doubleday, Page, 1916), 137–141; Al Jennings, *Through the Shadows with O. Henry* (New York: H. K. Fly, 1921).

48. Davis, *The Exiles and Other Stories*, 3, 21; Henry, *Cabbages and Kings*, 45.

49. Richard Harding Davis, *Soldiers of Fortune* (New York: C. Scribner's Sons, 1897).

50. *The American Almanac, Year-Book, Cyclopaedia and Atlas*, 2nd ed. (New York: W. R. Hearst, 1903), 446; "Again Seek Allen in Toronto on New Clue," *Boston Journal*, August 13, 1903, 3; "Questions and Answers," *Dallas Morning News*, April 17, 1904, 17; "Questions and Answers," *Dallas Morning News*, August 28, 1904, 17; "Bringing Them Home," *New York Times*, October 16, 1932, E1; "Foresight of Defaulters," *Washington Post*, March 8, 1903, 2.

51. The Solicitor to Gaillard Hunt, October 14, 1923, Box 3298, Folder 42, File 211.18, CDF, 1910–1929, RG 59, NARA (emphasis in original).

52. "Neely Released on Bail," *New York Times*, May 8, 1900, 2; "The Investigation in Havana," *New York Times*, May 8, 1900, 2.

53. "The Criminal's Last Haven of Refuge," *American Lawyer*, August 1903, 339.

54. Act of June 6, 1900, Ch. 793, 31 Stat. 656.

55. Neely v. Henkel, 180 U.S. 109 (1901).

56. Downes v. Bidwell, 182 U.S. 244 (1901). On the Insular Cases, see Bartholomew H. Sparrow, *The Insular Cases and the Emergence of American Empire* (Lawrence: University Press of Kansas, 2006). On Puerto Rico, see Christina Duffy Burnett and Burke Marshall, eds., *Foreign in a Domestic Sense: Puerto Rico, American Expansion, and the Constitution* (Durham, NC: Duke University Press, 2001).

57. Sparrow, *Insular Cases*, 133–136.

58. S. R. Gummeré, American Legation in Morocco, to Secretary of State, September 6, 1906, in *FRUS 1906* (Washington, DC: U.S. Government Printing Office, 1906), 1163; "Criminal Never Safe Anywhere," *Chicago Daily Tribune*, September 9, 1906, B3.

4

Extradition Havens

1. On arguments in the Moore case, see Federico T. Moore, *De la extradición: Alegato de Claudio Arteaga U., abogado por parte de los Estados Unidos de Norte América en la causa de extradición contra Federico T. Moore, pronunciado ante la exma. Corte suprema de Chile en las audiencias del 25, 26 y 29 de enero de 1900* (Santiago de Chile: Imprenta Barcelona, 1900). On the charges against Moore, see Extradition Case File of Frederick T. Moore, Entry 857, Box 53, RG 59, NARA. Moore's counsel, Enrique MacIver Rodríguez, is quoted in "Will Refuse Extradition," *Boston Daily Globe*, January 27, 1900, 3. On Moore's release, see "Refused to Extradite Boston Fugitive," *Washington Post*, March 10, 1900, 9; "No Extradition from Chili," *New York Tribune*, April 19, 1900, 10.

2. The various extradition treaties between the United States and Latin American nations are in Charles I. Bevans, *Treaties and Other International Agreements of the United States of America, 1776–1949* (Washington, DC: U.S. Government Printing Office, 1968), vols. 5–12.

3. On the history of the Monroe Doctrine, see Jay Sexton, *The Monroe Doctrine: Empire and Nation in Nineteenth-Century America* (New York: Hill and Wang, 2011); Brian Loveman, *No Higher Law: American Foreign Policy and the Western Hemisphere since 1776* (Chapel Hill: University of North Carolina Press, 2010).

4. The most complete account of Meiggs's life is Watt Stewart, *Henry Meiggs: Yankee Pizarro* (Durham, NC: Duke University Press, 1946). Meiggs also is discussed at length in J. Fred Rippy, "Henry Meiggs, Yankee Railroad Builder," in *People and Issues in Latin American History: From Independence to the Present*, ed. Lewis Hanke and Jane M. Rausch (New York: M. Weiner, 1993), 110–116; Lawrence A. Clayton, *Grace: W. R. Grace & Co., The Formative Years, 1850–1930* (Ottawa, IL: Jameson Books, 1985), 56–83; Jonathan V. Levin, *The Export Economies: Their Pattern of Development in Historical Perspective* (Cambridge, MA: Harvard University Press, 1960), 98–108; David M. Pletcher, *The Diplomacy of Trade and Investment: American Economic Expansion in the Hemisphere, 1865–1900* (Columbia: University of Missouri Press, 1998), 198–199.

5. Samuel Curtis Upham, *Notes of a Voyage to California via Cape Horn* (Philadelphia: The author, 1878), 150.

6. Stewart, *Henry Meiggs*, 18–21.

7. Thomas H. Nelson, Legation of the United States in Santiago de Chile, to William A. Seward, Secretary of State, December 16, 1863, in *FRUS 1864*, part 4 (Washington, DC: U.S. Government Printing Office, 1864), 168–169; *El Mercurio*, December 14, 1863, reprinted in translation in *FRUS 1864*, 171.

8. Alvin P. Hovey, Legation of the United States in Lima, to Hamilton Fish, Secretary of State, August 22, 1870, in *FRUS 1870–71* (Washington, DC: U.S. Government Printing Office, 1871), 507; Estuardo Núñez, *Biblioteca Hombres del Perú: A. de Humboldt, Enrique Meiggs* (Lima: Editorial Universitaria, 1966).

9. "A Remarkable Career," *New York Times*, October 12, 1877, 4.

10. "A Land of Thieves: Where Criminals Gather from All Parts of the Earth," *New Orleans Daily Picayune*, September 22, 1900, 7; Vicente Romero y Girón and Alejo García Moreno, *Colección de las instituciones políticas y jurídicas de los pueblos modernos, Apéndice III, Nuevos leyes y códigos de los estados americanos* (Madrid: Centro Editorial de Góngora, 1896), 381.

11. Nancy Peckenham and Annie Street, eds., *Honduras: Portrait of a Captive Nation* (New York: Praeger, 1985), 23–33; Darío A. Euraque, *Reinterpreting the Banana Republic: Region and State in Honduras, 1870–1972* (Chapel Hill: University of North Carolina Press, 1996), 3–4.

12. The best accounts of Burke's escape to Honduras are James F. Vivian, "Major E. A. Burke: The Honduras Exile, 1889–1928," *Louisiana History* 15 (1974): 175–194; Kathryn K. Conley, "The Making of an American Imperialist: Major Edward Austin Burke, Reconstruction New Orleans, and the Road to Central America" (master's thesis, University of New Orleans, 2012). Burke is discussed in the context of corrupt government officials in the post-Reconstruction South in C. Vann Woodward, *The Origins of the New South, 1877–1913* (Baton Rouge: Louisiana State University Press, 1951), 70–72.

13. "Hiding in Honduras," *Chicago Tribune*, December 25, 1889, 1; "Major Burke in Clover," *New York Tribune*, April 6, 1890, 4.

14. Invitation to banquet in honor of President Manuel Bonilla, May 16, 1903, EAB, LSU; Invitation to the wedding of Emma, daughter of Policarpo Bonilla, EAB, LSU; "Escritura de compraventa de la mitad de la zona Apamul," EAB, LSU; P. Bonilla to E. A. Burke, April 23, 1892, EAB, LSU; E. A. Burke to President Bonilla, December 10, 1897, EAB, LSU; I. K. Shuman, "Put Lindbergh to Flight," *New York Times*, January 6, 1928, 2; "Louisianian Left Half Estate to Honduras; Self-Exiled Treasurer Lived There 40 Years," *New York Times*, October 22, 1928, 1.

15. "Mayor Edward A. Burke, fallecido recientemente," *Renacimiento*, September 30, 1928, 12; "Eduardo Alfredo Burke," *El Democrata*, October 4, 1928 (emphasis in original), 3; "Muere un amigo de Honduras," *El Cronista*, September 24, 1928, 2; "Anoche falleció en esta capital el Mayor Eduardo A. Burke: Honduras está de duelo," *El Cronista*, September 24, 1928, 2. All newspapers are located in ANH.

16. Luis Lazo Arriaga, Legation of Honduras, to State Department, March 10, 1910, File No. 211.15, Box 3297, CDF 1910–29, RG 59, NARA.

17. Juan Manuel Aguilar Flores, "Árbol navideño en Tegucigalpa," *La Tribuna: Anales Históricos*, December 13, 2009; Charles D. White to Secretary of State, February 7, 1912, Box 3355, File 215.11, CDF 1910–29, RG 59, NARA; "Dr. Walther beyond Pursuit," *Chicago Tribune*, July 7, 1903, 13; "Protected in Honduras," *New York Times*, July 7, 1903, 5.

18. John Ewing to Secretary of State, December 8, 1915, Box 3354, File 215.11, CDF 1910–29, RG 59, NARA. Earl J. Davis to Secretary of State, March 7, 1924, Box 3355, File 215.11, CDF 1910–29, RG 59, NARA; Clayton, *Grace*, 56–60; "Describes Life of 'Big Dan,'" *Chicago Tribune*, April 10, 1909, 3.

19. Circular written by E. A. Burke, December 16, 1897, EAB, LSU. On Burke's frequent unsolicited advice to the State Department, see James Patterson, U.S. Consul in Tegucigalpa, to State Department, September 30, 1893,

Despatches from United States Consuls in Tegucigalpa, Honduras, 1860–1906, Roll 4, RG 59, T-352, NARA (microfilm).

20. Wayne E. Fuller, *Morality and the Mail in Nineteenth-Century America* (Urbana: University of Illinois Press, 2003), 211–212.

21. "The Lottery in Florida," *New York Times*, February 3, 1894, 4; Fuller, *Morality and the Mail*, 213–214; Richard Harding Davis, *Three Gringos in Venezuela and Central America* (New York: Harper and Brothers, 1896), 34–35, originally published as "The Exiled Lottery," *Harper's Weekly*, August 3, 1895, 728–729.

22. Fuller, *Morality and the Mail*, 213. Davis describes a lottery drawing in *Three Gringos*, 49–50.

23. "The Lottery's Refuge," *Outlook*, November 18, 1893, 883.

24. Frederick Palmer, *Central America and Its Problems: An Account of a Journey from the Rio Grande to Panama* (New York: Moffat, Yard, 1910), 143. On the end of the Honduran lottery, see "Honduras Lottery Downed At Last," *Los Angeles Times*, April 2, 1907, II1. President Theodore Roosevelt praised the Secret Service for the destruction of the Honduras National Lottery in a special memorandum to the House of Representatives, January 4, 1909, in Theodore Roosevelt, *Presidential Addresses and State Papers and European Addresses, December 8, 1908–June 7, 1910* (New York: Review of Reviews, 1910), 2036–2037.

25. *La Gaceta*, no. 3.255, March 13, 1909, 245, ANH; Hugh S. Gibson, American Legation in Tegucigalpa, to Secretary of State, November 18, 1908, Numerical and Minor Files of the Department of State, 1906–1910, File 12344/16, Roll 802, RG 59, NARA (microfilm). On Honduras as a banana republic, see Walter La Feber, *Inevitable Revolutions: The United States in Central America*, 2nd ed. (New York: W. W. Norton, 1993), 42. On United States military intervention in Honduras, see Richard Grimmet, *Instances of Use of United States Armed Forces Abroad, 1798–2001* (Congressional Research Service Report for Congress, 2002), available at www.fas.org/man/crs/RL30172.pdf.

26. "Crooks Raise Boodle Fund," *Los Angeles Times*, February 10, 1910, II14; Emily S. Rosenberg, *Financial Missionaries to the World: The Politics and Culture of Dollar Diplomacy, 1900–1930* (Durham, NC: Duke University Press, 2003), 68; La Feber, *Inevitable Revolutions*, 45; Extradition Treaty between the United States and Honduras, ratifications exchanged at Washington, July 10, 1912, in Bevans, *Treaties and Other International Agreements of the United States*, vol. 8, 892–897.

27. On racial ideas in Latin America, see Nancy Appelbaum, Anne S. Macpherson, and Karin Alejandra Rosemblatt, eds., *Race and Nation in Modern Latin America* (Chapel Hill: University of North Carolina Press, 2003); Richard Graham, ed., *The Idea of Race in Latin America, 1870–1940* (Austin: University of Texas Press, 1990); Nancy Leys Stepan, *"The Hour of Eugenics": Race, Gender, and Nation in Latin America* (Ithaca, NY: Cornell University Press, 1991); Jeffrey Lesser, *Negotiating National Identity: Immigrants, Minorities, and the Struggle for Ethnicity in Brazil* (Durham, NC: Duke University Press, 1999); Magnus Mörner, ed., *Race and Class in Latin America* (New York: Columbia University Press, 1970). Only a small percentage of European

immigrants to Latin America were "Anglo-Saxon"; most were Italian, Spanish, Portuguese, and German, as well as people from the Middle East who at times were considered white.

28. Julia Rodriguez, *Civilizing Argentina: Science, Medicine, and the Modern State* (Chapel Hill: University of North Carolina Press, 2006), 2–5. On science and the body politic in Argentina, see Kristin Ruggiero, *Modernity in the Flesh: Medicine, Law, and Society in Turn-of-the-Century Argentina* (Stanford, CA: Stanford University Press, 2004); Donna Guy, *Sex and Danger in Buenos Aires: Prostitution, Family, and Nation in Argentina* (Lincoln: University of Nebraska Press, 1990).

29. Juan Bautista Alberdi, "Immigration as a Means of Progress," in *The Argentina Reader: History, Culture, Politics*, ed. Gabriela Nouzeilles and Graciela Montaldo (Durham, NC: Duke University Press, 2002), 95–96.

30. *Message of the President of the Republic on Opening the Argentine Congress, May 1882* (Buenos Aires: Standard Printing Office, 1882), 5; Despatches from the United States Ministers to Argentina, 1817–1906, Roll 21, RG 59, M69, NARA (microfilm).

31. "Fugitives from Justice," *Buenos Ayres Standard*, clipping enclosed in John R. G. Pitkin to Department of State, April 14, 1893, U.S. Embassy, Argentina, Despatches, 1817–1906, Roll 25, RG 59, M69, NARA (microfilm).

32. Henry Cabot Lodge, *The History of Nations, Vol. 21: South America* (Chicago: H. W. Snow, 1910), 258; Frank G. Carpenter, *South America, Social, Industrial, and Political: A Twenty-Five-Thousand-Mile Journey in Search of Information* (New York: Western W. Wilson, 1900), 312.

33. Rodriguez, *Civilizing Argentina*, 54–55, 186–187, 194; Guy, *Sex and Danger in Buenos Aires*. On Vucetich and fingerprinting, see Julia Rodriguez, "South Atlantic Crossings: Fingerprints, Science, and the State in Turn-of-the-Century Argentina," *American Historical Review* 109 (2004): 387–416.

34. Bayless W. Hanna, U.S. Legation in Buenos Aires, to Mr. Porter, Acting Secretary of State, February 21, 1887, Despatches from the United States Ministers to Argentina, 1817–1906, Roll 22, RG 59, M69, NARA (microfilm); Extradition Treaty between the United States and the Argentine Republic, ratifications exchanged at Buenos Aires, June 2, 1900, in Bevans, *Treaties and Other International Agreements of the United States*, vol. 5, 67–71; Extradition Case File of William Hoeppner, Entry 857, Box 59, RG 59, NARA; "Clerk Charged with a $30,000 Defalcation," *New York Times*, September 28, 1901, 3.

35. Gustavus L. Monroe, U.S. Legation in San José, to Secretary of State, September 18, 1911, Box 3298, File 211.18, CDF 1910–29, RG 59, NARA.

36. Memorandum from Cleto González Víquez to the Costa Rican Ministry of Foreign Affairs, July 30, 1911, Caja 200, No. 32, Estados Unidos—Legaciones Extrajeras 1911, DRE, ANCR.

37. Lara Putnam, *The Company They Kept: Migrants and the Politics of Gender in Caribbean Costa Rica, 1870–1960* (Chapel Hill: University of North Carolina Press, 2002), 39. On Afro-Caribbean immigration, particularly as labor on Costa Rican banana plantations, see Aviva Chomsky, *West Indian Workers and the United Fruit Company in Costa Rica, 1870–1940* (Baton Rouge: Louisiana State University Press, 1996); Philippe I. Bourgois, *Ethnicity at Work: Divided*

Labor on a Central American Banana Plantation (Baltimore, MD: Johns Hopkins University Press, 1989); Quince Duncan and Carlos Melendez, *El Negro en Costa Rica* (San José: Editorial Costa Rica, 1981). On the "white legend" by Costa Rican elites that ignores discrimination against ethnic minorities, see Mavis Hiltunen Biesanz, Richard Biesanz, and Karen Zubris Biesanz, *The Ticos: Culture and Social Change in Costa Rica* (Boulder, CO: Lynne Rienner, 1999), 109–121. On the elites' insistence of their own European racial purity and their "bleaching" of their historical heroes to deny indigenous or African blood, see Lowell Gudmundson, *Costa Rica before Coffee: Society and Economy on the Eve of the Export Boom* (Baton Rouge: Louisiana State University Press, 1986), 86.

38. Clodomiro Picado, "Our Blood Is Blackening," in *The Costa Rica Reader: History, Culture, Politics*, ed. Steven Palmer and Iván Molina (Durham, NC: Duke University Press, 2004), 243–244.

39. Memorandum from Cleto González Víquez to the Costa Rican Ministry of Foreign Affairs, July 30, 1911, Caja 200, No. 32, Estados Unidos—Legaciones Extrajeras 1911, DRE, ANCR.

40. "Fugitives from Justice," *Buenos Ayres Standard*, clipping enclosed in Pitkin to Department of State, April 14, 1893, U.S. Embassy, Argentina, Despatches, 1817–1906, Roll 25, RG 59, M69, NARA (microfilm).

41. "Arrest of Francis H. Weeks," *New York Tribune*, September 12, 1893; "Weeks Will Be Here Soon," *New York Times*, September 27, 1893, 5. On Weeks's crime, see David Huyssen, *Progressive Inequality: Rich and Poor in New York, 1890–1920* (Cambridge, MA: Harvard University Press, 2014), 63–64, 86–87.

42. Harrison R. Williams, U.S. Consul in San José, to Department of State, September 15, 1893, Despatches from United States consuls in San José, Costa Rica, 1852–1906, Roll 5, RG 59, T 35, NARA (microfilm); Williams to Josiah Quincy, Assistant Secretary of State, September 18, 1893, Despatches from United States consuls in San José, Costa Rica, 1852–1906, Roll 5, RG 59, T 35, NARA (microfilm).

43. *El Diario de Comercio* quoted in "Protesting Costa Ricans," *New York Times*, October 31, 1893, 3.

44. Williams to the Department of State, September 15, 1893; Grover Cleveland, "Message of the President, Dec. 4, 1893," in *FRUS 1893–1894*, vol. 1 (Washington, DC: U.S. Government Printing Office, 1893–1894), vi.

45. On Costa Rica's refusal to sign an extradition treaty unless it prohibited the death penalty, see "No Extradition with Costa Rica," *Chicago Daily Tribune*, February 25, 1894; Correspondencia Manuel María Peralta, No. 303, ANCR. On the United States' inability to enter into such a treaty, see *Albany Law Journal*, March 3, 1894, 153. On the 1923 treaty, see Treaty Series No. 668, *Treaty between the United States and Costa Rica: Extradition and Exchange of Notes concerning Death Penalty* (Washington, DC: U.S. Government Printing Office, 1926); J. S. Reeves, "Extradition Treaties and the Death Penalty," *American Journal of International Law* 18 (1924): 298–300.

46. William Beach Lawrence, *American Law Review*, June 1881, 412. On the abolition of the death penalty in Latin America, see William Schabas, *The Abolition of the Death Penalty in International Law* (Cambridge, UK: Cambridge University Press, 2002), 311; Ricardo Ulate, "The Death Penalty:

Some Observations on Latin America," *Crime Prevention and Criminal Justice* 27 (1986): 12–13; "Growing Tendency in Latin America to Abolish the Death Penalty," *Bulletin of the Pan American Union* 58 (1924): 362–365.

47. Brazilian Extradition Statute No. 2416, of June 28, 1911, in *FRUS 1913* (Washington, DC: U.S. Government Printing Office, 1913), 26–28; Memorandum respecting proposed new extradition law of Brazil, handed to Dr. Martins of the Brazilian Foreign Office, May 5, 1910, File 22903/2, Record 232.00, CDF 1910–29, RG 59, NARA; Extract from Memorandum Prepared by the Counselor for the Department of State, Enclosure to Memorandum of May 5, 1910, File 22903/2, Record 232.00, CDF 1910–29, RG 59, NARA.

48. *The Steel Trap*, written and directed by Andrew L. Stone, 1952.

49. On politics in Costa Rica during this period, see Deborah J. Yashar, *Demanding Democracy: Reform and Reaction in Costa Rica and Guatemala, 1870s-1950s* (Stanford, CA: Stanford University Press, 1997).

50. The arguments from both sides of the Weeks trial are transcribed in full in Republica de Costa Rica, Ministerio de Relaciones Exteriores, *Documentos relativos a la extradición de Francis H. Weeks* (San José: Tipografia Nacional, 1893), 59, ANCR. On the Weeks trial, see Caja 113, No. 1, Estados Unidos, 1893, DRE, ANCR.

51. *La Prensa Libre* quoted in "Protesting Costa Ricans," *New York Times*, October 31, 1893, 3. Martí's most famous essay is "Our America" (1891); see José Martí, "Our America" in *José Martí: Selected Writings*, ed. and trans. Esther Allen (New York: Penguin Books, 2002), 288–295.

52. Harrison R. Williams, U.S. Consul in San José, to Josiah Quincy, Assistant Secretary of State, October 30, 1893, Despatches from United States consuls in San José, Costa Rica, 1852–1906, Roll 5, RG 59, T 35, NARA (microfilm); *El Heraldo de Costa Rica*, October 18, 1893, 2, Biblioteca Nacional de Costa Rica.

53. Williams to the Department of State, December 4, 1893, Despatches from United States consuls in San José, Costa Rica, 1852–1906, Roll 5, RG 59, T 35, NARA (microfilm); Williams to Edwin F. Uhl, Assistant Secretary of State, January 12, 1894, Despatches from United States consuls in San José, Costa Rica, 1852–1906, Roll 5, RG 59, T 35, NARA (microfilm).

54. Williams to Uhl, January 12, 1894; Frederick Augustus Henry, *Captain Henry of Geauga* (Cleveland, OH: Gates, 1942), 490, 492.

55. Memorandum from Cleto González Víquez to the Costa Rican Ministry of Foreign Affairs, July 30, 1911.

56. Uki Goñi, *The Real Odessa: How Perón Brought the Nazi War Criminals to Argentina* (London: Granta, 2002); Neal Bascomb, *Hunting Eichmann: How a Band of Survivors and a Young Spy Agency Chased Down the World's Most Notorious Nazi* (Boston: Houghton Mifflin Harcourt, 2009).

57. Arthur Herzog, *Vesco: From Wall Street to Castro's Cuba—The Rise, Fall, and Exile of the King of White Collar Crime* (New York: Doubleday, 1987).

5
Asylum No More

1. "Mrs. Mattie Rich Was Extradited," *El Paso Daily Times*, July 25, 1899, 8; "Dons Stars and Stripes," *Los Angeles Times*, July 25, 1899, 2; "How Mrs. Rich Went to Juarez," *San Antonio Express*, July 28, 1899, 6.

2. William McKinley, "Annual Message of the President, December 5, 1899," in *FRUS 1899* (Washington, DC: U.S. Government Printing Office, 1901), xxv–xxvi.

3. On the number of people extradited from the United States each year, see Warrants of Arrest and Extradition, 1843–1930, Entry 859, RG 59, NARA.

4. On the extradition of U.S. citizens, see Robert W. Rafuse, "The Extradition of Nationals," in *Illinois Studies in the Social Sciences* 24 (1939): 1–163; Daniel S. Margolies, *Spaces of Law in American Foreign Relations: Extradition and Extraterritoriality in the Borderlands and Beyond, 1877–1898* (Athens: University of Georgia Press, 2011), 231–272.

5. Thomas Paine, *Common Sense* (New York: Penguin Classics, 1986), 100. On the myth of the United States as an asylum, see Marilyn C. Baseler, *"Asylum for Mankind": America, 1607–1800* (Ithaca, NY: Cornell University Press, 1998).

6. Ruth Wedgwood, "The Revolutionary Martyrdom of Jonathan Robbins," *Yale Law Journal* 100 (1990–1991): 229–368; Christopher H. Pyle, *Extradition, Politics, and Human Rights* (Philadelphia: Temple University Press, 2001), 24–47.

7. Holmes v. Jennison, 39 U.S. 540 (1840). The extradition treaties signed by the United States are listed in Charles I. Bevans, comp., *Treaties and Other International Agreements of the United States of America, 1776–1949* (Washington, DC: U.S. Government Printing Office, 1968), vols. 5–12.

8. "National Requisition Case," *Niles National Register*, August 19, 1843, 1; Samuel Thayer Spear, *The Law of Extradition, International and Inter-state* (Albany, NY: Weed, Parsons, 1879), 27–30; *Report of the Trial of Mrs. Gilmour for the Alleged Murder of Her Husband* (Edinburgh: W. Forrester, 1844).

9. "The Extradition Case," *New York Herald*, July 18, 1843, 2. Many of the questions about process were resolved in 1848, when Congress passed a law setting forth the procedures that would govern every international extradition case. On the Kaine case, see Pyle, *Extradition, Politics, and Human Rights*, 100.

10. U.S. Const. art. IV, §2; Fugitive Slave Act, February 12, 1793, 1 Stat. 302.

11. Prigg v. Pennsylvania, 41 U.S. 539 (1842); Fugitive Slave Act, September 18, 1850, 9 Stat. 462. On the Minkins and Burns cases, see Steven Lubet, *Fugitive Justice: Runaways, Rescuers, and Slavery on Trial* (Cambridge, MA: Belknap Press of Harvard University Press, 2010).

12. On the number of annual extradition cases, see Warrants of Arrest and Extradition, 1843–1930, Entry 859, RG 59, NARA.

13. Ibid.

14. John Bassett Moore, *Report on Extradition, with Returns of All Cases from August 9, 1842 to January 1, 1890* (Washington, DC: U.S. Government Printing Office, 1890), 3. An important work on deportation that does not

mention extradition is Daniel Kanstroom, *Deportation Nation: Outsiders in American History* (Cambridge, MA: Harvard University Press, 2007).

15. Benjamin Franklin, "Rattlesnakes for Felons," *Pennsylvania Gazette*, May 9, 1751, in *A Benjamin Franklin Reader*, ed. Walter Isaacson (New York: Simon and Schuster, 2003), 149–151; Page Act, March 3, 1875, 18 Stat. 477. On the association between immigrants and criminality, see John Higham, *Strangers in the Land: Patterns of American Nativism, 1860–1925* (New York: Atheneum, 1963).

16. Henry Wheaton, *Elements of International Law* (Boston: Little, Brown, 1866), 189.

17. John Bassett Moore, *A Treatise on Extradition and Interstate Rendition*, vol. 1 (Boston: Boston Book, 1891), 152; Italian Penal Code of 1890, quoted in Charlton v. Kelly, 229 U.S. 447 (1913), 466.

18. Patrick Weil, *The Sovereign Citizen: Denaturalization and the Origins of the American Republic* (Philadelphia: University of Pennsylvania Press, 2013), 197; Linda K. Kerber, "Toward a History of Statelessness in America," *American Quarterly* 57 (2005): 727–749; I-Mien Tsiang, *The Question of Expatriation in America Prior to 1907* (Baltimore, MD: Johns Hopkins University Press, 1942); Rafuse, "Extradition of Nationals," 17.

19. Sir Edward Clarke, *A Treatise Upon the Law of Extradition* (London: Stevens and Haynes, 1888), 68; Moore, *Treatise*, vol. 1, 174–175.

20. Moore, *Treatise*, vol. 1, 157; Francis Wharton, *A Treatise on Criminal Pleading and Practice* (Philadelphia: Kay and Brother, 1880), 34; Francis Wharton, *A Treatise on the Conflict of Laws* (Philadelphia: Kay and Brother, 1872), 627–630; Spear, *Law of Extradition*, 26–27.

21. "Alexander Trimble: How His Release Is Viewed in Certain Quarters," *Galveston Daily News*, February 4, 1884. On the Trimble case, see Margolies, *Spaces of Law*, 254–257.

22. Secretary of State Frederick T. Frelinghuysen to President Chester A. Arthur, February 13, 1884, 48th Congress, 1st Session, Ex. Doc. No. 98, 5; Ex parte McCabe, 46 F. 363 (1891).

23. Extradition Treaty between the United States and Japan, ratifications exchanged at Tokyo, September 27, 1886, in Bevans, *Treaties*, 383–386 (emphasis added).

24. William Jackson Palmer to Frederick Frelinghuysen, February 7, 1884, AEMEUA T. 339, 608–11, SRE (emphasis in original).

25. Transcript of the extradition hearing of Francisco Benavides, beginning March 18, 1893, Extradition Case File of Francisco Benavides, Entry 857, Box 36, RG 59, NARA; Testimony before the U.S. Commissioner in the Extradition Hearing of Prudencio Gonzalez, May 6, 1893, AEMEUA T. 422, 149, SRE.

26. Governor Ireland's Second Inaugural Address, January 20, 1883, in *Collections in the Archives and History Department of the Texas State Library: Governors' Messages, 1874–1891* (Archive and History Department of the Texas State Library, 1916), 517–518. On the Rowe case, see "A Mexican Citizen," *Los Angeles Times*, July 22, 1895, 1; Extradition Case File of Chester W. Rowe, Entry 857, Box 42, RG 59, NARA; Margolies, *Spaces of Law*, 264–270.

27. Extradition treaty between the United States and Mexico, ratified at Mexico City, April 22, 1899, in Bevans, *Treaties*, vol. 9, 900–907, 903. On the history of extradition agreements between the United States and Mexico, see Bruce Zagaris and Julia Padierna Peralta, "Mexico–United States Extradition and Alternatives: From Fugitive Slaves to Drug Traffickers—150 Years and beyond the Rio Grande's Winding Courses," *American University Journal of International Law and Policy* 12 (1997): 519–621.

28. "The Mexican Treaty," *Arizona Republican*, June 1, 1899, 4.

29. Testimony of Mattie C. H. Rich, June 28, 1899, 1–2, Extradition Case File of Mattie Rich, Entry 857, Box 51, RG 59, NARA; New Mexico Marriages, 1727–1900, Ana County, ref. nos. 6019986–6019988, available at www .ancestry.com.

30. "El Paso Smallpox Scare," *Dallas Morning News*, December 18, 1898, 9; Mario T. García, *Desert Immigrants: The Mexicans of El Paso, 1880–1920* (New Haven, CT: Yale University Press, 1981), 37–38; Joseph Nevins, *Operation Gatekeeper: The Rise of the Illegal Alien and the Making of the U.S.-Mexico Boundary* (New York: Routledge, 2002), 193–194.

31. Testimony of Mattie C. H. Rich, June 28, 1899, 1–2; "J. D. Rich's Wound Proves Fatal," *El Paso Daily Herald*, May 2, 1899, 6. On working-class Americans and the American "colonies" in Mexico, see John Mason Hart, *Empire and Revolution: The Americans in Mexico since the Civil War* (Berkeley: University of California Press, 2002), 235–267; William Schell Jr., *Integral Outsiders: The American Colony in Mexico City, 1876–1911* (Wilmington, DE: Scholarly Resources, 2001).

32. "Mrs. Rich on the Stand," *El Paso Daily Times*, June 29, 1899, 7; Testimony of Mattie C. H. Rich, June 28, 1899, 26; "An Analysis of the Mystery," *El Paso Daily Times*, April 29, 1899, 7.

33. Mauricio Tenorio-Trillo, *Mexico at the World's Fairs: Crafting a Modern Nation* (Berkeley: University of California Press, 1996); William H. Beezley, *Judas at the Jockey Club and Other Episodes of Porfirian Mexico* (Lincoln: University of Nebraska Press, 1987), 10–11; Pablo Piccato, *City of Suspects: Crime in Mexico City, 1900–1931* (Durham, NC: Duke University Press, 2001), 41–45, 50–72; Paul J. Vanderwood, *Disorder and Progress: Bandits, Police, and Mexican Development* (Lincoln: University of Nebraska Press, 1981), 107–118.

34. "Mexico Requests Her Extradition," *El Paso Daily Herald*, May 5, 1899, 7; M. de Aspíroz to John Hay, May 18, 1899, in *FRUS 1899*, 497; "Dr. Jenkins Says He Knows Mrs. Rich," *El Paso Daily Times*, July 19, 1899, 6.

35. Testimony of Mattie C. H. Rich, June 28, 1899, 11; "Mrs. Rich on the Stand," *El Paso Daily Times*, June 29, 1899, 7.

36. "Mrs. Rich is Extradited," *New York Times*, July 15, 1899, 2.

37. "The Rich Case," *El Paso Daily Times*, July 16, 1899, 2 (emphasis added); Olive Ennis Hite, "Miserable Mrs. Rich," *Washington Post*, July 24, 1899, 3.

38. Hite, "Miserable Mrs. Rich," 3; "Prisoner's Eyes Glittered," *El Paso Daily Herald*, May 18, 1899, 3. On the deportation of Chinese, see El Paso Docket, Record 48-W-097, U.S. Commissioner, 1891–1900, NARA, Fort Worth, TX; Erika Lee, *At America's Gates: Chinese Immigration during the Exclusion Era, 1882–1943* (Chapel Hill: University of North Carolina Press,

2003), 179–187. On the extradition of Mexicans, see Extradition Case Files, 1836–1906, Entry 857, RG 59, NARA.

39. "Dons Stars and Stripes," *Los Angeles Times*, July 25, 1899, 2; Testimony of Mattie C. H. Rich, June 28, 1899, 3; "Mrs. Rich Is Delivered Up," *San Antonio Express*, July 25, 1899, 3. On the connections between gender and nationalism, see Amy Kaplan, "Manifest Domesticity," *American Literature* 70 (1998): 581–606; Kristin L Hoganson, *Fighting for American Manhood: How Gender Politics Provoked the Spanish-American and Philippine-American Wars* (New Haven, CT: Yale University Press, 1998).

40. Hite, "Miserable Mrs. Rich," 3. On Cuban imagery, see John J. Johnson, *Latin America in Caricature* (Austin: University of Texas Press, 1980).

41. "Extradition of Mrs. Rich," *Washington Post*, July 15, 1899, 9; "Mrs. Rich Surrendered," *Los Angeles Times*, July 15, 1899, 5; "Mrs. Rich Is Extradited," *New York Times*, July 15, 1899, 2; Hite, "Miserable Mrs. Rich," 3; "Is Sorry for Mrs. Rich," *El Paso Daily Times*, August 19, 1899, 3. On cultural representations of Mexico in the nineteenth century, see Shelley Streeby, *American Sensations: Class, Empire, and the Production of Popular Culture* (Berkeley: University of California Press, 2002).

42. "The Rich Extradition Case," *El Paso Daily Herald*, May 16, 1899, 2; "Mrs. Mattie Rich," *El Paso Daily Herald*, May 15, 1899, 6; Hite, "Miserable Mrs. Rich," 3.

43. "J. D. Rich's Wound Proves Fatal," *El Paso Daily Times*, May 2, 1899, 6.

44. "A Motive for Murder," *El Paso Daily Herald*, May 2, 1899, 3.

45. "Mrs. Rich on the Stand," *El Paso Daily Times*, June 29, 1899, 7; "An Analysis of the Mystery," *El Paso Daily Times*, April 29, 1899, 7; "Extradition Application," *El Paso Daily Herald*, May 5, 1899, 1.

46. On the "scatter syndrome," see Ruth Rosen, *The Lost Sisterhood: Prostitution in America, 1900–1918* (Baltimore, MD: Johns Hopkins University Press, 1982), 20–22, 30. On reform efforts in El Paso, see H. Gordon Frost, *The Gentlemen's Club: The Story of Prostitution in El Paso* (El Paso: Mangan Books, 1983), 80, 93–94, 125–126, 157; Leon Metz, *El Paso Guided through Time* (El Paso: Mangan Books, 1999), 123–124, 130.

47. Leon C. Metz, *Turning Points in El Paso, Texas* (El Paso: Mangan Books, 1985), 78–79; Metz, *El Paso Guided through Time*, 130.

48. "J. D. Rich Is Dead," *El Paso Daily Herald*, May 1, 1899, 3; "An Analysis of the Mystery," *El Paso Daily Times*, April 29, 1899, 7; "J. D. Rich's Wound Proves Fatal," *El Paso Daily Times*, May 2, 1899, 6; "The Verdict in the Rich Case," *El Paso Daily Herald*, January 27, 1900, 5; "Mrs. Rich Gets Fourteen Years," *El Paso Daily Times*, January 27, 1900; "The Rich Case," *El Paso Daily Times*, July 16, 1899, 2.

49. "Mrs. Rich Gets Fourteen Years," *El Paso Daily Times*, January 27, 1900, 7; "Hearing Tomorrow," *El Paso Daily Herald*, March 5, 1900, 1. On the diagnosis of hysteria, see Carroll Smith-Rosenberg, *Disorderly Conduct: Visions of Gender in Victorian America* (New York: Knopf, 1985), 197–216; Rosen, *The Lost Sisterhood*, 23.

50. John Hay to Powell Clayton, July 19, 1899, in *FRUS 1899*, 499.

51. "The Charlton Extradition Case," *American Journal of International Law* 5 (1911), 191. On crime in the Progressive Era, see Lawrence M. Friedman, *Crime and Punishment in American History* (New York: Basic Books, 1993), esp. chaps. 6 and 7; Jennifer Fronc, *New York Undercover: Private Surveillance in the Progressive Era* (Chicago: University of Chicago Press, 2009); Eric H. Monkkonen, *Police in Urban America, 1860–1920* (New York: Cambridge University Press, 1981); Kristofer Allerfeldt, *Crime and the Rise of Modern America: A History from 1865–1941* (New York: Routledge, 2011); David B. Wolcott and Tom Head, *Crime and Punishment in America* (New York: Infobase, 2010), 121–144.

52. Samuel Walker, *Popular Justice: A History of American Criminal Justice* (New York: Oxford University Press, 1998), 113, 117–119.

53. John Bassett Moore, *A Digest of International Law*, vol. 4 (Washington, DC: U.S. Government Printing Office, 1906), 287; "May Free Charlton Despite His Crime," *New York Times*, June 24, 1910, 2.

54. "Blas Aguirre's Case," *El Paso Daily Herald*, February 26, 1900, 4.

55. "First American Doomed to Die by Mexican Law," *St. Louis Post-Dispatch*, January 27, 1901, 34.

56. "The Crime of Fiends," *El Paso Daily Herald*, January 18, 1901, 1; "American Executed by Mexican Troops," *Atlanta Constitution*, June 15, 1901, 5; "With Back Turned to the Troops," *Cincinnati Enquirer*, June 15, 1901, 1; "Executed in a Mexican Prison," *San Francisco Chronicle*, June 15, 1901, 1.

57. "Mexico Wins Extradition Fight," *Washington Post*, August 15, 1901, 11; "Delivered to Mexico," *Los Angeles Times*, August 15, 1901; "Extradition of George Deering Reed to Mexico," in *FRUS 1908* (Washington, DC: U.S. Government Printing Office, 1908), 597–601.

58. Robert Thomas Devlin, *The Treaty Power under the Constitution of the United States* (San Francisco: Bancroft-Whitney, 1908), 588–604; Announcement by Ignacio Mariscal, December 21, 1903, Exp. 5, AEMEUA Leg. 262 (Guerra); Campos v. The State, 95 S.W. 1042 (Tex. Crim. App. 1906); "Extradition of Juan de Dios Rodriguez from Mexico," in *FRUS 1909* (Washington, DC: U.S. Government Printing Office, 1909), 415–425.

59. Extradition case file of Francis S. Mayer, Entry 857, Box 61, RG 59, NARA; "Japan Wants an American Citizen," *New York Tribune*, December 10, 1901, 9; "Must Answer in Japan," *New York Tribune*, February 7, 1902; Extradition Warrant for Yoshitaro Abe, October 9, 1908, Warrants of Arrest for Extradition, 1843–1930, Entry 859, RG 59, NARA.

60. "Slayer Charlton Tells His Story," *Chicago Daily Tribune*, June 24, 1910, 1; "Porter Charlton Confesses Crime," *New York Tribune*, June 24, 1910, 1.

61. "The Charlton Extradition Case," *American Journal of International Law* 5 (1911): 182–192; "Charlton Extradition Case (*Charlton v. Kelly*)," *American Journal of International Law* 7 (1913): 637–653.

62. "The Charlton Case," *New York Times*, June 25, 1910, 8; "Secretary Knox's Problem," *New York Tribune*, July 14, 1910, 6; "Seek Plot Proof in Como Murder," *Detroit Free Press*, July 15, 1910, 18; "Charlton Case Shows Need of Extradition Laws," *New York Times*, July 3, 1910, SM1; "Porter Charlton Still Held," *New-York Tribune*, August 6, 1911, 6.

63. "How a Murderer May Escape," *Boston Daily Globe*, July 5, 1910, 12; "Charlton Case Stirs Diplomats," *Chicago Daily Tribune*, July 3, 1910, A1.

64. Charlton v. Kelly, 229 U.S. 447 (1913); "Right in Law and Right in Policy," *Outlook*, December 24, 1910, 892; "The Charlton Extradition Case," *American Journal of International Law* 5 (1911), 191; "Charlton's Extradition," *New York Times*, June 12, 1913, 8.

65. "Charlton's Extradition," *New York Times*, June 12, 1913, 8; Will Irwin, "The American Newspaper: A Study of Journalism in Relation to the Public," in *Killing the Messenger: 100 Years of Media Criticism*, ed. Tom Goldstein (New York: Columbia University Press, 2007), 50.

66. "A Menace of Crime," *Outlook*, July 9, 1910, 502.

67. Charles E. Wesche to State Department, July 29, 1903, Despatches from United States consuls in Ciudad Juarez (Paso del Norte), Mexico, 1850–1906, RG 59, M-184, NARA (microfilm); "Is Still in Prison," *El Paso Daily Herald*, August 1, 1903, 1; "Returns to Juarez," *El Paso Morning Times*, September 4, 1903, 5; "The Prisoner of Juarez," *Los Angeles Times*, August 3, 1899, 9.

6
Camouflaged Extradition

1. "Recent Revolt in Mexico," *Dallas Morning News*, October 18, 1906, 14; "Del Rio Mexican Cases," *Dallas Morning News*, December 17, 1906, 11; "Mexican Consul Loses His Case," *Fort Worth Star-Telegram*, January 6, 1907, 4.

2. On the history of the political offense exception, see Manuel R. Garcia-Mora, "The Nature of Political Offenses: A Knotty Problem in Extradition Law," *Virginia Law Review* 48 (1962): 1226–1257; David M. Lieberman, "Sorting the Revolutionary from the Terrorist: The Delicate Application of the 'Political Offense' Exception in U.S. Extradition Cases," *Stanford Law Review* 59 (2006–2007): 181–212; Barbara Ann Banoff and Christopher H. Pyle, " 'To Surrender Political Offenders': The Political Offense Exception to Extradition in United States Law," *NYU Journal of International Law and Politics* 16 (1983–1984): 169–210.

3. "Their Arrest Political," *Atlanta Constitution*, January 6, 1907, B2; "Arredondo Crossed Border," *Atlanta Constitution*, January 7, 1907, 4; "Arredondo to Be Released," *Dallas Morning News*, February 1, 1907, 9; "Release Last One," *Fort Worth Star-Telegram*, February 3, 1907, 16; "Revoltoso en libertad," *El Clarin del Norte*, February 9, 1907, 1.

4. Joseph P. O'Grady, *Irish-Americans and Anglo-American Relations* (New York: Arno, 1976); Jonathan W. Gantt, "Irish American Terrorism and Anglo American Relations, 1881–1885," *Journal of the Gilded Age and Progressive Era* 5 (2006): 325–358; W. Dirk Raat, *Revoltosos: Mexico's Rebels in the United States, 1903–1923* (College Station: Texas A&M University Press, 1981).

5. Declaration of Independence, para. 2 (1776). On the early history of the political offense exception, see Christopher H. Pyle, *Extradition, Politics, and Human Rights* (Philadelphia: Temple University Press, 2001), 79–95; Lora L. Deere, "Political Offenses in the Law and Practice of Extradition," *American Journal of International Law* 27 (1933): 247–270. On the extradition of Jonathan

Robbins in 1799, see Ruth Wedgwood, "The Revolutionary Martyrdom of Jonathan Robbins," *Yale Law Journal* 100 (1990–1991): 229–368.

6. Article V, Extradition Treaty between the United States and France (1843), in Charles I. Bevans, comp., *Treaties and Other International Agreements of the United States of America, 1776–1949*, vol. 7 (Washington, DC: U.S. Government Printing Office, 1968), 831.

7. The text of every U.S. extradition treaty up to 1890 is reprinted in John Bassett Moore, *Report on Extradition, with Returns of All Cases from Aug. 9, 1842 to Jan. 1, 1890* (Washington, DC: U.S. Government Printing Office, 1890), 13–67.

8. A. E. Zucker, ed., *The Forty-Eighters: Political Refugees of the German Revolution of 1848* (New York: Russell and Russell, 1950); Michael A. Morrison, "American Reaction to European Revolutions, 1848–1852: Sectionalism, Memory, and the Revolutionary Heritage," *Civil War History* 49 (2003): 111–132; Chester Verne Easum, *The Americanization of Carl Schurz* (Chicago: University of Chicago Press, 1929).

9. William A. Marcy, Secretary of State, to Mr. Hülsemann, Austrian chargé d'affaires, September 26, 1853, House Ex. Doc. 1, 33rd Cong., 1st sess., 30.

10. On nineteenth-century Americans' reactions to anarchism, see James R. Green, *Death in the Haymarket: A Story of Chicago, the First Labor Movement, and the Bombing that Divided Gilded Age America* (New York: Pantheon Books, 2006); Richard Bach Jensen, *The Battle against Anarchist Terrorism: An International History, 1878–1934* (New York: Cambridge University Press, 2014).

11. James B. Angell, George Ticknor Curtis, and Thomas M. Cooley, "The Extradition of Dynamite Criminals," *North American Review*, July 1885, 47–59, esp. 49. On the Phoenix Park assassinations, see Tom Corfe, *The Phoenix Park Murders: Conflict, Compromise and Tragedy in Ireland, 1879–1882* (London: Hodder and Stoughton, 1968); Senan Molony, *The Phoenix Park Murders: Conspiracy, Betrayal and Retribution* (Dublin: Mercier, 2006).

12. Resolution, Senate Mis. Doc. 4, 47th Cong., special Senate sess. 1, March 14, 1881.

13. "International American Conference," vol. 2 (1890), 615, reprinted in *Proceedings of the American Society of International Law at Its Third Annual Meeting Held at Washington, DC, April 23 and 24, 1909* (New York: Baker, Voorhis, 1909), 150.

14. J. C. Burrows, "The Need of National Legislation against Anarchism," *North American Review*, December 1901, 738–740; William Preston Jr., *Aliens and Dissenters: Federal Suppression of Radicals, 1903–1933*, 2nd ed. (Urbana: University of Illinois Press, 1994), 27–29; James M. Beck, "The Suppression of Anarchy," *Twenty-Fifth Annual Meeting Proceedings of the New York State Bar Association, January 21–22, 1902* (Albany, NY: Argus, 1902), 159.

15. "Political Crimes," *San Francisco Chronicle*, September 4, 1892, 6.

16. Pyle, *Extradition, Politics, and Human Rights*, 108–109.

17. In re Meunier, 1 Q.B. 415 (1894), reprinted in *Cases and Materials on Terrorism: Three Nations' Response*, ed. Michael F. Noone and Yonah Alexander (The Hague, Netherlands: Kluwer Law International, 1997), 64–65.

18. In re Castioni, 1 Q.B. 149 (1891), reprinted in *Cases and Materials on Terrorism*, 62–63; Lieberman, "Sorting the Revolutionary from the Terrorist," 188–189.

19. In re Ezeta, 62 F. 972 (N.D. Cal. 1894).

20. "Gen. Ezeta's Ambition," *Washington Post*, September 25, 1894, 4; "Ezeta Is a Free Man," *San Francisco Chronicle*, September 23, 1894, 17; "Salvadorans Safe," *Los Angeles Times*, September 23, 1894, 2; "Ezeta Discharged from Custody," *New York Times*, September 23, 1894, 4; and "Judge Morrow Decides for Ezeta," *New York Tribune*, September 23, 1894, 1. John Bassett Moore, "The Case of the Salvadorean Refugees," *American Law Review* 29 (1895): 1–20.

21. Extradition Case File of Francisco Benavides, Entry 857, Box 36, RG 59, NARA; "The Benavides Case," *Galveston Daily News*, February 21, 1893, 3; "Insurgents or Cutthroats?," *Washington Post*, June 29, 1908, 6.

22. Price's decision is summarized in the Supreme Court's decision in Ornelas v. Ruiz, 161 U.S. 502 (1896). Maxey's decision of May 22, 1895 is reprinted in "Mexican Garza Revolution," *New York Times*, May 23, 1895, 5.

23. "Consistency in Extradition," *Washington Post*, February 24, 1893, 4; Matilda Gresham, *Life of Walter Quintin Gresham, 1832–1895* (Chicago: Rand McNally, 1919), 357–358.

24. Immigration Act of 1903 (Anarchist Exclusion Act), March 3, 1903, 32 Stat. 1213; J. C. Burrows, "The Need of National Legislation against Anarchism," *North American Review*, December 1901, 738–740. On Congress's earlier rejection of proposed immigration laws banning anarchists, see Preston, *Aliens and Dissenters*, 27–29.

25. "Urges Arbitration," *Washington Post*, April 24, 1909, 1.

26. Extradition of James Lynchehaun, Vol. 1 (1902–1903), FO 5/2568, NAUK; Extradition of James Lynchehaun, Vol. 2 (1904), FO 5/2569, NAUK; Attempts to Secure Return of Lynchehaun from USA to Ireland, HO 144/977/100676, NAUK. The Lynchehaun case is also chronicled in James Carney, *The Playboy and the Yellow Lady* (Dublin: Poolbeg, 1986); and John J. Cleary, "Lynchehaun: Patriotic Hero or Common Criminal?," *Irish Review* 4 (1988): 136–139.

27. This ballad is posted on the website for the Valley Inn, a hotel located at the estate in Achill, County Mayo, available at www.valley-house.com/history.htm.

28. Carney, *Playboy and the Yellow Lady*, 183–184; Pyle, *Extradition, Politics, and Human Rights*, 115–117.

29. Memorandum for Demanding Government, Extradition of James Lynchehaun, Vol. 1 (1902–1903), FO 5/2568, NAUK. *London Globe* quoted in "Angry over Lynchehaun Case," *Chicago Daily Tribune*, November 3, 1903, 5.

30. Percy Sanderson, British Consul in New York, to Secretary of State for Foreign Affairs, October 27, 1903, Lynchehaun File, NAUK.

31. On the Pouren case, see Herbert Parsons, *The Case of Jan Janoff Pouren: A Political Refugee from Russia* (New York: Royal Stationery, 1909). On the Rudowitz case, see Christian Rudowitz, *Before the Department of State: In the Matter of the Demand of the Imperial Russian Government for the Extradition of*

Christian Rudovitz (Chicago: n.p., 1909); Frederick C. Giffin, "The Rudowitz Extradition Case," *Journal of the Illinois State Historical Society* 75 (1982): 61–72.

32. Frederic R. Coudert, "Address of Mr. Frederic R. Coudert, of New York City," *Proceedings of the American Society of International Law at Its Third Annual Meeting Held at Washington, DC, April 23 and 24, 1909* (New York: Baker, Voorhis, 1909), 126. The same speech is reprinted in Frederic R. Coudert, *Certainty and Justice: Studies of the Conflict between Precedent and Progress in the Development of the Law* (New York: D. Appleton, 1914), 271–302.

33. Coudert, "Address," 141.

34. Petitions in Behalf of Jan Pouren, 1908, M862, Roll 1173, RG 59, NARA (microfilm); Mary Jo Deegan, *Jane Addams and the Men of the Chicago School, 1892–1918* (New Brunswick, NJ: Transaction Books, 1988), 117–118; Giffin, "Rudowitz Extradition Case," 65; "Political Refugee Defense League Made National in Scope," *Chicago Daily Tribune*, December 30, 1908, 4; "Czar Denounced at Big Meeting," *Chicago Daily Tribune*, November 30, 1908, 2.

35. Isaac A. Hourwich, "The Russian-American Extradition Treaty," *Yale Review* 3 (1894): 68–95; "Shall We Return the Fugitive to the Torture Chamber?," *Outlook*, September 5, 1908, 2–3.

36. "Deed of Infamy," *Boston Daily Globe*, March 7, 1893, 7; *Shall the American People Hand Over a Russian Revolutionary Refugee to the Czar?* (New Haven, CT: Pouren Defense Committee, Mudd Library, Yale University).

37. Moses Oppenheimer, "Jan Pouren and the Right of Political Asylum," address delivered before the Sunrise Club, New York, October 18, 1908, Box 99, Folder 5, Theodore Schroeder Papers, Southern Illinois University Special Collections.

38. Joseph Nevins, *Operation Gatekeeper: The Rise of the "Illegal Alien" and the Making of the U.S.-Mexico Boundary* (New York: Routledge, 2002), 193–194.

39. On the administrative process of deportation, see Daniel Kanstroom, *Deportation Nation: Outsiders in American History* (Cambridge, MA: Harvard University Press, 2007); Lucy E. Salyer, *Laws Harsh as Tigers: Chinese Immigrants and the Shaping of Modern Immigration Law* (Chapel Hill: University of North Carolina Press, 1995), 144, 147. On immigration legislation, see "U.S. Citizenship and Immigration Services, Legislation from 1790–1900," available at www.nps.gov/elis/forteachers/upload/Legislation-1790–1900.pdf.

40. John Bassett Moore, "Extradition," *American Law Register and Review* 44 (1896): 749–762, esp. 753.

41. Ibid., 749; John Bassett Moore, *A Treatise on Extradition and Interstate Rendition*, 2 vols. (Boston: Boston Book, 1891).

42. The one exception to the lack of judicial review was cases involving Chinese immigrants, who operated under a different set of laws. On the rules and procedures in an immigration hearing (or lack thereof), see Salyer, *Laws Harsh as Tigers*, 141–156.

43. Deirdre M. Moloney, *National Insecurities: Immigrants and U.S. Deportation Policy since 1882* (Chapel Hill: University of North Carolina Press, 2012); Jane Perry Clark, *Deportation of Aliens from the United States to Europe* (New York: Columbia University Press, 1931); William C. Van Vleck, *The*

Administrative Control of Aliens: A Study in Administrative Law and Procedure (New York: Commonwealth Fund, 1932).

44. Barfield, Henry A., Embezzlement, Returned as Unacceptable Immigrant, and Not by Extradition, by United States of America after Handing Over Money, HO 144/507/X60223 (1896–97), NAUK.

45. Charles Lanctot, Deputy Attorney General, Quebec, to M. F. Gallagher, Deputy Minister of Justice, May 1, 1929, Extradition File of David Sternshein (1929), Folder 778, Box 1002, Series A5, RG 13, LAC; "Article 33," *Mexican Review* 1 (1916), 11.

46. Fong Yue Ting v. U.S., 149 U.S. 698 (1893), 711, 730; Alona E. Evans, "Acquisition of Custody over the International Fugitive Offender—Alternatives to Extradition: A Survey of United States Practice," *British Yearbook of International Law* 40 (1964): 77–104; Alona E. Evans, "The New Extradition Treaties of the United States," *American Journal of International Law* 59 (1965): 351–362, esp. 358. On "disguised extradition," see Paul O'Higgins, "Disguised Extradition: Deportation or Extradition?," *Cambridge Law Journal* 21 (1963): 10–13; M. Cherif Bassiouni, "Unlawful Seizures and Irregular Rendition Devices as Alternatives to Extradition," *Vanderbilt Journal of Transnational Law* 7 (1973–1974): 25–70. Both O'Higgins and Bassiouni disapprove of irregular rendition, but stop short of denying its legality.

47. John Bassett Moore, "The Difficulties of Extradition," *Proceedings of the Academy of Political Science in the City of New York* 1 (1911): 625–634, esp. 631; Green Hayward Hackworth, *Digest of International Law*, vol. 4 (Washington, DC: U.S. Government Printing Office, 1940–1944), 30.

48. John Bassett Moore, "The Difficulties of Extradition," 630.

49. Michael Byrne File (1908–1909), Use of U.S. Immigration Laws in Lieu of Extradition Proceedings, HO 45/10391/172119, NAUK; Joseph Moloney File (1908–1909), Use of U.S. Immigration Laws when Fugitive Is Not Liable to Extradition, HO 45/10394/175113, NAUK. On Irish Republican Army (IRA) deportations, see Karen McElrath, *Unsafe Haven: The United States, the IRA, and Political Prisoners* (London: Pluto, 2000), 45–64.

50. Raat, *Revoltosos*; Thomas C. Langham, *Border Trials: Ricardo Flores Magón and the Mexican Liberals* (El Paso: Texas Western Press, University of Texas, 1981). For a biased but detailed account of U.S. deportation of Mexican revolutionaries, see John Kenneth Turner, *Barbarous Mexico* (Chicago: C. H. Kerr, 1911).

51. "No Change in Policy: Mexico Sets Up Claim for Villareal's Return as an Ex-Convict," *New York Tribune*, November 14, 1906, 1; "Mexicans in Terror: Revolutionists Here Feel They Will Be Deported," *Washington Post*, February 11, 1907, 5; "Rebel Will Be Deported," *Washington Post*, November 13, 1906, 12.

7
From the Pinkertons to the FBI

1. Mrs. Belle Cassidy, "Recollections of Early Denver," *Colorado Magazine*, January 1952, 52, in Box 1, Folder 6, PNDA, LOC.

2. Jeanette Gustin to the Pinkerton Agency, Box 1, Folder 6, PNDA, LOC.

3. Murray Kempner, "Son of Pinkerton," *New York Review of Books*, May 20, 1971.

4. Kenneth O'Reilly, "A New Deal for the FBI: The Roosevelt Administration, Crime Control, and National Security," *Journal of American History* 69 (1982): 638–658; Claire Bond Potter, *War on Crime: Bandits, G-Men, and the Politics of Mass Culture* (New Brunswick, NJ: Rutgers University Press, 1998), 4.

5. Frank Morn, *The Eye that Never Sleeps: A History of the Pinkerton National Detective Agency* (Bloomington: Indiana University Press, 1982), 192; Ward Churchill, "From the Pinkertons to the PATRIOT Act: The Trajectory of Political Policing in the United States, 1870 to the Present," *New Centennial Review* 4 (2004): 1–72, esp. 43–56; Kempner, "Son of Pinkerton."

6. A. W. Parsons, "Barrel-Maker Became the Most Famous Detective in the World," *Sunday Dispatch (London)*, March 26, 1950, in Box 3, Folder 7, PNDA, LOC; Ethan A. Nadelmann, *Cops across Borders: The Internationalization of U.S. Criminal Law Enforcement* (University Park: Pennsylvania State University Press, 1993), 177.

7. On the Homestead Strike, see Paul Kahan, *The Homestead Strike: Labor, Violence, and American Industry* (New York: Routledge, 2014).

8. Morn, *The Eye that Never Sleeps*, 102.

9. Act of March 3, 1893, 5 U.S.C. 53.

10. William R. Hunt, *Front Page Detective: William J. Burns and the Detective Profession, 1880–1930* (Bowling Green, OH: Bowling Green State University Press, 1990), 53.

11. "William J. Burns," *McClure's Magazine*, February 1911, 481; "William J. Burns," *The National Cyclopaedia of American Biography*, vol. 15 (New York: James T. White, 1916), 49. On the Hull case, see F. S. Alkus, Manager of the Burns Agency in Portland, to Director of the Consular Service, Department of State, August 23, 1915, Box 3411, CDF 1910–1929, RG 59, NARA; American Consulate General in Berlin to Secretary of State, October 26, 1915, Box 3411, CDF 1910–1929, RG 59, NARA.

12. Application for Requisition of A. B. Crouch, August 17, 1929, Box 3401, CDF 1910–29, RG 59, NARA.

13. Beverly Gage, *The Day Wall Street Exploded: A Story of America in Its First Age of Terror* (New York: Oxford University Press, 2009), 137–140, 267, 281; Nadelmann, *Cops across Borders*, 58; Hunt, *Front Page Detective*, 94; Charles A. Siringo, *Two Evil Isms: Pinkertonism and Anarchism, by a Cowboy Detective Who Knows, as He Spent Twenty-Two Years in the Inner Circle of Pinkerton's National Detective Agency* (Chicago: C. A. Siringo, 1915).

14. For an official history of the FBI, see Federal Bureau of Investigation, *The FBI: A Centennial History, 1908–2008* (Washington, DC: U.S. Department of Justice, FBI, 2008). For a more critical scholarly history of the FBI, see Rhodri Jeffreys-Jones, *The FBI: A History* (New Haven, CT: Yale University Press, 2007).

15. Mann Act, June 25, 1910, 18 U.S.C. 2421; Jack Johnson files, Box 3383, CDF 1910–29, RG 59, NARA; Theresa Runstedtler, *Jack Johnson, Rebel*

Sojourner: Boxing in the Shadow of the Global Color Line (Berkeley: University of California Press, 2012), 134–136, 230.

16. Franz von Rintelen files, Box 3368, CDF 1910–29, RG 59, NARA; Franz von Rintelen, *The Dark Invader: Wartime Reminiscences of a German Naval Officer* (New York: Macmillan, 1933); Tim Weiner, *Enemies: A History of the FBI* (New York: Random House, 2012), 6.

17. Hunt, *Front Page Detective*, 184.

18. Don P. Collins files, Box 3403, CDF 1910–29, RG 59, NARA; Warrants of Arrest and Extradition, 1843–1930, Vol. 5, Entry 859, RG 59, NARA.

19. W. J. Burns to William L. Hurley, February 7, 1922, Box 3355, CDF 1910–29, RG 59, NARA; Burns to Hurley, June 2, 1922, Box 3355, CDF 1910–29, RG 59, NARA.

20. National Bank Act, §5209 R.S.U.S., September 26, 1918; William Beverly, *On the Lam: Narratives of Flight in J. Edgar Hoover's America* (Jackson: University Press of Mississippi, 2003), 46.

21. David A. Langbart and Gerald K. Haines, *Unlocking the Files of the FBI: A Guide to Its Records and Classification System* (New York: Rowman and Littlefield, 1993), classification 88; Rinaldo DePietro File, Box 1140, CDF 1930–39, RG 59, NARA; James W. Borton File, Box 1141, CDF 1930–39, RG 59, NARA; O'Reilly, "A New Deal for the FBI," 643.

22. "Washington Develops a World Clearing House for Identifying Criminals by Fingerprints," *New York Times*, August 10, 1932, 2; Federal Bureau of Investigation, *The FBI: A Centennial History*, 18.

23. Federal Bureau of Investigation, *The FBI: A Centennial History*, 81.

24. J. C. Meinbress to State Department, April 17, 1930, Box 1095, CDF 1930–39, RG 59, NARA; J. R. Baker to Pinkerton's National Detective Agency, April 22, 1930, Box 1095, CDF 1930–39, RG 59, NARA; Meinbress to Baker, April 28, 1930, Box 1095, CDF 1930–39, RG 59, NARA; Green H. Hackworth to Pinkerton National Detective Agency, May 3, 1930, Box 1095, CDF 1930–39, RG 59, NARA.

25. Walter Carlson, "Pinkerton Force Is Family Affair," *New York Times*, August 16, 1964, 41.

26. "Robert A. Pinkerton, Chairman of Detective Agency, Is Dead," *New York Times*, October 12, 1967, 45.

27. "Allan Pinkerton: Pioneered on the Illinois Central," *Illinois Central Magazine*, January 1946, 22, in Box 4, Folder 11, PNDA, LOC; A. W. Parsons, "Barrel-Maker Became the Most Famous Detective in the World," *Sunday Dispatch*, March 26, 1950, in Box 3, Folder 7, PNDA, LOC.

28. This statistic is calculated based on CDF 1910–29, CDF 1930–39, and CDF 1940–44, RG 59, NARA.

29. Biographies of Insull include John F. Wasik, *The Merchant of Power: Samuel Insull, Thomas Edison, and the Creation of the Modern Metropolis* (New York: Palgrave Macmillan, 2006); Forrest McDonald, *Insull: The Rise and Fall of a Billionaire Utility Tycoon* (Chicago: University of Chicago Press, 1962).

30. McDonald, *Insull*, 277; Wasik, *The Merchant of Power*, 145; covers of *Time* magazine, November 4, 1929, and May 14, 1934.

31. Robert J. Casey and W. A. S. Douglas, *The Midwesterner: The Story of Dwight H. Green* (Chicago: Wilcox and Follett, 1948), 173; David Skeel, *Icarus in the Boardroom: The Fundamental Flaws in Corporate American and Where They Came From* (New York: Oxford University Press, 2005), 11.

32. "U.S. Voids Pact with Greece on Extradition," *Chicago Tribune*, November 6, 1933, 1; "Note to Greece in Insull Case Ends '31 Treaty," *New York Herald Tribune*, November 6, 1933, 4; Edmund Gale, "Insull-ated!," *Los Angeles Times*, December 29, 1932, 1.

33. Confidential letter from Lincoln MacVeigh, American Minister in Athens, to Secretary of State, December 15, 1933, Box 1167, CDF 1930–39, RG 59, NARA. On the surrender of Insull by Turkey, see *FRUS 1934* (Washington, DC: U.S. Government Printing Office, 1934), 576–583; "U.S. to Spirit Insull from Ship at Dawn," *New York Herald Tribune*, May 7, 1934, 1.

34. M. Cherif Bassiouni, "Unlawful Seizures and Irregular Rendition Devices as Alternatives to Extradition," *Vanderbilt Journal of Transnational Law* 7 (1973–74): 25–70, esp. 26.

35. Christopher H. Pyle, *Extradition, Politics, and Human Rights* (Philadelphia: Temple University Press, 2001), 266. On lawlessness in the borderlands during the Mexican Revolution, see W. Dirk Raat, *Revoltosos: Mexico's Rebels in the United States, 1903–1923* (College Station: Texas A&M University Press, 1981).

36. Clifford Berryman, "I've Had about Enough of This," March 10, 1916, Clifford Berryman Collection, NARA.

37. George Ellis, *A Man Named Jones* (New York: Signet Books, 1963), 12; Jones quote available at www.fbi.gov/sanantonio/about-us/history-1.

38. Acting Attorney General to Secretary of State, August 24, 1923, Box 3347, CDF 1910–29, RG 59, NARA; "Marsino's Arrest Ends Wild Episode in High Financing," *Washington Post*, August 28, 1923, 5; Department of State, Division of Mexican Affairs to Mr. Armour, August 28, 1923, Box 3347, CDF 1910–29, RG 59, NARA.

39. Bob Bates File, 212.11 B31, Box 3347, CDF 1910–29, RG 59, NARA; Warrants of Arrest and Extradition, 1843–1930, Vol. 5, Entry 859, RG 59, NARA.

40. "Dos Falsos Agentes Policíacos Llevan a Cabo por su Cuenta Una Extradición," *Excélsior*, December 7, 1940, in Box 1004, CDF 1940–44, RG 59, NARA; J. Edgar Hoover to Adolf A. Berle, Assistant Secretary of State, January 28, 1941, Box 1004, CDF 1940–44, RG 59, NARA.

41. "Un Verdadero Filón de Oro Constituyen Las Extradiciones al Margen de la Ley," *Excélsior*, December 9, 1940, in Box 1004, CDF 1940–44, RG 59, NARA.

42. File of Tomas Hernandez and Eduardo Villareal, Box 1097, CDF 1930–39, RG 59, NARA; "Held in Mexican Kidnapping," *New York Times*, May 14, 1934, 13; "Pair Ordered Extradited," *Valley Morning Star*, May 12, 1934, 1; "Texas Police Chiefs Complicate Extradition Proceedings," *South Texas Citizen*, May 18, 1934, 2.

43. Ex parte Lopez, 6 F.Supp. 342 (1934); Donald R. Rothwell, Stuart Kaye, Afshin Akhtarkhavari, and Ruth Davis, *International Law: Cases and Materials with Australian Perspectives* (New York: Cambridge University Press, 2011), 314.

44. "Imprisonment of Edward M. Blatt and Lawrence F. Converse in Mexico," in *FRUS 1911* (Washington, DC: U.S. Government Printing Office, 1911), 605–614.

45. Jonathan A. Gluck, "The Customary International Law of State-Sponsored International Abduction and United States Courts," *Duke Law Journal* 44 (1994–1995): 612–656, esp. 633; Green H. Hackworth, *Digest of International Law*, vol. 2 (Washington, DC: U.S. Government Printing Office, 1941), 310–311; "Kidnapping of Samuel Cantú, a Mexican Citizen, on American Territory by Mexican Officers," in *FRUS 1914* (Washington, DC: U.S. Government Printing Office, 1914), 900–904; "Man Kidnaped in Texas; Is Ordered Shot," *El Paso Herald*, January 27, 1914, 1; "Kidnaped Mexican Freed," *Austin Statesman*, February 2, 1914, 1.

46. On Lafond, see C. V. Cole, "Extradition Treaties Abound but Unlawful Seizures Continue," *International Perspectives*, March/April 1975, 40–41; Green H. Hackworth, *Digest of International Law*, vol. 4 (Washington, DC: U.S. Government Printing Office, 1942), 224. On Marker, see Cole, "Extradition Treaties Abound," 41; Hackworth, *Digest of International Law*, 226–227.

47. United States v. Unverzagt, 299 Fed. 1015 (1924); Unverzagt v. Benn, 5.F2d 492 (1925); Rothwell et al., *International Law*, 314.

48. "Dope Informer to Be Sent to Canada Court," *Sun*, June 18, 1931, in Box 1116, CDF 1930–39, RG 59, NARA; Extradition of Mertz, 52 F.2d 241 (1931); "Mertz Freed after Hearing over Slaying," *Houston Chronicle*, February 19, 1930.

49. "Kidnapping of Antonio Martinez," in *FRUS 1906* (Washington, DC: U.S. Government Printing Office, 1906), 1121–1122; "Wants Extradition Papers," *San Jose Mercury News*, June 4, 1905, 3; "Doomed to Die for Kidnaping Murderer," *Los Angeles Herald*, July 11, 1908, 5.

50. Cordell Hull quoted in Walter LaFeber, *The American Age: United States Foreign Policy at Home and Abroad, 1750 to the Present* (New York: W. W. Norton, 1994), 376.

51. "Dillinger Put behind Bars in Indiana Jail," *Baltimore Sun*, January 31, 1934, 1; "Is Dillinger Dead? Wounded? Or Fled U.S.?," *Atlanta Daily World*, May 8, 1934, 2.

52. Robert Talley, "Uncle Sam's Sleuths Pursue Lawbreakers: Mysteries that Would Defy Detective Story Writers Are Solved Daily by These Crime Experts," *Washington Post*, June 24, 1934, M3.

53. Dillinger, John, Box 1144, CDF 1930–39, RG 59, NARA; "Dillinger Hunted on Canadian Liner," *New York Times*, May 6, 1934, 2; "Dillinger Not on C.P.R. Liner," *Glasgow Herald*, May 6, 1934; "Britain Hunts for Dillinger," *The People*, May 6, 1934; "Killer Not on Liner at Greenock," *Sunday Post*, May 6, 1934; "Dillinger Man-Hunt," *Empire News*, May 7, 1934; "Dillinger Not on Board," *Liverpool Post and Mercury*, May 7, 1934. Dillinger's Freedom of Information Act (FOIA)-released FBI records are available at http://vault.fbi.gov.

54. Gillis, Lester M. aka Baby Face Nelson, Box 1142, CDF 1930–39, RG 59, NARA.

55. Heller, Nathaniel, Box 1142, CDF 1930–39, RG 59, NARA; "Link Karpis to Arrest of Man in Cuba," *Milwaukee Journal*, February 2, 1935, 1;

"Nathan Heller Freed of Charges," *Havana Post*, April 22, 1936; Enclosure to despatch No. 6011 from the Havana Embassy, April 22, 1926, in Box 1142, CDF 1930–39, RG 59, NARA.

56. A. A. Berle to Mr. Warren, June 3, 1940, Box 1000, CDF 1940–44, RG 59, NARA.

57. Luis Fernández to Cordell Hull, March 12, 1941, Box 1000, CDF 1940–44, RG 59, NARA; J. E. Hoover to Adolf A. Berle, April 3, 1941, Box 1000, CDF 1940–44, RG 59, NARA; Hoover to Berle, May 19, 1941, Box 1000, CDF 1940–44, RG 59, NARA.

58. Graham, Alexander, Boxes 1000–1001, CDF 1940–44, RG 59, NARA.

59. La Follette Civil Liberties Committee Files, Box 13, PNDA, LOC.

Epilogue: How Rendition Became Extraordinary

1. Steve Hendricks, *A Kidnapping in Milan: The CIA on Trial* (New York: W. W. Norton, 2010).

2. Rachel Donadio, "Italy Convicts 23 Americans, Most Working for C.I.A., of Abducting Muslim Cleric," *New York Times*, November 5, 2009, A15; Matteo M. Winkler, "When 'Extraordinary' Means Illegal: International Law and the European Reactions to the United States Rendition Program," *Yale Law School Student Scholarship Papers*, Paper 46 (2007), 4.

3. Louis Fisher, "Extraordinary Rendition: The Price of Secrecy," *American University Law Review* 57 (2008): 1405–1451, esp. 1416; Stephen Gray, *Ghost Plane: The True Story of the CIA Torture Program* (New York: St. Martin's Press, 2006), 135.

4. See, for example, Gregory S. McNeal and Brian J. Field, "Snatch-and-Grab Ops: Justifying Extraterritorial Abduction," *Transnational Law and Contemporary Problems* 16 (2006–2007): 491–522; Margaret L. Satterthwaite and Angelica Fisher, "Tortured Logic: Renditions to Justice, Extraordinary Rendition, and Human Rights Law," *Long Term View* 6 (2006): 52–71.

5. Attorney-General of Israel v. Eichmann, 36 I.L.R. 5 (1961); United States v. Sobell, 244 F.2d 520 (1957). Sobell describes his kidnapping in his memoir, Morton Sobell, *On Doing Time* (New York: Charles Scribner's Sons, 1974), 3–22.

6. Frisbie v. Collins, 342 U.S. 519 (1952).

7. Mapp v. Ohio, 367 U.S. 643 (1961); Christopher H. Pyle, *Extradition, Politics, and Human Rights* (Philadelphia: Temple University Press, 2001), 263, 269–271; United States v. Toscanino, 500 F.2d 267 (1974), 270, 273.

8. United States v. Herrera, 504 F.2d 859 (5th Cir. 1974); Lujan v. Gengler, 510 F.2d 62 (1975), 65; United States v. Lira, 515 F.2d 68 (1975).

9. Comprehensive Crime Control Act of 1984, 18 U.S.C. 1203; Omnibus Diplomatic Security and Antiterrorism Act of 1986, 18 U.S.C. 2331.

10. Pyle, *Extradition, Politics, and Human Rights*, 274–276; Arlen Specter, "How to Make Terrorists Think Twice," *New York Times*, May 22, 1986, A31; John Walcott and Andy Pasztor, "Reagan Ruling to Let CIA Kidnap Terrorists Overseas Is Disclosed," *Wall Street Journal*, February 20, 1987, 1; Satterthwaite and Fisher, "Tortured Logic," 55–56.

11. George P. Schulz to Joe Clark, Canadian Secretary of State for External Affairs, January 11, 1988, quoted in Kristofer R. Schleicher, "Transborder Abductions by American Bounty Hunters: The *Jaffe* Case and a New Understanding between the United States and Canada," *Georgia Journal of International and Comparative Law* 20 (1990): 489–504, esp. 490.

12. United States v. Noriega, 117 F.3d 1206 (11th Cir. 1997); Pyle, *Extradition, Politics, and Human Rights*, 277–279.

13. United States v. Alvarez-Machain, 542 U.S. 655 (1992). For the argument in favor of Álvarez Machain's habeas corpus petition, see Ruth Wedgwood, "The Argument against International Abduction of Criminal Defendants: Amicus Curiae Brief Filed by the Lawyers Committee for Human Rights in *United States v. Humberto Alvarez-Machain*," *American University International Law Review* 6 (1991): 537–569.

14. United States v. Alvarez-Machain, 682; Alan W. Clarke, *Rendition to Torture* (New Brunswick, NJ: Rutgers University Press, 2012), 83; Jonathan A. Bush, "How Did We Get Here? Foreign Abduction after *Alvarez-Machain*," *Stanford Law Review* 45 (1993): 939–983.

15. *USIA Daily Digest of Foreign Media Reaction*, June 22, 1992, Box 1, Mexico-General Files June 1992, Folder 1, Charles A. Gillespie Files, National Security Council, George Bush Presidential Library; Clarke, *Rendition to Torture*, 85.

16. Presidential Decision Directive 39: U.S. Policy on Counterterrorism, June 21, 1995, available at www.fas.org/irp/offdocs/pdd39.htm; Satterthwaite and Fisher, "Tortured Logic," 57; Douglas Kash, "Abducting Terrorists under PDD-39: Much Ado about Nothing New," *American University International Law Review* 13 (1999): 139–156; United States v. Yousef, 327 F.3d 56 (2d Cir. 2003); Kasi v. Angelone, 300 F.3d 487 (4th Cir. 2002).

17. Satterthwaite and Fisher, "Tortured Logic," 88; Jane Mayer, "Outsourcing Torture: The Secret History of America's 'Extraordinary Rendition' Program," *New Yorker*, February 14, 2005, 106.

18. Dana Priest and Barton Gellman, "U.S. Decries Abuse but Defends Interrogations," *Washington Post*, December 26, 2002, A1, quoted in Margaret L. Satterthwaite, "Rendered Meaningless: Extraordinary Rendition and the Rule of Law," *George Washington Law Review* 75 (2006–2007): 1333–1420, esp. 1335; Satterthwaite and Fisher, "Tortured Logic," 58–60.

19. McNeal and Field, "Snatch-and-Grab Ops"; Daniel Benjamin, "Five Myths about Rendition (and That New Movie)," *Washington Post*, October 21, 2007, B3; Clarke, *Rendition to Torture*, 86.

Acknowledgments

My intellectual debts start at Yale University, where this project began. Johnny Faragher trusted me as I took this project through various twists and turns. I received advice and support from Jean-Christophe Agnew, David Blight, Bill Deverell, Seth Fein, Beverly Gage, Jay Gitlin, Matt Jacobson, Gil Joseph, George Miles, Jen Van Vleck, and John Witt. I also thank Marcy Kaufman for her help and patience. Lisa Pinley Covert, Mary Greenfield, Sarah Hammond, Briallen Hopper, Julia Irwin, Carmen Kordick, and Andrew Sackett generously read drafts and helped my ideas and prose shine.

Various working groups allowed me to present portions of my work in progress: Yale's Writing History, International Security Studies, and Urban History workshops; the Georgetown Law Roundtable; and the Huntington-USC Institute on California and the West. During my final book revisions, I had the great fortune to receive helpful feedback at the University of Maryland's Miller Center for Historical Studies and the Global American Studies symposium held by Harvard University's Charles Warren Center.

This work would not have been possible without the foundations and centers that have provided me with fellowships and grants, including the American Historical Association (AHA), the Andrew W. Mellon Foundation, the Beinecke Rare Book and Manuscript Library, the Howard R. Lamar Center for the Study of Frontiers and Borders, the Jacob K. Javits Fellowship Program, and the

Smith Richardson Foundation. The Miller Center of Public Affairs at the University of Virginia gave me much more than just financial support; I particularly want to single out Brian Balogh and Lisa Cobbs Hoffman for their mentorship. I also would like to thank the dedicated librarians and archivists at the Beinecke Library; the Hiram College Archives; the Huntington Library; Library and Archives Canada; the Library of Congress (LOC); LSU Special Collections; the National Archives, College Park; the National Archives of Honduras, Costa Rica, and the United Kingdom; the SRE in Mexico City; and the Yale and Texas A&M Libraries.

I was tremendously fortunate to spend the summer of 2013 at the Kluge Center at the Library of Congress, thanks to funding from the American Historical Association. Among those who helped make the summer productive were Travis Hensley and Mary Lou Reker at the LOC, Dana Schaffer at the AHA, and my research assistant, Annadil Zaman, who went on the hunt for fugitives with enthusiasm.

At Harvard University Press, I received invaluable feedback from my editor, Joyce Seltzer, and the two anonymous readers. Brian Distelberg assisted with endless patience. It couldn't have been a smoother process.

Joining the history department at Texas A&M University has changed the direction of my life, both personally and professionally. I am truly lucky to be part of such a congenial and collegial department. My particular gratitude goes to those colleagues who have taken the time to mentor me, especially Quince Adams, Al Broussard, Olga Dror, Lorien Foote, Andy Kirkendall, John Lenihan, Jason Parker, and David Vaught. The Texas A&M College of Liberal Arts and the Department of History provided generous start-up and travel funds that enabled me to do the Central American research in this book. My writing group—Side Emre, Lisa Ramos, Brian Rouleau, Dan Schwartz, and Erin Wood—offered much-valued deadlines, feedback, and conversation.

Throughout the writing process, two cafés have provided inspiration, atmosphere, sustenance, and good company: Jojo's in New Haven, Connecticut, and The Village in Bryan, Texas. Good friends have come to Texas and supported me along the way, especially J. K. Barret, Briallen Hopper, Annie Ruderman, and Jessica Santonastaso.

Few people can say that they finished their manuscript drafts at Comic-Con, so I am indebted to my cousin, Elizabeth Unterman, for that wonderful, surreal experience in San Diego. Arthur Unterman and Catherine Zehr gave me a second home in New York and made me feel so welcome that I never wanted to leave. My sister, Laura Gershuni, struck the perfect balance of strict and supportive. Thanks to all of the Gershunis and to my aunt, Marian Unterman. My new family, the extended Rouleau clan, has welcomed me with open arms. I am forever grateful for the unconditional love and support from my mother, Susan Unterman. This book is dedicated to the memory of my father, Robert Unterman, who would have been proud.

Finally, the biggest thank you goes to my boys, Brian and Hudson. This book would not exist without Brian's love, laughter, inspiration, editing eye, encouragement, and cooking. Here's to many, many more years of making history together.

Index

abduction. *See* kidnapping
Abe, Yoshitaro, 154
Abu Omar, 210
Adams, George H., 26
Adams, John, 129–130
Addams, Jane, 174
Adee, Alvey, 96
Adler, William, 112
African Americans, 31, 34, 189. *See also* slaves, fugitive
Aguirre, Blas, 152–153
Aguirre, Jesús, 140–141
Ahern, P. K., 40
Alberdi, Juan Bautista, 113–114
Allen, Willis Boyd, 80
Álvarez Machain, Humberto, 215. *See also United States v. Alvarez-Machain*
American Bankers Association (ABA), 22, 36, 37, 64, 187
American Surety Company, 30, 34, 36, 67–71, 123
Anarchist Exclusion Act, 166, 170, 176
anarchists, 4, 54, 115, 151, 161, 162, 164, 165, 166, 167, 168, 170, 176, 181, 191
Andreas, Peter, 7
Angell, James B., 165
Argentina: fugitives in, 11, 84, 86–87, 114–115; Wild Bunch in, 64–65; abduction of fugitives from, 72, 73, 211; market in, 86; extradition treaties with U.S., 87, 101–102, 116; reasons for resisting extradition, 102, 103, 113–116; efforts to attract white immigrants, 113–116; crime in, 115, 118; extradition

treaties with European countries, 116; extradition in, 116, 118; standards of punishment in, 118–119; sheltering of ex-Nazis in, 125
Arguelles, José Agustín, 133
Around the World in Eighty Days (Verne), 1
Around the World in Seventy-Two Days (Bly), 1–2
Aspíroz, Manuel de, 142
assassinations, 54, 151, 161, 165, 166, 167, 168, 170
asylum: in the United States, 3, 128, 129, 130, 131; erosion of, 11, 128, 129, 130, 132–133, 161; in international law, 60; and extradition safeguards, 133; for political crimes, 133, 160–162, 163; right of citizens to, 133–139, 143–144, 146, 150; executive's power in, 135–136, 143, 149, 182; standards for, 166–170. *See also* havens, extradition; political offense exception
attentat clause, 167
Austria, 164
Austria-Hungary, 135, 165

Baca, Sabas (Samuel), 153
Baiata, Joseph, 200
Bailey, Francis, 112
Balfour, Jabez Spencer, 72, 118–119
banana republics, 94, 112
banks, 9, 15, 18, 23–24, 48–49, 53, 56, 63, 194. *See also* American Bankers Association (ABA)

267

Barfield, Henry Arthur, 178–179
Barrena, Juan, 201
Barrios, José María, 64
Bassiouni, M. Cherif, 197
Beattie, C. Stuart, 58, 59–60
Beck, James M., 166
Bee, Thomas, 129
Belgium, 71, 94, 114, 116, 117, 135, 167
Benavides, Francisco, 137–138, 139, 170.
    See also San Ygnacio Raid
Benavides, José, 201
Benjamin, Daniel, 218
Benyon, Abner, 32
Berkman, Alexander, 170, 191
Berryman, Clifford, 198
Bilodeau, Amedee, 204
Blaine, James, 45, 66, 87, 123
Blatt, Edward M., 202
Bly, Nellie, 1–2
Boards of Special Inquiry, 178. See also
    immigration
Bográn, Luis, 107
Bolles, Albert S., 23
Bonnie and Clyde, 184, 194
boodlers. See embezzlers; individual
    embezzlers
Borden, Lizzie, 145
borderlands, U.S.–Mexican, 10, 19, 54,
    136–138, 198
Border Patrol, U.S., 37, 198, 201
borders, international: feasibility of
    crossing, 2, 15, 18, 140; and jurisdic-
    tion, 3, 9–10, 41; as encouragement
    to crime, 4–5, 16, 23–26, 31; policing
    across, 5, 6–7, 9–10, 35, 52, 53, 55–56,
    62, 73; representations of, 26–29,
    198–199. See also Canadian border;
    Mexico
border towns, 7, 18, 22, 39. See also
    El Paso, Texas
Borton, James W., 191
Botsford, Harpin A., 69, 70
bounty hunters, 66–67, 214
Bowman, Joel W., 69
Brainerd, Lawrence, 40–41
Brazil, 10, 11, 45, 64, 69–70, 84, 87, 93,
    114, 118, 120, 121, 125, 212
bribery, 12, 16, 43, 44, 89–92
Brown, James L., 39
Bryan, William Jennings, 186, 203
Buchanan, James, 134

Bureau of Immigration, 162, 173, 177,
    180, 181, 182, 208. See also immigration
Bureau of Investigation. See Federal
    Bureau of Investigation
Burke, E. A., 63, 102, 107–108, 109–110,
    113
Burns, William J., 8, 186–188, 189–190
Burns International Detective Agency,
    65, 186–188, 209
Bush, George H. W., 214
Bush, George W., 12–13, 73, 217
Bushnell, William, 101
business, 15, 18, 24, 30, 36, 84, 110, 126,
    194. See also corporations
businessmen: reaction to boodlers, 14,
    23–24; targeted by FBI, 194–197, 209
Butler, Edward, 89
Byrne, Michael, 180–181
Byrnes, Thomas, 55

Cabbages and Kings (Henry), 94, 95
Cadwallader, Albert A., 69, 70
Callejas, J. M., 108
Camarena, Patricio, 200
Camarena Salazar, Enrique, 215
Canada: and fugitive slaves, 6–7, 31, 34;
    boodlers in, 15, 19–22, 33 (see also Eno,
    John Chester); extradition treaties
    with U.S., 15, 16, 36, 42, 45, 83, 130;
    control of foreign affairs of, 15, 38,
    44–45; as destination for fugitives, 16,
    18, 19, 23, 54, 90, 106, 188, 190; U.S.
    dollar in, 19–20; boodler colonies in,
    24, 32; American investments in,
    29–30; attraction of, 32; sovereignty of,
    35, 38, 41; diplomatic disputes with
    U.S., 35–36, 203–204, 214; American
    detectives in, 38–42, 55, 68, 69; view
    of boodlers in, 40, 42–44; cooperation
    with American detectives in, 40, 50,
    55, 68, 73, 192; and kidnapping of
    fugitives, 40–41, 72–73, 203–204, 205,
    214; corruption scandals in, 43–44;
    extradition from, 45, 83–84; King v.
    Walton, 72–73, 203; extradition to, 130,
    204, 214; deportation of fugitives by,
    179
Canadian border: ease of crossing, 15, 18,
    27, 37; and encouragement of crime,
    16, 23; and subversion of moral order,
    16, 31; law enforcement challenges

along, 18–19, 29; blamed for embezzlement, 24–25; allure of, 25–26; and sense of distance/proximity, 26–29; threat of, 32; preventing fugitives from crossing, 37–38; enticing fugitives across, 39; proposed restrictions on crossing, 41–42

Cané, Miguel, 115

Cantú, Samuel, 203

capital: Pinkertons as agents of, 9, 52–53; as international investment, 11, 29, 51, 84, 102, 104, 125–126, 137; mobility of, 15, 19, 27, 29, 36, 140; legal vs. illegal, 30, 49, 105, 110–112

capitalism: in the Gilded Age, 4, 15, 17; policing of, 9; and mobility, 15. *See also* banks; business; businessmen; corporations; markets; social order

capital punishment, 118, 120–122, 152–153

Capitals of Spanish America, The (Curtis), 86

Caribbean, U.S. troops sent to, 88, 112

Caron, Louis-Bonaventure, 21, 32

Cassidy, Belle, 183

Cassidy, Butch, 64–65

Castioni, Angelo, 168

Castro Quesada, Manuel, 116

Central America. *See* Latin America; *individual countries*

Central Intelligence Agency (CIA), 48, 210, 214, 217, 218

Charlton, Mary Scott Castle, 155, 157

Charlton, Porter, 154–157, 158

Charlton v. Kelly, 156, 157

Cheek, Silas E., 34

Chile, 11, 51, 57–58, 83, 87, 101, 102, 103–106, 113, 191, 213

China, 81, 133

Chinese Exclusion Act, 42, 140, 176

Christmas, Lee, 113

CIA (Central Intelligence Agency), 48, 210, 214, 217, 218

Citizen Kane (film), 195

citizens, extradition of, 127–128, 136–139, 150; to Mexico, 127, 141–142, 145–146, 152–154 (*see also* Rich, Mattie); protection from, 129, 133–138, 155; opposition to, 131, 143–146; in treaties, 135, 136, 138–139, 155; president's power in, 135–136, 139, 143, 149; and right to asylum, 143–144, 146; support

for, 146–149; 150–158; by Mexico, 154; Charlton, 154–157

citizens, naturalized, 109, 123, 134, 138

citizenship, 59, 87, 108, 134, 137–138, 150

civilization, and extradition, 6, 77, 80–81, 91, 93, 94, 103, 122, 145, 156, 157, 158

civil law, 98, 134

Clark, Samuel E., 109

Clarke, Edward, 79

clerks, 15–16, 17–18, 24, 33

Cleveland, Grover, 120

Clinton, Bill, 210, 216, 217, 218

Cockrell, Francis M., 90

Collins, Don P., 190

Colombia, 84, 111, 120, 165–166, 208

colonies, 5, 10, 11, 77; of Great Britain, 8, 72, 76, 82, 133; of fugitives, 24, 31, 32, 93–94, 95, 112. *See also* empire, U.S.

Commerce and Labor Department, 161, 177, 178, 181. *See also* immigration

Committee on Extradition, International Conference of American States, 87

common law, 21, 134

Common Sense (Paine), 129

communication, 2, 78. *See also* telegraph

Comprehensive Crime Control Act, 213

Conservative Party (Canada), 43–44

Constitution, U.S.: in territories, 9, 11, 73, 98–99; application outside U.S., 10, 60–61, 73; interstate extradition in, 22, 98, 99, 131–132; article 4, 60; Fourteenth Amendment, 60, 62; Fourth Amendment, 62, 130, 212; Sixth Amendment, 98; Fifth Amendment, 130

Converse, Lawrence F., 202–203

corporations, 9, 17, 21, 23, 29–30, 48, 49, 52–53, 61, 63, 126

corruption, Folk's campaign against, 12, 89–92

Costa Rica: fugitives in, 11, 45, 190; investments in, 11, 102, 104; Huntington in, 70–71, 123–124; and extradition, 88, 96, 102, 103, 116, 117, 118; immigration to, 102, 113, 116–118; West Indian workers in, 117–118; crime in, 118; opposition to death penalty, 118, 120; Weeks in, 119–120, 122–123; negotiations with U.S., 120; relationship with U.S., 122–125; Vesco Law, 125; Sandoval Lara, 207–208

Coudert, Frederic, 155, 171, 174, 175
Coughlin, Dan, 109
Crawford, Edward Sturgis, 63–64
crime: extraditable offenses, 15, 16,
    19, 36, 56, 90, 92, 95–96, 163; and
    immigration, 115, 132–133, 151
crime control, 128, 158, 191, 213, 218
crimes, federal, 185, 190–191, 194, 213
criminality, 4, 85, 103, 119, 132, 158
criminals: identification of, 2, 37, 47, 55,
    60, 179, 184, 192, 206; support for
    immigration of, 114–118; opposition
    to immigration of, 115–116, 133;
    extradition of, 116, 131, 132–133;
    removal of from society, 146. *See also*
    embezzlers; fugitives
criminology, science of, 4, 53, 141
Crouch, A. B., 187
Cuba, 55, 78, 88, 95, 97–99, 125, 133, 145,
    190, 191, 206–207
Curtis, William Eleroy, 83, 85–88
Czolgosz, Leon, 151, 170

Darrow, Clarence, 175
Daugherty-Burns scandal, 189
Davis, Jim, 109
Davis, Richard Harding, 77, 93, 94–95,
    102, 111
DEA (Drug Enforcement Administra-
    tion), 48, 215
death penalty, 118, 120–122, 152–153
Dellapiane, Antonio, 115
Department of Commerce and Labor,
    161, 177, 178, 181. *See also* immigration
DePietro, Rinaldo, 191
deportation: as disguised extradition, 6,
    161, 162, 177–182; goal of, 12; exclusion
    of felons by, 128, 133; and erosion of
    American asylum, 132–133; of
    naturalized citizens, 134; as a plenary
    power, 136; of Chinese, 144; used to
    avoid political offense exception, 161,
    162, 173, 180–182; as a substitute for
    extradition, 176, 177, 178–180, 182;
    proceedings, 178; of fugitives, from
    Mexico, 179, 200; of fugitives, to
    Mexico, 181, 200; of radicals, 182, 191.
    See also disguised extradition;
    immigration law
detectives, private: Burns, 8, 186–188,
    189–190; clients of, 9, 35, 36–37, 48, 56,

63, 194; legal constraints on, 9–10, 73;
    tactics of, 37–42, 48; kidnapping by,
    39–41, 48, 62, 73; international
    cooperation with, 40, 67; lack of
    constraints on, 48, 56, 60–61, 62,
    63–64, 73; as state-sanctioned nonstate
    actors, 49, 52; as private police, 52–53,
    55–56; Siringo, 53, 188; negotiations
    with foreign governments, 64, 70–71;
    Pinkerton competitors, 65–66,
    186–188; Burns International
    Detective Agency, 65, 186–188, 209;
    diplomatic problems caused by, 66;
    employed by surety companies, 68–71;
    decline of, 183–184, 192–194; influence
    on FBI, 184–186, 190, 197, 209;
    government banned from hiring, 186,
    188; investigations into, 208–209.
    See also Pinkerton National Detective
    Agency
Díaz, Porfirio, 19, 111, 141, 160, 162,
    169, 181
Dictator, The (Davis), 93, 95
Digest of International Law (Moore), 152
Dillinger, John, 184, 194, 205–206
Dimaio, Frank, 64
disguised extradition, 6, 161, 162,
    177–182
distance, psychological, 26
dollar diplomacy, 88, 113
dollars, U.S., 19–20
Double Life and the Detectives, A
    (Pinkerton), 58
Downes v. Bidwell, 98–99
Dreiser, Theodore, 25, 38
Drug Enforcement Administration
    (DEA), 48, 215
due process, 60, 62, 161, 182, 212, 219
dynamite, 36, 45, 164, 165

economics, 83; in the Gilded Age, 4, 15,
    24, 33, 49, 140; and U.S. empire, 10,
    11, 88, 109–110, 112, 122, 125; and
    development in Latin America, 102,
    106, 107. *See also* investment; markets
Edison, Thomas, 2, 78, 195
Eichmann, Adolf, 73, 125, 211
electoral politics, and extradition, 122,
    124, 175–176
Elements of International Law (Wheaton),
    133–134

Ellis, George, 199
Elmer, Richard Allison, 67
El Paso, Texas, 127, 147–148, 202
El Salvador, 84, 168–169
embezzlement: rate of, 14, 18, 45, 84; in
    extradition treaties, 15, 19, 36, 45; and
    clerks, 15–16, 17–18; definition of, 17;
    attempts to prevent, 18, 24, 35–42; rise
    in, 18–20; effects of on banks, 23–24;
    encouragement of, 23–26; Canadian
    border blamed for, 24–25; in literature,
    25, 38; and railroads, 25–26; insurance
    against, 67–68; as federal crime, 191;
    investigated by FBI, 194. See also
    embezzlers
embezzlers: meaning of boodler label, 14;
    destinations of, 15, 19, 45; in Canada,
    19–22, 32–33; Canadian, 21; attempts
    to trap, 21, 30, 36–42; in literature, 25,
    38; ethnicity of, 31; sensationalization
    of, 31–33; challenge of, to social order,
    33; image of, 33, 34–35; use of private
    detectives to pursue, 36–42; kidnap-
    ping of, 39–41, 58–59; view of, in
    Canada, 40, 42–44; in Latin America,
    83–84. See also fugitives; individual
    embezzlers
empire, U.S.: debate over, 5, 10, 77; and
    extradition, 8, 97–100, 123; link with
    law, 10–11; and reach of U.S. law,
    78–79, 80; and markets, 80; celebration
    of, 94–95; treatment of territories in,
    98–99, 150; fugitives' support of,
    109–110; Mexican War, 123
Eno, John Chester, 20–21, 22, 26, 30, 32,
    38, 44
Europe, 53–54. See also individual
    countries
Evans, Alona, 179
executive branch, 136, 162, 175–176,
    179–180, 182, 216. See also presi-
    dent, U.S.
executive order, 188, 216
"Exiles, The" (Davis), 93, 94
Ex parte Lopez, 202
Ex parte McCabe, 136, 157
Ex parte Scott, 71, 73
extradition: increased importance of, 3;
    as national accomplishment, 8, 79;
    expansion of, 76; and spread of
    civilization, 80–81; as instrument for

good, 82; resistance to, 122–125;
    opposition to in U.S., 128, 130;
    reciprocity of, 128, 132. See also
    rendition
extradition, disguised, 6, 161, 162,
    177–182
extradition, interstate, 22, 98, 99, 131–132
Extradition Act of 1848, 179
Extradition Clause of U.S. Constitution,
    22, 131–132
extradition-free zones, 93–95. See also
    havens, extradition
extradition havens. See havens, extra-
    dition
extradition law: goal of, 3, 12; expansion
    of, 3–4, 6; and encouragement of new
    crimes, 22; limits of, 22, 26–29, 95,
    97–98; Weldon Extradition Bill, 42–45;
    and international stature, 79, 81, 103;
    criticism of, 82–83; in popular culture,
    92–95; attempts to conceal limits of,
    95–97
extradition treaties: need for, 3–4;
    American resistance to, 3–4, 129;
    ideology of, 5–6; circumvention of, 6,
    62–63, 197; embezzlement in, 15; with
    Great Britain, 15, 16, 36, 45, 46, 92,
    129, 130; with Canada, 15, 16, 45;
    Webster-Ashburton Treaty, 16, 130;
    with Mexico, 19, 90, 130, 136, 138–139,
    141, 154, 155, 163, 198, 216; attempts to
    amend, 35–36, 45, 90; Phelps-Rosebery
    Treaty, 36, 42; effectiveness of, 45–46,
    218; enforcement of, 47; with Peru,
    57, 87, 163; with Chile, 58, 87–88,
    101, 102, 104; and legal protection, 60,
    61–62; necessity of, 63, 132; impor-
    tance of, 75–76; increase in number
    of, 76, 77–78, 82, 130, 132, 133;
    media attention given to, 76–77; and
    international stature, 79, 103; and
    civilization, 81, 103; with Latin
    American countries, 83, 84, 87–88, 101;
    reciprocity of, 83, 132; with Russia, 83,
    175; with European countries, 84; with
    Argentina, 87, 101–102, 116; with
    Brazil, 87, 121; with Guatemala, 88;
    with Costa Rica, 88, 96, 102, 116, 117,
    120, 124; with Cuba, 88, 97; with
    Honduras, 88, 102, 108, 112–113;
    published lists of, 95–96; concealment

extradition treaties *(continued)*
  of information about, 96–97, 192–193;
  with Japan, 103, 136, 155; and
  restriction of immigration, 116,
  132–133; and death penalty, 120–122;
  with Italy, 155, 156–157; and political
  offenders, 160, 163 *(see also* political
  offense exception); with France, 163,
  190; assassinations in, 167; *attentat*
  clause, 167; with Greece, 196;
  extradition of citizens in *(see* citizens)
extraterritoriality, 6, 81–82, 213
Ezeta, Antonio, 168–169

family deserters, 4
Farnsworth, Fred E., 187
FBI (Federal Bureau of Investigation).
  See Federal Bureau of Investigation
Federal Bureau of Investigation (FBI):
  founding of, 9, 183, 188; and abductions, 48, 199–201; Hoover at, 183,
  184–185, 189, 191–192, 201, 205; shift
  of authority to, 183–184; rise of, 184;
  connections with Pinkerton National
  Detective Agency, 184–185; international manhunts by, 185, 190, 205–207;
  mandate of, 185, 190–191, 194; early
  international cases, 188–189; Burns at,
  189–190; techniques of, 191–192,
  197–198; international cooperation by,
  192, 199–200; jurisdiction of, 194;
  targets of, 194–197, 209; search for
  foreign fugitives, 207–208
Felix, Antonio, 204, 205
Fernández, Luis, 207–208
Fernández, Mauro, 119, 122
fidelity insurance, 67–71. *See also*
  American Surety Company
Field, David Dudley, 16–17
Fifth Amendment, 130
Figueres, José, 125
fingerprinting, 2, 115, 184, 192, 206
Flores Magón, Ricardo, 181
Folk, Joseph W., 12, 88–92
Fong Yue Ting v. U.S., 179
foreigners, extradition of, 131
foreign intervention, 5, 75, 88, 95, 112,
  126, 205. *See also* influence, U.S.;
  power, U.S.
Forsee, W. F., 64
"Forty-Eighters," 163–164

Foucault, Michel, 4
Fourteenth Amendment, 60, 62
Fourth Amendment, 62, 130, 212
France, 3, 8, 53, 55, 69, 79, 81, 90, 132,
  163, 167, 190, 196
Franklin, Benjamin, 133
Frelinghuysen, Frederick, 135–136, 137
Frick, Henry Clay, 186
Frisbie v. Collins, 211. See also *Ker-Frisbie*
  doctrine
Froest, Frank, 72
fugitives: anxieties about, 4; subversion
  of social order by, 4; destinations of,
  11, 18, 45; benefits of sheltering, 11,
  101, 102, 103, 106, 113 *(see also* Burke;
  Meiggs); investment by, 30, 102;
  loyalties of, 109–110. *See also* criminals;
  embezzlers; manhunts, international
Fugitive Slave Act, 131–132, 175. *See also*
  slaves, fugitive

gamblers, 31
Gammell, William, 3, 80
gangsters: and rise of FBI, 184, 191, 194;
  international searches for, 205–207
Garfield, James, 165, 167
gender, 144–145, 146–147, 148, 157
geographical consciousness, 2, 7–8, 75
Gilded Age, 4, 13, 15, 16, 17, 49
Gillis, Lester Joseph, 206–207
Gilmour, Christina, 130–131
Gimbernat, J. Raymond, 156
Goldman, Emma, 134, 170, 191
Gonzales, Leonardo, 154
Gonzalez, Prudencio, 137–138, 139.
  See also San Ygnacio Raid
González Víquez, Cleto, 116–117, 124,
  126
Good Neighbor Policy, 204
Grace, J. W., 109
Grace, W. R., 109
Graham, Alexander, 208
Graham, Clasen, 37
Great Britain: British Empire, 8, 72, 82,
  134; extradition treaties with U.S., 15,
  16, 36, 45, 46, 92, 129, 130; control of
  Canadian foreign affairs by, 15, 35–36,
  38, 44–45; Webster-Ashburton Treaty,
  16, 130; Scotland Yard, 53–54, 72, 82,
  206; *Ex parte Scott*, 71, 73; extraterrito-
  rial abductions permitted by, 71–72,

216; Jay Treaty, 129; and strict territoriality, 134; and extradition of Irish radicals, 164; and extradition of Meunier, 167; *In re Castioni*, 168; and Lynchehaun case, 171–173; and use of immigration law to bypass extradition, 178–179; and deportation of Irish radicals, 180–181

Greece, 196

Gresham, Walter, 170

Grinnell, Julius, 38

Guantánamo Bay, 73

Guatemala, 64, 88

gunboat diplomacy, 88, 112

habeas corpus, 59, 60, 155, 202, 204, 210, 212, 215

Hackworth, Green H., 180

Hahn, Joseph J., 64

Hale, Samuel B., 86

Harlan, John Marshall, 98, 99

Harvey, David, 2

Haven, Gilbert, 19

havens, extradition: motivations of, 102–103; Honduras as, 106; Costa Rica as, 113, 116–118, 122–124; Argentina as, 113–115; Brazil as, 121; in later 20th century, 125. *See also* Argentina; Brazil; Chile; Costa Rica; Honduras

Hay, John, 90, 91, 142, 149

Haymarket Affair, 161, 164, 166

Head of Pasht, The (Allen), 80

Heaton, John Langdon, 93

hegemony, U.S. *See* influence, U.S.; power, U.S.

Heller, Nathaniel, 207

Henry, Charles E., 69–71, 123, 124

Henry, O., 77, 93–94, 95

Hernandez, Tomas, 202

Hervey, Robert, 59–60

Hill, W. P., 79

Hilliard, Louis Armstrong, 68

History of Nations, The (Lodge), 115

Hite, Olive Ennis, 144–145

Holl, Joseph, 187, 190

Holmes, George, 130

Holmes v. Jennison, 130

Homestead Strike, 53, 186, 209

Honduras: lack of extradition treaty with U.S., 7, 11, 63, 106, 107; Burke in, 63, 102, 107–108, 109–110; capture of

Crawford in, 63–64; extradition treaty with U.S., 88, 102, 112–113; depictions of, 93, 94; Henry in, 93–94; reasons for resisting extradition, 102, 103; debt of, 106–107; attempts to attract fugitive funds to, 106–110; negotiations over extradition treaty, 108; fugitives in, 108–109; and Louisiana State Lottery, 110–112; as a banana republic, 112; demand of fugitives from, 112; intervention in, 112, 126; relationship with U.S., 112–113; extradition of fugitives by, 113

Honduras National Lottery, 111–112

Hoover, J. Edgar, 183, 184–185, 189, 191–192, 201, 205, 207, 208

Hourwich, Isaac C., 175

Hovey, Alvin P., 105

Howard, Mattie. *See* Rich, Mattie

Howells, William Dean, 25, 38

human rights, 212, 218, 219

Hunt, Gaillard, 96–97

Hunter, Thomas J., 79–80, 81–82, 100

Huntington, Robert, 71, 123–124

Hussey, F. S., 40

IACP (International Association of Chiefs of Police), 192

ICPC (International Criminal Police Commission), 192

Identification Orders (IO), 192, 206

immigration: in Latin America, 113–118; belief in redeeming power of, 114, 115; and crime, 115, 128, 132–133, 151; Bureau of Immigration, 162, 173, 177, 180, 181, 182, 208; Boards of Special Inquiry, 178

immigration law: goal of, 12; Chinese Exclusion Act, 42, 140, 176; and race, 113–114; exclusion of felons by, 128, 133; and erosion of American asylum, 132–133; Page Act, 133, 176; and Mexico, 140; and anarchists, 166, 170, 176; and nihilists, 166; Anarchist Exclusion Act, 170; expansion of, 176; enforcement of, 176–177, 178, 182; ambiguous language of, 178; used to bypass extradition, 178–182. *See also* deportation

imperialism, U.S. *See* empire, U.S.

industrialists, targeted by FBI, 195–197

influence, U.S.: expansion of, 77;
    resistance to, 102–103. *See also*
    power, U.S.
information, dissemination of, 15, 20.
    See also press; telegraph
In re Castioni, 168
Insular Cases, 10–11, 73, 98–99
Insull, Samuel, 194–197, 209
insurance companies, 23, 30, 34, 36, 56,
    63, 67–71
International Association of Chiefs of
    Police (IACP), 192
International Conference of American
    States, 83, 87
International Criminal Police Commis-
    sion (ICPC), 192
Interpol (International Criminal Police
    Organization), 13, 192, 218–219
interrogation, 211, 212, 213, 217, 218
intervention, foreign, 5, 75, 88, 95, 112,
    126, 205, 214–215
investment: in Canada, 29–30; by
    fugitives, 30, 102, 104, 105, 106, 108,
    109, 125–126; and growth of extradi-
    tion law, 84–88; fugitives' links to, 110;
    in Mexico, 137, 141, 181
IO (Identification Orders), 192, 206
Ireland, John, 135, 138
Irish immigrants: voters, 36; fugitives,
    164, 165, 171–173, 180–181
Irish nationalist organizations, 36, 162, 172
Irish National Land League, 172
Irish Republican Army (IRA), 181
Irwin, Will, 157
Israel, 73, 125, 211
Italy: nonextradition of citizens by, 134,
    155; extradition of Charlton to,
    154–158; extradition treaties with, 155,
    156–157; image of, 157; kidnapping of
    Abu Omar in, 210

Jaffe, Sidney, 214
Japan, 81, 103, 136, 154
Jay Treaty, 129
Jennison, Silas, 130
Johnsen, Timm, 214
Johnson, Jack, 188–189
Johnson, O. W., 145–146
Jones, Gus T., 199–200
judges, authority of, in extradition cases,
    21, 151, 168–174

Judson, Harry Pratt, 80
Julian, Henry, 48, 52, 56–59, 60, 61,
    62, 72
jurisdiction: and subversion of moral
    order, 3; of U.S. laws, 7–8 (*see also*
    law, U.S.); expanded notion of, 9–10,
    78; and strict territoriality, 10, 61, 134,
    155; based on nationality of victim, 213
jurisdiction, extraterritorial, 6, 81–82,
    213
jurisdiction, territorial, 10, 61, 134, 151,
    155
Justice Department. *See* Federal Bureau
    of Investigation

Kaine, Thomas, 131
Kane, Charles Foster, 195
Karpis, Alvin "Creepy," 207
Kean, Samuel, 50
Kear, Daniel, 214
Keenan, John, 30, 44
Keith, Minor C., 104
Kelly, Daniel J., 90
Kempner, Murray, 183–184, 185
Keppler, Joseph, 26, 27
Ker, Frederick, 49–52, 56, 58–62, 219.
    See also *Ker v. Illinois*
Ker-Frisbie doctrine, 212, 213, 215
Kerr, Augustus, 69
Ker v. Illinois, 48, 49, 60–63; implications
    of, 62–63, 65; legacy of, 66, 68, 71, 73,
    74, 185, 198, 205; as a legal precedent,
    202, 204, 211–213, 218; and extraordi-
    nary rendition, 211, 218; distortion of,
    218–219. *See also* kidnapping
kidnapping: of fugitives in Canada,
    39–41, 204; opposition to, 40–41, 60,
    212, 216; legal justification of, 48, 49,
    60–61, 62; of Ker, 58–62; after *Ker v.
    Illinois*, 62–63, 65, 66, 71, 73; of
    fugitives in Mexico, 66, 198–202; by
    bounty hunters, 66, 214; permitted by
    Britain, 71–72; permitted by Canada,
    72–73; risks of, 75–76; by Mexican law
    enforcement, 202–203; by Canadian
    law enforcement, 203; of Abu Omar,
    210; in twenty-first century, 210–211,
    217–219; and *Ker-Frisbie* doctrine, 212,
    213, 215; in war on drugs, 212–213,
    214–215; in counterterrorism strategy,
    213–214, 216–218; of Noriega, 214–215;

Alvarez-Machain decision, 215–216, 218; and PDD-39, 216–217. *See also Ker v. Illinois; male captus, bene detentus;* rendition, extraordinary; rendition, irregular

King v. Walton, The, 72–73, 203

Kossuth, Louis, 164

Kratz, Charles, 90, 91, 92

Krug, John, 153–154

labor migrations, 117, 140

labor movement, 161, 164, 186, 209

La Follette Civil Liberties Committee, 208–209

Lanctot, Charles, 179

Lange, Albert, 39

Larrabee, Christopher A., 65

Latin America: irregular rendition in, 48; and Monroe Doctrine, 75, 87, 88, 102, 110; U.S. intervention in, 75, 88, 112, 214; fugitives in, effects on trade, 83, 85–87; asylum in, 83–84; extradition treaties in, 84, 87–88; investment in, 84–85, 125–126; resistance to extradition in, 101–102, 103, 124–125; capital punishment in, 120. *See also individual countries*

Latner, T. J., 66

Lavergne, Joseph, 44

law, disparities in, 119–122

law, U.S.: reach of, 7–8, 10, 75, 78–80, 82, 92, 185–186; jurisdiction of, 7–8, 60–61, 134; as justification for international action, 11, 91–92; failure to keep up with change, 15, 22; limitations of, 20–22, 61, 94; and expansion of influence, 77, 80; as a civilizing force, 77, 80–81, 93; critics of, 82–83. *See also* Constitution, U.S.

law enforcement, British, 8, 53–54, 72, 82

law enforcement, U.S.: and technology, 2–3, 13, 50, 78, 82, 192; justification of cross-border policing, 5, 92; internationalization of, 7; abilities of, 8, 52–53, 54–56, 185, 190–192; constraints on, 9–10, 22, 38, 63; expanding reach of, 12–13, 77–79, 91–92; by nonstate actors, 52; federal, 54–55, 183–186 (*see also* Federal Bureau of Investigation); in popular media, 78, 82; deprivatization of, 183–184. *See also* law, U.S.

Lawrence, William Beach, 120–121

legal consciousness, 7–8, 9–10, 22, 75, 77, 79

Lincoln, Abraham, 54, 165, 183

Lira, Rafael, 212, 213

literature: embezzlement in, 25, 38; extradition in, 77, 80; extradition-free zones in, 93–95

Lodge, Henry Cabot, 115

Lombroso, Cesare, 4

Longabaugh, Harry, 64–65

Lopez, Luis, 201–202

Louisiana State Lottery, 110–111

Lowe, D. Warren, 86–87

Lujan, Julio Juventino, 212, 213

Lujan v. Gengler, 213

Lyman, H. D., 36

Lynchehaun, James, 171–173, 180

Macdonald, John A., 40, 43

Madama Butterfly, 56

male captus, bene detentus, 62, 71, 72–73, 74, 211–212, 216, 219. *See also* kidnapping

Mandelbaum, Fredericka "Mother," 26, 27

manhunts, international: celebration of, 8, 58, 78; by Pinkertons, 9, 35, 37, 50–52, 53, 64–65, 72; legacies of, 13; and technology, 13, 50, 191–192; motivation for, 48–49, 64–65; by Scotland Yard, 53, 72; by FBI, 185, 188–189, 190–191, 205–207; Pinkertons shut out of, 192–193. *See also* Pinkerton National Detective Agency

Mann Act, 188, 190

Mapp v. Ohio, 212

Marcy, William A., 164

markets, foreign, 10, 78, 80, 83, 86, 89, 100. *See also* investment

Marsh, Gideon, 55, 86

Marshals, U.S., 54–55

Marsino, Joseph B., 200

Martí, José, 122, 123

Maxey, Thomas, 170

Mayer, Francis, 154

McCabe, Maria Inez, 136, 157

McKinley, William, 77, 127, 143, 149, 151, 161, 166, 170, 172, 173

media, 31–32, 76, 78, 93, 99, 145, 146, 184, 194. *See also* literature; press

Meiggs, Henry, 101, 102, 103–106, 109, 117
Meinbress, J. C., 192–193
Mengele, Josef, 125
Mercer, Sid T., 190
Mertz, Fred G., 204
Meunier, Théodole, 167
Mexican Revolution, 162, 181, 198, 202
Mexican War, 123
Mexico: and extradition of fugitive slaves,
    7; capture of fugitives in, 10, 54, 65, 66,
    92, 199–202, 211, 215; as destination for
    fugitives, 19, 90; extradition treaties
    with U.S., 19, 90, 130, 136, 138–139,
    141, 155, 163; Díaz, 19, 111, 141, 160,
    162, 169, 181; diplomatic disputes
    with U.S., 66, 198, 201–203, 215;
    kidnapping of fugitives from, 66,
    201–202, 204, 211, 215; extradition
    of U.S. citizens to, 127, 135–139, 149,
    152–154, 204 (see also Rich, Mattie);
    American investment in, 136–137, 140,
    181; and cross-border crime, 137, 198;
    San Ygnacio raiders, 138, 169–170;
    Americans in, 140; and immigration
    law, 140; image of, 141, 145, 157;
    prisons in, 145–146; capital punish-
    ment in, 152–153; extradition of
    citizens by, 154; refusal to extradite
    Arredondo to, 160–162, 181; chal-
    lengers to Díaz in, 162, 169, 181;
    deportation of fugitives by, 179, 200;
    deportation of rebels to, 181–182;
    Pancho Villa, 198; suspension of
    extradition with U.S., 198–200; and
    irregular rendition, 198–203, 204–205;
    sovereignty of, 202; kidnapping of
    fugitives by, 202–203
Miller, Samuel Freeman, 60–62
Minchin, "Doc," 86
miscegenation, 189
mobility: restraints on, 5; crisis of, 15;
    new forms of, 15; and crime, 17, 42; of
    capital, 19; and threats to social order,
    23; proposed restrictions on, 35, 41–42.
    See also transportation/travel
Monroe, Gustavus L., 116
Monroe Doctrine, 75, 83, 87, 88, 102, 110
Moore, Avery, 21–22
Moore, Frederick T., 101, 102
Moore, John Bassett, 3, 47, 48, 63, 133,
    134, 135, 152, 169, 177–178, 180, 182

Moores, Charles, 172, 173
morality, 16, 31, 168, 188–189
moral reformers, 25, 34, 110, 111,
    147–148
moral turpitude, 176, 178
Morgan, J. P., 112
Morocco, 10, 11, 79–80, 81–82, 93, 94, 97,
    100, 103
Morrow, William M., 168–169
Murrell, John K., 90, 91

Nadelmann, Ethan, 7
Nash, Thomas, 129–130. See also
    Robbins, Jonathan
Nast, Thomas, 55
National Bank Act, 191, 194
nationals. See citizens
Nazis, sheltering of, 73, 125, 211
Neely, Charles F. W., 97–99
Neely v. Henkel, 98, 99
Nelson, "Baby Face," 206–207
Nelson, John, 130
Newbury, George, 64
New Deal era, 184, 191, 197, 209
newspapers. See press
Nicaragua, 84, 111, 125, 168
nihilists, 165, 166
9/11, 12, 74, 210, 211, 217–218, 219
nonstate actors, 9, 41, 48, 49, 52, 62, 72,
    219. See also detectives, private
Noriega, Manuel, 214–215
"nowhere to hide" rhetoric, 78–79, 82,
    83, 95, 99, 100
Nye, Bill, 34–35

O'Brien, Frank A., 55
O'Brien, Thomas "Bunco," 86
Olney, Peter B., 21
Open Door Notes, 100
Opper, Frederick Burr, 27
Owens, Fred J., 109

Pacific Mail Steamship Company, 51
Page Act, 133, 176
Paine, Thomas, 129
Palmer, A. Mitchell, 182
Palmer, Frederick, 112
Palmer, William Jackson, 137
Palmer Raids, 182
Panama, 2, 51, 84, 88, 120, 124, 192, 214
panic, financial, 20

Parker, Robert Leroy, 64–65
Parsons, A. W., 185, 194
passive personality principle, 213
passports, 5, 12, 19, 27
PDD-39, 216–217
Pershing, John J., 198
Peru, 2, 11, 48, 51–52, 57–58, 59, 60, 61, 62, 84, 87, 92, 102, 104, 105, 109, 163
Phelps, Edward John, 36
Phelps-Rosebery Treaty, 36, 42
Philippines, 78, 79, 98, 99, 150
photography, 2, 37, 50, 55, 184
Pinkerton, Allan, 9, 37, 38, 50, 52, 53, 55, 58, 183, 184, 193
Pinkerton, Allan, II, 193
Pinkerton, Matt A., 66
Pinkerton, Robert, 55, 63, 66
Pinkerton, Robert A., 193, 209
Pinkerton, William, 40, 50, 55, 58, 66, 184
Pinkerton and Company, United States Detective Agency, 66
Pinkerton National Detective Agency: clients of, 9, 35, 56, 194, 195; as agents of capital, 9, 49, 52–53; tactics, 37, 39; contract with ABA, 37, 187; infiltration of labor unions, 39, 209; international networks, 40, 51, 53, 55–56, 64; lack of oversight of, 48, 56, 62, 63; as private police, 49, 52, 186; in Ker manhunt, 50–52, 56–58; resources of, 51; legality of actions of, 52; origins of, 52–53; cross-border work of, 53, 63, 64, 79; advantages in cross-border work, 55–56, 72; pursuit of Wild Bunch, 64–65; competitors, 65, 66, 186–188; as private security firm, 74, 193; hired by foreign governments, 171; influence on FBI, 184–185, 197; Homestead Strike, 186; reputation of, 186, 188; decline of, 186–188, 191–194
Pinkerton's, Inc., 193
Pinkerton v. Pinkerton, 66
Place, Etta, 64
police: municipal, in U.S., 9, 51, 55, 185, 218; European, 53–54; federal, in U.S., 54; international alliances, 192, 218
policing. See law enforcement, U.S.
political crimes: asylum for, 133, 160–162, 163; defining, 161, 162–163, 167; ambiguity of, 164–166. See also political offense exception

political offenders, 16, 131, 133, 163, 173. See also political offense exception
political offense exception, 133, 160; and Mexican revolutionaries, 160, 181–182; in extradition treaties, 163; and anarchists, 164, 167, 168; and Irish Republicans, 164–165, 180–181; and assassinations, 165, 167, 168, 170; standards for, 166–170, 174–176; uprising test, 168–170; and San Ygnacio raiders, 169–170; judicial inconsistency in, 170, 171; Lynchehaun case, 171–173; division over, 173, 174–175; and Russian radicals, 173–176; use of deportation to avoid, 180–182
Political Refugee Defense League, 175
Porter, William Sydney, 93–94. See also Henry, O.
porters, 34
Potter, Claire Bond, 184
Potter, H. C., 8
Pouren, Jan, 173–176, 180
power, U.S., 6, 10–11, 56, 77, 78, 80, 88, 92, 100, 122–124, 125–126, 150. See also empire, U.S.; influence, U.S.
president, U.S., 135–136, 139, 157, 191. See also executive branch; individual presidents
Presidential Decision Directive 39 (PDD-39), 216–217
press: portrayal of international policing in, 8, 82; sensationalization of boodlers in, 31–33; extradition treaties in, 76, 139; and improved policing, 82; depictions of extradition-free zones in, 93; Rich case in, 143–146, 147, 148–149; opposition to extradition of citizens in, 144–146; support for extradition of citizens in, 146, 156
Preston, Kean, and Company, 49–50
Price, Robert, 204
Prigg v. Pennsylvania, 131
prisons, Mexican, 145–146
procurement, 39
Progressive era, 13, 184, 209
Progressive reformers, 89, 147, 150, 151, 157, 174, 184
prosecution, for offenses committed abroad, 134, 138, 155–156
prostitution, 133, 148, 176, 188
Prussia, 132, 135

Pscherhofer, Charles, 45
"Public Enemy Number One," 205–207
public violence, 162, 164, 165. *See also*
    political crimes; political offense
    exception
Puck, 26–29, 31
Puerto Rico, 79, 98–99, 150, 155
punishment, standards of, 118–122.
    See also capital punishment
Punitive Expedition, 198

Qazi, Mir, 217
Quality of Mercy, The (Howells), 38

race: and immigration policies, 113–114,
    117, 118; and extradition, 144;
    miscegenation, 189
radicals, 4, 36, 161, 162, 164, 165, 170,
    173–176, 180–182. *See also* anarchists
railroads: and speed of travel, 2, 18; as
    means of fugitives' escape, 3; built with
    fugitives' funds, 11, 30, 102, 104, 105,
    108; and embezzlement, 15, 25–26; and
    connection with Canada, 18; and
    connection with Mexico, 19; Trans-
    Canada route, 30; porters, 34; train
    robbers, 37, 53, 64, 135; across Panama,
    51; as clients of private detectives, 56,
    64; intercontinental, 85; built by
    Meiggs, 104, 105, 109; in Peru, 104,
    105, 109; in Costa Rica, 104, 117; in
    Honduras, 106–107, 108; in U.S.-
    Mexican borderlands, 137, 140, 148;
    strikes on, 191
Rauscher, William, 61–62
Reagan, Ronald, 213, 214
Reed, George Deering, 154
Reese v. United States, 66
reform movements, 25, 31, 34, 110,
    111–112, 147, 151
Regina v. Sattler, 71
religion, 25, 31, 111–112
rendition: definition of, 5, 47, 210;
    informal types of, 6 (*see also* rendition,
    irregular); of fugitive slaves, 6–7,
    131–132 (*see also* slaves, fugitive); and
    geographical consciousness, 7–8; and
    legal consciousness, 7–8; increase in,
    10; from U.S., 11–12; in war on terror,
    13 (*see also* rendition, extraordinary);
    interstate, 22, 99, 131–132; in practice,

47; motivation for, 48–49; preference
    for extradition, 67, 76; to third
    countries, 217, 218. *See also* extradition;
    extradition treaties
rendition, extraordinary, 74, 210–211,
    213, 215, 216, 217–219
rendition, irregular: definition, 47–48,
    197–198; expansion of, 48; normaliza-
    tion of, 60–63, 71; by Britain, 72; by
    FBI, 185, 199–200, 201; categories of,
    197–198; and Mexico, 198–203, 205;
    discouragement of, 204, 214; and
    torture, 212, 213. See also *Ker v.
    Illinois*; kidnapping
Reno Brothers Gang, 53
revolutionaries, 162–164. *See also* political
    offense exception; radicals; uprising
    test
Rich, John, 139–141, 142, 148–149
Rich, Mattie, 127, 139–150, 157, 158–159;
    case as legal precedent, 127, 150, 152;
    and idea of asylum for citizens, 128,
    129, 139, 143–144, 150. *See also* citizens,
    extradition of
Riddleberger, Harrison, 36
Riley, Henry A., 25
Robbins, Jonathan, 129–130, 150
Rocas, Julio Argentino, 114
Rodríguez, José, 120, 122
Rogan, Octavia F., 96–97
rogues' colonies, 93–95
Rogues' Gallery, 37, 55, 184
Romero, Matías, 170
Roosevelt, Franklin D., 191, 195–196, 204
Roosevelt, Theodore, 12, 75, 77, 91–92,
    188
Roosevelt Corollary to Monroe Doc-
    trine, 75, 102
Root, Elihu, 176
Rosebery, Lord, 36
Rowe, Chester, 138
Rudowitz, Christian, 173–176, 180
rule of specialty, 133
Russell, J. C., 135
Russia: extradition treaty with, 83, 175;
    Russian radicals, 162, 164, 173–176

Salvini, Guido, 210
Sandoval Lara, José María, 208
San Ygnacio Raid, 138, 169–170
Sayers, Joseph D., 146

scatter syndrome, 148
Schick, Charles E., 69
Schreiber, William, 39
Schurz, Carl, 164, 174
Scotland Yard, 8, 53–54, 72, 82, 206
Scott, Richard S., 14, 19
Scott, Susanna, 71
Secret Service, 112, 187, 188
Secret Six, 195
Sexton, F. B., 142, 152
Shame of the Cities, The (Steffens), 89
Shearer, Ivan, 12
Sherwood, A. P., 40
Shultz, George P., 214
Siebrecht, George L., 127
Siringo, Charles A., 53, 188
Sister Carrie (Dreiser), 25, 38
Sixth Amendment, 98
slaves, fugitive, 6–7, 16, 31, 34, 131–132,
    175
Sobell, Morton, 211
social exclusion, 147–148
social instability, fears about, 4–5, 23, 158
social order, challenges to, 3, 4, 23, 33–34
social station, flexibility of, 4, 15
Soldiers of Fortune (Davis), 94–95
Soto, Marco Aurelio, 106
South America. *See* Latin America;
    individual countries
sovereignty: in extradition law, 6, 22, 46;
    in international law, 6, 215; and
    fugitive slaves, 7, 31; violations of, 7,
    38, 40, 48, 202, 210, 211; and resistance
    to U.S., 11, 102, 122–125; of Canada,
    35, 38; and apprehension of embezzlers,
    38–42; in U.S. territories, 73, 99; in
    Lopez case, 202; in Abu Omar case,
    210
Spear, Samuel T., 135
State Department: policy on extradition,
    63; discouragement of irregular
    rendition by, 76, 204; reluctance to
    share extradition information, 95–97;
    intervention in extradition cases, 176;
    and disguised extradition, 180
steamships, 2, 45, 51
Steel Trap, The (film), 121
Steffens, Lincoln, 89–90, 91
Stella, E. M., 109
Stensland, Paul, 100
Stevens, John Paul, 215–216

Stewart, Watt, 104
St. Louis Boodlers, 89–92
Stone, Melville, 21
Strakosch, Alexander, 208
Suburban Railway, 89, 90
success, views of, 33
Sundance Kid, 64–65
Supreme Court: Insular Cases, 10–11, 73,
    98–99; *United States v. Rauscher*, 61–62;
    Reese v. United States, 66; *Neely v.
    Henkel*, 98, 99; *Holmes v. Jennison*, 130;
    Prigg v. Pennsylvania, 131; *Charlton v.
    Kelly*, 156, 157; *Fong Yue Ting v. U.S.*,
    179; *Ker-Frisbie* doctrine, 212, 213, 215;
    Mapp v. Ohio, 212; *United States v.
    Alvarez-Machain*, 215–216, 218. See also
    Ker v. Illinois
Sûreté Nationale, 53
surety companies, 67–71. *See also*
    American Surety Company
Surratt, John, 54–55
Switzerland, 117, 135, 168

Taft, William Howard, 155, 175
Tammany Ring, 16. *See also* Tweed,
    William M. "Boss"
technology: telegraph, 2, 20, 50, 55, 82,
    136; fingerprinting, 2, 115, 184, 192,
    206; and law enforcement, 2–3, 13, 50,
    78, 82; and apprehension of embezzlers,
    37; and manhunts, 50; in extradition
    treaties, 136; used by FBI, 192
telegraph, 2, 20, 50, 55, 82, 136
temptation, and embezzlement, 24–25
Tenet, George, 217
territoriality, 10, 61, 134, 155
territories, U.S., 73, 98–99, 150. *See also*
    empire, U.S.
terror, war on, 12, 13, 210, 218
terrorism, 12, 164, 182, 210, 213–214,
    216–217
Thiel's Detective Service Company, 65
time-space compression, 2
torture, 175, 212, 213, 215, 217, 218, 219
Toscanino, Francisco, 212
transportation/travel, 1–2, 3, 18, 26. *See
    also* railroads; steamships
treaties, extradition. *See* extradition
    treaties
*Treatise on Extradition and Interstate
    Rendition, A* (Moore), 47, 63, 177–178

treaty making, increase in, 6, 76
Trimble, Alexander, 135–136, 137, 138, 139, 155, 157
Turkey, 78, 164, 196
Tweed, William M. "Boss," 16, 55
Two Evil Isms (Siringo), 188
Tyrrell, Frank G., 89

Underground Railroad, 34
United Fruit Company, 104, 109
United States: changing international role of, 7, 10, 77 (see also influence, U.S.; power, U.S.); opposition to centralized police in, 54; as international policeman, 75, 78
United States v. Alvarez-Machain, 215–216, 218
United States v. Rauscher, 61–62
United States v. Toscanino, 212
United States v. Unverzagt, 204
Unlawful Flight to Avoid Prosecution Act, 191
Unverzagt, Charles H., 204
Upham, Samuel Curtis, 104
uprising test, 168–170
urbanization, 4, 17, 115
Uruguay, 88, 120, 212
U.S. Marshals Service, 54–55

Vaccaro, Sarro, 204, 205
Van Dyne, Frederick, 96
Verne, Jules, 1
Vesco, Robert, 125
vice, attempts to eradicate, 43, 147–148, 188
Vidocq, Eugène François, 53
Villa, Pancho, 198
Villareal, Antonio, 181
Villareal, Eduardo, 201–202, 205
violence, legitimate, 49

violence, public, 162, 164, 165. See also political offense exception
Von Rintelen, Franz, 189
vote, Irish-American, 36
Vucetich, Juan, 115

Wainwright, Ellis, 90
Walther, Gustav Adolph, 108–109
Walton, A. R., 73
Warner, Frank, 58
War of the Pacific, 57–58
war on terror, 12, 13, 210, 217–218
Washburn, Edward S., 23, 24
Weber, Max, 49
Webster-Ashburton Treaty, 16, 130
Weeks, Francis Henry, 119–120, 122–123
Weldon, Richard Chapman, 42–44
Weldon Extradition Bill, 42–45
Welles, Orson, 195
Wesche, Charles E., 158
Wetmore, Claude, 89
Wharton, Francis, 135
Wheaton, Henry, 134, 152
Wild Bunch, 64–65
Wilkie, Franc Bangs, 59
Williams, Harrison R., 119, 123, 124
Winslow, Ezra, 86–87
World Trade Center bombing (1993), 216, 217
wrongly captured, properly detained, 62, 71, 72–73, 74, 211–212, 216, 219. See also kidnapping

Yglesias Castro, Rafael, 124
Younis, Fawaz, 214
Yousef, Ramzi, 217

Zaremba, Charles W., 66
Zemurray, Samuel, 109, 112–113